Psychoanalysis and Male Homosexuality

Psychoanalysis and Male Homosexuality

Twentieth-Anniversary Edition

Kenneth Lewes

With a Personal Reflection by Gilbert W. Cole
and a Foreword by Donald Moss

JASON ARONSON
Lanham • Boulder • New York • Toronto • Plymouth, UK

Published in the United States of America
by Jason Aronson
An imprint of Rowman & Littlefield Publishers, Inc.

A wholly owned subsidiary of
The Rowman & Littlefield Publishing Group, Inc.
4501 Forbes Boulevard, Suite 200, Lanham, Maryland 20706
www.rowmanlittlefield.com

Estover Road
Plymouth PL6 7PY
United Kingdom

British Library Cataloguing in Publication Information Available

Library of Congress Cataloging-in-Publication Data

Library of Congress Control Number: 2008944236

ISBN 978-0-7657-0647-8 (cloth : alk. paper)
eISBN 978-0-7657-0649-2

Printed in the United States of America

♾ ™ The paper used in this publication meets the minimum requirements of
American National Standard for Information Sciences—Permanence of Paper for
Printed Library Materials, ANSI/NISO Z39.48-1992.

They that have pow'r to hurt and will do none,
That do not do the thing they most do show,
Who moving others, are themselves as stone,
Unmoved, cold and to temptation slow;
They rightly do inherit heaven's graces
And husband nature's riches from expense;
They are the lords and owners of their faces,
Others but stewards of their excellence.
The summer's flow'r is to the summer sweet,
Though to itself it only live and die,
But if that flow'r with base infection meet,
The basest weed outbraves his dignity:
    For sweetest things turn sourest by their deeds;
    Lilies that fester smell far worse than weeds.

William Shakespeare
Sonnet 94

CONTENTS

PERSONAL REFLECTION

I have been invited to write a foreword to the twentieth-anniversary edition of Kenneth Lewes's book in a very personal voice, an appreciation of the book's impact on me when it first appeared. I felt not a moment of hesitation before agreeing to do so. The book was important to me then, and it remains important to me. The process of writing a detailed appreciation of its impact, though, has led back into memories that are painful and difficult for me to confront. It is impossible to contact an experience of my relationship with psychoanalysis prior to my awareness of the book because the book was formative of that relationship. While I cannot measure the book's influence against a time before I felt its influence, I can reach for a description of one analyst's development in the complicated context that included this book. It is my hope that this description imparts something of the value that this book continues to hold for a new generation of psychoanalysts.

When Kenneth Lewes's book first appeared in 1988, I was beginning to explore the options available to a person interested in training to become a psychoanalyst. I was quite naïve, fascinated by the psychoanalytic literature I was reading, and convinced as to the transformative power of psychoanalysis effectively practiced. Certainly the condition that Lewes so acutely identifies and analyses in this book had not been resolved then, and my education involved varying degrees of confrontation with an entrenched homophobia; sometimes obscure, sometimes clear as a summer noontime. That condition persists, though every analyst also knows that we are not supposed to harbor homophobic attitudes anymore. Would that it were so easy. Every analyst, regardless of sexual orientation, from the time they first consider analytic training, encounters these traces, gross or subtle, of a persistent homophobia that has occupied the psychoanalytic conversation since the inception of the field. And every analyst will confront the question as to whether, to what extent, and how they will engage this apparently intractable dynamic. For some analysts that question will bear more urgency than for others.

The cultural climate twenty years ago for gay people had a special urgency. It was six years into what once was referred to as "the AIDS crisis." Now what once was a crisis has become more simply, at least for those with access to adequate health care, life as we know it. HIV has become a fact, rather than an immediate or incipient terror. But twenty years ago sex, death, and how to make a life worth living were matters freshly called into question, and seemed to become saturated with meaning that called out for every strategy that could help find a way into that thicket of meaning. Those of us who found in psychoanalysis a useful way to think about our lives encountered a series of paradoxes. Most obviously, psychoanalysis demands a relationship to time that defies limits. Its practice requires a willingness to linger, to wait, to see what develops as time passes. For many in my age cohort, the time required for a psychoanalytic training seemed unreasonably protracted in an atmosphere where time had demonstrably run out for many of us.

If, however, one pressed on, employing that adaptive sort of denial, one was engaged in a psychoanalytic process and one encountered the theory, on the one hand, and on the other, the disposition of power within psychoanalytic institutions: those who train and analyze. More that one straight friend of mine wondered why I would be interested in psychoanalysis, since it was famously biased against homosexuals. For many gay men and lesbians, this undifferentiated understanding of "psychoanalysis" was another fact of life, more or less simply accepted. Having read some psychoanalytic theory long before I found my way to graduate school and analytic training, and having begun my own analysis, I knew this not to be the whole story. Ken Lewes's book helped me to understand much more of the story.

I distinctly remember spotting the announcement of the book's release, because I was in graduate school. I had just completed a project on homosexuality for that ubiquitous but oddly amorphous course that is found in every graduate program devoted to mental health, often called "Personality Development." A survey of psychiatric, psychological, and social work literature turned up the expectable but no less dismaying array of literature that described the homosexual in ways that confirmed a heterosexist bias and confused the signs and causes of psychic disturbance with a response to an oppressed and vilified condition. In my naiveté I wondered how it could be at that late date, nearly twenty years after the Stonewall uprising, that the literature for the most part languished so woefully behind, willing to regard human beings as meaningfully divided into two monolithic groups: homosexual and heterosexual, as if these categories tell us anything at all about the people sorted into them. What was particularly troubling and vivid to me was that for any prevailing psychoanalytic notion of what the term "the homosexual" could refer to with any agreed upon meaning, however tacit, there were those in the field who had to remain willfully blind to most of the salient evidence about the individuals they sorted into that category. If it is possible to infer anything about the psychic lives of individuals from the material facts surrounding them, there was something to be understood about those who creatively and aggressively challenged entrenched power deployed against them while building robust familial and community structures that celebrated and provided care, if only one could be bothered to look and to be curious. Certainly the psychoanalytic tendency to generalize based on a population seen in the clinical setting was the predominant cause of this tropism. But why is this an explanation? And what does it explain?

By this time in my education I was certain that the psychoanalysis I wished to be engaged with was predicated on an open-minded curiosity, and I was frustrated by what I found. A friend who'd seen a pre-publication announcement advised me that a book was about to be published that might provide some kind of answer to my dismay. In many ways, she was right. Ken's book strengthened my belief in psychoanalysis as a discipline I wanted to pursue, and my resolve.

Two years after the book appeared, I applied for psychoanalytic training at several training institutes. It is not possible to be certain, of course, as to the effect of my "coming out" in my interviews for admission, but if this first formal encounter with psychoanalytic institutions might usefully be thought of as an experiment, it was an opportunity to make a very preliminary and provisional observation. It also had the effect of a cautionary tale replete with lessons to be learned about the inevitability of disillusionment and the terrible lure and phony promise of the safety of the closet. As I try to reconstruct these long ago events, I cannot help but confront, to my shame and dismay, what learning these lessons required, for that is what I thought was possible, even necessary: a temporary, strategic return to the closet. It is certainly fair to ask of me, "What on earth were you thinking?" The best answer I can manage is, I wasn't able to think adequately at the beginning, and the trajectory of my training experience includes the developing capacity to think, which is, after all, one of the goals of the process.

My analyst was a member of the International Psychoanalytic Association, and so I applied to two institutes that were constituent members. One rejected me. This was the institute where my analyst was affiliated. It was in one of the interviews for this institute that I disclosed my homosexuality in response to a question about my current relationship status. The one that accepted me was the one to whom I did not disclose my sexual orientation. This was the institute where I began my psychoanalytic training. A single trial learning paradigm would clearly indicate that coming out was not the best course of action. I was a quick learner, and I signed on for my own version of a "don't ask, don't tell" policy.

It was a small class; I was the only male among four candidates. We were all new to the field, with varying amounts of clinical experience, but we all had been in our own psychoanalyses for some time. We were beginners, cordial, reticent, feeling our way. There was little precedent, indeed no occasion, in the group for dissent, largely, I think, because we didn't know enough about anything over which we could disagree. One evening, packed into an elevator on the way to a class, a colleague remarked in a voice that expressed a sense of outraged scandal that the author of the recently published biography of Freud (Peter Gay) was gay! I was suddenly, unaccountably, anxious. I had no idea as to whether this was a true description of an aspect of Peter Gay's life, and it had never struck me as important. But a moment had arrived in which I could point out the utter irrelevancy of sexual orientation to scholarly authority. Somehow, it suddenly and unaccountably felt dangerous to do so. To point out the absurdity of this bit of gossip as an occasion of outrage felt tantamount to coming out to my classmates. Already I was responding to an atmosphere in which the question of sexual orientation had an unreasonably intense charge to it. One of my other colleagues responded, "What difference does that make?" The outraged candidate spluttered something incomprehensible and trailed off. After a moment I quietly asserted that sexual orientation of an individual was not a meaningful marker of much of anything. But a line had been drawn.

That moment crystallized something that had been true since long before I'd ever thought of applying for psychoanalytic training, something that was salient for every lesbian or gay person who was interested in doing so. We all know that sexual orientation was and continues to be a meaningful social organizer in the wider world. It is to be hoped that it is equally widely known that the differences within the categories of sexual orientation defy any coherence within the given category. I had hoped that in the small and shrinking world of psychoanalysis, at least, that this would be true. But I was wrong. The meanings of sexual orientation have a remarkable and tenacious capacity to create boundaries, allegiances, sectors of safety and danger, even in the setting that purports to be one of open and nonjudgmental inquiry into human experience.

There were other moments that confirmed my sense of this pervasive, meaningful organizing principle. A respected instructor, illustrating a point about Freud's "On Narcissism," describes the treatment of "a homosexual, and he goes on his first date with a woman, probably someone he met at the Hamptons, and you learn that she has very short hair and small breasts. . . ." Again, the terrible moment when I knew that a challenging response was required, but I felt the irrational, fearful certainty that to challenge this remark would be to identify myself and jeopardize my psychoanalytic training. At first I was shocked to hear this statement, and I wondered if indeed I had heard accurately. When I was sure that I had heard this rather concrete and stupid collection of descriptors, it was clear that my decision to remain closeted inhibited my capacity to think, to function adequately in a psychoanalytic way, that is, to question and to understand what is being communicated. My determination to remain closeted, to tacitly endorse the prevailing division of humanity into hetero and homo, with all of the meanings encrusted to it, amounted to a requirement to lie in the course of training for a discipline founded on telling the truth.

This position was untenable. I could not go on being a liar, but I was uncertain as to how to pursue the aim of psychoanalytic training. I sought the advice of two of the instructors I had that year, analysts I trusted and who had let me know that they thought I had the potential to become an analyst. I described the awkward position I had placed myself in, and the tension I'd already experienced. I didn't ask either of them if they had an opinion as to whether I ought to disclose my sexual orientation. Both spontaneously discouraged me from doing so. They each told me they believed that there were senior analysts on the training committee of the institute who would not allow me to finish the training if it was known that I was gay. They also advised me to make sure that neither of my training cases be gay people, either. The logic of their advice went something like this: since being gay represented, at best, an inadequately resolved Oedipal phase, there could not possibly be a complete analysis of a gay person. No such case would be regarded by some at the institute as a demonstration of a candidate's adequate training.

It was clear to me that, if I were to continue in psychoanalytic training with any sense of integrity, I would have to find another training institute. There are many in New York City unaffiliated with either the American Psychoanalytic or the International Psychoanalytic Associations. Among these institutes there were at this time, I was shortly to learn, several that did not discourage lesbian and gay candidates from being open and honest about their sexual orientations. I transferred to one of these institutes and completed my training over the course of the following eight years.

In that span of roughly a decade things have changed a good deal for those seeking training. Most institutes with treatment services have discovered that lesbians and gays are one of the populations "underserved" by psychoanalytic treatment, and in order to ensure a pool of patients for their candidates have actively positioned their services as appropriate to this group. More significantly, many training institutes have seen the number of people seeking training drop and have become far more welcoming to lesbian and gay people wishing to enroll. Now not only are there analysts in training who may be far more sympathetic to the lesbian and gay population these institutes are seeking to treat, but the presence of these gay and lesbian candidates has made it impossible uncritically to make the routine kinds of remarks about an assumed psychic stereotype of gay people. Analysts know now that homophobia is something to be noticed, analyzed, and guarded against.

In a striking way, though, now that the field knows the attitudes it ought to have, it may be more difficult to analyze the persistence of the attitudes it knows it ought not to harbor. For example, some years ago, I was invited to present the "gay analyst's point of view" of love in the psychoanalytic setting. Clearly the organizers of the conference sought to make sure that homosexual analysts were represented in order to redress the long years of discrimination against homosexuals. What was more difficult to notice was the repetition of the splitting process that creates two monolithic groups and then assumes that a representative of one, a specimen who is also an expert, can speak meaningfully about some lasting, identifying features of that group to the other. The fact that an openly gay analyst was available to be invited, and that he was indeed invited to speak about love, is undeniable progress. But the resistance to a more thorough working-through may be more obscure than the old days when remarks about the first time a homosexual one is treating goes on a date with a woman can pass without challenge.

That progress was surely impelled in no small measure by this book. This book can impel and guide the work that remains to be done as clearly and vitally as it did twenty years ago. The book confirmed for me then the value of a psychoanalytic point of view despite the distorted uses to which its theories sometimes had been put. It is to be hoped that lesbian and gay people interested in psychoanalytic training need no longer wonder for a moment whether a "don't ask, don't tell" policy is a viable way to become an analyst. The extent to which this is now true is one indication of the change to which this book has contributed its particular impact. The book has lasting values, too, not least of which is its systematic analysis of the field itself to enable greater freedom and insight about its own anxieties and limitations.

Gilbert W. Cole, Ph.D., L.C.S.W.

FOREWORD

The republication of Kenneth Lewes's magnificent book would be a simple occasion for celebration were it not for the fact that, in spite of the twenty years since its initial appearance, much remains disquietingly fraught in the cultural sector marked out by the intersection of psychoanalysis and male homosexuality.

The changes in the sector have been both momentous and precipitous. Most obviously, of course, this sector is now gay-friendly. At a certain moment, pressures suddenly turned effective; progressive sentiments convincingly won the day. Decades of suspicion were transfigured into signs of welcome. Interdiction turned into affirmation, psychopathology into difference. By any measure, it seemed that all of the closed doors had suddenly opened.

And yet . . .

Despite the groundbreaking restructuring found in Kenneth Lewes's book, and despite the radical reordering of what can and cannot take place, of what can and cannot be said and thought, despite, that is, a radical reordering of the demands of conscience, there has still not been a thoroughgoing critique, a thoroughgoing reconceptualization, a thorough redoing of the foundational premises whose homophobic effects have infiltrated this sector for one hundred years.

Instead of a reconceptualization of the determinants of those effects, instead of a necessarily disruptive examination of how a systematized form of hatred—homophobia—found its way into the very foundations of liberatory psychoanalysis, we have, instead, in effect, a declaration that all expressions of that hatred are null and void.

From this day forward . . . homophobia will be banned and its long-standing targets, once excluded, will be welcomed. The enormity of this implicit declaration must be respected. Almost all of us are grateful for the change of tone, the change of constituency, the enfranchisement, and the transformed ethos that has reconfigured our borders, our interfaces, and the very fabric of our collegial and clinical lives. And yet, questions remain, fundamental ones, psychoanalytic ones.

Here are a few:

1. What, after all, are we witnessing when we witness, in effect, the absolute eradication of all signs of homophobia, all markers of it in official psychoanalysis; all published suggestions that male homo-sexuality might, in any way, pose a problem for psychoanalytic the-ory and practice; all barriers to candidacy for gay applicants?
2. Was the entire homophobic edifice so brittle, so fragile, so incapable of self-preservation, that its vanishing has left behind such little ap-parent trace?
3. Does what we are witnessing represent a radical change; are we in the midst of a fundamental rearrangement of thinking, feeling, and acting; or, contrarily, are we in the midst of what, to employ clinical jargon, might be called a "flight into health"?

I think that the asking of such unwelcome questions represents a proper modality through which to celebrate this book, pay homage to it, and continue its work.

Lewes' sober reflections certainly contributed to the changes of the past two decades. Those same reflections can also help us now as we try to make sense of what has happened, what is happening, and what might yet be needed to be done. Then, and now, Lewes, more than any other thinker I know, insists that this zone of intersection, where psychoanalysis meets male homosexuality, be looked at soberly. His insistence is con-veyed by example. There is no hectoring, no moralizing, as he indirectly alerts us to resist the pleasures of inebriation, whatever they might be, the ones offered by vicious targeting no less than the ones offered by manic denial. Lewes insists that we simply, and doggedly, think.

I suggest, then, that we follow his lead, that we postpone the noisy celebration for now. Lewes works slowly, painstakingly, and carefully. To best commemorate the republication of this monumental book, I think that we should too.

Lewes's book would not have had the power it once had, nor the power I think it will again have, were it, in fact, to have been a text of all sobriety and caution. It seems to me that Lewes actually wants us to join him in exciting, and usually interdicted, activities. The activities, of course, pertain to sexuality. They also pertain to thinking. He wants us, that is, to join him in thinking sexuality. Lurking in his argument is the notion that such thinking is itself sexual, and thus promising.

Lewes doesn't exactly ask us to join him, of course. Instead, he sets an example. He does what he likely wants us to do. And in doing it for us, and with us, he might likely expect or hope that we will see for ourselves some of the pleasures available to us in giving it a try.

What Lewes most exemplifies is daring. He perches on a kind of self-constructed ledge, on what Freud, regarding his own daring thought, referred to as self-constructed "scaffolding." From that ledge, Lewes looks out upon, with a fixed, riveted, and deeply interested gaze, the often brutal, occasionally pacified engagement that has, for a century now, bound psychoanalysis to male homosexuality.

The two seem bound no less intensively than, say, the police and black people are bound in every urban American center. In fact, one of the central activities I think that Lewes might want us to join him in is to wonder about how, and whether, psychoanalysis can "think" male homosexuality without, in fact, "policing" it. Can we construct a psychoanalysis that aims to establish conceptual order without at the same time aiming to establish law and order?

In some way, then, Lewes wants to "police" the psychoanalytic police, to reform them, to replace an order based on dominance and regulation with one based on structure and taxonomy. Instead of simply using psychoanalysis to generate a one-directional practice that orders and regulates the male homosexuality it runs into, Lewes means to use both psychoanalysis and male homosexuality to generate a two-directional practice that might order relations between the two. In some way, Lewes wants to use male homosexuality to think about psychoanalysis while simultaneously using psychoanalysis to think about male homosexuality.

The second of these activities is traditional and, by now, commonplace. The first, reversing direction, is astonishing. It is in this direction that Lewes almost beckons us to join him. It's an offer, not quite made, but nonetheless lurking in these pages, and one that, once it catches your attention, is nearly impossible to refuse, I think. It is seductive in the same way that Euclid might be or Newton, or, for that matter, Freud. That is, Freud, instead of simply adding to the regulatory apparatus of medical science, perched himself on the side of sexuality and, from there, one could say, wrote psychoanalysis. How could sexuality regulate and generate a new kind of thinking?, he might have wondered. This reversal of direction is what Lewes is doing here. What happens to psychoanalysis when we write it from over there, on the side of one of its long-suffering objects, male homosexuality? Lewes makes this move. This move is what makes this book as exciting as it is. It's a move that demonstrates a wonderful capacity of thought, and of thinking: the capacity to turn itself into an object and reflect upon itself from the point of view of its former object.

To return, for a moment, to the metaphor of police and black people: Lewes observes the interface, the points of contact, from the "community" side. He catalogs the violence, the apologias, the benighted good hearts, the efforts at reform and, in effect, concludes radically: there is something twisted in the premises that inform each and every interaction at the interface. These premises must be rethought. But, he writes, himself hopeful, that with psychoanalysis, we have the conceptual apparatus that will allow us to rewrite these premises, and re-write them he does.

Before encountering Lewes' re-writing, though, I think a series of preliminaries are called for.

Let's start with the title, *Psychoanalysis and Male Homosexuality*. The title invites us to imagine this pair of terms, *psychoanalysis* and *male homosexuality*, in some kind of relation to each other, at some point of intersection. The invitation cannot be refused. *Invitation*, then, is the wrong word. Better would be *stimulation*. The title stimulates, provokes, and reminds. That is, we see the title and, necessarily, imagine something; some kind of relation: conflict, resolution, harmony, opposition, synergy, indifference, antipathy. The range of possibilities is wide. The title gives us no hint as to where Lewes stands.

We begin, then, with the chance to catch ourselves in an act of prejudice, of prejudging, of lining up the pair in some particular way. Whatever this particular way turns out to be, Lewes's book means to take it up, take up our preconceptions. That is, Lewes will write of this pairing at its most fundamental level, will write of it as a pairing without intrinsic quality.

Lewes connects the two terms by that most noncommittal copula, *and*. The possibilities are limitless. I, for one, see the title and find a flurry of them. I find the *and* of Bonnie *and* Clyde; I find cops *and* robbers, black *and* white, doctor *and* patient, high *and* low. This is, of course, my own decidedly nonrandom list. What's important about the list is that I did not think it. I did not, in any commonsensical way, even construct it. The list found me as much as I found it. The list was there, waiting for me. That is the sense I have in mind when I refer to prejudgment: this list is a flurry of associations that precedes my thought, that tilts my thought, that simultaneously launches it and weighs it down. My thought both floats on and carries this load as I set out to read Kenneth Lewes's book. The load is not balanced; it lacks symmetry. The load is ideological—simultaneously private and public. It pulls from the most commonplace cultural shelves while simultaneously pointing to a reservoir of unarticulated private appetites. And what is the load? As I reflect on it, the load includes sexy criminals, law and order, good and bad, sublime and crude, illness and cure. This is just the beginning, of course, just a first flurry prompted by a neutral title. The point is that I cannot even make it through the title clear-headedly. None of us can. The best we can do, I think, is to be in a state of continuous self-reflection, a state in which we continuously try to assess the shifting load we're carrying and the consequent tilt our thinking must bear.

I think this associational exercise might be a good idea for readers of this book. It is likely to alert them to some of the psychic ground on which they stand when they begin to open themselves up to the prospect of a sustained encounter with "psychoanalysis" and "male homosexuality."

In mediating the construction of this associational list, the *and* of Lewes's title functions as a neutral connector: not entirely unlike a psychoanalyst: aiming to put commonly separated terms into novel relation to one another. Treating the connector as neutral frees us to treat anything we might sense in the connection as, in fact, coming from us.

The most obvious point of intersection of the title's two terms is *sexuality*. Psychoanalysis, in both theory and practice, is sexual. In taking sexuality as its primary object, from its inception it has necessarily become sexual itself. Whether interdicting or sanctioning, whether neutral or invested, the discipline is caught up with, and becomes part of, the sexualities on which it has so doggedly focused for more than one hundred years. It not only "discovers" the sexual lurking in the ostensibly driest of symptoms, it actually transports the sexual to those symptoms. Psychoanalysis sexualizes its objects while gazing at them. Psychoanalysis "thinks" sexuality, but, as it itself has consistently demonstrated, there can be no definitive line drawn that would separate sexual thinking from sexuality itself.

In thinking sexuality, psychoanalysis orders sexual ideas, sexual fantasies, sexual possibilities. Ordering itself turns into a sexualized and sexualizing activity. Despite its never-ending efforts to stay clean, to stay neutral, to resist its objects' seductions, psychoanalysis can never find a way to jump back quickly enough from the sexual ground it might wish to merely describe. It has sexual paint on the bottom of its shoes.

Again, as it itself so consistently demonstrated, its banner of "no" must affirm a hidden "yes." Its mood of austerity, its ethos of abstinence, its barriers against all forms of direct sensuous contact have the indirect effect of locating and sanctioning an alternative site—there and then—for what it—psychoanalysis—cannot permit—here and now. That alternative site, what Freud called an "other scene," is, in fact, in principle, everywhere and limitless.

Psychoanalytic thinking proceeds as though, for the moment, the sexual can be bracketed out, as though, for the moment, we can think about sexuality, without, in fact, enacting it. But this bracketing out is both temporary and contingent.

Psychoanalysis is seductive. It simultaneously speaks of, and promises, an expanded range of possibilities and a clear-eyed look at consequences. It exposes the costs and benefits of hiding, of disguising, of being open and direct. What do you want; what can you get; how can you get it; what must you pay—these are the kinds of questions that structure psychoanalytic sexuality. Psychoanalysis is, of course, a clinical-theoretical discipline, while less overtly (more sexually) it functions as a disciplinary discipline. It orders, yes, but in doing so it also gives orders.

Thinking of sexual economies, psychoanalysis is itself a discipline of sexual economy. Psychoanalytic treatment promises optimal sexual efficiency. Within the orienting frames of psychoanalysis, symptoms are symptoms because, in effect, they cost too much. They are not worth it. The sexuality they might permit comes at too dear a price.

Here at this point of exchange—some kind of satisfaction in exchange for, or even as an equivalent of, some kind of suffering—psychoanalysis does much of its sexual work. Perhaps the terms can be modified. Perhaps a better arrangement can be brokered, a better, more favorable, compromise worked out: more satisfaction at less cost, ancient debts eradicated, a little more freedom purchased.

The sexual/psychoanalytic labor of putting your dirty thoughts into words is worth it only because it promises to unburden you from having to wash and rewash your already red-raw hands. Psychoanalysis offers a way of sorting out sexuality, housing it differently; freeing those hands to touch something other than themselves, say. It establishes divisions, categories. It offers privacy, secrecy and control, a chance to carry on a sexualized life on terms that you might set yourself, a sexuality that is essentially imperceptible in the public sphere, a sexuality that allows you to assume the tasks of a citizen, that allows you, that is, to "function."

And here, with the notion of "function"—and its attendant elements of proper work, of appropriate limits, of good form, of the extrinsic burdens imposed by the necessity to integrate—we begin to sense that however liberatory the sexual economy offered by psychoanalysis, it too, like any economy it might displace, will have its costs.

And here, at this point where cost and "function" converge, we can, I think, locate the most volatile encounter between psychoanalysis and male homosexuality. How do we determine what something costs, what its intrinsic costs are? By costs, here, I mean sacrifice. What must be sacrificed in order to have what you want? How are those sacrifices determined? How are they measured? How essential are they? What are the fundamental structural costs of my desires? How can those costs be modified?

To think about the determinants of male homosexuality is, in effect, to think about the exchanges, the costs, that go into its production and maintenance. What must be sacrificed in order to live life as a male homosexual? Two terms shimmer in that question: *what* and *must*. These are psychoanalytic questions. They are also the questions of "male homosexuality." The two terms approach the questions from points of view that are not necessarily harmonious.

Psychoanalysis aims to separate the contingent from the essential. The aim of any psychoanalytic treatment is to expose desires, to illuminate their costs, to distinguish which of those costs are essential and which contingent, and to make possible a reconfiguration of desire and cost that increases the one and diminishes the other. Psychoanalytic treatment is painful to the extent that it affirms that sacrifice is necessary, that there is an essential gap between what can be imagined and what can be realized. Psychoanalytic theory and practice rest on the premise of that gap.

The particulars of that gap—its size and its contents—are, in effect, under constant surveillance. Clinical theory is the systematized record of that surveillance. But no clinical theory—none—can survive the assumption that the gap can be reduced to zero. That utopian assumption is necessarily in opposition to the working possibilities of psychoanalysis. That gap functions as the very premise of the discipline.

Traditional sexualities, all of them, including male homosexuality, aim to reduce that gap to zero. Psychoanalysis aims to preserve it. Here is a point of direct opposition.

Neither aim receives broad cultural support. Psychoanalysis, insisting on the irreducibly melancholy dimension of sexuality, takes a scornful view of the social/personal project of erotic perfectibility. It treats that view as an illusion, a kind of secular religion. For its trouble, then, psychoanalysis is consistently pushed to the margins where it struggles to survive. Male homosexuality, claiming desire's rights, also takes a scornful view of the widespread notion that desire must be sacrificed in the name of the greater good. It, too, like psychoanalysis, is consistently pushed to the margins where it too struggles to survive. Each looks for cover; each, perhaps, can look to the other for cover, but both, finding little, and embittered and proud, struggle to survive. The two are more competitors than allies, then, each vigilant, eager to survive, in a cultural setting, a niche, that is fundamentally hostile to both.

This shared burden of trying to survive—and perhaps having to compete—lends a strain of pathos to the ongoing interface between psychoanalysis and male homosexuality. The pathos is a product of necessity, the necessity a product of structure.

Kenneth Lewes means to write structure.

In some sense, then, Lewes writes from underneath both psychoanalysis and homosexuality. The book is a kind of anthropology. Its mood resembles the mood of Levi-Strauss' "Triste Tropiques" or "The Raw and the Cooked." Its mood also resembles Freud's in "Interpretation of Dreams." In effect, Freud asks there "What must be true of both dreams and psychoanalysis such that the two can inform each other and each be made sensible to the other? What must be true of mind such that it can simultaneously camouflage its desires in dreams and generate a theory that undoes the camouflaging work of dreaming?"

Levi-Strauss, Freud, and here Lewes are aiming to write from what might actually be an unattainable position: the position of the clear-headed outsider, the one who wonders how this, of all possibilities, is the way things are ordered. But the outsider may never quite achieve the wished-for clear head. His is also clouded with the self-same determinants that make the object of his attention, the order of things—the structural, often pathetic, order of things—an occasion for sadness. And with that phrase, the order of things, we can also attach the name of Michel Foucault to the mood-makers with whom Lewes's work is in harmony.

The mood is both dogged and melancholic. Lewes is writing alone. He pulls together some five hundred documents. He reads them all. He contends with the poignant liberal sentiments and the manic vitriol. And at no point does he break with his own project. At no point does he give up on structure and capitulate to emotional force. The integrity of this work is awesome: the capacity to maintain a singular point of view, a commitment to thought, to structure that no actual evidence supports. What is the payoff for such commitment? What is it worth? The melancholy that permeates this book is a marker that its author has embarked on a monumental task without consideration of payoff. Had payoff been taken into account, this book would never have been written.

After all, we all know the cynical fruits of experience. Theory is for losers. The search for structure, for pattern, for foundations leads nowhere. Go beneath experience, treat the empirical as merely empirical, and you wind up in the now transcended nether zone where thought seeks out imaginary prey while elsewhere predators find real prey. Join the predators. This is the cynical lesson of cynical experience. Practice/action/immediacy: this is where the rewards lie. Does it really matter how things are structured? Isn't the real problem the more concrete one? The one that presents itself today? The one that calls out now? Lewes, like Freud, like Levi-Strauss, and like Foucault, before him, says, in effect, no.

No, for Lewes, the basic issues, the ones that count, the ones that demand thought, are not, finally, whether homosexuality is classified as a psychopathology, say, or whether gay people ought to have the right to marry. These issues matter, of course, but they do not demand thought, at least not the kind on display in this book.

We can only marvel and feel grateful that a figure such as Lewes, and a book such as this one, actually emerges. Their emergence gives us the opportunity to reconsider our own relations to immediacy and common sense, to what feels right and necessary, to the soft satisfactions of proceeding in accordance with what our times and circumstances will dictate.

Reading Lewes might make us want to write our own book, say, one that would ask how it comes to be that such figures, such writing, is possible, how it comes to be that work this lonely can nonetheless be accomplished. What must be true of minds that allows any of us to endure the melancholy, the loneliness, necessary to think on our own, to leave behind life's comforts, life's companions, life's rewards, and to pursue, instead, the dry, sad zone of structure? What allows us, in effect, to temporarily think like angels?

No one before Lewes had done this kind of thing. And now, we can add that no one in the twenty years since the book has come out has substantively followed up on what Lewes has done. The book, and its author, stood alone and still stand alone. Think of Bruno Ganz, playing one of the angels in Wim Wenders's *Wings of Desire*; think of the way he looks on, lovingly, mournfully, at the mess, the frantic mess, of quotidian urban life. Lewes, in effect, has that look on his face; that mournful look, that sense that what he sees is such a mess, such a gratuitous, yet essential, mess. The task he sets himself is to think this gratuitous essential mess.

Gratuitous and essential; the terms are incompatible. Thinking this incompatibility, this is the impossible task that Kenneth Lewes gives himself as he looks, as though from the eyes of an angel, on the melancholy pairing of psychoanalysis and male homosexuality.

Donald Moss, M.D.

INTRODUCTION TO THE TWENTIETH-ANNIVERSARY EDITION: A CELEBRATION AND A WARNING

When I began working on this book more than twenty-five years ago, I had one primary purpose in mind, and that was to show that the traditional psychoanalytic theory of homosexuality was mistaken. At that time, I was nearing the end of a long and arduous process of completing the requirements for my doctorate in clinical psychology, having already earned a similar degree in English literature and having taught English at the college level for more than ten years. The transition that I was attempting to negotiate out of a literary milieu into a more nearly "scientific" one had been difficult and problematic for me in many ways. Most difficult of all, at least from my own personal point of view, was my repeatedly having to confront and somehow deal with old and entrenched psychoanalytic attitudes that maintained such a low opinion of people who loved and had sex with members of their own sex.

Although the American Psychiatric Association and the American Psychological Association by the mid-1970s had formally repudiated the labeling of homosexuality as a mental "disorder," the psychoanalytic establishment—that most mandarin of therapeutic and theoretical schools—persisted in claiming that it was one. This disparity was particularly troubling for someone like myself, who had decided to devote himself to the study and practice of psychoanalysis. Such a decision carried the implication that I had distinguished quite sharply between psychoanalysis, as I strictly defined it, and other more eclectic and positivistic forms of psychological investigation, and that I had made an intellectual commitment to the former.

Thus, I found myself—as they say in Michigan, where I had gone to pursue my graduate studies—caught between a rock and a hard place. Or, to characterize my anomalous situation a little more accurately, I found myself compelled to find a place somewhere among the peculiarly shaped nooks and crannies that existed around several hard places, and to adjust to it. I had newly learned to value the procedures and attitudes of academic and clinical psychology, with its emphasis on hypothesis-testing and statistical analysis. I still maintained my enthusiasm for the liberal traditions of world literature. I looked back with nostalgia to my previous immersion in the cosmopolitan outlook of a sophisticated Department of English, where the supreme achievements of artists who had been homosexual was taken as a matter of course. And, most important of all, I was myself homosexual, and I counted many people who professed a homosexual or a bisexual social identity among my closest friends and most valued associates.

As a consequence of my new acquaintance with psychoanalytic ideas, as well as my somewhat more complicated project of self-understanding, I was, of course, curious about what the classic psychoanalytic masters had to say about people who loved people of their own sex. Freud, whom I had read rather extensively before I returned to graduate school, once again proved to be interesting and informative on the subject. Despite some rather odd limitations that I noted in his sensibility, he never proved offensive to my experience of what homosexual people and their accomplishments were like. But when I began to read more systematically in the psychoanalytic literature of his followers, I was shocked and appalled by what I discovered.

The literature about homosexuality that I was reading—which by the time of my starting to write my book amounted to more than five hundred items—was almost uniformly negative and censorious. Almost all psychoanalytic writers considered homosexuality a profoundly disturbed psychological condition. Many analysts were eager to inform their readers that it was frequently found in association with vicious and bizarre behaviors of various kinds. Some analysts went so far as to assert that homosexuals were quite simply incapable of adequately loving another human being.

But even more striking than that, the tone of many of these pronouncements was infused with contempt, anger and hate. Today, it would be easy for a reader to recognize them as the homophobic exercises that they in fact were. But back then, they represented not only a majority of psychoanalytic opinion, but a near unanimity. Only a handful of analysts thought that they could dissent from this dark evaluation, and those who dared to do so at best adopted only an indirect and theoretical approach.

There were also several other characteristics of this chorus of condemnation that I would like to call attention to. First, the negative opinions and observations that these analysts espoused did not represent some unusual, quaint intellectual relic of the past or a residue of old-fashioned Victorian prudery. To the contrary, they represented the most up-to-date thinking on the subject. This psychoanalytic party-line remained pretty much what it had been since the death of Freud in 1939, and it continued in that path until literally the turn of the millenium in 2001, when the American Psychoanalytic Association officially changed its point of view and chose to honor one of its previously closeted homosexual members.

By then, of course, the social and intellectual environment that surrounded psychoanalysis had long since changed. Most important of all, following the Stonewall Riot of 1969, Gay Liberation had reached a kind of maturity and had formulated a cogent and persuasive critique of the psychoanalytic theory of homosexuality. Although this critique deeply influenced the theory and procedures of more eclectic psychotherapy as it was practiced by most professional groups, the psychoanalytic establishment remained relatively unaffected by it. Analysts claimed that they and they alone occupied a privileged position from which to view and evaluate issues of psychological and sexual functioning. According to them, any other view was necessarily based on superficial observations of the phenomena in question. In thus continuing to adhere firmly to its old formulations and in disdaining to acknowledge the new insights that were arising from psychiatry, clinical social work and nonanalytic psychology, as well as from historical and sociological studies, psychoanalysis left it to those other more nearly progressive disciplines to achieve new understandings of human sexuality.

To some progressive and understandably impatient critics of psychoanalysis, the old discipline, which had once been so deservedly proud of its history of providing a progressive and radical insight into individual psychological functioning within a society that demanded more and more instinctual renunciation, was beginning to seem as impervious to changing ideas and points of view as astrology or alchemy. But for an enthusiastic new student of psychoanalysis like myself, who by that time was deeply involved in his own classical analysis, the moral and intellectual scene around him was becoming more bifurcated and confusing. One of my primary personal reasons for feeling so uncertain was the fact that many of my most important teachers, some of whom I continue to this day to esteem for their sensitivity, wisdom and compassion, persisted in espousing the old analytic line. There were some, of course, who might publicly acknowledge the usefulness of the new attitude towards homosexuality, but they almost always reverted to more traditional ideas when it came to private case conferences or individual clinical supervision. Even now I wince with embarrassment when I remember some of the ideas I had to listen to when they were repeated again and again in classes and lectures I attended. Even now I find myself growing furious when I remember some of the demeaning treatment that I had to endure personally when some of my superiors became aware of my sexual orientation. At that time it was extremely difficult, if not impossible, for a person who was openly homosexual to receive training as an analyst at most of the more traditional institutes. There was thus no way of being heard if one wished to speak analytically and yet remain homosexual.

After having undergone one particularly egregious humiliating and infuriating experience at an analytic institute, I decided that my dissertation would be a critical history of the psychoanalytic theory of homosexuality. It had already occurred to me that such a study was long overdue. Although many books and articles had already appeared challenging the received psychoanalytic wisdom, and although popular and professional opinion had begun to turn against the old analytic orthodoxy, no extended critique of the psychoanalytic theory of homosexuality had appeared that had been mounted from *within* psychoanalysis itself. That is to say, none of the critical studies that I was familiar with employed psychoanalytic ideas and vocabulary to frame its critique. Consequently, the analytic establishment could ignore or dismiss most of the extra-analytic criticism that had already appeared as not really being addressed to psychoanalytic issues and ideas. Around the time that I was starting to write, one gay intellectual activist told that he sometimes felt like a member of a tribe of Indians in the Old West who were attacking a wagon train of settlers that had circled around itself for defense.

I therefore reached several decisions about what my book would be like. First, it would contain an *internal* critique of the psychoanalytic theory. Second, it would adopt the discourse of psychoanalysis as its own strategy in addressing phenomena that psychoanalysis had always claimed as its own property. By thus engaging in a characteristically analytic discourse—that is, by using its own ideas, vocabulary and procedures, I planned my project to show that the theory, as it had evolved in time, was mistaken. I also entertained hopes that the analytic establishment would be compelled to take serious notice of my ideas.

Looking back on the twenty years that have elapsed since the publication of *The Psychoanalytic Theory of Male Homosexuality*, I think I can say with some confidence that my primary aim for that book has been achieved. Of course, it was not the book itself that accomplished this goal. Instead, it was the larger surrounding intellectual and cultural progressive movement that should be accorded the credit. Gay Lib, Women's Lib, the Identity Movement, recent developments in literary criticism and sociology, as well as in hermeneutics and historical theory, have all contributed in important ways toward the development of new attitudes and ideas about the issue of sexual variance. The most significant contributors to this change, of course, have been gay people themselves, who came to insist on their right to formulate and direct a discourse that had always concerned primarily themselves. I am proud to number myself among this group of intellectual and cultural innovators.

And yet, and yet . . .

While I was writing, I frankly did have other aims in mind than simply to show that the psychoanalytic theory about male homosexuality was mistaken. One of my fondest hopes was that my work might contribute to a much larger reconsideration of the procedures and discourse of psychoanalysis itself. The deficiencies in psychoanalytic thinking that were occupying me at length, I had become convinced, were not confined to the discourse that had developed around homosexuality. As I continued to formulate and focus my critique of the psychoanalytic theory, I was becoming more and more convinced that its most glaring failures did not represent mere accidents or the results of some theoretical or procedural carelessness. It was clear to me that they were the consequences of *systematic* deficiencies and flaws in analytic discourse as it had evolved from the very beginning of analytic history. I therefore ventured to hope that psychoanalysis, once it began to understand these systematic flaws, might embark on a process of self-reconsideration and renewal. And having done that, it might then go on to purge itself of some of its old habits of insularity and smugness, and so once again assume its rightful position as a progressive—if not a liberationist—humane discipline. When I consider the present situation we find ourselves in—both intellectually and politically—I cannot claim that many of these larger goals have been achieved.

I had intended my book as something of a challenge—a gauntlet I had thrown down. I eagerly awaited a response. In my more grandiose moments, I even imagined that I had invited psychoanalysis to put itself on the couch. To put it less grandiosely, I thought that my historical and theoretical survey had uncovered evidence of a neurotic disturbance in the procedures and convictions of psychoanalysis itself. Specifically, the homophobia that I had attempted to identify and analyze seemed to me to represent a symptom of an underlying, more insidious and quite widespread mental disturbance.

As I read psychoanalytic ideas about homosexuality more extensively, the largeness and complications of my project became apparent. I became convinced that the ferocity of psychoanalysis's condemnation of homosexuality, which was obviously so disproportionate to its provocation, as well as the blatant inaccuracies of some of its social and historical claims, could only be accounted for as some kind of neurotic distortion. I could not understand why analysts—especially those without any apparent stake in maintaining this campaign of vilification and misinformation—failed to recognize and condemn what in any other context they would surely have labeled countertransferential distortions. There was no response to my charges.

But an even more baffling failure occurred later on. When psychoanalysis finally officially abandoned its previous condemnatory homophobic positions, it did not undertake a related program of trying to identify and understand what had caused this moral and intellectual failure. Instead, the discredited ideas simply disappeared. With the exception of the polemics of a few die-hard rear-guard activists, they were no longer even discussed. Consequently, their origins in a flawed intellectual discourse and in obscure processes of anxiety and defense were never understood. At one analytic conference I was invited to speak at, the organizers reported that they had encountered some difficulty in locating a single psychoanalyst who would be willing to argue in favor of the old, classic view. In the question period that followed the presentations, the semireluctant spokesman for the earlier orthodoxy, whom the organizers were able to locate, claimed that psychoanalysts had never espoused such untenable ideas.

For some of us in the room that day, the fact that the love that dared not speak its name had bequeathed its tattered veil of silence to an important group of previously vocal antihomosexual psychoanalysts was a symbol of the intellectual victory we had achieved. But in another sense, it was also a sad occasion, as well as a sobering warning, that the forces that had caused the widespread neurotic distortion in the first place had not been understood, analyzed and extirpated. Instead, they had simply gone underground, where they might continue to lead a furtive and unanalyzed life until they broke out again in forms that that none of us could predict.

This later moral and intellectual failure on the part of the psychoanalytic establishment continues to trouble me. If the psychoanalysis—that is to say, its ideology, procedures, practitioners, institutions and discourse—had been, as I had fantasized, a patient on the analytic couch, the standard analytic treatment would have been employed. Or to put it in somewhat less baroque terms, had an analytic patient reported that a neurotic process, which at one time had seriously distorted and debilitated his capacity for love and work, had suddenly and quite miraculously disappeared, any analyst would immediately have known what to think. He would have entertained the strong suspicion that only the most obvious of the symptoms of the disturbance had disappeared, but that the underlying disturbance was still lurking in the unconscious. Despite this, once psychoanalysis emerged from a century-long campaign of mistaken, driven and, I would claim, delusional hyperactivity, it did not attempt to understand the preconditions that underlay the onset of this illness. Nor did it stop to consider why its continued existence had been tolerated with so little sign of conscious anxiety on the part of the most prominent and embattled spokesmen. The apparent signs of the neurosis did seem to have passed quite mysteriously. But most of the people who had previously been infected by it, both its active and more nearly passive supporters, marked its passing by breathing a sigh of relief, as they collectively joined in a flight into health.

In this way, a rare opportunity for the acquisition of greater self-knowledge had been missed. Although the historical record of psychoanalytic animosity towards homosexuality was for the most part repudiated, it was also ignored. It should, on the contrary, have been examined closely, for it might have suggested an extremely important idea. The issue of homosexuality—both its experience and speculation about it—had from the beginning occupied a position of central importance in the concepts and procedures that psychoanalysis developed. One could quite legitimately claim that homosexuality always inhered essentially in the psychoanalytic project. With the almost sole exception of Freud, psychoanalytic writers had been promulgating and defending homophobic ideas for a century—that is to say, for the entire lifetime of the movement. It might therefore have occurred to analysts that the preconditions for this long obsessional preoccupation lay in a substrate of attraction and excitement, which could only be tolerated by a defensive strategy of disowning the wish, projecting it, and finally attacking it in whatever forms it assumed in the Other.

If these speculations are even remotely valid, there are two major reasons why psychoanalysis should have tried to understand its own complex relations to homosexuality. First, psychoanalysis can claim to have recovered its balance and clear-sightedness only if it has understood this phobic process and its connection to such other problematic psychoanalytic traits and characteristics as, for example, its previous insistence on analytic neutrality, its phallo-centric orientation, or its refusal to recognize its countertransferential participation in analytic constructions of many kinds. Second, and even more important, if the underlying illness has not been investigated and adequately understood, it is likely that entirely new symptoms will appear, and that these may turn out to be even more malign. As every competent practitioner of psychoanalysis has been trained to suspect, the apparent disappearance of a symptom is no guarantee that the underlying illness has been cured. Like all spurious claims to health, the recent repudiation by psychoanalysis of its previous homophobic fixations may amount to little more than an anxious flight into health.

There can be no question that psychoanalysis has undergone remarkable transformations over the past twenty-five years. These changes are not confined to the specific issue of homosexuality. The theory of psychoanalysis, its values, its procedures, and its characteristic discourse have all undergone major reconsiderations and reformulations. The emergence of a "gay-friendly" psychoanalysis is only one aspect of this change. Far more far-reaching changes can be observed in such developments as the rise of relational schools of psychoanalysis, the elaboration of feminist-inflected critiques, which have led to a general repudiation of a phallo-centric orientation, and a remarkable new sophistication about basic epistemological issues concerning the very possibility of eliciting valid psychological information, their interpretation and the construction of narratives. Psychoanalysis' new openness to previously marginalized voices, as well as the more literal opening up of its training institutes to candidates from sexual minorities, are equally important indications of these changes. All of these new developments are the happy results of a new receptivity on the part of psychoanalysis to variety and difference, as well as its turning away from a previous espousal of exclusivity and a habit of promulgating traditional social norms and prescriptions.

I certainly applaud all of these new developments. At the same time, however, I think that we should not lose ourselves in the chorus of applause and self-congratulation. Throughout the history of psychoanalysis, many newly arisen trends, which at first sight seemed to hold the promise of progress and greater enlightenment, have, in the light of later developments, turned out to be regressive. In our terms, they proved to be a new set of substitute symptoms arising out of never-dormant defensive responses to anxiety. Despite our intuition that these most recent developments are commendable, there are equally compelling reasons for us to be alarmed at such Janus-faced trends. We can begin to understand signs of our hopeful but dangerous times if we look at the vexed issue of theory and its place in psychoanalytic procedures and discourse.

Although I have been made very happy by the attention my book has received and by the way it has figured in some of the debates and reevaluations I have already referred to, I also feel something like regret for one of the uses to which my work has been put. One of my purposes in undertaking it was, as I have said, to show that the psychoanalytic theory of homosexuality was mistaken. The particular theory, in my view, had been carelessly and incoherently formulated, and more importantly, had operated in the service of more nearly unconscious needs and anxieties. As I delved deeper into the record, I became convinced that psychoanalytic theory had not been immune from the contagion that had affected the particular theory of homosexuality.

I had hoped that my work would be thought of as a call for a rethinking and reformulation of that particular theory. But in order to demonstrate its theoretical incoherence and to call for its reformulation, I had tried to be assiduous in making use of basic psychoanalytic theory, at least as I understood it. For this reason, I had always thought that my own critical exercise should properly be considered a *theoretical* refutation of a theory. For example, I had almost entirely ignored relevant sociological research findings in my arguments and focused my attention instead on the theory and its construction. Thus, I never thought that my work would be considered a denial of the importance and usefulness of theory, let alone a refutation of theoretical projects in general. Nevertheless, some readers of my book used my arguments to stake out an antitheoretical position of their own and to call for the repudiation of all theoretical endeavors in psychoanalytic discourse. They are, of course, entitled to embark on such project, but I would like to state my own opposition to such a program.

Contemporary clinicians who have objected to the use of theory in psychoanalytic discourse have succeeded in many areas of psychological investigation. To be sure, a great deal of theoretical work continues to appear regularly in contemporary psychoanalytic publications. Such efforts, however, are for the most part confined to questions that are quite abstract. They are essentially epistemological in nature. That is to say, they investigate the limitations necessarily placed around projects involving the gathering of psychological information or the formulation of valid generalizations and narrative constructions. The theory that we find still appearing nowadays thus aims primarily at negative and limiting conclusions. On the other hand, investigations that used to be called psychoanalytic theory—that is to say, Freud's "metapsychology" or the abstract logical procedures used to proceed from inference about abstract and theoretical constructs to clinical particularities—has, for the most part, been abandoned.

More than that, some of the most recent schools of clinical work show a distinct tendency to avoid theoretical speculation and inference entirely. Some contemporary practitioners urge us to replace theoretical interests with an emphasis on such notions as attentive and respectful listening to individual patients. They urge us to eschew norms and prescriptions and encourage the toleration, if not the celebration, of variety and difference. Specifically, some see the classical Oedipus Complex, as they interpret it, as containing a built-in teleology, from which norms for mental health and sexual normalcy have been derived. According to these critics, such theorizing represents the deployment of unexamined value judgments, which have not been adequately substantiated. They consequently urge us to discard it, along with such other outmoded concepts as the notion of optimal psychological development, which supposedly finds its fulfillment in "the genital personality," an essentially heterosexist position. According to this line of argument, the very concepts of "perversion" and "inversion" also should be rejected in favor of less judgmental notions of sexual variance, which invokes a difference that significantly does not imply any notion of inferiority or defect.

In a similar vein, many other critics have gone on to deny any essential difference between homosexual and heterosexual psychic organizations or their patterns of development. For them, even to entertain the question of why certain children became homosexual in their later object choice is a covert form of negative judgment and exclusion. After all, they claimed somewhat inaccurately, no one has ever been puzzled by why some people turn out to be heterosexual. It has even become fashionable in certain analytic circles to think that the only reliable difference between heterosexual and homosexual people is the latter's experience of social homophobia and heterosexism.

In many ways, this denial of theory can be justified as an appropriate response to a long history of misusing psychoanalytic theory, especially when it involved the issue of psychological norms and their reliance on the dialectically generated notions of deviance. Freud was clearer than most of his followers in seeing that arguments that promulgate notions of optimal emotional "health" or "normal" development have a contingent basis. He saw them as depending on particular historical and social settings, each with its own set of relinquishments, needs and imperatives. For Freud, current European standards of correct sexual behavior had absolutely no extra-historical validity to recommend them. He pointed out very acutely, for example, that the classical Greeks had their own notion of sexual normalcy, which, though valid for them, differed radically from European standards of morality and civilized behavior. He would not, I think, have been surprised by some of the ideas later put forward by Michel Foucault, for example. Freud's scrupulousness and general cosmopolitan outlook when he came to deal with these matters, however, was, for the most part, not shared by most of his disciples. And by the 1940s, it had almost disappeared from psychoanalytic thought.

In its place we find the analytic habit of freely setting out patterns of behavior that it considers optimal, normal and healthy. Looking back on these prescriptive norms today, we can see them as products of their times, determined by historical and cultural factors, of which their formulators were insufficiently conscious. This psychoanalytic freedom to pontificate and prescribe continued unabated almost until the end of the millenium. Much of the psychoanalytic movement's loss of prestige and influence in the culture at large, which it had suffered by the end of the century, can be largely attributed to its smug self-confidence, coupled with its cultural and intellectual insularity.

There are, therefore, substantial reasons for us to be skeptical of the usefulness of psychoanalytic theory. Nonetheless, while these revisionist antitheoretical developments are, as a whole, to be applauded, we can also recognize that the general attitudes that they offer in their stead are themselves insufficient guides to clinical work. They can even be misleading. They fail most egregiously by leaving an empty conceptual space at the core of the psychoanalytic project. In themselves, although they can serve as guarantees for the unbiased listening and nonjudgmental interpretation that these clinicians urge us to embrace, and although these ideas may seem to be more enlightened than the old ones, in the end they may amount to little more than wishful thinking.

I, for one, find the purity of this newly developing orthodoxy to be entirely unsatisfactory. I have many reasons for reaching this conclusion, both clinical and more generally philosophic, but the most significant one, I think, is the way it threatens to deprive psychoanalysis of one of its most useful and important social functions—its ability to stand outside of current social norms, conventions and fashions and to fashion a critique of society and the toll that it necessarily imposes on individual lives. My own view, of course, implies a real value judgment, but it is a judgment that I consider essential if a free and progressive discourse is to develop and legitimately sustain itself.

I have believe for a long time in the idea that psychoanalysis, if it wishes to provide an effective counterweight to political exigencies, must occupy a conceptual position located *outside* of these social values. And to do so, it must, in turn, possess a consciously acknowledged, examined and coherent set of theoretical propositions. Failing that, it may eventually find that that the empty conceptual space at its center has been usurped by another set of notions that are unconscious in nature. It may think that it is upholding values that are derived from commonsense, but such attitudes, admirable as they may appear to be, may from a wider perspective turn out to be operating in the service of power interests and prejudice, as well as providing disguise and camouflage for them. So-called commonsense, when it is examined carefully, often amounts to little more than unsystematic and unconscious ideology, a conviction that its view of the world sees things as they are, never acknowledging the necessity for articulating and criticizing itself, simply because such things go without saying.

On the other hand, the one distinct advantage that conscious theory, whatever its limitations, can always hold up to unconscious ideology is the simple fact that it is conscious. Because it is conscious, it remains at least possible for us to examine, criticize, evaluate and reformulate it. None of these critical procedures, however, are possible if ideas, attitudes and ideals, no matter how benignly and humanely intended, remain sealed off from conscious examination and criticism. The ideas that we are espousing nowadays may seem fashionable and attractive, but those reassurances are insufficient to ensure the integrity of our project. An important discipline like psychoanalysis must make another, higher demand of itself. It must employ a set of basic standards and commitments more substantial and enduring than mere fashion. And, equally important, they must be subjected to careful criticism and evaluation.

I am also calling for something else as well. Partly on the basis of the dreary and lamentable history of psychoanalytic homophobia, many critics deny psychoanalysts any right to assume a superior position with respect to their analysands' own perceptions, ideas and wishes. Instead, they claim that the analysts' most essential function is to listen "respectfully" and to accept whatever their clients wish to tell them. They argue that no one knows more about individual lives and experiences than the people who are living them. These arguments seem to me quite spurious and to stem from a peculiar kind of diffidence and pusillanimity. They deny the possibility that competent psychoanalysts who have been well trained, attempt seriously to keep themselves abreast of new developments, and try to remain aware of the distorting effects of their own neurotic countertransference do occupy a privileged position vis-a-vis what their clients tell them.

They know, for example, that what motivates all people is largely unconscious in nature, and that a complicated system of defense operates to keep it sealed off from consciousness. The goals that patients may set for themselves at the beginning of treatment often act in the service of preserving their debilitations and inhibitions intact. This is true for an overworked executive who announces that he wishes to learn to exercise greater control over his adolescent children as it is for an anxious young career woman who wishes to ignore her sexual yearnings. Analysts should, of course, listen to these communications, and their listening should be consistently careful and respectful. But they must also reserve the right to decide that such communications may disguise deeper meanings and wishes. Being aware of such possibilities is an essential component of an analyst's professional competence. Denying it seems amounts to a repudiation of any claims to be helpful in the first place.

It is, of course, an extraordinary act of arrogance for someone to claim to know better than people who come for help what their real interests are, especially if the understanding of their difficulties conflicts with the ideas they have been entertaining about themselves. Any reader of the present work knows the pernicious effects that follow when clinicians glibly assume a privileged position from which to adjudicate such issues. Analysts will never know, nor should they hope to discover, what Mother Nature intended when she gave us our sexual nature. Individual human lives are extremely complex matters. We should also approach them with respect and a sense of the limitations of our own skill and knowledge. Nevertheless, the humane ends that analysts have set for themselves require that they bear the burden of trying to discover a set of ideas that will help in distinguishing between beliefs and wishes that social systems, with their ideologies and complicated sets of coercions, require people to believe about themselves from what may turn out to have been genuinely motivating them.

This is a position that is intellectually enormously difficult to substantiate, and it is even more morally dangerous to maintain. In the past, what has been regarded as obvious aspects of an ahistorical "human nature" have revealed themselves to be little more than weapons in ideological struggles waged to maintain power. Ideologies are always rooted in specific historical moments. We must therefore be extremely wary of naively maintaining such hypostacized ideas and claiming them to be non-contingently true. Many currents in psychoanalytic history regarding its attitude towards women and homosexuals, for example, should warn us against undertaking this task without an adequate sense both of the risks involved and of our own limitations.

Having said that, however, I would argue that it is simply not possible to begin to assess the human costs that are exacted by any political or social system if we do not possess an articulated set of ideas about what human nature is and what its possibilities might be. We must deal with an extremely broad range of issues that when we undertake such a project. Nowadays, we may find ourselves condemning the practice of female circumcision and clitoridectomy, criticizing certain aspects of the institution of marriage, warning against the uncontrolled use of psychotropic medications, or expressing opinions about the legal issue of gay adoption of children. But to do any of these, we necessarily invoke a conviction about what we believe human nature to be like. This remains true whether we like it or not, or whether we do it in a covert or an articulate manner.

This is a difficult moral and intellectual position to find ourselves in. But we cannot avoid it. To refrain from asking certain questions concerning the relations between, on the one hand, social arrangements, conventions, roles and responsibilities, and, on the other, individual experiences, will most often lead to a tacit acquiescence in the forms that those social arrangements have assumed. While it is a legitimate aim of psychoanalysis to take the part of individuals in their essential opposition to societal norms and requirements, the contemporary ideal of "respectful" listening to what individual people want to say about themselves, commendable though it appears to be, unfortunately will take us only a short way in fulfilling this project. There is a simple reason for this. Fantasies, wishes and most expressions of human desire are among the first faculties that succumb to the pressures placed on individual consciousness by society. Especially now, with the triumph of advertising and consumerism and the systematic and unrelenting assault on the experience of privacy and inwardness, is it imperative that we be on our guard against the temptation to take the things people say about their wishes, aspirations and experiences as representing their real interests. But who can claim to know better?

An essential, though ultimately unattainable project of psychoanalysis has always been to locate itself among a constellation of other disciplines, not one of which has an unquestionable insight into human nature. But taken together, all them can afford an insight into this difficult but essential issue. Human nature, whatever it is, is hedged around by constraints imposed by biology and genetics. The full range of human possibility can never be understood and appreciated by considering one society or one historical epoch, least of all our own. History, sociology and literature have essential insights to offer about the possibilities of human experience. Finally, psychoanalysis has its own body of experience. By having listened to numberless accounts of individual lives, we come to some understanding, however limited, of how people manage to negotiate a path among the exigencies of their own needs and wishes, and social requirements.

Psychoanalysis was gravely injured by its excessive indulgence in theoretical speculation and normative prescription. It is therefore now quite understandably fearful of renewing contact with something that burned it so badly. But, in my view, it is currently engaged in replacing something that resembled an obsessional addiction with something else, which, in its turn, resembles a phobia. I myself think that the contemporary avoidance of theorizing represents the emergence of a new set of neurotic symptoms, which, like all neurotic symptoms, are being used to avoid something whose outbreak causes an almost intolerable anxiety. We would be wise to try to understand what this danger is before we find ourselves once again enslaved to it.

INTRODUCTION 1988: NORMALITY AND PATHOLOGY

I have written the following study with two aims in mind. First, I have attempted to set out, with reasonable fullness and complexity, the psychoanalytic theory, or theories, of male homosexuality. The subject matter of such an exposition is homosexuality. I undertook the task because of my conviction that psychoanalysis is a privileged mode of discourse and has developed a powerful and incisive system of description and explanation of that condition. Second, I have also tried to account for how that theory developed. The subject matter of this second narrative is psychoanalysis itself. Although both accounts have been evolved from *within* the discipline of psychoanalysis and have made use of its methods and theoretical orientation, my stance is critical, and I have ventured to point out deficiencies in the theory and to criticize both the way psychoanalysis has gathered its clinical data on homosexuality and the way the theory was formulated and developed.

For people who think about such things, homosexuality possesses an ability to provoke a kind of anxious curiosity. In the first place, exclusive homosexuality occupies an anomalous place in "Nature," denying as it does procreation, the end for which sexuality seems directed. In addition, the social arrangements of most societies with which we are adequately familiar, as well as traditional moral strictures, all support the notion of homosexuality as a deviation, a turning away from natural ends—in short, and quite literally, a perversion. But most important of all is the remarkable ambivalence most people, especially men, feel for the very idea of homosexuality. Eliciting a strange anxiety in those who are not themselves homosexual, it simultaneously inspires the fascination and repulsion that Freud himself noticed and tried to account for.

1

For some homosexuals, this condition of erotic experience is not the least bit problematic. It is to them as natural and irreducible a fact of their personality and experience as, say, being a twin is to others. Posing questions about its "unnatural" or pathological status seems to them about as sensible as doing the same for heterosexuality. While there is much to be said for this position, it does not represent the initial intuition of most people who are interested in such matters. But even if one is content to label homosexuality a perversion, it still does not occupy the same place as other perverse erotic phenomena which most people can comfortably consider merely strange or repugnant. The testimony of many people who are homosexual, what has come down to us about the erotic behavior of cultures such as the classical Athenian, and a large body of literary and artistic anecdotes and gossip all prevent our taking a distant and judgmental view of people who love members of their own sex. Finally, anyone who is minimally aware knows someone who is homosexual. Understanding such a phenomenon and the way in which it both unites and separates people is a project that will lead to an enlarged human sympathy and a deeper awareness of oneself.

The number of questions that one would like to ask is large, but perhaps the following list includes most of those that have occurred to thoughtful and intellectually curious people. Is homosexuality an "unnatural" condition? Why do some people become homosexual: are they born that way or have they been made so by some psychic injury and stunting? Does the fact of choosing sexual partners of the same sex imply limitations of other kinds, especially in the capacity to form deep, complex, lasting, and satisfying relations with other people? Can homosexuality be "cured"? Should it be? What relation does homosexuality have to such aspects of heterosexual experience as friendship, cooperation, admiration, and loyalty? Is there something special and privileged about the homosexual condition, either in its very experience or in its relation to creative achievement? Does heterosexuality represent a corresponding limitation in possibility, so that becoming exclusively heterosexual involves the relinquishment of important potentialities? What finally is that urge to unite sexually with someone whose body is like one's own and not complementary to it? And what is that dread that accompanies the very idea of homosexuality for most people?

It was with such questions in mind that I began the following study, turning to psychoanalysis as the discipline most likely to answer them. Its attention to nuance and detail and to the particular quality of individual experience offers a special stance from which to understand as complex and personal a phenomenon as sexuality, and the theory it espouses seems suited to deal with the very questions I had posed. Although I shall have occasion later to qualify this generalization, I may nevertheless state that for psychoanalytic theory, the motivating force behind human behavior and the shaper of experience and personality is sexuality, which can serve as a causal explanation in two ways. Psychoanalysis can relate conscious experience and behavior, which may or may not appear to be sexual in nature, to an unconscious sexual drive. Or it can relate present experience and behavior to an earlier, more primitive and infantile sexuality. But in both cases, a basic sexual drive is transformed into recognizable experience and behavior. What is especially relevant for our purposes here is that many of the psychoanalytic rules of transformation specify the preservation of the sexual drive itself as a motivating force and the displacement of the original object of that drive. More precisely, although the infant's first sexual object is the mother, that attachment is neither heterosexual nor homosexual, but unfocused, uncoordinated, and all-inclusive. In Freud's phrase, it is "polymorphously perverse." In these terms, psychosexual development is a process of progressive focusing and exclusion, and it is this process that seemed to me most likely to account for the development of homosexual object choice.

With such considerations in mind, I set out to find what the most important analytic statements about homosexuality had to offer. What I found surprised and sometimes shocked me. While some analytic writers profoundly and powerfully illuminated the phenomenology and meaning of homosexual thoughts and actions, by far the greater number considered that condition as gravely disturbed and characterized by serious limitations in personal and creative capacities. For example, Edmund Bergler, the most important analytic theorist of homosexuality in the 1950s, was unequivocal in his estimate of homosexual people:

> I have no bias against homosexuality . . . [but] homosexuals are essentially disagreeable people . . . [displaying] a mixture of superciliousness, false aggression, and whimpering, . . . subservient when confronted with a stronger person, merciless when in power, unscrupulous about trampling on a weaker person.[1]

Bergler was an extreme figure in his views and rhetoric, but his statements represent with great clarity the general psychoanalytic consensus that no homosexual was capable of achieving any peace of mind, any satisfying relations with other people, or any genuine artistic accomplishment. Faced with the evidence of high artistic achievements by homosexuals, many analysts were quite confident in their explanation: "if a homosexual is a great artist, this is so *despite,* and not because of his homosexuality."[2]

These opinions are nonsense, and they are a particularly pernicious form of nonsense in their both repeating popular clichés and serving the purposes of those who wish to justify their own prejudices. For example, the author of an article in *Policy Review* sought to address the question, Is homosexuality normal? Declining to acknowledge any distinction between homosexuality on the one hand and necrophilia and coprophilia on the other, he invoked the authority of "Freudians" to claim that homosexuality is in fact abnormal because of the abnormality "of the causal factors that generate the behavior."[3] Although the reader who perseveres through the following pages will discover that no such etiology has ever been demonstrated that can be accepted by informed "Freudians," he (or she) will also find that by far the largest proportion of analytic writers have never really departed from the mass of popular prejudice and clichés and that their discourse, thus limited, has not included a serious consideration of the kinds of questions I listed earlier.

With this discovery, my task suddenly changed. My own primary intellectual allegiance had been and still is to psychoanalysis as a privileged mode of describing and understanding human experience, but my acquaintance with a larger culture as well as my personal and clinical experience all convinced me that the official, published analytic theory of male homosexuality was incomplete, partial, and frequently in error. Moreover, its failure to address the project with open-mindedness and objectivity pointed to serious deficiencies in the ways it gathered its data and formulated its theories. My task was now to trace how psychoanalysis, with respect to the subject of homosexuality, had moved from the humane and cosmopolitan system of investigation it had been with Freud and his circle to a rigid and impervious set of values and judgments.

The task I set myself seemed uncomplicated enough: I would read every article and book on homosexuality that assumed an analytic stance, and I would provide the reader with an account of how the analytic theory of male homosexuality developed, giving notice of particular advances in the theory and showing how analysts were influenced by previous work. Although this undertaking proved more substantial than I had expected—more than five hundred items are cited in the text—I think I have fulfilled this primary goal. Some items may unintentionally have been omitted, but they do not figure prominently in our history and are not cited in subsequent literature.

It soon became evident to me, however, that a compilation of published writings constituted only a partial history. Part of the difficulty lay in the selectivity I had exercised in compiling my bibliography. In the first place, I had chosen to deal with only strictly analytic work. Such figures as Stekel, Jung, and Fromm lay outside the perimeter I had drawn around my subject. Luckily, such peripheral figures had little influence on mainstream analytic thought on homosexuality. Further, the very breadth and complexity of my topic required that I exercise even more selection. Beginning with Freud and continuing through to the contemporary orthodox analytic school, bisexuality remained a cornerstone of analytic thought, and any adequate analytic description of an individual would necessarily have to deal with the fate of bisexual strivings and the way they inform both heterosexual and homosexual wishes and behavior. It followed, then, that any but the most limited and circumscribed analytic article bears on our history, whether it deals explicitly with bisexuality or not. A complete history of our subject would therefore require that every analytic article and book be considered, a task the present author must decline.

These caveats to the reader, important as they are, are not extraordinary in any history, which necessarily has to limit and focus its scope. But there is another set of considerations that renders our history far more problematic and that has to do with what is *not* articulated and written about in the published literature. In its simplest form, we may discern in some analytic writers a reluctance to deal with homosexuality when they are discussing an individual who for other reasons claims their affection and respect. We may see this in Lewy's long biographical article on Frederick the Great, in which he steadfastly refused to acknowledge that monarch's manifest homosexual interest, even while discussing at length the single most crucial episode in Frederick's life, his failed elopement with his male lover.[4] Similarly, Hitschmann, an earlier analyst who wrote on homosexuality and who occupies a modest place in our history, devoted an article to the psychology of Johannes Brahms. Though he dwelt in detail on Brahms's apparent effeminacy, his high-pitched voice, and his avoidance of close relations with women,

Hitschmann was at pains to argue that such characteristics did not indicate homosexual proclivities, but something else.[5] What Lewy or Hitschmann really thought about the relation of homosexuality to cultural or artistic achievement we will never know, and the historian can only point to the space left by the anxiety they felt at having to reconcile a repugnant idea with a figure whom they respected. Paradoxically, then, a complete account of psychoanalytic writings on homosexuality would necessarily but impossibly have to include what is not written.

There is an even more troublesome issue. An attentive reading of the psychoanalytic literature on almost any analytic topic suggests that published views constitute only a portion of the total analytic discourse. Much of the formulation of psychoanalytic theory and technique takes place informally, at analytic conferences and symposia or even more privately in supervision. Apart from actual analytic sessions, these are perhaps the most fruitful exchanges of ideas and information, and the glimpses one catches of them in published paraphrases tell much about the actual procedures of analytic discourse. But these exchanges take place among analysts and are not intended for the ears of laymen. Official, published analytic pronouncements, then, can be quite distinct from more complex ideas still undergoing final formulation. Often these differences are only matters of emphasis or qualification, but they are crucial to the question of how open such debates really were. This history, then, cannot claim to present what analysts actually have thought, but only what they have decided to publish, and the sense of analytic discourse being a unified set of ideas and procedures may be an illusion. The real history of psychoanalytic ideas can therefore never be written using only published sources. Nonetheless, these sources have a history of their own, and it is this history that is the subject of the following survey.

Before I end these introductory remarks, I must acknowledge that the three groups of readers for whom this history is primarily intended, apart from the general reader—psychoanalysts, feminists, and homosexual men—may find much here that is disappointing and even offensive. Although I cannot consider their objections fully, I should like briefly to note them.

Analysts are likely, and not without justification, to feel exasperated and offended by my account of analytic theory and by the many harsh judgments I pass throughout the following history. This is particularly troublesome to me because my intellectual allegiance, as I have suggested already, is to the theory and methodology of psychoanalysis. It is for me the only nearly adequate means of discovering the meaning of individual experience and, when appropriate, of removing blockages to a freer and fuller capacity for authenticity and richness. It can achieve these goals through the exercise of a deep human compassion informed by intellectual clarity and depth. I see no conflict between the heart and the brain in such an undertaking. It is precisely because of the importance and seriousness of the project that my standards have been so high, my demands so imperious, and my judgments so harsh. The "power to hurt" I invoke in my epigraph, in these terms, is the reverse side of an equal capacity for good, and my rebukes and criticisms have, I should like to think, been impelled by a deep hopefulness.

Still, the best intention cannot compensate for the real shortcomings of the present history. Psychoanalytic theory, even the portion of it that constitutes my exposition, is extremely complex and, by virtue of its dealing with unconscious motivation and the maneuvers that aim at keeping it unconscious, quite implausible. Any adequate exposition, therefore, would have to begin with basic principles, offer clinical evidence, and defend obvious offenses against common sense. But because of the limitations of space and the particular angle of approach I have taken, I have, for the most part, eschewed all three. The unfortunate result of such a decision is, therefore, a rather cursory treatment of extremely complex ideas. The general readers will find much in the following pages that is obscure and knotted, but those who know and use the theory daily will undoubtedly find my account superficial. I can offer no defense against such a finding and can claim in extenuation only that the very number of articles and books considered necessarily required compression and simplification. My aim has been to provide a sense of the formation of the psychoanalytic theory of male homosexuality, so that the readers may be able to place any individual contribution into a developmental context and thereby be able to understand novel developments and to identify logical inconsistencies and slippages. No important item here is discussed with the completeness and subtlety it rightly deserves. Theoretically sophisticated readers must, therefore, if they are to understand it at all adequately, return to it. If they find the present study useful, it can be so only as a contextual guide.

I am so explicit about this because I do not wish my summary treatments to be construed as dismissive or sardonic. There are, in the course of the following account, several items that I judge to be intellectually shabby or morally repugnant, and I have tried to be explicit about the reasons for my judgments. Others I have found deficient in their failure to limit the scope of their application, but they are powerful contributions to the theory and have important practical implications. I would not want my readers to dismiss them as fanciful or preposterous. I should like to think that the very length and painstakingness of this work is sufficient testimony to my respect for figures I have been bold enough to criticize. I am prepared to accept fully the criticism that I have not understood everything I have read or that my discussion is inadequate, but I reject in advance the accusation that I have approached the task with disrespect or with the intention to trivialize and ridicule.

As for the second group of skeptical readers, those with a feminist orientation, their legitimate objection begins with my title: the following is an account of the psychoanalytic theory of *male* homosexuality. I have avoided any discussion of female homosexuality and have referred to it only when it is relevant to a point I am making about its male equivalent. I have done so because of my impression that female homosexuality is not as well understood from an analytic point of view as the male variety and also because the dynamics that analysts have uncovered for it are quite distinct from those characterizing the latter. More important, however, the animus against male homosexuality which is an important aspect of the history I am tracing is muted, if not absent, from discussions about the female variety. The central text on female homosexuality is still Clara Thompson's article of 1947, in which she emphasized the meaning such relations have "in interpersonal terms" and concluded by finding that some female homosexual relations are reasonable and appropriate arrangements.[6] This open-minded attention to the meaning such relations have for their participants is, with the exception of the earliest contributions, almost entirely absent from the literature on male homosexuality. Why this should be so, and what effect the personal lives of female analysts have had on the developing theory, are questions that cannot be answered here, although they are extremely interesting and important.

Nevertheless, it may be charged that I find the subject of female homosexuality less interesting and important than its male equivalent. But the charge is untrue. Though the literature on female homosexuality is much smaller and the theory less developed, it focuses in a particular way on one of the most vexed and important issues in psychoanalysis—its male-centered, phallically oriented basis. This is an issue that is now only beginning to receive the attention it deserves, and, in a peculiar way, I consider the following survey a contribution to that growing discussion. I shall, in fact, argue in my concluding chapter that the psychoanalytic bias against male homosexuals derives from an initial gynecophobic stance in psychoanalysis and that the fear and denigration of women which hover at the perimeter of analytic discourse became displaced onto the theory of male homosexuality. The crucial study of the analytic theory of femininity has yet to be written, and the present author would be gratified if his history were cited in that future book as contributing to its findings.

The last group of readers, homosexuals themselves, have the weightiest accusation to make, and their suspicions and distrust of psychoanalysis are, in many ways, well founded. They derive, it seems to me, from two sources. The first is the way too many analysts have violated basic norms of decency in their treatment of homosexuals. The enmity between homosexuals and psychoanalysis is extremely unfortunate, but the blame for its emergence rests squarely on the analytic establishment alone. Second, it need hardly be argued that homosexuals have been and continue to be the victims of prejudice and discrimination both subtle and blatant. While the deepest roots of this animus lie in intrapsychic fears and defensiveness, the intellectual rationalizations that have been invoked to justify such unreasoning hatred and fear have frequently been psychoanalytic in nature. Official discriminatory immigration policies, the slow and grudging governmental response to the AIDS epidemic, and the vulnerability many homosexuals must suffer on their jobs have all been justified by recourse to psychoanalytic ideas, and analysts, for their part, have generally been content to have their work misunderstood and pressed into the service of prejudice.

That groups of homosexuals see the analytic community as aligned with those who seek to legitimate prejudice and hatred is understandable, and the historian must acknowledge the substantial reasons for this view. On the other hand, it takes in only a partial version of what analysts have thought and does not consider the important efforts at understanding and aid that have characterized analytic work throughout the history of that movement. The author undertook the present work not to accuse and harangue, but to communicate his conviction that the discipline of psychoanalysis provides the most nearly adequate understanding of homosexuality and the only possibility not of "curing" people of that particular form of sexual experience but of helping troubled and dissatisfied people who happen to be homosexual.

The last objection some homosexuals might raise to the following study is both more substantial and more complicated. It is that any undertaking that seeks to discover the causes of homosexuality is itself a form of prejudice since it isolates that phenomenon as a form of abnormality in need of an explanation and thereby assumes beforehand that it is an "unnatural" and "unhealthy" disturbance of human experience and behavior. Implicit in such a charge is the view that psychoanalysis is the study of pathology, so that any object of psychoanalytic investigation is assumed to be pathological. While, no doubt, a few analysts and many amateur students of psychoanalysis espouse such a position, it does not represent the central motivating core of analytic thought. Instead, psychoanalysis has always striven to account for all human experience and behavior, pathological and "normal." In these terms, homosexuality can be viewed as only one variety of human experience to be understood, and statistically more normal development also represents a valid object of research.

There can be no doubt that some forms of homosexuality are psychopathological, but the same is true for heterosexuality. Whether some forms of homosexuality are, on the other hand, "normal" and "healthy" is a question that spurs a continuing debate that is one of the primary points of interest in the following survey. Readers may already have formed their own opinions. But it seems to me that it is a legitimate project to attempt to discover what some of the most trained, scrupulous, and subtle minds have thought about the subject. Their conclusions can, of course, be pressed into the service of malign ends, and they have been. But it can do nobody any good to ignore what may turn out to be true and useful, and all readers must decide themselves how the theories we are about to present can appropriately be evaluated and criticized. If the theory has festered and brought harm, it is partly because it is largely unknown to educated and thoughtful people and has for the most part been available to analysts alone. I have tried in the present work to bring these theoretical obscurities out into the light of day so that they may be subjected to examination and criticism.

Homosexual people do not need the analytic establishment, and they will continue to lead their lives as they have done in far more hostile and dangerous circumstances. But the acrimony and alienation that characterize the relation between homosexuals and psychoanalysis are wasteful and unnecessary, and healing that breach will profit both groups. I should like to think that a major conclusion to be drawn from the following history is that, despite the enmity, a tradition has always existed within psychoanalysis that operates through respect, compassion, and fairness. That tradition remains available to be claimed and validated, and, it seems to me, it is only fitting that psychoanalysis now frame the first gestures of reconciliation.

Chapter II

FREUD

No reader will be surprised to hear that a psychoanalytic discussion of homosexuality must begin with Freud. His work on homosexuality is interesting primarily for two reasons, quite apart from his substantive contributions. First, it implicitly established the conceptual limitations and unexamined moral and aesthetic judgments that are evident in much later writings on homosexuality. Second, because Freud was always conscious of stating only preliminary ideas and findings, his work has a tentative and open-ended quality that is often lacking in later, more formalized writing on the subject. Thus, my interest in Freud will be exercised in two, perhaps opposite, directions. I see it as a kind of microcosm, in both its strengths and limitations, of later work, and, with its sensitivity to qualification and complication, as a standard against which to measure later, more nearly resolved ideas about homosexuality. In short, it is both a model and a reproach for what followed.

Although Freud probably saw his place as being within the history of biological science, he was also rooted in a cultural tradition that can provide focus and enrichment for many of his ideas, particularly the more complicated ones. Perhaps second only to Plato, Freud is the West's great philosopher of love, and, like Plato, he devoted much attention to the relationship between spiritual love and a basic sexuality. In grounding the higher functions firmly on biological drive and in allowing for the sometimes destructive power of lust, Freud was able to discard many of our sentimental and self-serving ideas about human nature, motivation, and childhood experience. In this, he ranks as one of the great modernists. Nonetheless, we can also take some measure of

Freud's achievement when we place him against contemporaries who were dealing with similar issues, but in different media and modes of thought. There is no question that Freud is one of the greatest of intellectual liberators, but it must also be observed that in many ways his outlook was quite provincial.

Let us recall that Freud did not live in Ann Arbor. He lived in Vienna during one of the most compressed innovative periods in modern culture, from the revolutions of 1848 to the beginning of World War II. The astonishing artistic and intellectual achievements in several capitals—Paris, London, and Petersburg, most notably—during that time are remarkable for their coherence and, in particular, for their relevance to Freud's work. Two ideas central to the Viennese achievement were the reconsideration of the role of sexuality—especially in its extreme and even morbid forms—in high cultural activity and the reevaluation by the young of the traditional, stable paternal cultural patterns of that time.

Surprisingly, Freud was reticent in reevaluating many of these cultural norms, most especially in contrast to other contemporary achievements that directly took on the moral issues obviously inherent in Freud's more nearly scientific project. Two relevant examples are Robert Musil's *Die Verwirrungen des Zoeglings Toerless* (*Young Toerless*), written in 1905, the same year as Freud's *Three Essays on the Theory of Sexuality*,[1] and Thomas Mann's *Der Tod in Venedig* (*Death in Venice*), published in 1911, the same year as the Schreber case.[2] These literary achievements are not, of course, the systematic and sustained researches of Freud, but the moral issues they treat are not separable from Freud's work, since the very idea of pathology assumes an ideal of health or "normalcy," a concept left largely unargued in Freud, even though it was undergoing profound investigation and transformation at the hands of his contemporaries.

In the visual arts, the relation of the beautiful to the morbid was being completely transformed, most obviously by the Secessionist movement, its publication *Ver Sacrum*, and the achievements of such artists as Gustav Klimt and Egon Schiele. This transformation was accomplished through the efforts of allied movements in other countries as well. For example, the decadence of the English Aesthetic movement influenced the poetry of Hugo von Hofmannsthal and the music of Richard Strauss, while the dark Expressionism of the Scandinavian Edvard Munch profoundly affected the artistic strategies of Oskar Kokoschka.[3]

In many ways, Freud was at the center of this turmoil, although he himself did not directly participate in it. His great love was literature, but his taste was resolutely Victorian and Anglophile. Still, he was aware that such figures as Arthur Schnitzler and Hofmannsthal were attempting to combine classical German traditions with the extremities of the Decadence and the subversive, alien quality of a Jewish sensibility.[4] His personal contact with such writers as Thomas Mann surely provided an awareness of the transformation of values taking place around him. His professional association with Lou Andreas-Salome[5] put him in personal contact with Rainer Maria Rilke and the radical developments in Prague and Paris.[6] His meeting with Mahler is similarly suggestive.[7] Nevertheless, Freud did not consider himself part of the cultural avant-garde. Instead, he was an heir to the classical and cosmopolitan tradition of Goethe, and although he was well aware that his discoveries were revolutionary, he thought that they would allow for the endurance rather than the destruction of traditional, liberal European values, much as the analysis of the id would foster and strengthen the ego.

I have presented the reader with this little bouquet of proper names in order to suggest that by considering Freud's exposure and reaction to this transformation of values, we can better judge his relation to traditional morality and aesthetics. In particular, we are interested in his attitudes toward traditional values and sex roles, the relation of the individual to the family, the notion of normalcy, and the amount of sexual relinquishment that society could appropriately require of its members. These issues are all crucial in determining what he considered to be necessary pathology, avoidable neurosis, or maladaptation that could be changed and ameliorated with understanding. Freud's response to these issues was, I think, rather disappointing. Although he almost always adopted the decent, liberal, and progressive point of view on such specific issues as the legal rights of homosexuals[8] or the variety of sexual identifications found among women,[9] he inadequately examined the larger moral and aesthetic issues underlying these particular ones and, consequently, left them to assume traditional, bourgeois forms. In assessing Freud's momentous contributions to the transformation of values we have alluded to, it is absolutely essential that we distinguish those statements and ideas of his that belong to the progress of science from those that properly belong to the history of opinion.

I think that many of Freud's moral and aesthetic values were simply quite limited. Certainly by our standards his opinions seem provincial, but even in his day they were unnecessarily stuffy and peculiar. While this adds a certain charm to the reading of Freud, it also marks a serious limitation in his theorizing about homosexuality, which depended as much upon personal moral judgment as upon objective clinical data and the requirements of formal metapsychological conceptualization. At its most innocent and beguiling, Freud's provinciality manifested itself in opinions that seem rather peculiar to all but those who have a middle-European mother. Thus, in arguing for a strong constitutional femininity in Leonardo da Vinci, Freud cited his "physical beauty and his left-handedness."[10] More serious, however, Freud would often put forward a personal preference or judgment as a fact unqualified by historical or cultural conditions. In *Three Essays*, for example, he related, almost as if it should pass without further remark, "the fact that the genitals . . . can really never be considered 'beautiful,' "[11] an observation that would surprise a visitor to an anthropological museum. And in the monograph on Leonardo, he insouciantly judged fellatio to be "a loathsome sexual perversion,"[12] an opinion that perhaps will surprise others as well. He makes even more disturbing judgments in his discussion of "normal" sexual tastes:

> If one makes a broad survey of the sexual life of our own time
> and in particular of the classes who sustain human civilization,
> one is tempted to declare that it is only with reluctance that the
> majority of those alive today obey the command to propagate
> their kind; they feel that their dignity as human beings suffers and
> is degraded in the process. What is to be found among us in the
> way of another view of sexual life is confined to the uncultivated
> strata of society.[13]

Similarly, his view of sexual *pudor* as a spur to excitement seems quite strange and even repugnant. According to him, women avoid intercourse during their menstrual period, and this variety of shame only enhances their desirability to men.[14] Men by nature demand that their sexual partners be virgins[15] and, finding female repression exciting, demand that their wives and mistresses be sexually hesitant.[16]

These peculiarities throw suspicion on some of his larger assertions. Was Freud's claim that women want to be loved more than they wish to love[17]—a crucial idea in his theory of narcissistic object choice—

really based on unbiased and representative clinical observation or on the projected confirmation of a culturally limited provincialism?

The issue of homosexuality engaged Freud's interest throughout his career, but his most important writings on the subject range from *Three Essays on the Theory of Sexuality*, written in 1905, to "Certain Neurotic Mechanisms in Jealousy, Paranoia and Homosexuality," written in 1922. Although Freud addressed inversion in the first of the *Three Essays*, wrote a paper on the etiology of a case of female homosexuality,[18] and summarized his work on the various etiologies of homosexual object choice in "Certain Neurotic Mechanisms in Jealousy, Paranoia and Homosexuality," no major work of his deals exclusively with male homosexuality. For the most part, his contributions to the theory of homosexuality are scattered throughout his corpus and are frequently the results of a discussion of some other psychoanalytic topic.

Freud's direct contributions to the subject of homosexuality were complete by the time he wrote "Certain Neurotic Mechanisms," but in this late work he explicitly called attention to the incompleteness of his prior formulations and offered yet another, though again expressing doubt about its exact applicability to his subject:

> We have, however, never regarded this analysis of the origin of homosexuality as complete; and I can now point to a new mechanism leading to homosexual object-choice, although I cannot say how large a part it plays in the formation of the extreme, manifest and exclusive type of homosexuality.[19]

Furthermore, in the monograph on Leonardo da Vinci, one of the works central to the subject, after denying any wish "to exaggerate the importance of these explanations of the psychical genesis of homosexuality," Freud clearly indicated his sense that the phenomenon was more varied and complex than any one explanation could suggest:

> What is for practical reasons called homosexuality may arise from a whole variety of psychosexual inhibitory processes; the particular process we have singled out is perhaps only one among many, and is perhaps related to only one type of "homosexuality." We must also admit that the number of cases of our homosexual type

on which it is possible to point to the determinants which we require far exceeds the number of those where the deduced effect
actually takes place; so that we too cannot reject the part played
by unknown constitutional factors. . . .[20]

In the same work, he called attention to the "small number of persons"
on whom his conclusions were based. More important, however, was
Freud's admitted uncertainty about whether homosexuality, even confined to the male variety, was a unitary phenomenon. Thus, in the
section above, he wryly referred to "what is for practical reasons called
homosexuality," and, in a later essay, he referred to "the various forms
of homosexuality, which, to be sure, are manifold."[21]

A more difficult issue in Freud is the relation of homosexuality to
psychopathology. One extreme position is that homosexuality is in itself
a psychopathological entity that necessarily involves other inhibitions of
function. A more moderate position is that homosexuality is a feature of
other pathological conditions, and, while it may generally be thought of
as pathognomonic, it cannot be used for diagnostic specification. The
other extreme position is that no necessary connection exists between
homosexuality and psychopathology. According to this view, homosexuality represents a variation in the direction the sexual instinct may take,
and it can be considered "abnormal" only in a statistical sense.

To the end, Freud seemed to have been undecided on the relationship between homosexuality and psychopathology, and he advanced
statements that can be located in all three positions. Nor does attention
to the chronology of his works yield a sense of changing views. Therefore, his explicit statements and their legitimate implications must be
considered carefully within their own contexts. The issue of pathology
would be clearer if Freud considered homosexuality necessarily to be
one of the perversions, which for him were clearly pathological. But he
did not. Instead, he consistently distinguished between "perversion" and
"inversion," the term he frequently used for homosexuality.[22] Although
one recent commentator on Freud claimed that by the time he wrote the
essay on libido theory and narcissism in 1916[23] he had come to consider
homosexuality as a kind of perversion,[24] the claim is untrue, since he
carefully preserved the distinction in his essay three years later on
beating fantasies.[25] Nonetheless, the common etymological root in both
inversion and perversion, apparent in the German as well, suggests the
similarity of a psychic process of "turning away" from what is normal

and an instinctual "turning inward" and illustrates how close in meaning the two terms were. It also suggests the delicate balance Freud had to maintain in order to draw such subtle distinctions.

But if for Freud homosexuality was not a perversion, it was always for him determined by an inhibition of normal development. Thus, he found "in every aberration from the normal sexual life, a fragment of inhibited development and infantilism."[26] Later this idea was worded specifically to include homosexuality: "Sexual aberration in adults— perversion, fetishism, inversion— . . . will reveal a fixation in childhood."[27] Finally, in the posthumous *Outline of Psycho-Analysis*, homosexuality was cited as an example of "an inhibition in development of the consolidation of component instincts."[28]

Still, if homosexuality is at least partly the result of an inhibition of "normal" psychosexual development, might it not necessarily involve a stunting of other aspects of mental life or behavior? Surprisingly, Freud explicitly denied such a deduction. "The inversion is found in people who otherwise show no marked deviation from the normal," he wrote, citing evidence from "ancient nations at the height of their culture." Furthermore, he noted that while an "abnormality in other relations of life will always show an undercurrent of abnormal sexual behavior," the reverse is not necessarily so. Finally, Freud clearly implied that homosexuality can exist alongside other aspects of normal mental life or is a possible aspect of such normalcy when he observed that among men "the most perfect psychic manliness may be united with the inversion."[29]

Throughout his career, but especially in his later work,[30] Freud believed that an adequate psychosexual development, a tolerable adjustment to society, and a life of productivity and pleasure were all predicated on a shifting balance of instinctual gratification, renunciation, and sublimation, not on any ideal of absolute mental health.[31] In fact, in his last major work, the posthumous *Outline of Psycho-Analysis*, he made this point specifically: "We have seen that it is not scientifically feasible to draw a line of demarcation between what is psychically normal and abnormal; so that that distinction, in spite of its practical importance, possesses only a conventional value."[32] Indeed, for Freud, the connection between homosexuality and psychopathology was always uneasy, and he consistently took pains to call attention to the apparent absence of a pathological inhibition of function among certain homosexuals. Though Freud most often seemed to believe that the "natural" end of psychosexual development was heterosexual object choice for both pleasure and procreation, he clearly recognized that homosexuality could result in extraordinary cultural and humanitarian accomplishment. The two artists to whom Freud devoted monographs, Michelangelo and Leonardo, were "manifest inverts,"[33] and, in the first, he named Leonardo "among the greatest of the human race." In addition, Freud often stressed the remarkable social feeling and responsibility of many homosexuals. Thus, in an essay that can be considered to be an early version of *Civilization and Its Discontents*, he claimed that homosexuals are "often distinguished by the sexual impulse lending itself to 'cultural' sublimations in a special degree."[34] He made the same point at length in his discussion of the famous Schreber case.[35] For Freud, this coincidence seems not to have been a mystery, since he attributed this "special development of the social instincts and . . . devotion to the interests of the community" to the fact that for homosexual men, other men are regarded not so much as rivals as potential love objects.[36] It must not be forgotten that Freud was consciously writing in a German tradition that venerated the achievements of such "manifest inverts," from the greatest of Enlightenment monarchs, Frederick the Great, to Freud's contemporary, the openly homosexual poet Stefan George, not to mention Freud's beloved Latin and Greek writers, homosexual or bisexual almost to the man.

Luckily, the vexed question of whether Freud practically thought that homosexuality was necessarily a mental disturbance can be resolved somewhat by looking at his formal pronouncements on the subject. He was, first of all, consistently opposed to treating homosexuality as a criminal activity, and in 1930 he signed a public appeal to decriminalize homosexuality in Austria and Germany.[37] Two years earlier, he contributed to the Festschrift for Magnus Hirschfeld, a manifest homosexual and pioneer researcher and activist for homosexual rights and *Sexualwissenschaft*. This contribution is most striking in light of the fact that twenty-five years before, Freud began his discussion of homosexual inversion in *Three Essays* with an explicit refutation of Hirschfeld's claims.[38] In addition, at just about the same time, he answered a question about homosexuality posed to him by the Viennese newspaper, *Die Zeit*:

> I am . . . of the firm conviction that homosexuals must not be treated as sick people, for a perverse orientation is far from being

a sickness. Would that not oblige us to characterize as sick many great thinkers and scholars of all times, whose perverse orientation we know for a fact and whom we admire precisely because of their mental health? Homosexual persons are not sick.[39]

Moreover, Freud's most famous statement on the subject is the note he wrote to an American mother of a homosexual, which was published in 1951, sixteen years after it was written. The mother's letter seems not to have been preserved, but, judging from Freud's reply, she had apparently asked whether psychoanalysis could change her son's sexual orientation. Significantly, she could not bring herself to mention his condition by name, and it is with this fact that Freud began his reply. He answered in English:

> I gather from your letter that your son is a homosexual. I am most impressed by the fact that you do not mention this term yourself in your information about him. May I question you, why you avoid it? Homosexuality is assuredly no advantage but it is nothing to be ashamed of, no vice, no degradation, it cannot be classified as an illness; we consider it to be a variation of the sexual function produced by a certain arrest of sexual development. Many highly respectable individuals of ancient and modern times have been homosexuals, several of the greatest men among them (Plato, Michelangelo, Leonardo da Vinci, etc.). It is a great injustice to persecute homosexuality as a crime and cruelty too.[40]

Still, even with this clear statement, certain ambiguities remain. The note is personal and is meant both to reassure and to challenge. In this, it seems to have succeeded. The mother who offered the letter to the journal where it was published signed herself "Grateful," and she characterized the author as "a Great and Good man." The theoretical issues, however, remain. Homosexuality is not "an illness"; it is a mere "variation of the sexual function." Yet it is caused by an "arrest of sexual development." Freud's position on the legal and moral issues is clear, but his thinking on the specific issues of the pathological nature of homosexuality is not.

A document rediscovered in 1977, however, casts important light on this question. In 1921, the British psychoanalyst Ernest Jones had written to Freud informing him that it had been decided to reject the application of a manifest homosexual for admission into his psychoanalytic society on the grounds of his acknowledged homosexuality. Jones went on to bemoan the intractability of the condition in analysis. If the candidate could not be analyzed himself and instead persevered in his pathological orientation, he could not, Jones decided, be entrusted with the analysis of others. The response that Freud made, cosigned by the analyst Otto Rank, is surprising:

> Your query, dear Ernest, concerning prospective membership of homosexuals has been considered by us and we disagree with you. In effect we cannot exclude such persons without other suffi-cient reasons, as we cannot agree with their legal prosecution. We feel that a decision in such cases should depend upon a thor-ough examination of the other qualities of the candidate.[41]

This is the clearest acknowledgment on Freud's part of the lack of a necessary connection between homosexuality and psychopathological conditions. At least here, homosexual object choice implied nothing conclusive about other areas of mental functioning or behavior. Still, there are, as we have seen, sufficient ambiguities and hesitations in Freud's work to allow later analysts to draw the opposite inference. In Freud and his immediate circle, however, the reluctance to see homo-sexuality as a disturbance seems to have been partly determined by the palpable and readily attestable fact of normal or high functioning in ancient and modern homosexual figures. Later analysts, however, found such evidence less compelling than what they saw as the necessarily opposite deductions to be drawn from analytic theory.

Finally, Freud's theories of the etiology and dynamics of homosexual object choice were quite separate from his thoughts on the possibility of correcting this condition with psychoanalytic therapy. Quite simply, Freud was pessimistic on that subject. In the letter to an American mother, just cited, Freud directly addressed the question of a psycho-analytic cure:

> By asking me if I can help, you mean, I suppose, if I can abolish homosexuality and make normal heterosexuality take its place. The answer is, in a general way, we cannot promise to achieve it. In a certain number of cases we succeed in developing the blighted germs of heterosexual tendencies which are present in every homosexual, in the majority of cases it is no more possible.

Still, he continued, psychoanalysis did promise a certain kind of improvement:

> What analysis can do for your son runs in a different line. If he is
> unhappy, neurotic, torn by conflicts, inhibited in his social life,
> analysis may bring him harmony, peace of mind, full efficiency,
> whether he remains a homosexual or gets changed.[42]

In a more technical paper, Freud again affirmed his pessimism: "in actual numbers the successes achieved by psychoanalytic treatment of . . . homosexuality . . . are not very striking," and "in general to undertake to convert a fully developed homosexual into a heterosexual is not much more promising than to do the reverse." Part of the reason for this lack of success, he thought, had to do with the superficiality of motivation on the part of the patient to be cured: "the homosexual is not able to give up the object of his pleasure, and one cannot convince him that if he changed to the other object he would find again the pleasure that he has renounced." Most homosexuals appear for treatment because of "external motives, such as social disadvantages and danger attaching to his choice of object," and after analysis begins, it becomes apparent that the real motivation for treatment is the wish *not* to be cured. In this way, the homosexual can assure himself that he has done everything possible to change and "can now resign himself with an easy conscience" to his sexual pleasure.[43] The happily adjusted homosexual was a figure about whom Freud had no knowledge. As he wryly observed elsewhere, "perverts who can obtain satisfaction rarely have occasion to come in search of analysis."[44]

These observations were to play an important part in the history of psychoanalytic ideas about homosexuality and were sometimes seized upon to justify many extreme views.[45] They do not, however, represent Freud's complete thought on why psychoanalytic treatment failed. While he maintained that behind every homosexual lay an earlier heterosexual nature, he also recognized that homosexuality could not be explained solely by a particular family's stresses at the time of the child's oedipal period. For Freud, there was always an irreducible biological component to predispose the child to homosexuality, which he conceived of as an inborn, genetic endowment, existing, at least *in potentia*, prior to events in the child's psychosocial environment. Sometimes such a component was specified as the child's tendency to make narcissistic object choices or to linger at the anal stage of psychosexual development. Other times it involved the adoption of a "negative" Oedipus complex instead of the more usual positive one.[46] But even this was itself reducible to a more basic and universal bisexuality, which varied only in the proportion of active to passive, masculine to feminine, in each individual.[47] Even after uncovering the dynamics that powered the etiology of homosexual object choice, Freud found himself forced to confront an unanalyzable component—in the case of his twenty-year-old female homosexual, a strong "masculinity complex"—which belonged more to biology than to psychoanalysis:

> It is not for psychoanalysis to solve the problem of homosexuality.
> It must rest content with discovering the psychical mechanisms
> that resulted in determination of the object-choice, and with trac-
> ing the paths leading from them to the instinctual basis of the
> disposition. There its work ends, and it leaves the rest to biologi-
> cal research.[48]

Even though this was for Freud a more general and theoretically more important reason for the failure of psychoanalysis to "cure" homosexuality, it was not given its full measure of attention by later writers and was, in fact, rejected by some for reasons that reach to the very foundations of analytic assumptions.

As a final introductory consideration, Freud's attention to homosexuality throughout his career should perhaps be best understood primarily as an interest in a common variation of sexual development. He did not see same-sex object choice as sufficient grounds for establishing it alone as a category with distinguishing characteristics. "Psychoanalytic research very strongly opposes the attempt to separate homosexuals from other persons as a group of a special nature," he wrote. Indeed, he found heterosexual object choice as puzzling a phenomenon and one that required explanation. "In the psychoanalytic sense the exclusive interest of the man for the woman is also a problem requiring an explanation, and is not something that is self-evident."[49]

Freud proposed several theories to account for the etiology of homosexuality. They are scattered throughout his writings, and references to them range from a single footnote or sentence to extended exposition and discussion. They are not entirely consistent among themselves, and it is sometimes difficult to decide whether one statement represents an extension of a previous one, a refinement, or an alternative to it. I have, however, distinguished what seem to be four separate theories.

The first is the clearest of the four and the least problematic. Delineated in the case study of Little Hans[50] and in the monograph on Leonardo da Vinci,[51] it derives directly from the Oedipus complex, and, in its straightforwardness, seems almost a corallary of it. According to the theory, the young male child begins with an erotic bond with the mother, which is perfectly normal except perhaps for an "excessive tenderness" on the part of the mother and a consequent overestimation of the penis on the part of the child. The distinction between self and other has not yet been made distinct, and the child assumes that his mother is genitally equipped in the same manner as himself.[52] With the emergence from the narcissistic period, the child begins to sense his separateness from the mother and, simultaneously, to apprehend a castration threat, which, he feels, might be a punishment for his own erotic strivings for her. When the child discovers that his mother does not in fact have a penis like his own, he is both horrified and disgusted. His loved mother now becomes an object of loathing to him, and he recoils in horror from the thought that he too may share a similar fate. From then on the thought of the penisless mother is intolerable, since it automatically elicits an overpowering castration anxiety.[53] He therefore severs the erotic bond with the now despised mother and henceforth chooses a compromise figure for his sexual object: a "woman with a penis," a boy with a feminine appearance.

This theory was an essential complement to the broader theories about psychosexual development that Freud was constructing around the time of the *Three Essays*,[54] and, in certain ways, it seems to flow from them logically. In this respect homosexuality represents just one of the possible resolutions of the Oedipus complex, with its driving force of castration threat. It occupies a position equal to that of fetishism, which it resembles in many ways. Both fetishism and the form of male homosexuality described by this first theory are responses to the discovery that the mother has no penis. But where the homosexual is driven to seek objects who can satisfy his unconscious need for a woman with a penis and finds them in feminized men, the fetishist continues to seek women, but to equip them with the missing organ. According to Freud, the fetish, whatever particular form it may take, always unconsciously represents the mother's imagined penis. Thus, both the fetishist and the homosexual are driven by the same anxiety, but the mechanisms they use to assuage the anxiety are different. As Freud observed, the fetish keeps the fetishist from becoming homosexual, since its presence allows the penisless women to remain a tolerable sexual object. [55]

Implicit in this etiology are the reasons for considering homosexuality a pathological condition. Freud himself did not articulate these implications, but they are reasonable inferences to be drawn from his theory, and they have been used in later discussions on the relation of homosexual object choice to psychopathology. First, this form of homosexuality is powered by an extreme castration anxiety that operates not only at the initial crisis of the Oedipus complex, but every time a homosexual object choice is made or a heterosexual one is rejected. Male homosexuality in these terms cannot be considered primarily as the love of men for other men, but as the acceptance of these objects *faute de mieux* in face of a horror at the sight of mutilated female genitals. Like the fetishist, the homosexual, in finding an acceptable sexual object, reinforces his belief in the possibility of a woman equipped with a penis. Thus, this particular crisis of the Oedipus complex is never really resolved or mastered, but only sinks into the unconscious, where it endlessly seeks confirmation and reassurance by a repetition of symbolic or ritual acts.

In addition, such a solution to the Oedipus complex represents a regression to a more primitive phase in Freud's theory of psychosexual development. [56] As the child approaches the Oedipus complex, he has just emerged from the anal stage of late narcissism and entered the phallic stage just before true object-relatedness. His object relations, such as they are, are primarily need-gratifying, and his transactions with the outside world are negotiated primarily by such transitional objects as his feces. His location in the phallic stage with its first true object relations is a recent and unstable achievement, and he is not yet committed to object-relatedness. All children suffer the same shock at discovering that their mothers have no penis, but boys who will become heterosexual in their object choice in later life are impelled by this shock further into object-relatedness. They enter a period of latency in which they will consolidate and elaborate their object-relatedness until the onslaught of puberty. For some boys who will become homosexual, however, the shock is so great that they are forced to relinquish their tenuous achievement of the phallic stage and to retreat back into the anal stage, regressing from the oedipal stage, with its true object relations, back into narcissism, with its more primitive need-gratifying object relations.

Specifically, the object choices of this kind of homosexual must have not only genital equipment like his own, but some semblance to the self that was once loved by the mother. His love object may be like him as he now is, as he once was, or as he would like to be, or it may resemble someone who was once part of him.[57] All future love relations would then seem to be oblique strategies for loving himself. Formally speaking, the development from autoerotism to object love "has been reversed and they [these homosexual men] have remained at a point of fixation between the two."[58] Such a view takes into account the importance of the anal zone in homosexual lovemaking,[59] since it involves a regression from oedipal object relations back into a world of narcissistic and anal need gratification. The strongest argument for considering homosexuality a serious borderline disturbance derives easily from this first theory, as it does, we shall see, from the third as well.

The second theory is distinct from but not incompatible with the first, and can, in fact, reinforce or be reinforced by tendencies implicit in the first. This second theory seems to have been a favorite of Freud's. He fully presented it for the first time in the *Three Essays*[60] and repeated it without much change in later writings on sexual development, including the monograph on Leonardo da Vinci,[61] the essay on the psychology of groups,[62] and the later paper on the relations among jealousy, paranoia, and homosexuality.[63] According to this theory, the male child who is to become homosexual enjoys a particularly long relation with the mother—so long that the child rather excessively overvalues his penis. Partly because of the mother's oversolicitude the child refuses to relinquish this relation with her, his first love object. Freud does not specify the event that disrupts this bond, but the child, in order to preserve it unconsciously while relinquishing it in reality, now identifies with his mother and selects future love objects who resemble himself. In loving them, he can reexperience the erotic bond that once united him to his mother. He is able to continue loving his mother in himself, and simultaneously to be loved himself. Where once he was loved, he will now love, turning passive into active. Although one object has essentially substituted for another, the more important change has taken place in the ego, which has been remade into the image of the mother. Thus, the former love object has been preserved in unconscious fantasy at the expense of a distortion of the ego through a process of introjection, much as it is in the process of pathological mourning.[64]

These two theories seem opposite insofar as the first is the conscious relinquishing of the bond with the mother, while the second is the unconscious preservation of that bond. In the first, the child rejects women to relieve his loathing and horror of the mother, while in the second he flees them to ensure his fidelity to her. However, these two mechanisms can be seen as complementary, leading to a complex compromise formation, as the child flees from castration anxiety, yet maintains the libidinally gratifying bond with the mother.

Such a theory of homosexuality implies several pathological factors, only some of which were articulated by Freud. The most important is the introjection of the mother and the consequent remaking of the ego along the lines of a sexual character that is biologically inappropriate.[65] The emotional tie for all male children is, originally, identification with the mother, since ego and object have not yet been differentiated. The child who will be heterosexual renounces this tie, being propelled by castration fear and drawn by a new identification with the father. Thus, the ego of the heterosexual male child is preserved with respect to its sexual character. On the other hand, some male children who will become homosexual incorporate the love object into their ego, transforming it into the character of the object. These children identify with the mother and henceforth love men as she would. This process normally works to shape and solidify the identity of female children as they move from their "masculine" phallic stage into a "feminine" latency period.[66] In certain ways, this form of homosexuality is more pathological than the first, in which the male's identity can remain firmly male. In this second schema, the child suffers a basic unsureness and confusion about what will later in psychoanalytic theory be called his core sexual identity.

The third theory is the most difficult, filled as it is with paradoxes and contradictions. Fully set forth in the case study of "the Wolf Man,"[67] it is popularly known as the "negative" or "inverted" Oedipus complex, and its mechanisms are paradoxically both begun and terminated by the Oedipus complex. Oddly, Freud described it in the case history of someone who was not homosexual, after having excavated a hidden layer of psychosexual development that had been superseded yet remained alive in the unconscious. Peculiarly, this particular form of homosexuality is more common than the other three and can be found, for example, in the transferences in therapy of men who are not primarily homosexual. The exact way in which the circumstances of this particular case can be generalized is not at all clear. It is important partly because of its ubiquity and partly because it anticipates with great acuity the vexed subjects of activity and passivity, as well as that of bisexuality.

In this particular case, the Wolf Man's previous identification with the father was undone when an older sister seduced him. The boy's libidinal position, already tending to a rather narcissistic masculinity, then shifted from a masculine, "active" phallic character to a feminine, "passive" anal one. The father, who once served as the core for a masculine identification, then became the boy's object choice. Rather than be like the father, the boy chose to be loved by him. In addition, the boy related his mother's attack of dysentery to a primal scene he had witnessed performed *more ferorum ab tergo* (in the manner of beasts from the rear), which refueled his jealousy of his mother and sister and led to a new identification with the mother and a shift in primary erotogenic zone to the anus. Hence, he showed a willingness to surrender his masculine identity in order to be loved as a woman.

For the Wolf Man himself, however, this feminine identification was repudiated by the horror he felt at viewing what were to him the mutilated genitals of his mother. Thus, paradoxically, the same factors that led to homosexuality in the first theory—the horror at female genitals and the consequent intensified castration fear—now led to a recovery of masculine identity and of heterosexual object choice. This last contretemps is most peculiar, if not contradictory. At first, the boy was willing to relinquish his masculine identity and embrace a feminine ego in order to be loved as a woman by the father. Then, he was willing to surrender the love by the father in order to preserve his masculine identity.

One can make sense of this conundrum only by understanding that the psychic preconditions for such shifts are themselves in a state of flux. In particular, the predisposition to either a masculine or feminine libidinal position, while varying from individual to individual, also varies within the individual. Throughout his analysis of this case, Freud viewed the passive and active mode, the homosexual and heterosexual, as existing side by side. Elsewhere, in fact, Freud saw a bisexual wish in hysterical fantasies[68] similar to the Wolf Man's unconsciously passive homosexual and masochistic wishes, which had been superseded by active heterosexual ones. He interpreted the Wolf Man's wish to return to his mother's womb as a superimposition of opposites of this kind. On the one hand, it represents a desire to be inside the mother's genitals, as the child imagines himself to be a penis. In this sense the fantasy of rebirth is primarily a symbol for having intercourse with the mother. On the other hand, the wish to be in the mother's womb also represents the desire to be copulated with by the father, and therefore both to be born of him and to present him with a child. Thus, these two fantasies "give expression, according as the subject's attitude is feminine or masculine, to his wish for sexual intercourse with his father or with his mother."[69] Despite whatever mechanisms determine object choice, the outcome is at least partly influenced by a psychic predisposition toward a masculine or feminine stance.

The peculiar and singular circumstances of the Wolf Man's case confuse the issues of the negative Oedipus complex. Most simply, the negative Oedipus complex is one variation of the general Oedipus complex and results from the particular proportion of activity and passivity, masculinity and femininity, in any individual.[70] The sexual constitution of most male children contains a larger proportion of activity than of passivity,[71] and therefore inclines the child toward adopting an active stance with respect to the mother. In some children, however, the proportion of passivity is greater than that of activity, so that the child is more inclined to adopt a passive sexual stance.[72] Rather than attempting to penetrate his early sexual object, he desires to be penetrated himself by seeking the attentions of the father or the phallic mother, who, he assumes, is able to penetrate him.

In some children, Freud considered the negative Oedipus complex to be the natural result of their biological sexual constitution. For others, however, such an outcome can result from the crisis of the Oedipus complex occurring during the secondary passive substage of the phallic stage. For others still, it can represent a regression to an earlier object tie with the father, brought on by a particularly difficult positive Oedipus complex and by an unmanageable castration anxiety. Thus, we have at least three subvarieties of the negative Oedipus complex: a "natural" development of a biologically given sexual constitution; the accidental product of the chance alignment of several separate maturational schemes; or the result of a neurotic compromise. As we shall see later, it is crucial to keep these varieties clear, since upon them rests the critical difference in diagnosing homosexuality as "normal" or as pathological.

Freud's fourth theory of homosexuality, his last major contribution to the subject, was discussed only once, in the essay dealing with the relations among jealousy, paranoia, and homosexuality.[73] It represents the most significant divergence from the other theories, since it involves neither identification with the mother nor a fear of female genitals brought on by intense castration anxiety, nor does it involve a narcissistic object choice. Hence it describes a form of homosexuality entirely distinct from the others. As in the others, however, the transformation of the sexual object begins with an intense love for the mother, which, in this case, leads to extreme jealousy of siblings as well as, presumably, of the father. This jealousy mobilizes death wishes and sadistic fantasies of great violence. It is unclear what forces the child to relinquish and transform these wishes, but "under the influence of training," they are repressed and transformed into feelings of homosexual love through a process Freud called "reaction formation." Most likely, the child is predisposed for such a transformation, since competitive or "normal" jealousy is often experienced bisexually, and the strength of the murderously jealous feelings inclines the child toward the choice of reaction formation as a defense mechanism.

Quite interestingly, the process of converting rivals into love objects is the mirror image of the process by which passive homosexual love is transformed into persecutory or delusional paranoia. In the latter case, the intolerable homosexual impulse, "I love him," is transformed by negation into "I hate him," and then rationalized through projection into "He hates me," so that paranoia keeps the subject from becoming homosexual. Moreover, this theory accounts for the notable correspondence between homosexuality and highly developed social feelings and altruism, since the mechanism of reaction formation transforms violently murderous fantasies into exaggerated social impulses and intentions.

According to Freud's fourth theory, the shift from heterosexual to homosexual object choice occurs earlier than it does in the other theories. In addition, the child has no pathological identification with the mother. While there has been, of course, a preoedipal symbiotic attachment to her, he has passed through this narcissistic identification and entered the oedipal stage with a vengeance. More important, there is no necessary horror of female genitals, and, consequently, the possibility of heterosexual feeling as well as behavior is not excluded. This theory does not require relinquishing the mother as the prototypical sexual object nor turning against her with fear and loathing. Instead, a later heterosexual object choice based on a normally transformed bond to the mother is quite possible, and this form of homosexuality need not be exclusive.[74]

I have tried to be very clear about what Freud actually wrote about homosexual object choice and am confident about accurately presenting his theories of its etiology. However, it is not so clear how pathological homosexuality can be thought to be according to these theories. This is partly because of Freud's own uncertainty and equivocation and partly because of the difficulty in determining what is pathological, since it depends as much on cultural judgments of morality and aesthetics as on theoretical and clinical psychoanalytic issues. Still, several broad inferences can be drawn from Freud's theories about the question of the pathological nature of homosexual object choice. Freud himself never articulated them directly, but he might have held them to be true had he been asked.

First, according to these formulations, homosexual object choice cannot be considered simply as the love of one man for another. At the basis of such a choice is an unconscious and unresolved fixation on the mother. Choosing an object of the same sex, in these terms, is a second-order phenomenon that both denies and protects the cherished infantile bond. The homosexual lover is not drawn to his object through preference, but is impelled to it by the horror of the mutilated female genitals and the possibility of suffering a similar fate, a force that operates each time a homosexual object choice is made or a heterosexual one repudiated. Behavior that is propelled not by desire, pleasure, or the need for discharge but by anxiety is by definition pathological.

Second, although identification with the mother, even for a male child, is a necessary stage in psychic development, the kind of identification with her that occurs at the climax of the Oedipus complex and results in remaking the ego according to her sexual character suggests grave pathology. For one thing, identification with the father at the resolution of the Oedipus complex allows the child his first real connectedness with social reality as his newly formed superego develops, thus internalizing social, moral, and aesthetic norms. Such a result, however, cannot be expected with an identification with the mother because she is the love object and not the ambivalently loved prohibitor of love. The renunciation of the love object through identification does not have the same significance for the formation of the superego. Instead of leading to an internalization of a portion of social reality with its norms of prohibition and reward, the resolution here reinforces a tendency to sexualize these new ego and superego formations.

Moreover, the child's new feminine sense of self, with its implied feminine values of receptivity and passivity, is biologically inappropriate to the male child, so that he has a mistaken, even delusional sense of the possibilities of physical sexuality. In adopting a passive libidinal stance, the male child, consciously or unconsciously, fantasies using his anus as a vagina and derives gratification from the fantasy of presenting the father with a baby in the form of feces. But these fantasies are, in any case, necessarily ambivalent and leave unresolved all the anxiety and depression of a psychic castration initiated by the child himself. Thus, from the beginning, the ego he begins to develop is prone to extraordinary castration fear, ambivalent love, hatred, loathing, and depression, such as we find in the ambivalent process of incorporation in pathological mourning.[75]

Finally, the child's tendency toward narcissistic object choice in homosexuality seriously limits the possibility of his sexuality resulting in mature object relations. While the fully formed genital character is able to perceive objects as truly independent of the self, the narcissistic character is always partly dependent upon his objects for reassurance that he has not been castrated or will not be in the future. His sexual character can be maintained only if his sexual object fulfills whatever requirements have been set up in the unconscious of the narcissist. Any violation of these unarticulated requirements would therefore be experienced as narcissistic injury. Moreover, the lack of firm ego boundaries suggested by such psychic contingency necessarily results in the shadowy world of mirror object relations. The narcissistic lover can never be involved primarily with objects distinct from him. Instead, he is dealing with a complex system of projections and ritual reassurances whose purposes have never been articulated or understood.

One last point. All these theories impinge on one large theoretical subject—the psychoanalytic notion of genitality—which bears directly on the question of the pathological nature of homosexuality. Having biological, psychological, and cultural implications, it occupies a difficult and curious position in psychoanalytic theory. Psychoanalysis, for the most part, has been the study of psychopathology. With such notions as "abnormality" and "perversion," it has only inadequately described what ideal such pathological conditions deviate from. Freud claimed that "it is impossible to define health except in terms of meta-psychology, *i.e.* of the dynamic relations between those agencies of the psychical apparatus,"[76] and "it is not scientifically feasible to draw a line of demarcation between what is psychically normal or abnormal; so that that distinction, in spite of its practical importance, possesses only a conventional value."[77] Yet he nonetheless indiscriminately laid down such requirements in at least four essays: one of the *Three Essays*, the essay on "civilized" sexual morality, the Clark University lecture on infantile sexuality, and *An Outline of Psycho-Analysis*.[78]

For Freud, since every sexual aberration represented an inhibition in development or an "infantilism,"[79] all forms of individual sexuality had to be measured against a putative mature form, which was genital sexuality.

> The final outcome of sexual development lies in what is known as the normal sexual life of the adult, in which the pursuit of pleasure comes under the sway of the reproductive function and in which the component instincts, under the primacy of a single erotogenic zone, form a firm organization directed towards a sexual aim attached to some extraneous [i e , external] sexual object.[80]

In this short comment, Freud laid down requirements for genitality: the pursuit of sexual pleasure now serves the function of reproduction; the component instincts are unified; the genitals assume primacy as the erotogenic zone; the component instincts, insofar as they operate at all, subserve the genital function; sexual striving is directed toward an object that is external to the self.

All but the first of these requirements for mature genital sexuality can easily be used to define characteristics of a mature and healthy psychological functioning. Only the requirement that sexuality must subserve a reproductive function seems to lie outside a pure psychological discourse and seems to represent the intrusion of some extrapsychological value of Freud's, about which he nevertheless felt a deep conviction.

For example in the essay " 'Civilized' Sexual Morality and Modern Nervous Illness," a precursor in certain respects to *Civilization and Its Discontents*, Freud began by locating modern sexual practices between the two extremes of untrammeled gratification and sexuality in the service of society. He criticized the effects of present-day sexual customs and established three levels of sexual function in our culture: first, the free expression of sex without procreation; second, the exercise of sex for purposes of procreation; and, third, the exercise of sex for legitimate procreation. According to Freud, the third level characterizes "civilized" sexual behavior. However, he blamed this requirement for the high incidence of "modern nervous illness" and argued that "a certain amount of direct sexual satisfaction" is absolutely necessary to the individual's psychic well-being. One might therefore expect Freud to have argued for the desirability of level one, the free exercise of sex without procreation. But instead, he saw level two—the exercise of sex for procreation—as "our standard," a position he shared, startlingly, with Plato in The Laws,[81] who also legitimated sexuality only by yoking it to a reproductive function.

If for Freud the ideal sexuality necessarily fused pleasure and procreation, homosexuality was necessarily "perverse," "abnormal," or "unhealthy." Such a decision, in fact, underlay Freud's understanding of the difference between perversion, which involved a fixation on infantile sexual aims so that procreation did not predominate sexual striving, and inversion, whose identifying characteristic was a deflection of sexual aim away from its biologically appropriate object in the opposite sex. Henceforth sexual aberrations would be thought of as deflections of the sexual instinct away from its dual goals of pleasure and procreation. They would not be measured according to the quality of the sexual experience itself or the way in which they satisfied more nearly human goals of the exchange or expression of meaning and affection.

In an essay on female homosexuality,[82] Freud noted that homosexuality could really be a question of three distinct characteristics: it might involve physical sexual characteristics, as in the case of physical hermaphroditism, but that is a rare condition; it might involve mental sexual characteristics, but the universality of bisexuality and the ubiquitous mixture of masculine and feminine attitudes makes such a characteristic unusable for identifying that condition; or it might involve a particular kind of object choice. Although Freud could have considered other characteristics, such as sexual fantasies or sexual practices, he settled on the last of the three, even while explicitly noting in the same essay that homosexual object choice could correspond in men with unalloyed psychic manliness:

A man with predominantly male characteristics and also masculine in his erotic life may still be inverted in respect to his object, loving only men instead of women. A man in whose character feminine attributes obviously predominate, who may, indeed, behave in love like a woman, might be expected, from this feminine attitude, to choose a man for his love object; but he may nevertheless be heterosexual, and show no more inversion in respect to his object than an average normal man. The same is true of women; here also mental sexual character and object choice do not necessarily coincide.

The legacy that Freud left to psychoanalysis concerning homosexuality can be divided into two major portions: a clear and coherent theory of its etiology and dynamics and a somewhat confused and equivocal understanding of the relationship of homosexuality and "normal" functioning and behavior. The first part of this patrimony was claimed by his followers, but the second remained obscure, contradictory, and subject to the vagaries of convention and individual opinion. On the one hand, Freud's own attitude toward homosexuality included a profound respect for the achievements of homosexuals as well as an interest in the way homosexuality threw a new light on more usual behaviors and orientations taken for granted. On the other hand, Freud subscribed, explicitly as well as implicitly, to cultural norms that defined healthy psychic and sexual functioning by the way it corresponded to historically contingent establishments and customs. Whether or not this position was correct, it was never substantiated adequately, even though most later analysts would claim it as a cornerstone of their theory.

THE EARLY FREUDIANS:

1900–1930

The first generation of Freudians—those in Freud's immediate circle or those writing before the thirties—contributed very few innovative or important additions to the theory of homosexuality. Instead, they seemed to think that their task was to substantiate the ground-breaking discoveries of Freud. These early psychoanalysts, such as Isidore Sadger and Felix Boehm, were not particularly distinguished and are virtually unknown today, except to specialists. In their rather large corpus of articles on homosexuality, there is very little disagreement or original contribution. In fact, there is something rather touching in the careful piety of these workers in the field, gleaning in the trail of their master. Ernest Jones bestowed more than mere filial flattery when he observed in 1926 "the ever pioneering nature of Freud's work and the fact that his mind remains the youngest and freshest of any among us."[1] Just such an example of Freud's fresh thinking appeared in the *Internationale Zeitschrift fuer Psychoanalyse* of 1922, in which both Felix Boehm[2] and Nachmansohn[3] separately accepted and elaborated Freud's earlier theory of homosexuality involving the male child's identification with the mother and a consequent narcissistic object choice.[4] But startlingly, in the very same issue, Freud himself challenged the universality of this particular theory and added a new one that explained homosexuality as a reaction formation against murderous feelings toward rival siblings.[5]

In general, after Freud's initial findings, the field of homosexuality was worked by dutiful and unoriginal minds such as Sadger and Boehm, with the possible exceptions of Otto Rank and Hanns Sachs, who attempted to raise the subject of the sexual perversions to the level of theory,[6] and Sandor Ferenczi, who attempted the first serious nosology of homosexuality.[7] Isidore Sadger began his contributions in 1908 with an analysis of a homosexual, later followed by several articles, including an assessment of the value of psychoanalytic treatment for "contrary sexual feeling," a case of multiple perversions, a couple of specialized articles on the varieties of anal erotism, some general remarks on the perversions, and in 1921 his magnum opus, *Die Lehre von den Geschlechtsverwirrungen auf psychoanalytischer Grundlage.*[8] None of these was important enough to translate from the German, and they appear infrequently in later discussions, and then only for the sake of completeness. Sadger is principally important for illustrating Freud's idea that the homosexual unconsciously desires to castrate the father by rendering his male partner flaccid through orgasm and thus magically incorporating his masculinity so that he may finally obtain access to the mother.

Boehm's contributions are a little more substantial. In addition to his major work, a four-part series on homosexuality published in the *Internationale Zeitschrift fuer Psychoanalyse* from 1920 to 1933, in which he attempted to present and illustrate the most up-to-date psychoanalytic thought on homosexuality,[9] he wrote several related articles on prostitution, transvestism, and the femininity complex in men.[10] Finally, he also provided a collective review of the current literature on the sexual perversions for the *Internationale Zeitschrift*, including a more particular one of Sadger's *Lehre.*[11] Only his article on the femininity complex, however, appeared in English, and, apart from providing detailed case illustrations, his original contribution is quite minimal. His only truly theoretical statement was an attempt to distinguish between two types of homosexuality.[12] But this too, in hindsight, appears to be simply a restatement and elaboration of Ferenczi's earlier attempt,[13] yet without Ferenczi's lucidity and theoretical precision.

Still, this period of confirmation, illustration, and theoretical consolidation was extremely important for the psychoanalytic history of homosexuality, despite the fact that no new theories were put forth, since it firmly established the habits and conventions of discourse, the evidence to be considered, the problems to be discussed, and the general attitude toward the subject.

The importance of such a period can be seen more clearly by contrasting the history of the analytic theory of homosexuality with that of femininity. From the beginning of the psychoanalytic movement, theories of femininity, especially those concerning penis envy, the "phallic" nature of primary feminine sexuality, and "normal" feminine masochism were the subjects of intense debate. Significantly, both the supporters and rebutters of the original theory were frequently women. Thus, the theory of femininity was necessarily open-ended from the beginning, and fresh ideas and perspectives were assimilated into it, thereby enriching and deepening its insights. With the theory of homosexuality, on the other hand, since none of the contributors was admittedly homosexual, the viewpoint was always and without exception external to the subject. Any dissenting voice was thought to be outside of and inimical to psychoanalytic traditions and discourse. This early period, then, was one of consolidation and the formation of an orthodoxy.

Before we examine this period in detail, however, I should like to recommend some of its work to the reader's attention. Most of it has never been translated from German and is consequently unavailable to most readers, which is a pity, since an entire aspect of this early movement is represented here. Quite distinct from the magisterial formulations of Freud or the later lucid expositions of Otto Fenichel, these early accounts more nearly resemble the gossipy and curious details of, say, the Dora case. Ranging sometimes from the prurient to the hilarious, they include astonished accounts of the drinking bouts of *Studentenverbindungen* (i.e., college fraternities),[14] detailed analyses of brochures for German houses of prostitution,[15] rather literal equations between urethral fixations and "water sports,"[16] an interesting account of a homosexual seduction by a nine-year-old German baron,[17] indignant denunciations of the fashions worn at aristocratic spas which only serve to gratify *Gesaesserotik* (i.e., buttocks erotism), and extremely prurient though amusing accounts of Prussian officers and their ex-prostitute wives and of what they do in those resorts they go to.[18] Such finds sweeten the task of the historical researcher, but, more important, they suggest very strongly that psychoanalysis did not develop in a social vacuum or in strict adherence to the nature of its subject matter, but at least partly grew out of its practitioners' own curiosity, envy, and intrapsychic defenses.

In reading this literature, one is struck by its quaint and evocative aura and also by its genuinely humane and sympathetic tone. The view of homosexuals as lying and exploitative psychopaths was to come later.[19] Here they are, for example, suffering people who frequently commit suicide out of despair,[20] overly sensitive and highly refined individuals,[21] or people who manage to derive satisfaction and should be left alone to do so.[22] In fact, it is not at all clear whether these early writers considered homosexuality pathological in itself. Boehm, for example, considered a cure to consist of restoring enjoyable (*genuessreiche*) heterosexual functioning, and he freely allowed for the persistence of homosexual behavior.[23] Similarly, though Ferenczi hoped for a complete cure of certain types of homosexuality and attempted to abate the homosexual's hostility toward women, he was content with establishing "amphi-erotism" with both men and women.[24] Brill, addressing a meeting of the American Medical Association in New York City, claimed that "most of these patients recover, though they are content to remain homosexual."[25] Similarly, Rank saw his therapeutic goal as "solving the neurotic conflict . . . [and removing] the neurotic inhibition disturbing the patient's life," but was quite content to let the now conflict-free homosexual pursue his sexual activity in peace. He wrote that sometimes the analyst "can see no better outlet for the patient's sexual life than to sanction, so to speak, the perverse tendency."[26] Such a tolerant attitude characterized even those analysts who held out for a complete cure. Sadger answered "*mit einem runden Ja!*" ("with a round Yes!") the question of whether "contrary sexual feeling" was curable. Nevertheless, he permitted his patients to "regress" to homosexual activity during treatment because "behind it, a heterosexual can again be found."[27]

More important, many of these early figures shared Freud's complex attitude toward the homosexual condition. For example, even though Brill thought that homosexuality was closely aligned to self-love and that "the road to homosexuality always passes over narcissism, that is, love for one's self," he still maintained that the question of object choice was essentially independent of any notion of psychopathology. Addressing a group of physicians, he said, "homosexuality may occur in persons just as healthy as normal heterosexual persons." Interestingly, in the same address, he slyly impugned the interest and treatment the medical community afforded its homosexual patients: "I can never comprehend why physicians invariably resort to bladder washing and rectal massage when they are consulted by homosexuals."[28] Finally, as we have already seen, Rank and Freud cosigned a communication to Jones disagreeing with the policy of refusing admission to psychoanalytic institutes on the grounds of homosexuality alone.[29]

These tolerant, seemingly modern attitudes by early analysts were not isolated opinions, but sprang from a generally cosmopolitan and sophisticated world view. More than one analyst referred to the prestige attached to homosexuality in other cultures, not so much to call attention to an anomaly as to place his own culture's attitudes within a larger context. Freud's notion that heterosexuality was a phenomenon in as much need of explanation as homosexuality was deeply shared by many of his circle. For example, Ferenczi concluded an important article that attempted one of the first nosologies of homosexuality by noting the impoverishment of friendship in Western culture, which, he thought, was due to the general disdain and loathing felt for homosexuality. "It is in fact astounding to what extent present-day men have lost the capacity for mutual affection and amiability. Instead there prevails among men decided asperity, resistance and love of disputation." Although he had not solved "the problem of homosexuality," one of its more pressing aspects for him was the toll that homophobia took in society. The price of repressing homosexual feelings, he thought, was dueling, alcoholism, and decadently androgynous sexual tastes. "I quite seriously believe that the men of today are one and all obsessively heterosexual . . . ; in order to free themselves from men, they become the slaves of women."[30]

It is against this background of ideas being formulated and tested, of general tentativeness about therapeutic claims, and of honest uncertainty about certain issues that we should consider this early work, which, despite its engaging though somewhat naive eagerness, was quite modest in its aims. In general, these early Freudians pursued their work for three reasons: to confirm Freud's ideas; to illustrate them with specific case material; and to generalize these ideas to realms other than the clinical, such as art, anthropology, or education. Any theoretical progress they made on such topics as superego formation, the substages of the phallic phase, or the general theory of perversions was peripheral to the main subject of homosexuality. They made the first contributions to various debates unresolved today, surrounding the question of whether homosexuality is a unitary phenomenon, the classification of the varieties of homosexuality, and the theoretical, moral, and technical questions of treatment, prognosis, and cure.

The most significant of these peripheral contributions was by Hanns Sachs on the perversions in general. Its importance for our particular history, however, did not become apparent until a later period, when the absence of guilt for the perverse sexual behavior was taken as a distinguishing characteristic of certain types of homosexuality. In this early article, Sachs developed and refined Freud's idea that perversions represent the endurance of a portion of infantile sexuality into maturity and that what distinguishes the perversions from the neuroses is the ego-syntonic quality of the perverse tendency with respect to the ego, that is, the absence in them of guilt or anxiety. According to Sachs, the components of infantile sexuality undergo a kind of refraction through the Oedipus complex, whereby one component escapes repression and enters the ego in the service of repressing the other components. Hence perversions are not the global, undifferentiated, and primitive affairs that might have been suggested by Freud's earlier theory, but are quite capable of a great deal of elaboration and refinement. Significantly, for Sachs the choice of which element of infantile sexuality would survive repression was a question of constitution.[31] These were important and fruitful ideas, but they were not developed until a later generation began to direct attention to preoedipal stages of psychosexual development.

As for the task of generalizing Freud's ideas outside the clinical realm, there is not much to say. Most of these contributions range from the banal to the fanciful. Sadger, for example, claimed to have exposed the anal erotism lurking behind the fashions then current at the bathing spas and explained the popularity of *Uncle Tom's Cabin* in sexual terms.[32] Boehm attempted to distinguish between Protestant and Catholic German student culture on the basis of how latent homosexual strivings were handled. He also claimed that the Old Germanic tribes were monogamous and never engaged in homosexual activity.[33] Eduard Hitschmann speculated on the relations among urethral erotism, an interest in water sports, and a "burning ambition."[34] Hárnik wondered about the possibilities of intrauterine narcissism and of a cathexis of "the brain," and revealed why the penis on classical representations of Herakles was, to his eye, undersized.[35] These were amiable, if harmless, pursuits and do not substantially affect our history. The more important questions were left to later periods to discuss, such as the relation of homosexuality to such sociopathic phenomena as alcoholism and to certain forms of creativity, and the apparent prestige attached to pederastic homosexuality by what Freud called "ancient nations at the height of their culture."[36]

The first task of confirming Freud's ideas on homosexuality, however, was a more serious undertaking that included two large aims. The first concerned a general attitude and point of view in Freud's work on the sexual disorders, in which he sought to refute the prevailing medical opinion on the influence of heredity and genetic degeneration. The second was more specific and sought to elaborate and affirm Freud's particular ideas about the etiology of homosexuality. The first aim, by far the more important, was quite satisfactorily achieved, and we accept it today as self-apparent. At that time, however, even the current and enlightened view was that perversions were caused by "degenerescence," a hereditary weakening of genetic stock, which resulted in physical and moral weakness as well as specific sexual deviation.[37] Echoed in such literary works as Ibsen's *Ghosts* or Thomas Mann's *Buddenbrooks* and "The Blood of the Walsungs," this view was, in fact, a progressive development, insofar as it turned away from the older view of the sexual disorders as primarily moral phenomena.[38] Partly under the stimulus of the work of Magnus Hirschfeld,[39] with whom he disagreed, Freud argued in *Three Essays* for accidental and environmental causes, as well as for individual developmental and constitutional factors, as opposed to broader evolutionary ones. "The diagnosis of degeneration," he observed, "is generally of very little value."[40]

Freud sought to derive homosexual orientation from a constitutional disposition triggered by chance environmental factors that prevailed in the family during childhood. However, by "constitutional disposition" Freud did not mean a simple tendency toward homosexuality, but rather a complex sensitivity to certain strains and tendencies that were not in themselves homosexual in nature. Thus, an early and strong efflorescence of heterosexuality in a child could lead ultimately to homosexual object choice, or a strong aggressive instinct could be turned around by reaction formation and thereby result in homosexuality. In addition, these tendencies and dispositions could not be considered degenerative since, according to Freud, they were found in individuals of extraordinary moral and cultural achievement,[41] nor did they indicate a gradual decline of healthy genetic stock, but rather the random variation of personal characteristics.

Genetic degeneration as a cause of homosexuality is, among those of enlightened opinion, pretty much a dead issue, but in the early days of psychoanalysis it occupied these early writers' attention. Many of them seemed to think that a solution to the problem lay in establishing the proportion of environmental and genetic influences. Thus Sadger for the most part argued for the importance of accidental familial events, but frequently reported a family history of sexual inversion.[42] It is not clear why he did so, but his writing gives the distinct impression that he was not so much interested in family dynamics, or in unconscious identifications with inverted parents, as in a genetic predisposition.

Other analysts, however, entirely denied the importance of an inherited tendency to homosexuality. Ferenczi, for example, clearly stated that he did not believe in "innate homosexuality. . . . The sexual constitution is something potential." He went on to ground homosexual object choice in an "excessively powerful heterosexuality (intolerable to the ego)."[43] In an address to an American nonpsychoanalytic audience, Brill began with the issue of degeneration and claimed that from his experience with homosexual patients he could not connect homosexuality with any necessary emotional disturbance: "Homosexuality may occur in persons just as healthy as normal heterosexual persons." He argued against the importance of congenital causes and remained "convinced that homosexuality as such is entirely independent of any defective hereditary or other degenerative trends."[44]

Still, the debate over whether the determinants were hereditary or acquired continued to interest these early psychoanalysts. Their final resolution was a compromise of sorts, though it did stress the acquired determinants. It held that certain tendencies could be thought of as innate, but not a tendency toward homosexual or heterosexual object choice. Rather, such characteristics as a tendency toward narcissistic, as opposed to anaclitic, object choice, or the early efflorescence of heterosexual striving, or other factors like them, acting through accidental familial situations, could affect the later sexual choice or the kinds of identifications the child might make with each parent. By the end of the twenties, no analytic writer was claiming a direct link between innate constitution and later sexual object choice.

For example, when Nachmansohn discussed the issue in an article he wrote in 1922, he decided that homosexuality was the result of various defenses against incest, especially with the sister. He listed ten generalizations he was willing to make about the etiology and cure of homosexuality. Seven of these concerned accidental familial circumstances and two of them were quasi-constitutional factors, including an ascetic masochism and an abnormally strong impressionability. But the first, quite simply, was a strong disposition toward homosexuality.[45] By 1926, however, the balance in the debate clearly swung in favor of acquired determinants of homosexuality.[46] Significantly, in 1937 an American psychiatrist published an article on the psychogenic factors in homosexuality. He himself did not belong to the psychoanalytic camp, but referred with respect to the "theoretical generalizations of the Freudians." Primarily interested in prophylaxis, he listed ten generalizations. He thought that a large proportion of homosexuality was "predisposed by constitution and environment," and suggested taking a family history back at least to the grandparents, not as a way of assessing genetic degeneration, but as a way of exploring sets of emotional relationships in the family.[47] Thus, as a result of the growing eminence of psychoanalysis in medicine and education in America at least, the educated public generally assumed that homosexual object choice was determined by environmental and familial factors. The early analysts, through painstaking though unimaginative efforts, had succeeded in establishing Freud's innovations against the previously accepted medical and psychiatric wisdom.

The second task of confirming Freud's specific ideas of homosexuality was to replicate his findings on the etiology of homosexual object choice. Freud's ideas on the subject are scattered throughout his writings and were developed almost throughout his entire productive life. By far the richest source of them for early psychoanalytic writers was the monograph on Leonardo da Vinci,[48] although some writers found equally useful ideas in the essay on the relations among jealousy, homosexuality, and paranoia[49] and in the Schreber case.[50] Boehm, in fact, in his collective review of analytic publications on the sexual perversions for the *International Journal of Psychoanalysis* in 1921, after discussing the views of Adler, Blueher, Sadger, and Ferenczi, among others, specifically stated that the most important contribution to the subject was still Freud's monograph on Leonardo, written more than ten years earlier.[51]

The task of the early analysts ranged from confirming the largest of Freud's ideas, such as the crucial importance of the Oedipus complex, to confirming his rather more detailed and technical notions, such as the exact nature and extent of anal erotism. It is a measure of the coherence of the early psychoanalytic movement and a testament to its members' understanding of incipient ideas that the first confirmation of

Freud's ideas in the Leonardo monograph appeared the same year he wrote it.[52] In an article later singled out by Boehm as exemplary,[53] Sadger stated that he saw the Oedipus complex as central in the development of homosexual object choice, and emphasized castration wishes directed against the father, while pointing out the identification with the mother and the choice of a love object as a substitute for the self. The case he cited, one of "multiple perversions with hysterical absences," now seems almost like a museum of mechanisms that could lead to homosexual object choice, and its lack of logical coherence dates it back to the early days of discovery. An American psychiatrist elaborated a theory about the relations among the "mother complex," narcissism, and homosexuality, but his article was rather too general to have had much influence on psychiatric thought, although he does seem to have anticipated some later theories[54] that derive some forms of homosexuality from a failure to have emerged from a symbiotic relation to the mother.[55]

By 1926, however, Boehm was writing "Homosexualitaet und Oedipuskomplex," the third part of his four-part series on homosexuality, and could claim that "in the treatment of manifest homosexuality, one must see its development out of the normal Oedipus complex just as with other perversions."[56] His article detailed the steps from "an early strong attachment to the mother with outspoken erotic wishes," through intense "hatred . . . and death- and castration-wishes directed toward" the father, aided by "the inverted Oedipus complex," to the attempt "to call forth an ejaculation in the partner in order to render him impotent, so that he may approach the woman sexually." His major point throughout the article was that all apparently homosexual ideation and behavior are really displacements of a prior and more basic heterosexual nature, whose rediscovery and reactivation are the task of psychoanalysis. By this time, the importance of the Oedipus complex was an article of faith, so that Fenichel, the Walafrid Strabo of psychoanalysis, could roundly declare that "*all* perversions . . . are . . . intimately connected with the castration complex."[57] He too emphasized the identification with the phallic mother, and took exception with Sadger only over the question of whether the crucial organ is the mother's imagined phallus or her vulva.[58]

Similarly, all analytic writers agreed on the crucial importance of narcissism in the development of homosexual object choice. Even as early as 1913, Brill was able to summarize psychoanalytic thought on homosexuality and to declare that "the road to homosexuality always passes over narcissism, that is, love for one's self."[59] Narcissism, as we shall discuss in the next chapter, does not in fact mean "love for one's self," but any possible clarification of this concept had to await Freud's definitive formulation.[60] Primarily, the term narcissism in discussions of homosexuality came to mean the tendency to preserve the object tie to the mother by identifying with her and by seeking to regain her love by loving a partner who resembles the self.[61] The concept appeared in virtually all writing on the subject and served, for example, as the basis for the division of homosexuality into the varieties "anal-sadistic" and "narcissistic."[62]

In general, the twenty years that passed after the publication of the Leonardo monograph witnessed a progressive refinement of the ideas it contained. While these ideas became clinically more useful, there also occurred a progressive scholasticization (or, if one prefers, Talmudization) of them as analysts refined their distinctions again and again and uncovered and discussed new relationships, often without sufficient basis in clinical experience. Just as Fenichel and Sadger inconclusively squabbled over the fine point of whether the mother's phallus or her vulva is involved in narcissistic identification, another similarly inconclusive debate took place over the relationship between active and passive homosexuality. Ludwig Jekels asserted, without citing any evidence, that "active homosexuality is only apparently active; it is de facto passive, so that there exists no other homosexuality at all [ueberhaupt keine andere] but passive."[63] Boehm, on the other hand, citing the evidence of active castration wishes, claimed that all passive homosexuality changes during analysis into a more basic active form.[64] Finally, Ferenczi used a distinction between active and passive homosexuality as the basis for his nosology and observed that one could be a mask for the other.[65]

Still, much useful clinical data emerged during this period. These analysts first discussed the relationship of womb envy to castration anxiety, an issue still debated today in analytic circles.[66] They listed and illustrated the various symbolic forms the penis could assume for the homosexual, from the mother's breast[67] to his own turd (der Kot).[68] The notion of the retreat from heterosexuality as a defense against incest was broadened to include relations with the sister.[69] Finally, Sadger seemed to have made a minor career at explicating the varieties of anal erotism, from buttocks erotism (Gesaesserotik)[70] to urethral erotism, which, rather surprisingly, was no longer to be considered a form of phallic erotism,[71] a claim reaffirmed by Hitschmann.[72]

Significantly, these early writers seemed not to have taken up the only important new idea about homosexuality after 1910, Freud's theory of reaction formulation against murderous feelings of rivalry toward siblings and the father. Boehm made much of active castration wishes directed against the father and went so far as to see the homosexual's love of men as a mask for his hatred of the father, whom he views as a rival for the mother.[73] He found such wishes even in passive homosexual acts and saw the fear of the phallic mother as a displaced terror of the gigantic *Vaterpenis*. But he missed a major innovation in Freud's new theory when he continued to see homosexual object choice as necessarily dependent on an identification with the mother. So even for him, homosexuality meant a mistaken gender identity. While this may seem like a minor oversight, it had important implications for future psychoanalytic theorists, who, like these early writers, confined their attention to Freud's early ideas on homosexuality at the expense of his later ones.

Even more important for future psychoanalytic discourse about homosexuality was the curious fact that much of the early writing on homosexuality was not concerned with homosexuality at all, but with paranoia. In fact, at least one third of all psychoanalytic articles from this period dealt with the transformations of intolerable passive homosexual feelings into paranoid ideas of persecution, based on Freud's derivation of paranoia from passive homosexuality in the Schreber case. There Freud showed how the paranoid transforms the intolerable statement "I (a man) love him (a man)" to make it tolerable to consciousness. One of these transformations is "I don't love him; I hate him" and its necessary delusional consequence, "I hate him, because he persecutes me."[74]

Analysts quickly confirmed this extraordinarily simple but profound discovery in numerous cases of delusional paranoia, and used it as an example of the theoretical and clinical insights that psychoanalysis could produce. Such a finding was invaluable for the early psychoanalytic movement, since it could be proven empirically, unlike other "soft" claims difficult to test. In fact, it was used in one of the first analytic studies to employ a large number of subjects.[75] However, even though this new insight helped establish the new science's prestige, it also had long-term deleterious effects on the particular subject of homosexuality, which came to be associated with paranoid conditions and serious mental disturbance. Virtually every study mentioned here dealt with either frank psychotics or what we would call today "low-level borderlines."[76]

The association of homosexuality with paranoia represented a real confusion. Freud meant to show that the homosexual component of mankind's universal bisexuality served as the driving force behind these paranoid delusions. Strictly speaking, paranoia was a disturbance confined to those who found their own passive homosexual yearnings intolerable to consciousness. The existence of manifest homosexuals who were paranoid was in fact thought by some analysts to impugn the theory.[77] But most psychiatrists who sought to adopt an analytic point of view had only limited contact with homosexuals who suffered no paranoid thought disorder. The small number of highly refined, wealthy, and sometimes titled individuals described in the psychoanalytic journals of the time did not figure importantly in the caseloads of most psychiatrists. Instead, they faced a much larger number of bizarrely disturbed people, all of whom showed the suspected homosexual strivings. Few psychiatrists could hope to conduct treatment in the large Victorian leisure of Boehm or Sadger. Most found themselves face to face with frantic and confusing maniacs who came to represent for them the "typical" homosexual. It seems odd that this very difference in the severity of disturbance did not suggest a basic nosology of homosexuality, but no one seems to have thought the project worthwhile.

In short, while the early writers on homosexuality themselves understood that manifest homosexuality was not necessarily evidence of a paranoid condition, the sheer amount of case material presented in that period on the phenomenology and dynamics of homosexuality represented, in effect, a study of paranoid schizophrenia. Rank, who warned against this sloppy and dangerous tendency to confuse the two,[78] thought that homosexuality was a feature of other conditions—neurotic, psychotic, or even normal—and should be named after the complexes, not the other way around. Such advice, however, went unheeded, and this failure contributed later to gross misunderstandings about the condition itself and severely distorted all future psychoanalytic discourse about homosexuality.

The early psychoanalytic writers fulfilled the task of confirming Freud's ideas by illustrating them with case material in their theoretical discussions as a matter of course, but it is remarkable how frequently some of them made rather sweeping claims without offering one bit of clinical evidence. Thus, Jekels could maintain that all homosexuality was essentially passive, regardless of its manifest signs, without offering any clinical material whatever.[79] Most others, of course, supported their claims with evidence, however unsystematically. Hárnik speculated freely on intrauterine narcissism, relating it to men who dedicated themselves to athletics,[80] while Hitschmann correlated urethral erotism to an interest in water sports and a "burning ambition."[81] This sort of undisciplined method of gathering anecdotes was used to support Boehm's two early articles on homosexuality as related to polygamy and prostitution.[82]

There were two alternatives to this unsystematic approach, but both presented serious problems. First, one could systematically and "scientifically" collect data from large samples, but unfortunately large samples of representative homosexuals did not exist at the time. Thus, one writer could claim a large acquaintance with homosexuals, but only with those who were alcoholic.[83] The only truly large-scale survey, using a sample of 120, dealt with people suffering from *dementia praecox*, a synonym for schizophrenia.[84] It does seem that a study of 100 "socially well adjusted homosexual men and women" was undertaken by a "Committee for the Study of Sex Variants," but I have found only one reference to the study or the committee, and its results were never, to my knowledge, made known.[85] Therefore, whatever "hard" data these psychoanalysts presented only tended to confirm the misconception of homosexuals as severely disturbed individuals, either psychotic or sociopathic.

The other alternative was the detailed presentation of one or a few cases in depth. This approach was always characteristic of most important articles. Boehm's work from 1920 to 1933 is extremely rich in clinical vignettes, random observations, and interesting anecdotes. In one article he presented a detailed analysis of a single dream of a homosexual patient.[86] More ambitiously, Sadger and Nachmansohn each presented a case of a homosexual in treatment, one occupying twenty journal pages, the other seventy-five. However, most impressive was Sadger's detailed account of an entire analysis of a homosexual patient, almost one hundred pages long.[87] While such accounts immeasurably enriched the psychoanalytic literature on homosexuality, they did not have quite the full effect desired. None of these three was ever translated from German. Thus, though Melanie Klein and Boehm both referred to and discussed Sadger's case of multiple perversions,[88] one wonders how familiar American psychoanalysts were with the details of the case. While they could, no doubt, read the conclusions of more eminent and widely translated figures, they were probably unfamiliar with the clinical data on which these widely propagated generalizations were based. Moreover, it would have been difficult for them to evaluate to what extent any particular homosexual patient of their own resembled in dynamics, history, or experience the melancholy Danish count analyzed by Sadger. Nor could they surmise, if they had not read the original, that Sadger's detailed analysis lasted for only thirteen days and was suddenly and unilaterally terminated by the patient, whose sexual orientation was unaffected by treatment.

It is quite baffling how quickly "deep" material began to emerge from the extremely short duration of these analyses. Freud's prematurely terminated analysis of "Dora" lasted only three months, but even by such standards, it is amazing to learn of the speed at which these analysts uncovered material and effected cures. While Boehm criticized Sadger's *Lehre*[89] for the brevity of his analyses, most of which lasted only weeks or months,[90] Boehm himself recommended a particular finding in his work because it had emerged "after an analysis of many months [*nach mehrmonatiger Analyse*]."[91] Based on our own experience of psychoanalyses lasting ten and fifteen years, it is surprising that Sadger thought a mere thirteen-session analysis was exemplary,[92] but perhaps we should readjust our own expectations. Ferenczi, after all, gives us the measure we should apply when he suggests what he thought were the reasonable limits of an incisive analysis:

> I have had the opportunity of treating psychoanalytically a number of male homo-erotics; many for only a short period (a few weeks), others for months, a whole year, and even longer.[93]

Nonetheless, these analysts' recommendations must be considered against their ambitious claims. Ferenczi was attempting a nosology of male homosexuality based on "a number of patients," a few of whom were seen for "a whole year, and even longer." Similarly, Sadger substantiated his claim that homosexuality was curable by psychoanalysis with the details of a four-month analysis of a patient whose crucial memories "had been wholly unconscious and first had to be unearthed very laboriously through a month-long analysis [*vollstaendig unbewusst gewesen und erst durch monatlange Analyse sehr muehsam ausgegraben werden mussten].*" In the same article, Sadger argued that "behind homosexuality, a heterosexual can be found," by offering as proof the case of a twenty-one-year-old patient "of an apparently pure inversion" who began to entertain heterosexual masturbation fantasies in the tenth day of analysis.[94] Finally, Boehm claimed to have heard the following dream from one of his homosexual patients in the very first hour of analysis: "He lay with his mother in bed. The father assigned him the task of dissecting the mother."[95]

It is quite clear from such accounts that these early patients, whatever else their ailments, were what is thought of today as "good hysterics," extremely impressionable and eager to please. Much of the material these patients provided must have been at least partly influenced by their analysts' own expectations and hopes. In the case of conditions other than homosexuality, such as hysterical or obsessive-compulsive neurosis, the clinical material, however contaminated, formed a coherent body of conjecture and theory, which could be confirmed and replicated by any competent analyst in his own practice. But there was no such coherent or universal clinical experience with homosexuality. The theory remained, for the most part, in the preliminary stage at which Freud left it, and the number of homosexuals seen in treatment who were not disturbed remained extremely small.

Thus, until the thirties, the psychoanalytic theory of homosexuality remained unchanged from Freud's initial findings. Published in 1945, Fenichel's summary of the theory in his grand *Glossa Ordinaria, The Psychoanalytic Theory of Neurosis*,[96] serves as a lucid exposition of what the most competent and informed analysts thought about homosexuality during this period. His work reveals that even as late as 1945 mainstream psychoanalytic ideas about homosexuality were essentially Freud's, virtually unchanged and unaugmented since 1905, 1910, and 1922. Indeed, many of Freud's complex attitudes and ideas about the varieties and interconnections among mechanisms of homosexuality had been transmitted almost intact. Even Freud's irreducible ambiguities about the pathology of homosexuality remained. Fenichel thought that exclusive homosexuality was a disorder, but could not be considered "an infantile partial instinct," which would make it a perversion. Nor could it be considered a neurosis, since the neurotic fends off and represses the intolerable impulse, while the homosexual indulges in it. Indeed, Fenichel wrote that "a certain amount of sexual feeling toward one's own sex remains in everyone," and, like Freud, he thought that heterosexual object choice needed as much explanation as homosexuality. He also believed that bisexuality was a fundamentally biological phenomenon that could express itself through object choice, through a desire to penetrate or be penetrated, or through the manifestation of active or passive attitudes in social life. Most important, Fenichel wrote that homosexuality resulted from defenses aimed at assuaging the anxiety attendant upon the Oedipus and castration complexes. And although he mentioned the importance of some "pregenital fixations," it is quite clear that he believed that the crisis that determines object choice occurs at the climax of the Oedipus complex.

To summarize, informed psychoanalysts by 1930 would have agreed or disagreed on several ideas on the subject of homosexuality, and were undecided about others. By that time, all would have agreed that it could only be explained by accounting for intrapsychic conflict and defense mechanisms. Although biological constitutional factors were important, they could not be used to bolster the now discredited doctrine of degenerescence, the generational deterioration of genetic stock. In addition, despite the general interest in the relationship of homosexuality to paranoia, all would have agreed that simple homosexual object choice, unconnected with other psychic disturbance, was essentially an oedipal-level phenomenon, that is, the result of defenses against castration anxiety attendant upon genital strivings toward the mother.

As for the etiology of homosexuality, there was general agreement that homosexuality was an aspect of a basic and universal bisexuality, which remained a fundamental principle of psychoanalytic theory until it was challenged after Freud's death.[97] Consequently, the view that homosexuality was a variant manifestation of the sexual instinct could easily have been accepted by most early psychoanalysts. What made some boys homosexual and others not could, according to them, be accounted for by such constitutional factors as a tendency to narcissistic object choice, a lingering at the anal zone in psychosexual development, and a tendency to substitute identifications for object ties, particularly with the mother. But even so, all of them allowed for the qualification that certain kinds of homosexuality did not involve a "countersexual" identification.[98] While the task of psychoanalytic theory, as it is in all sciences, was always to account for variety with a minimum of constructs, all the writers of the period would have been prepared to admit that homosexuality might not be a unitary phenomenon.

As for their disagreements about homosexuality, these are more complicated and center on three related issues: the degree of psychopathology in homosexuality, the project of developing a theoretically coherent nosology of its varieties, and the possibility of curing the condition through psychoanalysis. On the question of pathology, Freud himself was equivocal. While, according to him, "the most perfect manliness may be united with the inversion,"[99] it also represented for him "an inhibition in development."[100] Such an uncertainty characterized the psychoanalytic movement as a whole, but there is a shift discernible from the early period, when homosexuality was freely admitted to be nonpathological in certain cases, to the end of the twenties, when most assumed, without discussion, that the condition was pathological. Thus, in the early years, Brill maintained that "homosexuality may occur in persons just as healthy as normal heterosexual persons,"[101] but by the twenties, most of the case material seemed to confirm the pathological nature of the condition. This period witnessed not simply a failure to expand upon Freud's ideas about homosexuality, but a marked constriction of them. But even with these assumptions, homosexuality was unanimously considered to be a disturbance of a neurotic level of severity.

The inability to decide upon the degree of pathology inherent in homosexuality also affected the lack of agreement about how to categorize its varieties. Rank, agreeing with Ferenczi, warned that homosexuality was not a unitary phenomenon. He suggested that it should be categorized and named by the neurotic complexes with which it was associated,[102] an idea that was quite in keeping with the spirit of Freud, who recognized at least three varieties: narcissistic object choice, a "negative" or "inverted" Oedipus complex, and a reaction formulation, each of which differed in highly significant ways. It is striking that after a reasonable amount of discussion of the possibilities for a more sophisticated nosology, this three-part division was the one referred to in general discussions of the subject.[103] Even a definition of homosexuality was extremely difficult due to the range of homosexual content in any one individual, which could be unconscious, latent, paranoid, or any number of other possibilities.

Most of the nosologies suggested during this period were consequently quite trivial, and either they were so superficial as to offer no aid in understanding the dynamics and treatment of the condition or they were tautological. Brill suggested that a classification be attempted on the basis of the latent content of dreams,[104] although considering the universality of unconscious homosexual object choices, it is difficult to see how such an approach would not serve to obliterate distinctions rather than to sharpen them. Sadger suggested that homosexuals could be divided into three groups, corresponding to the age of their preferred sexual object: younger, older, or the same age. But he offered as an illustration a case who singly embodied all three types.[105] Vinchon and Nacht also proposed a three-part classification, those with glandular abnormalities, the sexual perverts, and the neurotics. They washed their hands of the second: such a homosexual is "comfortably settled in his vice . . . and will never be cured."[106] They also avoided the problem posed by Fenichel when he found he could not place homosexuality among either the neuroses or the perversions. The only serious attempt to suggest a useful nosology and one that still merits our attention today was Ferenczi's, who distinguished between a "suffering" type, who is inverted with respect to his own identity, and an "acting" type, who is inverted with respect to his object choice. He concluded, however, by disclaiming any intention of having "exhaust[ed] all the possibilities."[107] Boehm, in one of his last articles twenty years later, proposed a distinction quite similar to Ferenczi's, although he did not credit his predecessor. He posited a narcissistic and an anal-sadistic type.[108] Fenichel had the last word: "Since narcissistic and anal fixations may occur in the same person, combinations of both types of homosexuality occur. Terms like *subject homoerotic* and *object homoerotic* have only a relative significance."[109]

On the subject of the likelihood of a psychoanalytic cure of homosexuality, there was a general, if by no means unanimous, pessimism. Psychoanalysis had always been both a therapeutic technique and a method of intrapsychic investigation. While analysts were confident about the ability of psychoanalysis to penetrate into the psychodynamics determining homosexual object choice, they were less sanguine about their ability to change any particular patient's sexual orientation. The question of whether homosexuality ought to be cured, which involved important and difficult moral and cultural issues, was not discussed except in the very earliest period. Homosexuality was, by the twenties, assumed to be pathological and hence suitable for treatment. Psychoanalysts' humane statements arose not so much from a doubt about whether such people should be changed as from a resigned recognition of psychoanalysis' modest abilities in that area. Freud himself was quite pessimistic about the possibility of curing homosexuality. "It is not for psychoanalysis to solve the problem of homosexuality," he wrote, since its roots are biological in nature, and the psychic mechanisms that give rise to homosexuality are only mediate in their operations. He concluded that "in general, to undertake to convert a fully developed homosexual into a heterosexual is not much more promising than to do the reverse," and that the number of successful psychoanalytic treatments of homosexuality "are not very striking."[110] Fifteen years later, these words were echoed by Isador Coriat, an American analyst: "In psychoanalytic theory, the analysis can not change conscious homosexuality to heterosexuality any more than psychoanalysis can change a heterosexual to a homosexual."[111]

It was generally thought that forms of homosexuality that were technically perversions were not curable. Often such perverts were dismissed contemptuously as "comfortably settled in [their] vice" and consequently would "never be cured."[112] Similarly, a homosexual who suffered a grave confusion about his sexual identity, who felt himself "to be a woman with the wish to be loved by a man," could not be considered a promising case for cure.[113] In the early days, as we have seen, a cure meant bringing the patient to heterosexual potency, while leaving it to him to decide if he wished to continue to pursue his homosexual activities. If he wished to do so, the analysis could make him more comfortable with his orientation. Thus Brill claimed to cure his patients, although many remained homosexual,[114] and Ferenczi could not report complete cures, even among his "object homoerotics." All he hoped to achieve was to cause an abatement of their hostility toward women, to help control their sexual urgency, and to restore their heterosexual potency with women. The final choice of sexual preference was their own. Still, he held out the hope for complete cures in the future, when psychoanalytic technique would be improved.[115] Rank too claimed that he could resolve the neurotic conflicts of his homosexual patients, but he advised the analyst to sanction the homosexual activity that remained after a successful treatment,[116] thus sharing Freud's therapeutic aims. With Boehm, the situation is unclear. Although he claimed to have cured homosexuals, in the case he presented as illustration, "the homosexuality never became conscious for the patient and had never expressed itself in manifest activity [die Homosexualitaet dem Patienten nicht bewusst geworden war und sich nie in manifesten Handlungen geaeussert hatte]."[117] As for his "manifest" homosexuals, they frequently bolted treatment, hating the analyst, just when they began to approach heterosexual functioning, a situation that Boehm found "almost as a rule [*fast regelmaessig*]."[118]

Only Sadger held out for the real promise of psychoanalysis as a cure. For him it was not enough to restore a spurious kind of heterosexual functioning, a mere "*masturbatio per vaginam*." Instead, he sought to change the patient's very "*Sexualideal*" (i.e., the internal image of the sexual object). He responded to the question of curing homosexuality "with a round Yes! [*mit einem rundem Ja!*]" although he offered no information about the fate of his patients after treatment was over. Finally, he saw the issue of prognosis as essentially moral in nature:

> The best chances favored those at whose throat the knife stood, who truly wanted to become healthy at any price and last but not least who were also honorable [*ehrlich*]. . . . Whoever is of a willing and honorable spirit with respect to his physician, who swears himself to discretion and silence [*Verschwiegenheit*], and who shrinks from no uprightness [*Aufrichtigkeit*] will find liberation from his perversion.[119]

From this distance, it is not possible to say for certain whether Sadger's tone was humane and tolerant or merely sanctimonious. Either way, however, even in his qualified confidence, he stood pretty much alone.

CHAPTER **IV**

THEORETICAL OVERVIEW I

The last two chapters have traced the very beginnings of our history: the positing of fundamental principles by Freud and their substantiation by his followers. Yet the future development of these theories was even by this point being biased by certain accidental circumstances and conditions. The difficulty in obtaining a representative clinical sample and the then-current interest in paranoia both served to emphasize certain implications in Freud's original theory, thus shifting its direction toward seeing homosexuality as a disturbed mental condition. But even more decisive in its influence was the failure of these early theoreticians, for all their carefulness, to address and resolve certain ambiguities and difficulties in the theory itself. While the circle of early psychoanalysts shared certain convictions about biological endowment and psychological development, these assumptions went largely unargued and unjustified. Their failure to address such issues had an extremely important effect on later stages of our history, since the gap left in theoretical discourse was to be filled by unexamined popular assumptions and judgments, from which the theory never freed itself. In particular, there are four general issues that these analysts neglected: the exact status of homosexuality as a clinical entity, the relevance of narcissism to the pathological nature of homosexuality, the Oedipus complex, and the notion of "natural" psychosexual development.

The first issue is the status of homosexuality as a clinical entity. Quite simply, early psychoanalytic theorists were never able to determine what homosexuality exactly was, beyond the simple definition of same-sex object choice. In fact, the word *homosexual* was introduced only as recently as the late nineteenth century by German psychologists, and it was not accepted into English until the twentieth century. The classical world, by contrast, did not have a word for homosexuality, and when Plato, for example, in the *Symposium* wished to discuss it, he had to resort to various periphrases.[1] The Greeks also found it worthwhile to describe still other sexual practices, such as the sexual interest of an adult male for another adult male, or a citizen's seeking an active sexual partner who was not a citizen, just as a Marxist sociologist in modern times might be more interested in sexual relations that cross class lines than he would be in homosexuality per se. The intuitive sense that homosexual object choice somehow constitutes a unity has a history itself.[2] Psychoanalysts, by comparison, proceeded on a historically based intuition and raised homosexuality to the level of a clinical entity, without adequately justifying such a procedure or even specifying the kind of entity homosexuality might be.

Oddly enough, it is not clear when and how psychoanalysis began accepting homosexuality as such an entity. Freud himself did not believe it was, but by the thirties a gradual shift in thinking had occurred. This important metapsychological decision was never argued or substantiated. Instead, it just happened, and we cannot speak of an important step having been taken so much as of a shift in opinion having occurred. For Freud, it was important to keep open the question of whether homosexuality was a unitary phenomenon, since it was always unclear whether "manifest" homosexual object choice was different from the homosexual object choice that results from the universal bisexuality in all individuals, or whether the object relations of a "neurotic" homosexual were essentially different from those of a psychotic. Quite early in this period, Brill called attention to the impossibility of using the term *homosexuality* diagnostically, since the term could refer to manifest, unconscious, latent, or paranoid homosexuality.[3] Unfortunately, however, not all the early analysts maintained the precise distinction that Brill observed, a confusion that resulted in several misleading ideas in the early psychoanalytic movement. Boehm, for example, cited the case of a patient whose "homosexuality was never conscious . . . and never had revealed itself in manifest behavior."[4] It seems likely that this patient was in fact not homosexual at all. Instead, the homosexual trends that Boehm detected were part of his normal bisexual psychic constitution, which could be expected to surface in the course of any adequate analysis. Thus, Boehm based some of his general knowledge on a patient whom he cured of a condition that he did not suffer from. Because of its failure to delineate the relationship between "normal" and "manifest" homosexual behavior, the psychoanalytic theory of homosexuality always found itself in danger of collapsing into generalizations about the psyche. On the other hand, because most analysts tended to blur the distinction between the diagnosis of homosexual paranoid and paranoid homosexual, there was always a tradition in psychoanalytic thought that viewed the psychosis of a homosexual paranoid, or the defective superego of a homosexual sociopath, as essential to the homosexual condition. And, by a strange twist of logic, homosexuality was seen to cause paranoid schizophrenia. Shackley, in an early article intended to provide illustration for Freud's set of paranoid transformations, concluded that unconscious homosexual impulses, working along with certain defense mechanisms, "produce a *dementia praecox* of the paranoid type."[5] Consequently, all homosexuals could be seen as at risk for this grave disturbance. No one in this period claimed that all homosexuals were on the borderline of psychosis or that they were all liars and swindlers, but when such claims came to be made in the forties, authors could refer in a vague way to a long-standing though never clearly articulated body of opinion and tradition within psychoanalysis.[6]

We can easily see now that the kind of homosexual impulses that would give rise to paranoid schizophrenia would involve preoedipal oral fantasies of incorporation and engulfment, not such oedipal wishes as passive surrender or the penetration of another male. Or we can see that schizophrenic disorganization causes such homosexual impulses to be handled in a paranoid fashion. It was possible then, of course, to suggest such ideas, and many did. This distinction of whether homosexuality is a clinical condition itself or a feature of a prior condition is extremely important—because it determines the category into which clinical material and certain case studies are to be put. Most psychoanalysts believe that one case, despite its particularity and even its extreme features, is prototypical of a whole category. However, the category is established by the clinical entity, not by the features, so that it is important to be clear about what category a certain case is taken as being prototypical of. If, for example, a prototypical patient is diagnosed as being paranoid with homosexual features, we may generalize categorical characteristics of that case to other paranoids. If, however, he is diagnosed as homosexual with paranoid features, his characteristics will be applied to all homosexuals. We can see now that if these early writers had more clearly conceptualized the difference between homosexuality as a condition and homosexuality as a feature, they could, for example, have seen homosexual object choice as a feature of psychotic, borderline (the term was not used then), neurotic, or essentially normal conditions. And if that last possibility had been acknowledged, as it had been in the early days by Freud and Brill among others, there might have been discussion of a question that concerns us today, but seems not to have occurred to anyone then: should it be treated at all? Such a discussion would have required examining difficult ideas of "health," "normalcy," and what is "natural." Psychoanalytic theory would have been richer and deeper for it, and many of the vexed questions we shall later look at could have been clarified. But this discussion never took place, and personal opinion, cultural values, and limited clinical experience instead determined the shape of future analytic discourse about homosexuality.

In addition to this larger, more general issue, there were other more specific and highly theoretical issues that the early psychoanalysts failed to address adequately. The first of these centers on the theory of narcissism. One idea concerning essential relations between homosexuality and narcissism was that homosexuality is necessarily more primitive than heterosexuality because it is narcissistic, while heterosexuality is developmentally more advanced and "object-related." Such a view makes three basic claims about the pathological nature of homosexuality: that it is not truly object-related, that it involves impoverished object relations and consequently operates through a primitive and defective superego, and that its mental organization is basically preoedipal.

For Freud, narcissism was something quite specific: a stage of psychosexual development occurring between autoerotism and alloerotism (or object-relatedness). In this stage, the libidinal object is the ego itself, not an external object.[7] Narcissism was also for him a later pathological condition in which libido has been withdrawn from objects and has been invested in the ego.[8] However, in later psychoanalytic writing based on Freud's ideas, the concept narcissism signifies the preoedipal stages of psychosexual development in general, including the oral stage as well as the anal, which use, though well established by convention, runs counter to Freud's primary use of the term.

In a child's earliest stage, autoerotism, the sexual instincts have not yet been unified and coordinated. Instead, each component (or partial) instinct seeks its own gratification independently. As yet, these instincts have not focused on an object, but instead are satisfied by local bodily gratifications. In the later stage, alloerotism, these component sexual instincts have become unified and seek gratification in an object distinct from the ego superordinate to them. The object may have a real existence in the outer world, or it may be merely fantasied, but its distinguishing feature is its separateness from the ego. Formally, the separation of ego from object defines the transition from autoerotism to alloerotism, which, however, proceeds by means of narcissism. Here, the component sexual instincts have been unified, but they are now directed toward an object of sorts, but this object is identified with the ego, which has been newly constituted. What is revolutionary about this stage for psychosexual development is the emergence of the ego, which was not present at birth, and the unification of the sexual instincts, which were present from the beginning. More precisely, the ego itself is cathected.

From the beginning, almost all analytic writers agreed upon the close and necessary connection between homosexuality and narcissism. To Freud, "the homosexual choice of object is originally more closely related to narcissism than the heterosexual." Since the most salient characteristic of the ego that is cathected during narcissism is the genitals, this period of self-love is essentially homosexual. Thus, the transition from narcissism to heterosexual alloerotism occurs through homosexual alloerotism. [9] These proved fruitful ideas to early analytic theorists. In 1910, Sadger maintained that "the road to homosexuality passes over narcissism," [10] and this aphorism was quoted shortly thereafter by Brill. [11] The connection between homosexuality and paranoia was strengthened because of their joint origin in narcissism. [12] To Ferenczi, this was the distinguishing characteristic of homosexual object choice: "Homosexuals are only more strongly fixed than other people in the narcissistic stage." [13] Fenichel was more subtle and attempted to untangle the narcissistic and object-related trends in the various perversions. [14] And Boehm based his bipartite nosology of homosexuality on whether the narcissistic stage had been achieved, regressed to, or a fixation there had suffered a reactivation. [15]

Freud claimed that for several varieties of homosexuality, object choice is predicated on the child's yearning for the lost love relation with his mother. The child's love objects are, however, real objects insofar as they are external to his own ego, but they are narcissistic in that they necessarily resemble it in any of four ways: by being what he is, what he once was, what he would like to be, or what was once part of himself. Such object choice is distinguished from "anaclitic" object choice, in which the object can resemble either "the woman who tends" or "the man who protects." Narcissistic objects represent transformations or derivatives of the ego, while anaclitic objects represent transformations or derivatives of external figures. Further, the narcissistic love of objects is a roundabout way of being loved, essentially a passive erotic stance, while anaclitic love is an active way of loving. For Freud, anaclitic object choice was characteristic of the heterosexual male, while narcissistic object choice was characteristic of most homosexual males and, an extremely important point to note, of the female.

But from this close connection between homosexuality and narcissism, several mistaken conclusions were drawn: that homosexuality is not truly object-related, that it involves impoverished object relations, and that its general organization is essentially preoedipal. Some analysts maintained that homosexuality was therefore necessarily a more primitive condition than heterosexuality. Since homosexual object choice was narcissistic and not anaclitic, it must therefore not be object-related in a strict sense. But Freud did not think that narcissistic object choice was disturbed or primitive. The narcissistic choice of the homosexual male could not be considered inferior to that of the heterosexual male simply because it resembled that of half the race: the normal heterosexual female. Although Freud may seem to have made such adverse judgments occasionally, he was at pains to deny the relative superiority of either mode:

> Perhaps it is not superfluous to give an assurance that, in this description of the feminine form of erotic life, no tendency to depreciate woman has any part. Apart from the fact that tendentiousness is alien to me, I also know that these different lines of development correspond to the differentiation of functions in a highly complicated biological connection.[16]

All that can be claimed about this distinction is that both are simply modes of relatedness. Further, both are represented in any individual's psychology. Finally, for Freud, the narcissistic libidinal position was not a "perversion, but the libidinal complement to the egoism of the instinct of self-preservation, a measure of which may be justifiably attributed to every living creature."[17] Freud's coinage, *narcissistic object choice*, was particularly unfortunate since it suggested a closer relation of that choice to the psychosexual stage of narcissism than Freud himself would have maintained. He was at pains to deny that narcissistic object choice was characteristic of narcissism, since for him the choice of any external object was not possible during narcissism. He wrote: "primary narcissism . . . lasts until the ego begins to cathect the ideas of objects with libido—to transform narcissistic libido into object libido."[18]

But even this clear formation conceals an ambiguity. What do we mean when we say that one set of object choices is based on the self and another on external objects? On the one hand, we may be implying that when the self is the basis for an object choice, what may seem like an act of loving another is in reality a passive state of being loved, with no real relation to an object. On the other hand, we may be claiming merely that certain kinds of object choice have their origins in the infantile experience of having been loved, which has been transformed at a higher level into a more complex relation to a separate and distinct object.

The most that can be legitimately claimed is that there is an innate tendency for homosexual object choice, when it is narcissistic, to drift toward more primitive narcissistic pathology. It does not seem at all unlikely that the ego, which serves as the prototype for later object choice, should exert a kind of centripetal influence, drawing erotic activity back to passivity and self-orientation. But it is important to see that an analogous innate tendency to drift to pathology can be discerned in anaclitic object relations. While narcissistic homosexual object choice tends to narcissistic (in the pejorative sense) passive self-gratification, its heterosexual equivalent tends to an equally primitive orientation around need gratification, which relates it in important ways to pathological borderline conditions.[19] But in both cases we are discussing the regression of advanced conditions to other more primitive states.

Later psychoanalysts also claimed that those who make narcissistic object choices necessarily suffer from defective superegos. While Freud maintained that the superego is constructed step by step by the introjection of cathected objects, so that they finally become identifications,[20] there is nothing in this theory to suggest that narcissistic objects, when they are true objects, are not just as suitable for this process as are anaclitic ones. In addition, the process that leads to the formation of the superego draws on large amounts of narcissistic libido, as the ego says, as it were, to the id, "Love me; I am just like the lost object."[21] For Jones, the establishment of the superego required the transformation of a certain amount of object libido into narcissistic libido, as the superego, having incorporated the lost love object, now itself serves as an object for the id.[22]

In general, while only a few classical psychoanalysts were once prone to view homosexuality as a protopsychotic condition,[23] many later psychoanalytic writers have seen overt homosexuality as stemming from an essentially borderline personality structure with its characteristic primitive object relations. It involves a kind of fixation at the narcissistic stage intermediate between autoerotism and object-relatedness, and thus midway between the neuroses and the psychoses. So this view has a certain symmetry and consistency to recommend it. The unstable self structure characteristic of this condition implies rather severe pathologies in object relations, which are transitional, between objectless autoerotism and an object-related oedipal situation. I do not claim that this view necessarily is untrue, only that it is based on an inconsistent interpretation of the theory that it claims as its metapsychological justification. The theory really allows for the possibility that such narcissistic object choice can serve as the ontogenetic basis for the later object choice, but it can also involve the same processes of elaboration, differentiation, and sublimation as its corresponding anaclitic object choice. Moreover, just as anaclitic object choice, in its developed form, need not be need-gratifying (although it is in its paradigmatic, original form), narcissistic object choice need not be a strategy for a passive state of self-love.

Much larger claims were based on a particular interpretation of how the Oedipus complex determines the "normal" conclusion of psychosexual development. From the beginning of the psychoanalytic movement up to the present day, most have claimed that psychosexual development, if left unhampered by trauma or some previous constitutional peculiarity, will naturally result in heterosexual object choice. Freud almost consistently maintained that homosexuality results when a more basic and natural heterosexuality is blocked. In his letter to an American mother, he explained that though homosexuality is "no vice, no degradation . . . [no] illness," it still is the result of a "certain arrest of sexual development."[24] "In every aberration from the normal sexual life a fragment of inhibited development and infantilism" can be found, he wrote,[25] and he later cited homosexuality specifically as "an inhibition in development."[26] Had this inhibition not occurred, psychosexual development would presumably have resulted in heterosexual object choice.

The primary mechanism for this natural and orderly achievement of heterosexual object choice was thought to be the Oedipus complex, which for Freud was "the central phenomenon of the sexual period of early childhood."[27] Although the term was first used in 1910, it was implicit in all of his work from the beginning, and he referred to it in passing in the Dora case of 1905. Its importance has not diminished for later theorists[28]; it occupies the same place in psychosexual developmental theory as the big bang does in modern cosmology. It marks the end of autoerotism and narcissism and ushers in true object-relatedness. For Freud, it was abolished in the unconscious by the threat of castration, to survive only in traces in pathological psychic structures.[29] Many of the arguments about the "unnaturalness" of homosexuality maintain that the persistence of homosexual object choice is prima facie evidence either that the Oedipus complex has not been worked through or that its experience was so traumatic that it caused a major psychosexual regression to a primitive preoedipal stage.

Although accounts of the Oedipus complex are scattered throughout Freud's work, the clearest, most concise, and most nearly complete formulations occur in *The Ego and the Id* and "The Dissolution of the Oedipus Complex." The male child takes his mother as his first object choice, which, developing from his attachment to the breast, is anaclitic in nature. Insofar as he is aware of his father, he identifies with him. But when his sexual desire for his mother becomes more urgent, the inherent ambivalence of his relationship to his father becomes apparent. The Oedipus complex begins as he starts to experience his father as a rival, and their relationship becomes hostile. The climax of the complex occurs when the child, who has overvalued his penis, discovers, after seeing female genitals, that, contrary to his previous assumption, it is possible to be without a penis. Castration thus becomes "imaginable" as punishment for his own importunate and jealous sexual strivings. So to preserve his organ, and because of his horror of the mutilated female genitalia, he must surrender his love object. The child abandons his sexual strivings in general and enters a period of latency, only to renew the quest with the onset of puberty. In addition, of great importance to his development is the introjection of his lost object, which now forms the basis for the development of his superego. Finally, infantile, un-coordinated sexual strivings are partly sublimated, thus enhancing the newly formed superego.

According to Freud himself, however, this short account of the Oedipus complex is the "simplified form." Other schemata are also possible. After outlining what he called a "simplification" of the disso-lution of the Oedipus complex, Freud posited two possible outcomes: an identification with the mother or an intensification of the primary identification with the father. He then added laconically, "We are accustomed to regard the latter outcome as the more normal." Later he remarked that "one gets the impression that the simple Oedipus com-plex is by no means its commonest form." And in another essay, he qualified his "simplified" account and added, "I do not maintain that this type is the only possible one. Variations in the sequence and the linking up of these processes must be very significant in the develop-ment of the individual."[30] Fully elaborated forms of the Oedipus com-plex, on the other hand, are extremely complex and ambiguous. Their mechanisms are not straightforward and unidirectional, and the rele-vant component forces undergo a bewildering variety of transforma-tions, repressions, and conversions into their opposites. Moreover, individual psychosexual development is not finally a function of the Oedipus complex alone but of it along with the peculiar psychosocial forces and the combination of instinctual drives and developed ego functions of the individual's "constitution."

The complicated issue of the fully elaborated Oedipus complex can perhaps most easily be approached by asking a simple question: If the child can relinquish his object tie to his mother only through a corre-sponding introjection and identification, much as mourning is resolved, then why is the image of the father introjected and identified with, not that of the mother? If the Oedipus complex were resolved like the process of incorporation in mourning, then all boys, if all went well, would become homosexuals.

Indeed, all preoedipal children, male and female, are psychically, if not functionally (in the case of little girls), homosexual. Up to the Oedipus complex, the only sexual organ that exists for children is the phallus—the penis for boys and the clitoris for girls. The mature female organ, the vagina, is, until puberty, "undiscovered." Thus, we may state that all preoedipal children are psychically phallic male homosexuals.[31] This state of affairs obtains until the child discovers the genitals of a member of the opposite sex. Before then the child assumes that all people have genital equipment like his own, including his first and prototypical love object, his mother. For the male child, then, the task is one of describing how he moves from psychic homosexuality through a mechanism biased toward identification with the lost female object to a final heterosexuality.

Nor is this all. The dilemma posed by castration threat—choosing between two unsatisfactory libidinal roles, an active and a passive one—leads in both directions to the surrender or paralysis of the penis, which has served as the basis for male sexual identity. If the child chooses the active role, laying claim to his object and insisting on his libidinal interests, his fate is to suffer enormous castration anxiety. He will remain "fixated" on his mother as an object choice. Though he has chosen an active identity, he will be unable to exercise or enjoy its function. If he chooses the passive role and surrenders his object in order to preserve his penis, he will be unable to exercise it on his object, having suffered a kind of self-castration. Even in optimal cases, the "normal" active phallic phase is relinquished in favor of a "neurotic" passive one,[32] a situation that is almost "universal."[33] This passive phallic phase also predisposes to "a certain type of homosexuality,"[34] as it defends against anxiety at female genitals with a "highly exaggerated and narcissistically cathected phallic phase."[35]

Finally, the unidirectional process to heterosexuality is further complicated by the bisexuality that Freud found "in the innate constitution of every human being."[36] This concept was a basic presupposition of psychoanalysis, which he thought it shared with biology. Classical orthodox psychoanalysis has pretty much accepted this idea, although it was later challenged.[37] But for most analysts, even in the most normative masculine development, there are important feminine trends, characteristics, and strivings that are simply not reducible to transformed masculinity. Implicitly, there is always at least a partial disposition to feminine identification, which becomes quite important because the Oedipus complex uniformly impels the male child away from a masculine libidinal stance.[38] So the choice between an active and passive outcome can be seen as favoring a homosexual resolution. Even if the child chooses the active alternative, he may unconsciously preserve his tie to his mother by identifying with her and consequently choosing future objects on a homosexual narcissistic basis. Or, if he chooses the passive alternative, he may try to preserve his penis, but in so doing he may have to be subject to his father and adopt the "inverted" Oedipus complex, thus becoming the father's passive sexual object. [39]

The only way we can continue to maintain that heterosexuality is the natural resolution of the Oedipus complex is further to complicate its mechanism. But this further weakens the claim that such an outcome is a foregone conclusion. The fully elaborated, complicated "fourfold" Oedipus complex takes into acount the constitutional bisexuality of the child and recognizes that his relation to his parents is more ambiguous and manifold than in the simpler version. The child is seen as bound to both parents by positive libidinal ties. Because of his preoedipal identification with his father, which corresponds to his identification with his mother, the child's relation to his father is not simple rivalry, but rather a developing ambivalence. And just as his primary bond with his father is libidinal and not simply aggressive, his relation with his mother is not simply affectionate and libidinal, but includes the same ambivalence and rivalry. Thus his relations with his parents are "fourfold." The child takes his mother as a libidinal object and regards his father as a rival. But he also takes his father as an object, and hates and competes with his mother as a rival for the loved father.

This conception of the Oedipus complex allows us plausibly to answer the question raised at the beginning of this section. The child can relinquish his libidinal tie to his mother by introjecting and identifying with his father because the basis for this identification, which the child effects at the end of the Oedipus complex, is not an entirely new relationship. It is built upon a previous, preoedipal primary identification. [40] In addition, the fear and loathing the child experienced at the sight of his mother's mutilated genitals prevent him from identifying with her. So he flies to the father. Paradoxically, this identification with the father both allows a future object tie to women and replaces the previous libidinal tie to the father.

What factors determine whether a child will intensify his identification with his father or identify with his mother? Apart from the character of particular families, the operations of constitutional bisexuality determine the final identification in two opposite ways. Freud observed that a passive, feminine predisposition will lead to a tendency to identify with the mother, and an active, masculine predisposition to a tendency to identify with the father. [41] "The relative intensity of the two identifications in any individual will reflect the preponderance in him of one or other of the two sexual dispositions." [42] This outcome, however, represents the last stage of the identification. Its earlier mechanisms have a more ambiguous direction because of a prior, irreducible ambiguity in sexual nature that determines the final outcome of the complex itself, rather than the Oedipus complex causing ambiguity in sexual nature. "It may even be that the ambivalence displayed in the relation to the parents should be attributed entirely to bisexuality and that it is not, as I have represented above, developed out of identification in consequence of rivalry."[43] When we look closely at this fourfold mechanism as it is powered by constitutional bisexuality, however, the startling conclusion is that a strong homosexual component in libidinal striving paradoxically leads to final heterosexual object choice, while a stronger than usual heterosexual libido will conversely tend to homosexual object choice.

When the child sees his mother's mutilated genitals and makes the horrified discovery of the difference between men and women, he is forced to relinquish his object tie to her and to replace it with an identification. But if his attachment to her is too strong—that is, if his libidinal position is excessively heterosexual—he will preserve the tie either by identifying with her or by seeking to deny her castrated state. Thus he may become a certain kind of homosexual or a fetishist. If, on the other hand, his attachment to his father is strong enough to withstand the threat of castration—that is, if he has a strong enough homosexual component in his sexual nature—he will adopt a heterosexual object choice by identifying with the father.

At the height of castration threat, a similar preponderance of homosexually related libido—specifically, the relative amounts of narcissistic and object libido—allows for a heterosexual outcome. Whether or not the child surrenders the object tie to the mother depends to a large extent on the amount of narcissistic libido, which is now directed toward the ego. The child's choice at the height of the Oedipus complex is between a narcissistic cathexis of his own penis and the object cathexes he has established with his mother. In most cases, narcissistic interest wins out, and the child turns from the Oedipus complex and enters latency, having thus established the preconditions for later heterosexual object choice, which will be exercised at the onset of puberty. But if his object cathexes are too strong, he will remain fixated at the erotic tie with the mother, or regress in the face of castration threat. Thus, in order for later heterosexual anaclitic object choice to occur, the child's narcissistic libido must be strong enough to outweigh the strength of his object cathexes. This was Freud's view, but it runs counter to that of certain early theorists.[44] In addition, the newly formed superego, itself the product of the child's relinquishing his object tie to the mother, aids him in consolidating this act of renunciation.

Tracing these paradoxical mechanisms counters the extremely common notions in psychoanalytic theory that heterosexual object choice is the "natural" outcome of the Oedipus complex, and that any other outcome is evidence of its defective workings. Implicit in this view is the notion that heterosexual object choice inheres in mental organization before the onset of the Oedipus complex as its telos and that it exfoliates during the process as direct fulfillment of that potentiality. Yet there is no straight line from preoedipal constitution to postoedipal result. There is instead a bewildering series of transformations, some of which turn preoedipal conditions into their opposites. It is not accurate to speak of "normal" or "natural" development in the case of the Oedipus complex, since these terms suggest an orderly efflorescence of possibilities inherent in the individual before he enters the oedipal stage. The mechanisms of the Oedipus complex are really a series of psychic traumas, and all results of it are neurotic compromise formations. Since even optimal development is the result of trauma, the fact that a certain development results from a "stunting" or "blocking" or "inhibition" of another possibility does not distinguish it from other developments. All results of the Oedipus complex are traumatic, and, for similar reasons, all are "normal." Some are more pathological than others, but the reason for considering them so cannot be derived from the operations of the Oedipus complex. Those writers who think otherwise ignore the traumatic origins of even optimal results and, in effect, disguise a moral judgment about what is "natural" as a pseudobiological argument.

From structural considerations alone, there are twelve possible resolutions of the Oedipus complex, in terms of sexual identity and object choice. Six of these are homosexual—those using as object-paradigms the self or the father. Of the twelve, only one is traditionally considered "normal" or "natural": the one based on an identification with the father, employing an anaclitic mode of object choice, with the castrated mother as paradigmatic object. For those who find such things helpful, the table on page 83 summarizes the final results of the Oedipus complex and the mechanisms that lead to them.

There may be reasons—empirical, clinical, ethical, aesthetic, or political—for considering any of these twelve resolutions pathological,

Table 1.
Sexual results of the Oedipus complex as determined by identifications (or instinctual aims) and object choices.

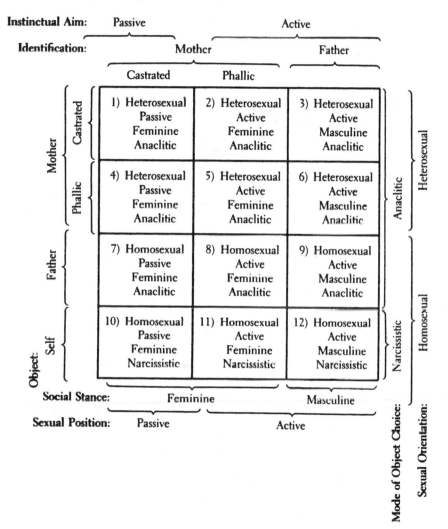

unnatural, or undesirable. But strictly speaking from structural considerations alone, all twelve are simply alternative resolutions. Whether a child will become homosexual or heterosexual is a question of sexual identity and object choices, and these are determined respectively by the primary identifications made at the height of the Oedipus complex and by the mode of object choice—anaclitic or narcissistic—he employed. Similarly, since the object the instinct focuses on for its discharge is almost entirely detachable from the aim that the instinct pursues, each aim can involve either anaclitic or narcissistic object choices, and anaclitic choices may be heterosexual or homosexual, since the father may be chosen as the prototypical anaclitic object.

Usually, two figures in childhood are available for identification, the mother and the father, and both are present and used as primary and secondary identifications. The mother, however, can serve as the model for identification in her "phallic" preoedipal guise, in which she is thought to be equipped with a penis, and in her "castrated" postoedipal guise, in which she is understood as not having a penis. An identification with the "castrated" mother—that is, a remaking of the ego into the semblance of the penisless mother—will involve, not surprisingly, a passive libidinal stance and a feminine identity, just as identification with the father will involve an active libidinal stance and a masculine identity. It is important to recall that the determinants of such identifications are quite complex. An identification with the castrated mother, for example, may require either a passive predisposition or a previous active libidinal stance so strong as not to permit relinquishing this primary object tie. Similarly, an identification with the father may require either an active predisposition or a weak libidinal stance. With any of these identifications, however, we are dealing with homosexual and heterosexual possibilities, since it is quite possible for a male with a primary identification with the castrated mother to make heterosexual object choices.

Strictly speaking, the distinction between homosexual and heterosexual can be made only with reference to object choice. Narcissistic object choices, those made for objects on the basis of their resemblance to the self, are homosexual. Anaclitic choices, that is, those made for objects on the basis of their resemblance to a lost, infantile object, can be either homosexual or heterosexual, depending on whether the infantile object was the mother or the father. And again, the mother may serve as the prototype for all later objects in either a "phallic" or a "castrated" aspect, so that a man who is libidinally passive and chooses an active partner may still be heterosexual in his object choice.

The question of sexual disposition is, however, even more complex than our table would suggest. Each cell is meant to represent an alternative solution to the Oedipus complex, and, for structural reasons alone, none can be considered any more "natural" or "primary" than any other. But clinically, such distinct and equivalent cells cannot be maintained. As Fenichel observed, one identification does not preclude another; simultaneous identifications are possible and indeed ubiquitous.[45] And, rather than speaking of a certain figure as the nucleus for an identification, it is more accurate to specify what aspect of that figure is being internalized, as in the case of the mother, whose phallic and castrated aspects have been distinguished. Similar distinctions could have been made about the self as the prototype for narcissistic object choice; it can be what one is, what one was, what one wished to be, or someone who was once part of one. Similar distinctions are conceivable for the father.

It often happens that one alternative can be a defense against another,[46] or a regression from another solution in the face of an overwhelming castration anxiety.[47] It is important to be very clear here that such a regression or defense, while quite common, should be considered as a secondary solution to the Oedipus complex. Any of the twelve alternatives can serve as such a secondary solution. But, more important, any of them can also serve as a primary solution. There is nothing structurally or dynamically inherent in any of the twelve that makes it necessarily one or the other.

The "negative" Oedipus complex (number 7), for example, can serve as a defense against another solution that, although it resulted from the operation of the Oedipus complex on a particular psychological constitution, was intolerable to the subject, such as a passive submission to the phallic mother (number 4). But it can also be the primary solution for another constitution, which, because of its attendant anxiety, might be replaced by another solution. This point is important because in later periods, as we shall see, the "negative" Oedipus complex has been claimed to be a necessarily "neurotic solution" to the Oedipus complex.

Some individual solutions, with their particular underlying constitutions, dynamics, and family relationships, are pathological, but they are not necessarily so. Nor can they be considered so merely because they are neurotic compromises determined by traumatic stresses during the oedipal period. All twelve solutions are the result of trauma; they are all compromise formations and are, even at their optimum, neurotic. They cannot be distinguished on the basis of whether they are "healthy" or "neurotic," since the Oedipus complex operates by trauma and necessarily results in neurotic conditions. It is not possible for any solution to be "normal," not even the normative number 3.

By contrast, a psychic mechanism that is not traumatic in its operations acts on a certain preexisting mental organization and, unless something goes wrong, mediates its full development. The final result of the operations of the Oedipus complex, however, whatever its form, does not represent a later development of an earlier stage. Instead, that precondition may have been transformed utterly, its direction reversed and its tendencies transformed into their opposites. We have already seen how homosexual tendencies, with respect to libidinal position and object choice, have been transformed into heterosexual equivalents, and heterosexual tendencies into their homosexual equivalents, or how object libido has been converted into narcissistic libido, and vice versa.

But most important, the phallic stage itself has been transformed from a "natural" maturational stage into a neurotic compromise formation. Boehm first called attention to the universality of this "passive" stage and saw the predominance of constitutional femininity there as occurring at the expense of constitutional masculinity.[48] And Jones explicated how this necessary trauma occurs. According to him, the phallic stage is divided into two subphases, one "innocent" and the other "anxious," depending on the child's knowledge of sexual differences and his consequent castration anxiety. The castration threat strengthens the homosexual attitude of the boy and pushes him from the innocent "protophallic" to the anxious "deuterophallic" substage, where his interest in penetrating with his penis is replaced by a voyeuristic interest in the penises of other men. Jones saw this not as a natural development but as a necessary though temporary "perversion," a neurotic compromise between libido and anxiety that had to be undone at puberty if heterosexual functioning was not to continue being suppressed.[49]

Jones's ideas were reaffirmed in the next few years by Benedek and Loewenstein. Benedek too saw the second subphase as traumatic and neurotic, a "highly exaggerated and narcissistically cathected phallic phase," which, if it persisted, often would result in homosexuality. For her too it was a "neurotic compromise" that permitted a narcissistic identification with the father as a defense against castration anxiety and the boy's own femininity. The penis here became an essentially passive organ of pleasure, but if this stage persisted, the Oedipus complex could not be considered to have been terminated.[50] Loewenstein repeated these formulations, emphasizing the passive nature of the subphase and the corresponding desire to receive caresses rather than to penetrate. Only with the reappearance of the active subphase could the genitals again assume primacy. He too related the persistence of this subphase to certain forms of homosexuality.[51]

Jones saw quite clearly that the deuterophallic stage was unlike most other stages in psychosexual development, which seemed to proceed by means of a nontraumatic maturational scheme:

> [It] is a deviation from the direct path of development, and is a
> response to anxiety, but nevertheless, for all we know, research
> may show that the earliest of infantile anxiety is inevitable and
> that the phallic defense is the only one possible at that age.[52]

Freud, too, insisted on the absolute destruction of the Oedipus complex. Mere repression was not sufficient, because later psychopathology would develop. In "The Dissolution of the Oedipus Complex,"[53] he listed the ways in which the complex brings about the destruction of the child's preoedipal psychosexual organization. His language there was quite strong, but it is somewhat obscured by the weak English translation. Freud's word for "dissolution" is *Untergang*, which can mean either a relatively mild setting, sinking, or fall (as Spengler meant by *Der Untergang des Abendlandes*) or a more violent downfall, ruin, or destruction. Freud's English translators favored the first sense, rendering it even milder as "The Passing of the Oedipus Complex." But it is clear that Freud did not intend this weaker sense, since he did not use the milder German word for "dissolution," *Aufloesung*. He also used *Untergang* in *The Ego and the Id*, where he coupled it with *Zertruemmerung*, which signifies shattering or demolition. *Truemmer* are ruins, and the prefix *Zer-* signifies "to pieces." Its best translation is probably the Latin *vastatio*.

I have subjected the reader to this little philological exercise in order to suggest that speaking of the "resolution" of the Oedipus complex begs the question. Implicit in all this is a metaphor of natural process. And this leads easily and insidiously to the sense that the various "resolutions" of the Oedipus complex can be distinguished by the extent to which they were produced by such an orderly and gradual natural process. Such a conception finally leads to the notion of "natural" and "unnatural" conditions. Yet Freud's language and Jones's explicit formulations do not permit such a view. Parenthetically, the question of whether animals practice homosexuality in their natural state is almost entirely irrelevant to the question of the pathological nature of human homosexuality. The sexual development of animals, as far as we know, is straightforward and unidirectional, pointed toward procreative competence and entirely maturational, since it is biologically determined. The final result of human psychosexual development, however, is only partially biological. It is, in addition, postulated on trauma, a blocking of "natural" sexual development, and a sharp swerve in the direction of that development.

Still, there are "solutions" to the Oedipus complex that are pathological, and it is important to be precise about the theoretical ways in which they can be distinguished. Psychoanalysis has based its determination of sexual pathology on the extent to which any particular psychosexual organization deviates from a putative norm of heterosexual genital competence. Though Freud claimed that he could not define psychic health in any theoretically cogent manner,[54] he did establish the characteristics of a "mature" and "normal" psychosexual organization:

> The final outcome of sexual development lies in what is known as the normal sexual life of the adult, in which the pursuit of pleasure comes under the sway of the reproductive function and in which the component instincts, under the primacy of a single erotogenic zone, form a firm organization directed towards a sexual aim attached to some extraneous sexual object.[55]

Everything but the first requirement—that the pursuit of pleasure be united with the reproductive function—seems sensible. The first, however, is ambiguous. It is unclear if Freud only meant to say that pleasure was henceforth to be derived from discharge associated with the reproductive organs, or if he meant more stringently that sexually pleasurable activity should essentially involve the physiological goal of reproduction. The distinction has, of course, crucial implications for psychoanalytic attitudes toward homosexuality.

For the most part, psychoanalytic writers have adopted the second reading and have consequently seen homosexuality as pathological. The editor of a recently published symposium on psychoanalytic views on sexual deviation, for example, explained that his group decided to ignore Freud's distinction between inversion and perversion since it "is not generally used," and instead "used the term 'perversion' for both":

> In subscribing to this view the group seemed to be adopting norms suggested by biological—that is, reproductive—function. Yet this judgment was rooted in an aggregate of clinical experience which suggested that deviant behavior conforming to this definition was usually accompanied by other signs of mental illness, and that if these defining factors were absent, other indications of pathology did not appear nearly so consistently. [56]

What was ambiguous in Freud became a doctrine in later psychoanalytic writing: "normal" and "healthy" sexual life required pleasurable genital competence in the service of a reproductive—that is, a heterosexual—aim.

In order to evaluate the validity of this definition of *normal* and *healthy*, we have to look more closely at what Freud meant by "the final outcome of sexual development." For him, the genital stage was the last and fulfilling stage of the four stages of psychosexual development: oral, anal, phallic, and genital, with a period of latency intervening between the last two. Each is under the sway of its own erotogenic zone, and each presents certain psychological tasks and goals for the developing individual. [57] Consequently, a fixation at, or regression to, any of the stages but the last represents a pathology with identifiable characteristics of personality, ego development, defensive strategies, and sexual functioning.

Despite this rather clear-cut scheme, however, the last stage presents certain anomalies. For one thing, in the case of the male, the genital stage is, in certain respects, a repetition of the third, since the primary erotogenic zone in both is the genitals. Nonetheless, the two stages are quite distinct. For one thing, the first "phallic" stage corresponds to the entry into the Oedipus complex, and as that complex is "shattered," the phallic stage, instead of being consolidated, is repudiated and relinquished under the onslaught of castration threat. The child then enters a period of "latency," in which sexual strivings are set aside, and other psychological goals, now freed from their thralldom to sexuality, are able to develop. With the beginning of puberty, the genitals again become the focus of psychological development, and a new psychosexual stage begins, or, rather, a previous one is taken up again. Thus, the last, genital stage centers on both the development that originally inhered in the first phallic stage and the new possibilities that have been prepared by the latency period. In other words, the genital stage is both the third stage of a rather straightforward maturational scheme and the fourth stage in a more complex developmental process.

The maturational scheme, for all its crucial psychological achievements, is primarily biological, though it has important effects on ego functioning, defensive strategies, and the like, which are all propelled by the pursuit of pleasure. In fact, the more primitive or basic the psychosexual stage, the tighter the fit between biology and psychology. Thus, in the oral stage, the infant's pursuit of pleasure—the sexual gratification arising from stimulation of the lips, tongue, and mouth—is aligned with his survival as an organism and his ability to take in nourishment. This is one of the meanings Freud intended when he discussed "anaclitic" instincts, which "lean on," as do their corresponding psychological achievements, a more basic biological drive. From this alignment, the psychological importance of this stage arises. But in the total psychosexual achievement there is no separation of biological, psychological, and social interests.

As psychosexual development proceeds and as new stages are embarked upon, this tight alignment of interests begins to unravel. The anal stage is often equivocal, but by the time of the first phallic stage, a clear separation of biographical and individual goals can be discerned. The genitals have become the primary focus of attention and pleasure, but they serve only a negligible biological function, since the child is not capable of sexual reproduction, nor will he be until puberty.

With puberty, and the inauguration of the genital stage, pleasure and procreation must be united, but this goal can be achieved only in a curiously asymmetrical manner. By this time, the adolescent's interest in his genitals and his ability to derive pleasure from their use have existed for years. Now he must coordinate and reconcile his striving for pleasure with his social and emotional connectedness to other people, in order to sustain an adequate relation with a sexual partner. This is a purely psychological task that is gradual and extends over the entire latency period. The child has matured cognitively and affectively, and his object relations have similarly developed. He has progressed from the crisis of the Oedipus complex through latency to the beginning of puberty. The second task of puberty is more sudden. With the maturation of the genitals, the adolescent suddenly assumes the role of representative of the race, faced with the responsibility to reproduce. But this task does not essentially involve the pursuit of pleasure or of his own self-interest. Instead, it is a social goal, and the adolescent's ability and will to fulfill it depend on the socialization that has occurred during the latency period.

As we move from the simple, biologically determined, and conjunctive oral stage to the more complex and at least partially socially conditioned and disjunctive genital stage, our descriptive and normative discourse must necessarily change. If, for example, we wish to prescribe what a "normal" or "healthy" oral stage should be, we may lay down certain psychological requirements that have the authority of ineluctable biology, since most psychological achievements at this stage are closely aligned with the function of taking in nourishment. But as the features of any stage become more disjunctive, as they do at the genital stage, we cannot prescribe with such unitary authority. The primacy of the genitals is a biological fact, but not whether an individual uses them for reproduction or pleasure or both. Our prescriptions become matters of judgment, involving ethics, politics, and aesthetics as well as biology. The failure to understand this has resulted in a curious truncation of psychoanalytic discourse and an entanglement in a pointless paradox.

By insisting on prescriptions for "health" and "normalcy" that are not psychological in nature, psychoanalysis turned away from issues that are its legitimate concern—specifying the conditions and characteristics of mature and healthy mental functioning. To do so, psychoanalysis must be prepared to acknowledge that certain behavior may not be congruent with them. Freud saw this clearly when he recognized the discrepancy among physical characteristics, mental characteristics, and object choice:

> A man with predominantly male characteristics and also masculine in his erotic life may still be inverted in respect to his object, loving only men instead of women. A man in whose character feminine attributes obviously predominate, who may, indeed, behave in love like a woman, might be expected, from this feminine attitude, to choose a man for his love object; but he may nevertheless be heterosexual, and show no more inversion in re-

spect to his object than an average normal man. . . . [Mental]
sexual character and object choice do not necessarily coincide.[58]

Why, in the face of such obvious discrepancies among overt behavior,
psychological experience, and "mental sexual character," did Freud
choose nonetheless to define a healthy mental organization partly on
the basis of object choice? For Freud, the act of procreation was the
central fact of human existence. Psychosexual development led up to it,
and all higher mental functions, as well as the very experience of one's
own psychology, were later developments and elaborations of it. So the
notion of "natural" and "unnatural" has a very particular meaning for
Freud. It simply describes the extent to which any particular activity
contributes to or detracts from the act of procreation. In fact, the very
idea of "masculine" and "feminine" could only be defined unequivocally as "active" and "passive" in the act of copulation.[59]

In attempting to ground human psychology in biology and all higher
activities in the act of reproduction, Freud turned the course of psychoanalysis away from the individual's experience and ascription of
meaning to his own instinctual life, and from the ways in which history
and society impinge on that life and give it form. In other words, Freud
removed sexuality from the realm of humane discourse, and placed it
inappropriately in the objective immutability of the natural sciences.
This conversion of what could have been an *ars erotica* into a *scientia
sexualis* led, among other things, to a hypostatization of sexuality, so
that it was now seen as a biological and anatomic given, having an
immutable teleology, without a history and resistance to individual
human meaning.

We can see the effects of this quite clearly in Freud's discussion of
instincts and how they are transformed in individual experience. In
"Instincts and Their Vicissitudes," he proposed that instincts could be
considered through four of their aspects: their impetus, or the force
required to power them; their aim, or the ways they attain their satisfaction in discharge; their object, or what or who it is through which
they achieve their aim; and their source, or what organ gives rise to the
corresponding somatic process. This exhausts Freud's analysis of the
instincts.

Strikingly absent is any systematic consideration of the quality of the
instincts. While Freud did speak of the union of sex, aggression, and
affection necessary for mature genital sexuality, he did not discuss at

length the quality of pleasure involved in the sex act, or the meaning of its affectional exchange. Still, in a footnote in *Three Essays* appended to the discussion of deviation in respect to the sexual object, Freud observed:

> The most pronounced difference between the love life of antiquity and ours lies in the fact that the ancients placed the emphasis on the instinct itself, while we put it on its object. The ancients extolled the instinct and were ready to ennoble through it even an inferior object, while we disparage the activity of the instinct as such and only countenance it on account of the merits of the object.[60]

Here I throw up my hands in admiration and exasperation. Freud recognized the point exactly, but he did nothing to answer his own objection.

This omission has not been rectified to this day. While every practicing clinician is constantly attentive to the quality of experience reported by his or her patient, the theory of sexuality offers little understanding of how individual experience relates to the broad categories of sexual orientation. A few attempts have recently been made in this direction,[61] but they are located in *terra incognita* or, more properly, *terra ignota*. No one would think of constructing a classification of modern eating habits based only on nutritional concerns, with such varieties of "perverts" as gourmets, gourmands, epicures, and nibblers, and in which the "forepleasures" of the table have replaced the primary nutritional aim. While eating is, no doubt, based on the biological need for nourishment, other values arise that are "anaclitic" to this need and relate more to the quality of the activity itself than to its aim or its instrumental objects.

The fact is that modern sexual activity has little to do with the act of procreation, and it is a form of moral atavism to continue to think that it does. It is engaged in for its pleasure or its possibility of intimacy, and there is no reason to think that procreative goals are essential or necessary, even unconsciously. The values that do operate are psychological and should be considered by means of the appropriate psychological discourse. And the propriety of any particular sexual activity for procreation is, strictly speaking, a matter of biology. The two discourses are related, but nevertheless quite distinct.

The heritage that the early psychoanalytic movement bequeathed to its heirs, for all its powerful and useful insights, and despite an early though short-lived tolerance, was most deficient in failing to provide a theoretically unambiguous account of homosexuality. In addition, ambiguities in the theory were exploited to lend support for certain judgments and presuppositions that do not belong in the body of psychoanalysis proper. Finally, the attempt to ground the theory of psychoanalysis on "hard" biological principles had the deleterious effect of relegating more nearly humane concerns to a kind of clinical twilight. We shall see how these concerns have continued, though in the case of homosexuality they have scarcely been acknowledged, into a later period. Only very recently has a debate begun on the relation of this underground tradition to the dominant one. For the greater part of the history we have been tracing, however, this relation has been one of silence, and the preconditions for that silence were set down in these early years of the psychoanalytic movement.

CHAPTER V

THE THEORISTS OF THE ORAL PERIOD: 1930–1948

In the next twenty years, from the end of the classical period to the postwar era, we can see a major and unanticipated shift in the psychoanalytic theory of homosexuality, reflecting larger developments in psychoanalysis as a whole. From the early thirties to the late forties, less attention was paid to drive theory and the vicissitudes of the id and more to the development of the ego and to how it modulated and coordinated such drives,[1] sometimes even apart from the operations and pressures of the id, as in the notion of "conflict-free" ego functions and development.[2] This led to a "psychosocial" consideration of how the ego developed and functioned in the social environment.[3] But this movement "out" from the private world of the unconscious is not crucial to our topic. More relevant to the psychoanalytic theory of homosexuality is a corresponding movement "down" to deeper and more primitive psychic strata. The primary interest of early theorizers was in the Oedipus complex, which was for Freud quite simply "the central phenomenon of the sexual period of early childhood."[4] Although it was preceded and partly determined by earlier developments at the oral and anal stages, the complex stood as the great gateway into object relations and true relatedness to the world. Early psychoanalysis was largely the analysis of the Oedipus complex. The oral stage was, of course, basic to Freud's theory of psychosexual development, and he dealt with preoedipal development in the Dora case, in which he detected powerful oral trends and fixations.[5] Regressions to stages earlier than the Oedipus complex were seen as involving such grave disturbances as the "paraphrenias" (e.g., paranoia and schizophrenia) and as being, for the most part, outside the pale of psychoanalytic treatment. We can see this procedural orientation as late as 1945, in that classic compendium, *The Psychoanalytic Theory of Neurosis*, in which virtually every emotional disturbance was explained by recourse to the operations of the Oedipus complex.[6]

But even by the thirties, major objections were being raised to dwelling on this universal and "monotonous" etiology.[7] As our present period began, there was a widespread interest in the precursors of the Oedipus complex, particularly the oral stage, even among analysts working within the classical psychoanalytic tradition. By far the most revolutionary work concerning the oral stage, which transformed psychoanalytic theory and also fragmented the movement, was by Melanie Klein,[8] in particular her lectures on preoedipal psychosexual development, published later as *The Psycho-Analysis of Children*.[9] Her insights provided the basis for the entire object relations school, and her influence on those who wrote after her was enormous.

During this period, such an influence can be seen in the tendency to emphasize the oral trends in homosexuality and to see homosexuality as a perversion—although most analysts would have agreed that it was developmentally the most advanced perversion—instead of as a neurosis. These are, of course, related, since perversions, in the technical sense, represent a disturbance in development that occurred at a stage earlier than the phallic oedipal crisis. In his textbook of psychoanalysis, Alexander saw homosexuality as a perversion that included both a "distortion in the quality of the sexual strivings" and a displacement in "the object of the sexual striving." And he further related such disturbances to "a failure in the integration of the pregenital components of sexuality into a mature form."[10] Similarly, Glover, in his handbook of psychoanalysis, defined homosexuality as a perversion representing "regression to an earlier stage of sexual development," although, he added, it was the "most advanced and organized form of sexual perversion."[11]

The watershed in the history of the psychoanalytic theory of homosexuality occurred with this identification of homosexuality as a perversion, which was to have profound effects on later discourse. It remained for a later period seriously to raise the question of whether nonperverse forms of homosexuality might exist. But by that time, the consensus was well established and reinforced by other developments in theory and discourse.

The other main development was not so much a theoretical development as a shift in tone and rhetoric, a freedom on the part of some analysts to engage in rather sadistic abuse and ridicule at the expense of their homosexual patients. Admittedly, such a development is peculiar, and its contemplation can offer satisfaction to no one, but it seemed to have sprung from the description of the character traits of "the typical homosexual," as well as from the more theoretical discussion of such oral traits as spite.

Still, the usual business of psychoanalytic research continued, much as it had in the earlier period. The classic theories of homosexuality, strengthened and deepened by new insights, served as the basis for psychoanalytic contributions to other fields. Karpman, for example, published a study of Tolstoi's "The Kreutzer Sonata," which was to be part of a more extended psychobiography of the author. He interpreted the misogyny and hatred of sex of the protagonist, Pozdnuishef, as due to his inability to love, itself a result of unconscious homosexuality. The period's interest in the oral stage was apparent in Karpman's attributing Pozdnuishef's fantasies of self-castration to his wish to castrate others, which derived from premature weaning and the resultant oral frustration and rage.[12] To illustrate his contention that homosexuals were incapable of sublimating their homoerotic libido, Bychowski applied psychoanalytic insights to Walt Whitman, who, he claimed, struggled in vain for such a sublimation.[13] To Nunberg, writing after World War II and concerning himself with Jewish history and consciousness, the practice of circumcision helped determine Jewish consciousness by handling the homosexual attitudes implicit in the ambivalence toward the father: "Man has always rebelled against this attachment" to the father. By giving up part of the genital to him, Jews were able to "renounc[e] instinct gratification and at the same time initiat[e] sublimation of their homosexuality."[14] In a similar spirit, Wittels argued in "Collective Defense Mechanisms Against Homosexuality" that societies must find ways of sublimating homosexual trends in the population, lest the entire society adopt collective paranoid defenses. His example was, of course, Nazi Germany,[15] and his examples drew heavily on work by Boehm on German drinking fraternities.[16]

The most ambitious application of psychoanalytic insights into homosexuality to a related field, in this case to anthropology, was Horney's explication of the universal dread of female genitalia. According to her, "male homosexuality has for its basis, in common indeed with all the other perversions, the desire to escape from the female genital, or to deny its very existence." Here too the interest in the oral precursors of the Oedipus complex is apparent. The fear of the female genital is not due primarily to castration fear, which only masks a fear of the mother that "is more deep-seated, weighs more heavily and is usually more energetically repressed." Furthermore, castration anxiety itself springs from a deeper source, "the ego's response to the *wish to be a woman*." Much of her article seemed to be an effort to push the determinants of neurosis back to earlier stages of development, but it was also an attempt to impugn the very notion of penis envy. Thus, narcissistic "scars" that result from the boy's humiliation in face of the "sinister female genital" drive him to attempt to prove himself with women sexually, to "debase women," and to "diminish the self-respect of women."[17] Later analytic writers largely missed these last implications, especially insofar as they suggested some countertransferential reasons for positing female penis envy, but they did accept the existence of a preoedipal dread of the mother's genitals that would often result in later homosexual object choice.

The usual work of analyzing and interpreting homosexual object choice as a neurosis also went on. Wulff, for example, published an account of male homosexuality that seemed to fit "none of the patterns that have hitherto been put forward." The patient, who was married, displayed considerable hatred of his father, who had been quite brutal to him during childhood. As it turned out, the case involved intense love of the father's penis during the phallic phase, which was later reaction formed when the patient was replaced in the father's affection by a stepmother. What was unusual was the apparent absence of any deep attachment to the mother, of excess narcissism, and apparently of castration anxiety at the sight of female genitals.[18] These findings seem to have been accepted, and they were referred to by several subsequent writers.[19]

In addition, Lorand further clarified the relationship between homosexuality and fetishism by means of the traditional psychoanalytic theory of responses to the discovery that the mother has no penis. Lorand claimed that this discovery had three possible consequences: homosexuality, fetishism, and normalcy. The first was caused, he thought, by a "tendency to female identification," which led to complete identification with the mother and an acceptance of her damaged genital.[20]

The publication of cases that confirmed classical psychoanalytic theories of homosexuality continued. Lagache's analysis of a homosexual illustrated the relation of active to passive forms of homosexuality and showed what defensive maneuvers mediate between the two. In this case, when the patient shifted from homosexual to heterosexual interests, he experienced a stage of intense, though "normal," jealousy, which Lagache regarded as both a sign of progress and a resistance. The patient was defending against passive homosexuality, which had previously been defended against by active homosexuality. The passive form was intolerable to the patient's consciousness because it was associated with castration, but it was deeply rooted in the patient's psychology because "submission and obedience to the father [had] as their aim the right to take his place."[21]

Although such dynamics fell well within the traditional psychoanalytic theory, they introduced an important technical distinction that was confirmed at about the same time by Anna Freud, who, in a series of unpublished lectures, reported on the successful analyses of homosexuals, whom she treated as neurotics. She maintained that it was important to pay attention to the interplay of passive and active homosexual fantasies, and to interpret to the patient that his choosing a passive partner allows him to enjoy vicariously a passive or receptive mode, while his choosing an active partner allows him to recapture his lost sense of masculinity. Such interpretations, she claimed, would reactivate repressed castration anxieties, and childhood narcissistic grandiosity and its complementary fear of dissolving into nothing during heterosexual intercourse would come with the renewal of heterosexual potency.[22] For Anna Freud, the original interplay of active and passive strivings prevented an adequate identification with the father. Thus, she resolved the question, unanswered in the earlier period, of whether active or passive homosexuality was the more basic condition.

The interest in the connection between homosexuality and paranoia also continued throughout this period. For Klein, the paranoid anxiety that resulted from the projection of primitive aggression was handled by allying with a "good penis," which guarded against fear and hatred of the love object:

> The mechanisms, which are dominant in cases of paranoic character, enter, though to a lesser degree, into every homosexual activity. The sexual act between men always in part serves to satisfy sadistic impulses and to confirm the sense of destructive om-

nipotence; and behind the positive relation to the "good" penis as an external love-object there lurk to a greater or lesser extent, according to the amount of hatred present, not only hatred of the father's penis but also destructive impulses against the sexual partner and the fear of him that they give rise to.[23]

These ideas spurred a great deal of discovery and publication. Kaufmann illustrated such projective identification operating both homosexually and heterosexually in one patient.[24] In addition, Nunberg emphasized the aggressive content of homosexual fantasies and reasserted that paranoia and homosexuality were intimately connected and could be distinguished only on the basis of the degree and quality of projection involved and of the conversion of sadism into masochism in the latter case.[25] Finally, Rosenfeld offered an overview of the kinds of relationships that exist between homosexuality and paranoia. He began with Freud's transformations in the Schreber case, but also maintained the reverse transformation: homosexuality, especially in its passive form, could defend against paranoia and, in both latent and manifest forms, could be a cover for this more serious disturbance. Specifically, paranoid persecution could be appeased by passive homosexual submission or by homosexual idealization. In both cases, however, projection was a triggering defense mechanism. Such traits and tendencies are to be found, he asserted, even in homosexuals who are not psychotic.[26]

Quite important for later developments, there was a brief flurry of discussion of bisexuality, although there was no substantive theoretical advance until later, when it was assimilated into the general discussion of homosexuality. As we have seen earlier, bisexuality occupied an important place in Freud's theoretical ideas. In "normal" development, the homosexual component is sublimated, but the implication of Freud's view is that the appearance of manifest homosexuality in adult life is at least partly due to an innate and irradicable tendency and not solely to emotional trauma or to a warping of the sexual constitution. In short, the argument about the naturalness or unnaturalness of manifest homosexuality largely concerns the precise and appropriate implications to be drawn from the concept of bisexuality.

All analysts seemed to have accepted Freud's notion. Karl Menninger, for example, criticized the author of an article on the varieties of homosexuality for not having emphasized the importance of homosexuality for all people.[27] The issue of bisexuality, however, was not a focus of discussion until 1930, when Bryan observed that it had until then been neglected, perhaps because of "deep resistances" on the part of analysts. He connected the countersexual organs in each gender, the clitoris in women and the sinus pocularis and ejaculatory ducts in men, to corresponding psychological traits, and related these to the impregnation of the ovum by the spermatazoon. His correspondences were fanciful and even silly—the similarity in shape between the "rod-like" spermatazoon and the penis, and the notion that male sexual response first begins with the stimulation of such "female" organs as the eye, mouth, and arms. His adducing such current expressions as "she's a peach" adds to one's discomfort with his ideas, as does his explanation of why exhibitionists derive no satisfaction from exposing themselves to blind women. All this was intended to support Bryan's contention that all people have characteristics of the opposite sex in their psychological constitution. [28]

Today's reader may well wonder how such undisciplined thinking could find its way into the *International Journal of Psychoanalysis*, but anyone who has browsed through issues of this publication published during the twenties will recognize that article as not very unusual. The early history of psychoanalysis included a tradition, now for the most part extinct, of fanciful speculation; and its various splinter groups, from the earnest and scholarly Jungians to the later zealous Reichians, are important examples of such a tradition. It is one of the achievements of the psychoanalytic movement that such tendencies were pretty much kept in check and, by and large, subsequently corrected. It is unfortunate, however, that certain important concepts, such as bisexuality, were discredited by being discussed with such soft mindedness. Implicit in Bryan's self-indulgent whimsy was the important notion that constitutional homosexuality might reveal itself in the thoughts and actions of "normal" men and women. But such a possibility was squelched by impatient critics.

Ten years later, for example, Rado rejected entirely the notion of physical bisexuality and constitutional homosexuality. He began by reviewing the anthropological evidence for the widespread belief in bisexuality and hermaphroditism and concluded that "the idea of bisexuality far antedates the scientific era and owes its origin to primordial, emotional need of animistic man." After discussing the anomalies of hermaphrodites, he asserted that "there is no such thing as bisexuality in man or in any of the higher vertebrates," and that what could be observed clinically of abnormal sexuality represented "abnormal conditions of *stimulation*," the causes for which should be located in childhood anxiety, and not in biological constitution. Reviewing the findings of contemporary biology, he observed that "the old speculative notion of bisexuality is in the process of withering away," and then attempted to ground the definition of sexuality in the action of the reproductive system. He rejected the notion of a constitutional "homosexual component," and maintained that such an idea contained several "flaws," including the failure to distinguish between adult and childhood sexuality, since "a fantasy whose content is unquestionably male or female in an adult, might in a child reflect nothing but complete ignorance or deliberate misinformation." In addition, not all relations between members of the same sex are homosexual, and to think so only adds unnecessary difficulties to psychoanalytic treatment and often causes "discouragement or panic" in a patient. He concluded that "it is imperative to supplant the deceptive concept of bisexuality with a psychological theory based on firmer biological foundations."[29]

We can see that Rado, under the guise of a tough-minded scientific stance, made the same error of analogy as his opponent. Bryan, having established what he thought was the existence of biological bisexuality, posited a corresponding psychological bisexuality, never stopping to consider how these two might be similar or different. Rado labored to show that no such biological bisexuality could be maintained or demonstrated. He insisted therefore that psychological bisexuality also could not exist, while likewise neglecting to discuss the relationship between the two. Behind Rado's argument lurked the specter of homosexuality. He was most exercised when he warned against the danger of finding signs of constitutional, biological homosexuality where there can be none, and of attributing such causes of behavior to normal as well as disturbed people. This is not so much an inference from his argument as it is its motivation; his unwillingness to acknowledge a biologically determined, instead of a traumatically caused, homosexual tendency can be seen against a larger distaste for all forms of homosexuality that became apparent around World War II. It is perhaps worth noting that Rado's article was published the year after Freud's death. One wonders if Rado was reluctant to challenge the founder on one of his favorite abstract theories, pitting an old-world cosmopolitanism against the modern positivism of the time.

The most important development in the period we are considering was the attention paid to the oral precursors of the Oedipus complex, and the single most important figure was Melanie Klein. Her seminal book, *The Psycho-Analysis of Children*, based on lectures she delivered to the British Psychoanalytic Society in 1925, appeared in 1932. But even before then, attention was being directed toward mechanisms and stages earlier than the Oedipus complex. Jones had already begun to doubt the centrality of castration fear and to regard the phallic phase as primarily defensive in nature. For him, castration fear was the phallic manifestation of a more basic anxiety that he called *aphanisis*. In addition, Freud's own attention in the last years of his life to aggression as the counterpart of libido corresponded to a general shift in emphasis, especially in London. Finally, the growing interest in psychosis[30] also focused attention on preoedipal stages of psychosexual development.

Klein's ideas are often difficult and obscure, and sometimes they seem quite implausible. But her most general insight is probably that even the very entry into the Oedipus complex is based on the previous modulation and mastery of primitive anxiety in the oral and anal stages. If these tasks are not accomplished or are accomplished inadequately, any development in the oedipal stage, such as the formation of a superego, will be unstable and primitive. So the complete analysis of people with such equivocal psychic organization would have to involve uncovering and interpreting early, primitive infantile concerns centered on the oral and anal stages. And the analysis of homosexuality would center on those paranoid trends associated with the oral stage.

In fact, Klein's book on child analysis ends with the analysis of Mr. B., a male homosexual in his mid-thirties. Although her description suggests that he was a special case—apparently with good object relations, but prone to regress profoundly into bizarre paranoid ideas—she nevertheless claimed that his psychology illustrated the general dynamics that "enter . . . into every homosexual activity." The characteristic defense mechanism of homosexuality, she claimed, was the "overemphasis of reality" as a way of controlling infantile paranoid anxiety. By that, she meant that the homosexual's idealization of "the good penis" of his partner serves to allay the fear of attack that came from the infant's having projected all his paranoid hatred onto the imagined, hidden "bad penis" of his mother. If this belief in the good penis fails, paranoid ideation is likely to surface. The analysis of Mr. B. consisted of uncovering and interpreting these layers of projection and delusion. Mr. B.'s homosexual behavior decreased after he ceased to adore the good penis of an idealized man. Recoverable through analysis was his belief in the good mother and in his ability to bring her sexual gratification with his "good" penis and his "good" and plentiful semen: "he had always unconciously kept the heterosexual aim . . . [and] to his unconscious his various homosexual activities represented so many bypaths leading to this unconsciously desired goal."[31]

In the year following the publication of Klein's lectures, but several years after she had first delivered them in London in 1925, two important articles appeared that presented findings roughly corresponding to Klein's—Eidelberg's on the perversions and Eidelberg and Bergler's on the "breast complex," or, as it is more beguilingly called in German, Der Mammakomplex. They suggest the period's general interest in the oral stage. Eidelberg attempted to account for the orgasmic gratification characteristic of the perversions and for its ego-syntonic quality—that is, its failure to provoke anxiety. By adopting Waelder's idea of "multiple function"—that is, that every action serves the ego, id, and superego,[32] Eidelberg thought that he had explained the characteristic alloplastic distortion of the perversions, as opposed to the autoplastic distortions of the neuroses. In his illustrative case of male homosexuality, he offered the usual etiology of the flight from incest and the fear of castration, but also emphasized the oral nature of this condition. The oral tie that was "characteristic" of homosexuality led to the marked megalomania, the sense of "absolute omnipotence," and the experience of any frustration as mortification. The flight from women gratified the aggressive idea, "I don't need women." In addition, the infant had attributed the disappointment experienced at weaning to his own oral aggression and biting. To achieve a kind of restitution, he substituted the penis for the breast and henceforth endeavored to make the passive experience of loss an active one. Thus he identified with the phallic mother and chose his love objects on a narcissistic basis.[33]

Eidelberg further developed these ideas jointly with Bergler in describing a "breast complex," which they thought was a universal inheritance of weaning, found in normal as well as in pathological conditions, especially "a type of homosexuality." It begins with the child's reacting violently to weaning. He attempts to inhibit his frustrated aggression, but this attempt only heightens it. Hence all identifications, object choices, and narcissistic compensations are ambivalent. Nonetheless, cathexes are displaced from the breast onto the penis, and as the infant substitutes urine for milk, he attempts to make active what once was passive. He tries unsuccessfully to transfer hatred of the mother onto the father, but because of the unresolved deep ambivalence of the oral period, the Oedipus complex does not reach normal intensity. Hence whatever unstable organization was achieved at the oedipal period regresses to an earlier stage with its fixation on the oral mother, whose vagina, conflated with the infant's own cannibalistic mouth, transmutes into the *vagina dentata*.[34]

What is of particular importance about these two articles is their attempt to displace the Oedipus complex, in certain cases, as the "central event of the sexual period of childhood," and to replace it with a corresponding crisis in the oral stage, the "breast complex." Indeed, the very name given to this crisis suggests a desire to rival the omnipotent mechanism of Freud and Fenichel. Both these articles and Klein's researches maintained that unless an adequate achievement in these preoedipal stages has occurred, the Oedipus complex cannot be considered sufficiently intense or focused to have led to such psychic developments as a properly functioning superego or the relinquishing of the incestuous erotic tie to the preoedipal mother. In addition, such a fixation at the oral stage would give rise to corresponding oral character traits: for Klein, a tendency to persecutory delusions; for Eidelberg and Bergler, spite and libido charged with aggression.

The general movement to push back psychosexual birth from the phallic to the oral stage can be seen in other ways. Bergler's paper, "Preliminary Phases of the Masculine Beating Fantasy," for example, while seemingly quite arcane, was a response to Freud's attempt in " 'A Child Is Being Beaten' " to explain this extremely common fantasy and to relate it to the development of perversions. Although working with only a small number of cases, Freud was able to account for its genesis in girls, for whom it goes through three phases. In the first, the child who is being beaten is not the subject herself, but often a sibling rival, and the beater is most frequently the father. The influence of guilt, however, transforms the fantasy into one of being beaten by the father, which in turn becomes unconscious. Here sadism turns into masochism, and there is a regression from the phallic to the anal period. This passive phase represents a kind of punishment for the incestuous relationship with the father, but it is also a "regressive substitute" for it. The third phase develops after the second has been repressed, and the fantasy is of the father or a father-substitute beating boys. When Freud came to consider the corresponding fantasy in boys, however, he could not identify the first stage. Instead, the transformation begins with the second phase. Because of castration fear and the struggle against passive wishes directed toward the father, this phase is repressed and replaced by the fantasy of being beaten by the mother. What is important for our purpose is the centrality of the Oedipus complex in all these transformations, and, in particular, of its "inverted" form in boys. For both girls and boys, the entire evolution of the fantasy begins with a passive incestuous attachment to the father that is not reducible to a more basic attachment to the mother. Freud did, however, leave open the possibility that a preliminary active and sadistic phase might exist for boys that would correspond to the first stage for girls. [35]

Bergler maintained that he had detected such a preliminary stage for boys. Related to the "breast complex" he had described five years earlier with Eidelberg, the phase begins with the weaning shock, which mobilizes enormous sadistic rage against the breasts of the depriving phallic mother. But, like the girls' preliminary stage, it is transmuted because of guilt into a masochistic fantasy of being beaten by the father, substituting the subject's own buttocks for the mother's breasts and idealizing the father out of intense hatred for the mother. The first is an attempt at narcissistic restitution for the lost breasts of the mother, and involves both the anus and the buttocks. The second involves substituting a homosexual for a previous heterosexual bond. [36]

Bergler's paper had important theoretical effects on the theory of homosexuality. First, it maintained that the important stage in the development of homosexual perversion, among others, occurs not during the Oedipus complex, but earlier, in the oral stage, in which the crucial figure is not the oedipal love figure—heterosexual or homosexual, mother or father—but the preoedipal phallic mother. Bergler believed this so strongly that ten years later he maintained that a previously undetected stage of the beating fantasy occurs for girls, which involves a corresponding oral sadistic wish. [37] Second, Bergler minimized the importance of object libido in the face of more primitive narcissistic oral rage. This was to have great importance in his delineation of the oral traits of "the typical homosexual." Third, for boys, the psychosexual development of the homosexual pervert could no longer be seen as based on a prime and irreducible homosexual attachment to the father. Instead, there was always an earlier heterosexual attachment to the mother.

In other words, the "negative" or "inverted" Oedipus complex was no longer seen as a prime mechanism of psychosexual development, which would for certain people outweigh the effects of its "positive" equivalent. Instead, it was seen as a regressive defense against a more basic heterosexual proto-oedipal stance toward the mother. According to Bergler's view, it was no longer possible to maintain that all twelve oedipal outcomes discussed in the last chapter are "prime" and "natural" results of the operations of the Oedipus complex. By implication, all those employing a passive homosexual stance toward the father are "perverse," because they involve a regressive denial of the possibilities contained in a previous "active" relationship with the mother. Such a view directly contradicted that of Bergler's contemporary Wulff.[38] In short, the emphasis on the oral stage of psychosexual development and the denial of the centrality of the Oedipus complex, at least for such extreme figures as Bergler, meant that no outcome of the Oedipus complex, with the exception of the single normative variety, could be considered "natural."

Two articles specifically on homosexuality, one by Bibring and the other by Nunberg, were both affected by this shift in emphasis and in turn affected later writers on homosexuality. Both writers would have located themselves centrally within the classic psychoanalytic tradition; they cited Freud approvingly and invoked the importance of the Oedipus complex. But in their interest in severely disturbed patients with bizarre perverse ideation and in their recourse to oral trends as explanations, they were typical of this second generation of theorists. Nunberg began his article, "Homosexuality, Magic and Aggression," by disclaiming any intention of "solving the problem of homosexuality," which, he agreed with Freud, was "rooted in an organic substratum." He was also careful to qualify the generality of his findings, thus displaying certain affinities with earlier writers. In addition, he cited the traditional etiologies of homosexual object choice as put forward by Freud in previous decades. But he made two major additions to the theory: the notion that just as the homosexual object was a "compromise figure" of masculine and feminine traits, the homosexual aim was a compromise of libido and aggression; and the notion that certain homosexual activities could be understood as delusional attempts to appropriate a lost and injured masculinity by magically incorporating it.

The prominent aggression in the severely disturbed case Nunberg offered, "possibly . . . something intermediate between neurosis and psychosis," resulted from the severe narcissistic injury inflicted by the mother. The desire to take revenge on her led to intense ambivalence toward her and all future homosexual love objects. Still, the patient's homosexual behavior was understood as an attempt to regain his lost masculinity in order to gain access to the mother and to be sexually potent with her. To accomplish this, the patient sought to absorb the masculinity of his idealized male love objects, and the desire to have big and strong men disguised and gratified the wish to be big and strong himself. The oral rituals to strengthen the self, according to Nunberg, resemble "magical measures carried out by schizophrenic hypochondriacs." They recapitulate infantile wishes to incorporate the father "in order to rob him of his potency and gain possession of the pregnant mother," but the implicit aggression prevents any adequate identification with the father because of the anxiety attending primitive cannibalistic fantasies. In any case, the failure to incorporate the father leaves the patient with only a defective superego to control his primitive impulses. [39]

Operating from the same basis in classical psychoanalytic theory and an interest in the oral stage, Bibring, in her pointedly titled article, "On an Oral Component in Masculine Inversion," reached conclusions similar to those of Nunberg, whom she cited with approval. Her ideas were probably known to prominent Central European analysts before their dispersal during the Second World War, though her article, which was based on a lecture she delivered in Vienna in 1934 and appeared in 1940 in German, was apparently never translated into English. She began by referring to Boehm's finding that latent homosexuals often go to prostitutes in order to gain access to other men, while observing that manifest homosexuals use men as sexual objects in order to gain access to women: "both the amorousness [die Verliebkeit] and the oral aggression against the man stand in the service of the tendency to use the masculine love-object in order to attain the woman." For her, the "primary goal [Hauptziel] of homosexual activity was "the winning of the woman (mother)." The case she offered, "a passive homosexual strongly orally fixated on the mother," arrived at his object choice through forming reactions against feelings of envy and hatred directed at a younger brother, much as Freud had outlined earlier. The patient yielded all prerogatives to this idealized brother, but also attempted to drain him, in the form of his love-object substitutes, of his manhood, in order to be potent with women. He was trying "to crawl into . . . a handsome man [in einem schoenem Mann . . . hineinzukriechen]" by sucking on his penis. Yet the oral aggression originally directed at the mother led to an intense ambivalence toward all his love objects, whom he both blamed for his narcissistic injury and loved as his only possible healers. In one crucial session, the patient recalled the promised healing of Amphortas: "*Die Wunde heilt der Speer nur, der sie schlug* [Only the spear that struck the wound can heal it]."

Bibring, unlike Bergler, did not deny the crucial importance of the Oedipus complex, but she saw the patient's oral frustration and consequent aggression as acting through it. Oedipal castration wounds are superimposed upon earlier oral and narcissistic injuries, and the patient seeks to heal both by incorporating the penis orally as well as anally. But does the shock of oedipal castration cause a regression to earlier traumatic fixation at the oral stage, or is the operation of the Oedipus complex determined by unresolved oral disturbances? The distinction is crucial, as Bergler was to argue later,[40] but here Bibring seemed to think that the two views were not incompatible. She concluded that "this homosexuality is, as it were, a point of fixation on the never relinquished road to the woman."[41]

With the growing sophistication of clinical technique and the increasing subtlety and complexity of insight, a full-fledged psychoanalytic theory of homosexuality was finally able to emerge. The two figures who formulated and articulated it were Glover and Bergler, who are particularly interesting for several reasons. First, they continued to make important contributions to the theory until the 1960s, so they had to respond to subsequent theoretical ideas and new empirical information. Second, although their most important contributions were theoretical and sometimes quite abstruse, especially Glover's, they also wrote major papers for a lay audience, attempting to apply their theoretical insights to concrete social and political issues. Third, although both agreed on such issues as the importance of the oral stage in the etiology of the perversions, the two disagreed on such issues as the necessary pathology of homosexuality, the character traits associated with it, and its status as a clinical entity. Finally, and quite important for our history, each expressed his views in quite distinct tones.

Glover's is the first important work on homosexuality as a perversion. He intended his theory of perversion to apply to homosexuality as well as to such conditions as fetishism, exhibitionism, sadism, and the like. Recall that Freud's distinction between "inversion" (or homosexuality) and "perversion" had been ignored for the most part by the time of the

1930s. Glover subscribed to this conflation of inversion and perversion, and the importance of his ideas only reinforced this connection for later writers. But he himself was always attentive to how homosexuality might differ essentially from these other conditions, although he saw the difference as primarily one of degree. For him, homosexuality was developmentally the most advanced of the perversions because it "reassures [i.e., assuages anxiety] mainly in respect of *complete objects not of primitive 'part' objects*," as the other perversions did. And it was a "defensive and restitutive system," which attempted to master "early anxieties as well as . . . later purely genitosexual anxieties."[42] In addition, he acknowledged the discrepancy between theoretical deductions and clinical experience: "In many cases apart from the denial of heterosexual genital and reproductive function the manifestation of homosexual love-feeling and the attitude to the love object cannot be distinguished from those associated with normal heterosexual love."[43]

He was forced to deal with the perversions as a result of difficulties he encountered in trying to classify the mental disorders on a continuum on the basis of the predominance of such defense mechanisms as primitive introjection and projection. He maintained that between the neuroses and the psychoses belonged not "borderline psychoses" but "transitional states" such as drug addiction. They belonged there because projection is more localized than in paranoia, but more prominent than in the obsessional neuroses. In addition, in obsessional neuroses this defense mechanism is mitigated by the developmentally more advanced defense of reaction formation.[44] The scheme broke down, however, when Glover attempted to place the perversions in the series.

He attempted to rectify this deficiency in a theoretically more sophisiticated paper the next year. Glover observed that "some perversions may be found in association with a fairly normal ego or with quite definite forms of psychosis." They could be arranged in an orderly continuum based not on their corresponding defenses, but on "the aim and completeness of object." This series could not be assimilated into the larger continuum of mental disorders, but instead ran parallel to it, with correspondences throughout to the "psychoses, transitional states, neuroses and social inhibitions." The most advanced of the perversions, homosexuality, could be found in association with the mildest of mental disturbances, the "social inhibitions."

Still, for him all forms of perversions signified a disturbance in the "reality sense," which he defined as "the capacity to retain psychic contact with the object that promotes gratification of instinct." Such a disturbance could not be derived, as Fenichel had maintained, from the operations of the Oedipus complex, strictly defined. Maintaining his allegiance with Freud's view, however, Glover interpreted the Oedipus complex broadly, including preoedipal relations to objects that would ultimately be "refracted" through the complex. Disturbances in the reality sense, he claimed, agreeing with Klein, were due to the failure to master primitive anxieties associated with the introjection of objects and the projection of primitive impulses. Characteristic of the perversions was the attempt to master these anxieties by "a process of excessive libidinization," which acts to neutralize infantile sadism. Hence, "perversions help patch over flaws in the development of reality-sense" over a wide area, at the expense of some specific, localized distortion, as in the case of fetishism. And the perversions could be arranged in a series on the basis of the corresponding "stages in the mastery of anxiety," which correspond to the transition from part objects to full objects. It is in this sense that homosexuality is developmentally the most advanced of the perversions.[45]

Glover's article helped resolve at least three important incoherences in the earlier psychoanalytic theory of homosexuality. First, it offered a theoretical rationale for considering homosexuality as a kind of sexual perversion on the basis of etiology and of the internal experience of sexuality, with its emphasis on the defensive functions involved in object choice. Second, it now became possible to consider homosexuality as a unitary phenomenon based on its characteristic mode of dealing with infantile anxiety. Third, it also allowed for a range of disturbances associated with such object choice, extending from the psychoses to the relatively mild "social inhibitions" or even "a fairly normal ego."

Glover's contributions to the theory of homosexuality resulted from his basic theoretical orientation. His interest in the larger issues of psychic development and the characteristic defense mechanisms of the perversions could be focused on the specific question of homosexual object choice. Bergler, on the other hand, had a primary interest in homosexuality and tried to apply ideas from other topics to it. Both rhetorically and substantially, Bergler frequently distanced himself from the central, classical psychoanalytic tradition, while at the same time claiming a position of importance within it. He thought of himself as a revolutionary who would transform the movement. We have already seen how he and Eidelberg attempted to supplant the "superficial" Oedipus complex with their own "breast complex," and how Bergler tried to establish the priority of oral concerns at the expense of oedipal, phallic ones. He continued to wage this campaign in his later articles, beginning one on the treatment of homosexuality by reviewing Freud's theories, but ending it by asserting that the Oedipus complex was secondary to the much more determinative oral breast complex.[46] And when Anna Freud lectured on the treatment of male homosexuality, Bergler used the question period to emphasize the patient's oral fears and to minimize the phallic castration concerns she had just emphasized.[47]

His major statement on homosexuality, which he was to repeat for fifteen years, was an article he wrote on its treatment. Freud thought that "to undertake to convert a fully developed homosexual into a heterosexual is not more promising than to do the reverse."[48] Bergler held out higher hopes, claiming that "99.9 percent of all cases of homosexuality" could be cured if the clinician observed the principles that Bergler had learned in ten years of treating such cases. Of the seven principles he listed, six concerned the oral nature of homosexual object choice. According to Bergler, the oral, preoedipal basis of homosexuality had been "confirmed without exception." Homosexual behavior represented an attempt to take revenge on the breast for having gotten too little from it through what Bergler called "the mechanism of orality," which was a repetitious and unchanging ritual of "moral masochism" acted out in the patient's life and in the clinical transference. The patient provokes a situation that recalls the initial withholding of the breast by the preoedipal mother. The patient's guilt at the consequent aggression leads to a defense of "pseudoaggression" and outbursts of righteous indignation, resulting in a gratifying state of self-pity.[49] Consequently, Bergler found it imperative that the therapist work through this defense of pseudoaggression. Then the patient could be expected to approach heterosexual functioning, but first he would go through a transitional phase of premature ejaculation, through which he would avenge himself on the depriving mother. This would involve unconsciously equating the penis with the breast, the vagina with the mouth, and sperm with milk. The equation of penis and breast was "more than an equation; it is an impressive clinical fact."[50] He concluded: "the psychic center in male homosexuality is the preoedipal mother attachment [and] the breast complex. . . . [T]he fate of the Oedipus complex is of merely secondary importance for these patients." Analysts who continue to concentrate on this later crisis "merely touch the surface layer of their patients' pathology."[51] Bergler continued to repeat these formulations in article after article and in several books until 1962. Often he quoted himself at length. Although he claimed to have analyzed "dozens" of homosexuals, he frequently used the same case to make a general point in different publications.

Bergler did, however, make an important contribution to the psycho-analytic theory of homosexuality by distinguishing between "spurious homosexuality" and "perversion homosexuality." This distinction had not been made clearly enough in the previous period, muddling, for example, the formulation of Boehm, who cured a patient of a condition he was in no danger of suffering from.[52] Bergler maintained that the two were entirely distinct, with no transitional condition existing between the two. "Perversion homosexuality" represented a regression to the oral stage of psychosexual development and involved a compulsive repetition of the "mechanism of orality." In this condition, the Oedipus complex was not decisive, since the patient was lingering at a preoedipal fixation and still deriving gratification from the various maneuvers that consti-tute a kind of "moral masochism." Very pointedly, Bergler claimed that Freud was wrong to think "that homosexuals . . . were . . . specific aberrations of the Oedipus complex." "Spurious homosexuality," on the other hand, was such an aberration, resulting from a fixation at the "negative" Oedipus complex. Patients with this condition were neurotic hysterics with an unconscious feminine identification. Frequently, in response to the superego's objection to such passive wishes, they would overcompensate and appear to be "super he-men" instead of their un-derlying "Milquetoast" true selves. They were often accused of being homosexual, but such accusations were made, according to Bergler, "unjustly."[53]

What is so extraordinary about Bergler's work on homosexuality is the intemperate and abusive tone he adopted when describing his patients. He was frequently annoyed and exasperated by their behavior, by their "unique . . . megalomaniacal superciliousness" and their "amazing degree of unreliability." He repeated these rhetorical formulations ver-batim in several different papers, approvingly crediting such stereotypes to "the unpsychological but accurately observing outside world."[54] And he deliberately argued for establishing other stereotypes. Though he had analyzed "dozens" of homosexuals, he concluded that "they all labor under" the same mechanism. "There are no happy homosexuals," he claimed, denying his patients' assertions to the contrary. "The amount of conflicts, of jealousy, for instance, between homosexuals surpasses everything known even in bad heterosexual relationships." Claims of bisexual potency are spurious: "Nobody can dance at two weddings at the same time, not even the wizard of a homosexual." The hostile complaining of his homosexual patients seems to have filled him with scorn: "homosexuals . . . pull a 'nobody loves me,' to quote a witty patient." And Bergler never ceased to be amazed at what he saw as "the great percentage of homosexuals among swindlers, pseudologues, forgers, lawbreakers of all sorts, drug purveyors, gamblers, pimps, spies, brothel-owners, etc."[55]

It would simplify matters if we could divorce this tone of abuse and scorn from Bergler's substantive ideas, but such a distinction is neither possible nor desirable. Whatever the truth or usefulness of Bergler's ideas, his tone clearly suggests extremely strong countertransference reactions that simply would not be tolerated by psychoanalysts, for example, in supervised training. That a psychoanalyst should be so angry at his patients or make jokes at their expense surely must have affected the course of treatment. So Bergler's reports of noncooperative patients must be regarded as suspect. It is shocking that Bergler's colleagues let such unprofessional conduct and attitudes go without rebuke. Such intemperance severely compromised psychoanalytic discourse about homosexuality for future generations and sullied the psychoanalytic tradition of sympathy and tolerance. Bergler and those who allowed it to pass without remark are at least partly responsible for the hostility and mutual enmity between the psychoanalytic community and groups of informed homosexuals. In the years around and after Bergler, we can no longer simply consider ideas according to rules of logic and evidence, but must now take into account the political and polemical forces that surrounded them and gave them form. Henceforth, the history of ideas about homosexuality is at least as much the history of opinion as it is of ideas.

We may see the stirrings of this new development in several articles that appeared around the time of Bergler's first contributions and that shared many of his presuppositions and attitudes. All of them are remarkable for their tone of irritation and condescension. Significantly, all refer in one way or another to *the* homosexual, *the* homosexual marriage, and the like, thus simultaneously reifying their patients and assuming without argument or demonstration that all forms of homosexual behavior are really the same. The first article, by Silverberg, belongs to the tradition of applying psychoanalytic insights to other social issues, in this case, to formulate an enlightened social policy toward passive male homosexuality. Although he offered only three cases in support of his generalizations, Silverberg claimed that the deepest aim of all passive male homosexuality is to separate the parents. All other explanations were "ramifications of secondary by-products of a consistent deeper motivation" that he had uncovered. The boy offers himself to the father so that the latter will no longer need the mother sexually and thus will leave her to be enjoyed by the boy. Passive homosexuals never approach women sexually after having seduced their men, Silverberg explained, because they "despair . . . of attaining [their] original aim." This explained the proverbial instability of homosexual marriages, since passive homosexuals are interested only in men who are attractive to and potent with women.

Because he approved of the general hostility to passive male homosexuality, Silverberg went on to speculate, in a parody of Freud in *Totem and Taboo* or *Moses and Monotheism*, that the social hostility to passive homosexuality had a historical basis:

> It is quite possible that our own social taboo concerning homosexuality originated in various small groups which were threatened with extinction because in each of these groups someone had the strategic pattern of passive homosexuality as his aim, and was succeeding in diverting *all* of the men (of the small group) from all the women until someone realized what was happening.

Silverberg thought it was unreasonable for society to penalize such homosexuals for not reproducing, because they would not reproduce anyway. But since "the passive homosexual is trying to extinguish the race," he felt that "society is justified in its violent feeling towards him and . . . in taking steps against him." He cautioned, however, that before it could take such steps, society was obliged "to prove that the act in question was intended to separate, or an actual separation" had occurred.[56]

It is easy to ridicule such nonsensical paranoia and the low opinion Silverberg seemed to have of the charms of the fairer sex as well as of the strength of character of such easily corruptible heterosexual men. But this article appeared in *Psychiatry*, and it met with no published disagreement. In fact, Bergler referred to it with approval in his important article on the treatment of homosexuality.[57] Perhaps such obviously unreasonable prejudice disguised as an idea went without rebuke because of the larger historical moment. The rise of Nazism, the imminence of a world war, and the official persecution of psychoanalysis in its birthplace in Germany and Austria may have made some of its practitioners nervous about the institutions of modern civilization. Although Silverberg thought he was arguing for "enlightened policy," the roots of his ideas in political and intellectual impotence are visible to the attentive reader. The important question of how this historical trauma caused a rigidification of psychoanalytic theory has not yet been investigated. Nonetheless, Silverberg's attempt to legitimate "society's violent feelings" toward homosexuals should be called by its right name. It is hate-mongering, and it is entirely antithetical to the ethical basis of psychoanalysis as a humane discipline.

A similar concern for the fragile institutions of society informs an article written by Robbins on homosexual marriages, which appeared during World War II. Here too the writer used the fashionable vocabulary of the oral phase to support his presuppositions. Based on only two cases, his findings he felt were applicable to all homosexuality, or, in the grammar of the times, to "the homosexual": "Suffering, unhappiness, limitations in functioning, severe disturbances in interpersonal relationships, and contradictory internal tendencies . . . are all present in the homosexual." According to Robbins, homosexual unions are unhappy because they are motivated by a deep sadistic trend that employs narcissism and masochism. Such "marriages" are attempts to merge two people for purposes of "enslavement." The sadism behind this, Robbins claimed, "determines the distinguishing symptom, homoerotism." In fact, he went so far as to speculate that the so-called "latent homosexuality" of all people really derives from universal sadism, again revealing the period's reluctance to acknowledge the universal bisexuality that was a cornerstone of Freud's larger theory.[58]

The more sophisticated Bychowski, explicating the characteristic ego of "homosexuals," went so far as to compare them to Nazis. In his theoretical approach Bychowski belonged to the central psychoanalytic tradition, yet he showed the influence of the new interest in both ego psychology and the oral stage. In seeking to account for the ego functioning of homosexuals, for instance, he referred to injuries sustained during the narcissistic phase. Bychowski's article is also noteworthy for his pervasively contemptuous tone and the general aura of enmity that seemed to infuse the analytic sessions. The patient he discussed hated Bychowski, finding him intrusive. Bychowski appeared that way in the patient's dreams. But Bychowski interpreted this therapeutic failure as resulting from the patient's hostility:

> This attitude manifested itself during the treatment as an absolute resistance against final improvement and the acceptance of virility. The patient resisted coming close to a girl he was seeing at that time because he felt that the analyst was so much interested in his giving this final proof of his virility.

Finally, Bychowski, like many other analysts, was quite willing to apply his rather limited experience to the entire condition of homosexuality. Though he claimed that his conclusions were "based on a large amount of material," he reported only two cases, both of whom seemed quite disturbed, one probably with a severe narcissistic personality disorder, and the other probably with an infantile personality disorder. Bychowski began by noting the similarity between the egos of schizophrenics and those of his homosexual patients, but he seemed not to have considered seriously the possibility that his patients were not representative.

Bychowski tried to relate homosexual object choice to Eidelberg's notion that the ego of perverts never surrenders the megalomania of early narcissism.[59] Bychowski found that his patients showed striking narcissistic features, including grandiosity and an attempt to avoid injuries and failures by avoiding any substantial involvement in the real world. Passive masochistic traits were prominent. Bychowski claimed that because the infantile erotic bond to the mother had never been severed, the patients were never able to develop their virility. Instead it was projected onto idealized men to whom the patients submitted and whose virility they were thus able to share. They defended their imaginary world of magical incorporation by means of spite and opposition. In examining the patients' lability of ego feeling and ego boundaries, Bychowski went even further than his colleagues who stopped at the oral stage of psychosexual development. He claimed that his patients had regressed to "prenatal narcissism," which manifested itself in the infuriating character traits of dreaminess and insubstantiality.[60]

This article is particularly important because for the first time a theoretical account was offered of the characteristic defective superego of homosexuals, mentioned earlier by Nunberg.[61] According to Bychowski, the fact that an identification with the mother replaced a previous object tie leads to the homosexual's inability to introject libidinal objects and consequently to form the nucleus of a superego. Here, narcissistic object choice precludes the appropriate libidinal attachment. In addition, the very fact of manifest homosexual activity is proof of the patient's inability to sublimate his homosexual trends, further weakening his already defective superego and leaving him incapable of forming adequate social ties. Thus Bychowski reversed Freud's contention that some homosexuals are remarkable for their elaborate and subtle social feeling. Finally, Bychowski's moralistic tone was to characterize much later writing on homosexuality: the homosexual avoids women because he dreads the "colossal" heterosexual task. We are back again with the view of homosexuals as only half-men and sexual intermediates, the view of Magnus Hirschfeld, whose refutation marked the beginning of Freud's interest in homosexuality.

Thus, the major tradition in psychoanalytic discourse on homosexuality, or at least its most audible voice, was established around World War II, both substantively and rhetorically. There were, to be sure, important psychoanalytic writers who maintained the tradition of tolerance and tentativeness established by Freud himself. Anna Freud continued to treat her patients humanely and successfully, but her methods were unspectacular and, to some, rather old-fashioned.[62] And the larger philosophical and ethical issues that the discourse on homosexuality raised or should have raised were, for the most part, neglected.

The only analyst during the period to deal with some of these issues in an extended manner was Schilder. But except for a brief reference by Bergler, who ignored the larger questions Schilder raised,[63] his paper went largely unnoticed. He began by listing ten distinct etiologies for homosexual object choice, adding that "it would be easy to make this list much longer and bring forward many more types of homosexual attitudes." Then he tried to make some basic categorical distinctions in this open-ended list. Two major groups could be established on the basis of the homosexual object: those of a mixed sexual character and those of the same sex as the subject "in the full meaning of the term." In addition, some homosexual tendencies could best be understood as a desire to be the other sex, rather than as an interest in the same sex.

Moreover, Schilder attempted to unsettle some of the basic assumptions of psychoanalytic theory. The very relation between behavior and sexual activity and passivity is not at all clear. Although there is clearly an influence of one on the other, it cannot be said that one is "an expression" of the other. In addition, when we speak of sexual differences in behavior, we cannot, strictly speaking, identify activity with males and passivity with females, simply because the female is more active during certain phases of sex. It would therefore be more accurate to specify a difference in the "curve of activity and passivity" or in "the phase difference in male and female activity." But most important, the entire project of basing a psychology of sex on biology is deeply misguided. Sexual attitudes and sexual behavior are not simply innate; they are learned in a social context, and the forms of sexual behavior that we can observe are historically contingent, determined at least partly by "the ideologies under which an individual lives and which force him to make a psychological connection between" biological function and psychological sexuality. Thus, "the constructive side of human life" is at least as determinative of sexual attitudes and behavior as the biologically fixed anatomy and process of maturation.

From these ideas, several important implications follow. First, "heterosexuality is not merely due to an instinct and a process of maturation but . . . it is due to a process of continuous construction and adaptation." Second, sexuality must be approached from the perspective of both biology and culture. "Natural," "normal," and "healthy" are not transcendent categories of sexuality:

> One has very often completely neglected that every society and culture has created a pattern of masculine and feminine which is much more an expression of cultural conditions than of biologic attitudes. . . . The tendency to accept these cultural patterns as the expression of an ultimate truth concerning masculine and feminine must be combated.[64]

In the early period of psychoanalysis the conceptual means were available to ask such questions. The indeterminacy of the Oedipus complex, for example, left open the question of what relation biological maturation had to final human psychological health. Although the earlier period was philosophically quite innocent, it was impelled by a cosmopolitan, liberal, and humane spirit that Freud inherited from

Goethe. But as psychoanalytic theory became more sophisticated, it became conceptually more limited, so that the questions Schilder raised were probably felt to be too general and "philosophical" to be of much interest to the practice or theory of psychoanalysis—as if such a separation could ever legitimately be made. The psychoanalytic theory of homosexuality in particular remained naive and uninterested in its place in larger historical and cultural movements, or in larger questions of epistemology and ethics. Freud's healthy cultural relativism simply faded, while some of the important deficiencies of the earlier period were not corrected in the later one. In particular, the formal problems of sampling and of generalizability of clinical findings based on atypical samples remained egregiously unscientific.

The single most productive trend from around 1930 to the postwar era was the shift in interest away from oedipal-level conflicts toward those of the more primitive oral stage. There was also a certain undisciplined and "wild" theorizing that extended from some of the more lurid mythologizing extremes of Melanie Klein to the confident bluster of Bergler. But these theoreticians of orality were finally able to describe homosexuality as a unitary phenomenon and to account for its striking range of variation in forms and degrees of pathology. The time was simply inauspicious for asking whether homosexuality might be neurotic or essentially normal, since the most important theoreticians were looking successfully at primitive psychic organizations. The present historian can offer no explanation why analysts interested in ego psychology and "psychosocial" development did not provide a counterweight to these theoreticians of orality. Psychoanalysts were making much more confident prescriptions about normalcy and optimal psychic development, and these prescriptions grew increasingly more conservative and bourgeois in nature. The experience of World War II, the Holocaust, and the atomic bomb may have caused a rigidification of American values and a consequent denial of some of the forms of cosmopolitan "decadence."

The sheer weight of insights resulting from attention to the oral phase was too impressive to deny or even to question. Specifically, such notions as the "negative" Oedipus complex came to be seen not so much as alternative and parallel to its positive form, but as a secondary, defensive form, which was necessarily disturbed. Similarly, heterosexuality was assumed to be the "natural" final result of psychosexual development. Homosexuality was not a mere variant of development as it implicitly was for Freud, but the result of trauma. Yet this point was never argued formally. In addition, the emphasis on the oral precursors of the Oedipus complex in our period reinforced the conviction that the primary attachment for all males was to the mother and, in particular, to the breast. Hence, the later appearance of homosexual object choice was prima facie evidence that development had been thwarted. What "constitution" was to Freud and his circle, preoedipal development was to later analysts. And for Freud, the determinants of homosexual object choice resided preponderantly in such irreducible "constitution," while for later analysts they were quite suitable for analysis, resolution, and "cure." Such a conceptual shift also affected more specific formulations. The description of homosexual character traits also became markedly oral in nature, as analysts emphasized the masochism, oral spite, and suffusion of libido with aggression in their homosexual patients. In addition, the notion of the invariably defective superego of homosexuals became general after it was first promulgated by Nunberg and elaborated by Bychowski. Freud's observations to the contrary were no longer repeated. In a period of impressive clinical and theoretical achievements, many figures, whatever their other contributions to psychoanalysis, failed egregiously in their professional dedication to humane discourse and compassion. Their failures are an embarrassment to the sympathetic historian and a stain on the history of psychoanalysis.

CHAPTER VI

ANALYTIC RESPONSES TO THE KINSEY REPORT

When the present history was being planned, I anticipated that this chapter would be central to my subject, and that the psychoanalytic response to the publication of the first Kinsey Report, *Sexual Behavior in the Human Male*,[1] would represent a turning point in psychoanalytic ideas about homosexuality. One of the most important points to be derived from this history as a whole, however, is that no such crisis occurred. I can say without much exaggeration that, for the most part, the psychoanalytic theory of homosexuality was, surprisingly, unaffected by it. Contrary to expectation, I could omit this chapter without losing track of theoretical or practical developments in psychoanalysis, which proceeded undeflected by what many analysts saw at the time as findings of "tremendous value"[2] and as "the most important addition which has ever been made to our information" on human sexual behavior, and which "merits detailed study from everyone who is concerned with human nature."[3] The psychoanalytic response to Kinsey, and in particular to his findings about male homosexuality, was prompt and sometimes not unsympathetic, but it was partial, unilateral, and ephemeral. The only finding of Kinsey's that seems to have affected psychoanalytic theory permanently, the prevalence of clitoral orgasm, was found in his second Report, dealing with female sexuality.[4]

The importance such a report might have had for our history is easy to imagine. From the beginning, psychoanalytic ideas about homosexuality had been based on extremely small samples of clinical experience, and some analysts, especially the earlier ones, had suspected that their patients might be entirely unrepresentative. Analysts had decided the question of whether homosexuality was necessarily pathological on the basis of their acquaintance with those who had come for treatment because they were distressed and badly adjusted to their lives. A sizable group of content, adjusted, and "normal" homosexuals might exist who never came for treatment, but their existence could not be determined by the data of psychoanalysis. As Freud remarked, "perverts who can obtain satisfaction rarely have occasion to come in search of analysis."[5] Kinsey purported to supply information that bore directly on such questions. He employed a sample of fifty-three hundred, by far the largest ever tabulated,[6] which he argued was, with certain exceptions (it included no Negroes), representative of the population of American males. Among his findings were: 37 percent of all men had had some homosexual experience to the point of orgasm between adolescence and old age; 18 percent of all men were at least as homosexual in fantasy or behavior as they were heterosexual; and 13 percent were more homosexual than heterosexual. Even if such prevalence was even only roughly valid, many psychoanalytic ideas and presuppositions about healthy sexual behavior would have had to be reconsidered and probably adjusted. For the most part, most psychoanalysts writing on sexual deviance seemed to assume that they dealt with only a small segment of the population. Few would have guessed that more than one third of all men had engaged in "unnatural" homosexual practices or that such practices constituted a major portion of the sexual life of one male out of seven. While it might be maintained, as indeed it was, that prevalence should not be confused with normalcy, it could still be argued that the direction of psychosexual development was more indeterminate than most psychoanalytic writings would suggest.

The psychoanalytic response to the first Report was prompt. Bergler published his rebuttal in January of the year it appeared[7] and later boasted of having written "immediately."[8] Symposia that included psychoanalysts were organized within a year,[9] and dozens of articles by psychoanalysts appeared in popular magazines as well as in professional journals. Bergler published with a gynecologist a book-length refutation of Kinsey when the second Report appeared, but dealt at length with his objections only to the first.[10] The quality and tone of these responses varied from the thoughtful and discriminating evaluations of Kubie and Knight[11] through the rather unfocused but shrill criticism of Kardiner and the pious warnings of Karl Menninger[12] to the ad hominem vituperations of "Hewitt,"[13] a pseudonym for an unidentified analyst. Several welcomed the study and praised its results, though they all had specific criticisms of its method or its assumptions. A few condemned it utterly and warned against the danger it posed to American society and way of life.[14]

Lacking in this response, with a very few exceptions,[15] was any sense that psychoanalysis could learn something from the Report. Instead, most analysts thought that their duty and prerogative was to criticize the Report from the point of view of their discipline. Many welcomed the confirmation of points of psychoanalytic doctrine, but criticized the Report when it impugned other points.[16] There was a general consensus that psychoanalysis enjoyed a privileged stance from which to judge both clinical and demographic data. If Kinsey and psychoanalysis clashed, some analysts were ready to assert the reliability of "clinical facts" over Kinsey's "entirely misleading" evidence.[17]

It is also noteworthy that the formal psychoanalytic community was not directly involved in the debate. Analysts wrote as individuals and not, for the most part, as formal representatives or spokesmen for analytic organizations. Sometimes their articles were to be found in popular magazines[18] or in journals of such specialized, nonpsychoanalytic fields as pastoral counseling.[19] But most of them appeared in psychiatric journals that professed no real allegiance to psychoanalytic theory or practice. Only five of the approximately three dozen items in the bibliography for this chapter appeared in psychoanalytic journals. One was a reprint of an article by the literary critic Lionel Trilling, which appeared originally in *Partisan Review*,[20] and one was a one-page review of Bergler's long article, which appeared in *Psychoanalytic Quarterly*.[21] The entire official psychoanalytic response to Kinsey's two reports consisted of the remaining three articles, published in *Psychoanalytic Quarterly*, *International Journal of Psychoanalysis*, and *American Journal of Psychoanalysis*. One was quite general, discussing at length the unconscious motivations of Kinsey's subjects, but not even mentioning homosexuality.[22] Another noted Kinsey's confirmation of psychoanalytic ideas, but dismissed his disagreements.[23] The third rejected Kinsey's findings because the study did not understand that homosexuality "indicates an extreme alienation of the person from his real self."[24] We may contrast this paucity of response with that of other fields and of the public at large, which, according to one bibliography, amounted to 260 items in the American press alone.[25]

Still, the psychoanalytic response is quite instructive. For one thing, Kinsey's antipsychiatric bias and his attack on what he conceived of as psychoanalytic ideas prompted analytic spokesmen to articulate their position clearly and unequivocally. This exposed both vagueness in the theory and clear disagreements among practitioners. More important is how the Kinsey Report implied that psychoanalysis, at least with respect to the topic of homosexuality (and certain aspects of female sexuality), had devised unrealistic norms of health and "naturalness." The discipline either had to attempt to revise some of its central tenets in the light of new important information or had to challenge the validity of these new findings. As we shall see, by far the greater effort went toward the latter goal, in some cases thoughtfully and in good faith, in others disingenuously, irresponsibly, and even dishonestly.

Before we consider the psychoanalytic response in detail, we should describe the Kinsey Report itself. It is a large volume, containing 804 pages, including the index, filled with charts and tables that deal primarily with frequencies, sample sizes, demographic information, and ages at which certain events occurred. Details of sexual practices are not the subject of such tabulation, and charts delineating "Source of Respondents' Orgasm/Body Contact Frictation" or "Frequency of Urination by Respondent on Same-Sex Partner" would not be published until thirty years later as "Marginal Tabulations."[26] The prose sections are devoted to reviews of the literature, explanations of the charts and tables, and occasional discussions of implications. There are no case histories or behavioral vignettes. Reading it is hard going and quite boring. The advertising campaign accompanying its publication was similarly chaste, merely listing bibliographical information and containing a scholarly blurb recommending the volume for the importance of its statistical findings. There is absolutely nothing salacious, exciting, or "sensational" about the Report, and those who purchased it at the time for titillation or as an aid to solitary pleasure must surely have been disappointed.

Although Kinsey claimed to have been completely neutral and detached in gathering and tabulating his data and to have "avoid[ed] social or moral interpretations of the facts," the Report is peppered with commentary and interpretation that reveal Kinsey's strong biases. He was by training a biologist—in particular, an entomologist—and his primary interest was in describing human behavior as it really occurred, eschewing any *a priori* notions of normal or abnormal. He claimed that he offered "no objection to any type of sexual behavior in which the subject could possibly have been involved," and his long and moving description of his interviewing technique is quite convincing in substantiating this claim. Securing unprejudiced data was important, he claimed, because only then could one frame realistic norms of behavior and devise sensible and humane treatment for people who had difficulties in their lives:

> Psychiatrists and analysts find that a majority of their patients
> need help in resolving sexual conflicts that have arisen in their
> lives. . . . Before it is possible to think scientifically on any of
> these matters, more needs to be known about the actual behavior
> of people, and about the inter-relationship of that behavior with
> the biologic and social aspects of their lives.

Although he singled out the New York Psychoanalytic Society and Institute for special thanks for its cooperation, and although he enlisted the aid of many analysts in his study, he frequently criticized, ridiculed, or refuted psychoanalysts and psychoanalytic ideas and suppositions. His most substantial criticism was that the psychoanalytic notion of "normal" or "natural" was *a priori* and failed to take into account what people really do or what their biological nature inclines them to do. He leveled this charge of naïveté in particular against psychoanalytic ideas about homosexuality, although other topics such as premature ejaculation were also involved. Frequently, he sniped at the provincial, ignorant, and rigid attitudes of analysts: "there are several dozen psychoanalysts who have contributed histories to this study who have insisted that they have never identified homosexual experiences or reactions in their own life histories." Kinsey also thought that his data explicitly disconfirmed certain points of psychoanalytic doctrine—sublimation, pregenital sexuality, polymorphous perversity, and narcissism as a developmental stage—though he sometimes misunderstood what these ideas really meant.[27] He argued that the emotional disturbance found in conjunction with sexual deviance was due to society's intolerance and was not itself the cause or a necessary correlate of that deviance.

Karl Menninger referred in brief to Kinsey's "somewhat hysterical antipathy" to psychoanalysis.[28] Yet in many ways, Kinsey's data, to quote Fromm, "suppor[t] the general trend of the psychoanalytic position,"[29] although Kinsey himself would have been the last to admit it. While denying the existence of polymorphous perversity, he provided evidence for its existence under his own definition, "the capacity to respond (sexually) to sufficient stimulation" of a nongenital nature. In addition, he offered some support for the analytic idea that homosexuality is favored by an early and strong efflorescence of sexuality in children, and he confirmed the idea that homosexual proclivities are "basic to the species," just as Freud had contended. He also agreed that homosexuality is acquired and not inherited, and specifically argued for the childhood determinants of adult sexual orientation. His data ended the debate on the existence of childhood sexuality, which was still current in certain disciplines. He also presented less conclusive evidence for a latency period. Finally, he saw clearly that heterosexuality and homosexuality, rather than being two distinct categories, define a continuum of human sexual behavior. And in giving an account of the varieties of homosexual behavior, he supported a major strain in psychoanalytic theory that held that the category of homosexuality was spurious and that it really represented an agglomerate of different nosologies and etiologies.

Kinsey found that thirty-seven percent of all men had had a homosexual experience to the point of orgasm at some time in their lives from adolescence onward. It is important to note that this figure does not include preadolescent homosexual activity, and that it does not distinguish between men who had had a single homosexual experience in their entire postpubertal life and men who had maintained a consistent pattern of homosexual activity. To estimate the number of homosexuals in the population, Kinsey devised a scale, "The Heterosexual-Homosexual Balance," in which subjects were asked to rate themselves "based on both psychologic reactions and overt experience" as follows:

0. Exclusively heterosexual with no homosexual
1. Predominantly heterosexual, with only incidental homosexual
2. Predominantly heterosexual, but more than incidentally homosexual
3. Equally heterosexual and homosexual
4. Predominantly homosexual, but more than incidentally heterosexual
5. Predominantly homosexual, but only incidentally heterosexual
6. Exclusively homosexual

He found that in at least a three-year period, for all males:

30% have had at least incidental homosexual experience (ratings 1 through 6)

25% have had more than incidental homosexual experience (ratings 2 through 6)

18% have had at least as much homosexual as heterosexual experience (ratings 3 through 6)

13% have had more homosexual than heterosexual experience (ratings 4 through 6)

10% have been more or less exclusively homosexual (ratings 5 through 6)

8% have been exclusively homosexual (rating 6)

4% have been exclusively homosexual all their lives

These data omit preadolescent sexual activity and also distinguish several varieties of men between the two extremes. Other tabulations were made to describe the proportion of heterosexual and homosexual activity for a single year, the age at which homosexual activity began, the frequency of homosexual activity, and the like.

Kinsey, however, did not limit himself to simply reporting his data, but readily offered interpretations and inferences. The Report includes a long section describing checks that were performed on the sample and interviewing technique, and concluded that the figures on the frequency of homosexual activity "must be understatements." Kinsey was confident that the larger study he was planning, which was to involve one hundred thousand subjects, would yield an even higher incidence and prevalence of deviant sexual behavior. But even from the present data, he concluded that "it is difficult to maintain the view that psychosexual relations between individuals of the same sex are rare and therefore abnormal or unnatural," and went on to deny that "they constitute within themselves evidence of neurosis or psychosis." Any disturbance found in association with such behavior was not a question of psychopathology, but was due to "society's reaction to the individual who departs from the code, or the individual's fear of social reaction."[30] Thus, Kinsey both provided data that could have augmented psychoanalytic knowledge of human behavior and attempted to remove an important and large aspect of that behavior from the purview of psychoanalysis by blaming psychoanalysis for ignorantly considering such behavior pathological.

Apart from such editorializing, Kinsey's statistical findings, at least with respect to male homosexuality, seem to have been quite robust. He reviewed previous studies, but discarded most of them because of their extremely selective sample (e.g., prisoners), their avoidance of the issue of homosexuality, or their obvious bias in questions such as "Has anyone tried to give you the mistaken notion that sex intercourse is necessary for the health of young men?" Studies that were minimally acceptable reached results not too discrepant from Kinsey's.[31] Thirty years after the publication of the Report, Kinsey's assistant retabulated some of the results in more detail, taking into account some of the criticisms of the statistics, and confirmed Kinsey's conclusions.[32] He also reviewed surveys of homosexuality in Western Europe and concluded that one quarter to one third of all males from all socioeconomic levels have had some homosexual experience since puberty.[33] Closer in time to Kinsey's findings was a survey of collegiate males conducted through the more conventional questionnaire method, which found results almost identical to Kinsey's.[34] As a more general confirmation, the Yale University Institute of Human Relations Cross-Cultural Survey found "widespread" homosexuality in the diverse cultures it surveyed.[35] And two studies of noninstitutionalized homosexuals, one English, the other South African, found no significant deviation from psychic normality in that group.[36] None of these studies, of course, provided conclusive demonstration of Kinsey's results or attempted to replicate his study fully, but they did provide general support. Significantly, no study claimed to refute Kinsey.

It is well known that the general public as well as many culturally conservative establishments reacted with surprise and horror to Kinsey's findings. Bergler called them "fantastic" and rejected them outright.[37] It is, however, not at all clear if these results were really that surprising to clinicians. Certainly Schilder, with his emphasis on the culturally determined learning of sexual preferences and behavior, could have accepted Kinsey's findings with equanimity, although he might have been surprised by the prevalence of such deviance in America. Moreover, there are signs scattered throughout the psychoanalytic literature that many took such prevalence as a matter of course. It will be remembered that Freud observed that homosexual object choices continue to be made throughout life, although they might (or might not) be unconscious.[38] Similarly, Fenichel claimed that few people escape making homosexual object choices in life.[39]

The reader is probably at a loss to decide whether these early writers meant that normal people, to use Kinsey's phrase, have a homosexual experience to the point of orgasm, or whether they had some more general sense in mind. Occasionally a clear statement emerges from the circumlocutions of the period. Henry, a psychiatrist with sympathy for both psychoanalysis and homosexuals, stated outright that "few people escape an overt homosexual experience at some period in life."[40] And startlingly, the snide and intemperate Robbins rejected entirely the notion of a healthy homosexual relationship, but nevertheless acknowledged those "transitory homoerotic episodes that punctuate almost every life history."[41]

The relation of these discrete acknowledgments to the more audible mainstream psychoanalytic tradition is not at all clear. Perhaps most practicing analysts knew of such deviant behavior from their patients or from their own experiences, and declined, for unexplained reasons, to acknowledge it, let alone discuss it. Or perhaps some analysts knew while others did not. Even if the second alternative is true, it suggests that no discussion took place between the two groups, or perhaps that no such discussion was possible under the conditions of psychoanalytic discourse.

What is of particular interest about the psychoanalytic response to the Kinsey Report is how the fact of important disagreement did not lead to debate about that disagreement. Trilling, for example, accused Kinsey of exaggerating the rigidity of the psychoanalytic position on sexual deviance: "no one," he claimed, "except a straw man would insist that *any* departure from sexual mores, or *any* participation in sexually taboo activities indicates a neurosis or a psychosis."[42] Of course, Trilling was a literary critic and not an analyst, and although his knowledge of analytic theory was as sophisticated as that of many of the figures we have considered, and his article was published in the *Bulletin of the Menninger Clinic*, he really cannot be said to speak for the psychoanalytic establishment. But Kubie was such a spokesman, and he leveled a similar accusation at Kinsey, who, he claimed, unjustly accused psychoanalysis of thinking that homosexuality was necessarily abnormal and pathological. The real analytic position, Kubie explained, was that "masturbation or homosexual behavior or other deviations may be either normal or neurotic or . . . a mixture of both." The psychoanalytic view of homosexuality, he insisted, was more qualified and *nuancé* than Kinsey thought:

The psychiatrist is far from believing that homosexuality is in and
of itself an index of psychopathology . . . but if the analyst's selected experience is in any way characteristic of the whole group
. . . the role of unconscious and unattainable goals is greater in
the homosexual than in the heterosexual adjustment.[43]

Such humane and temperate sentiment to the contrary, most psychoanalysts did indeed consider homosexuality as necessarily pathological and deeply disturbed. Bergler unequivocally claimed that
"psychoanalysis has always considered the homosexual a frightened
fugitive from misconceptions he unconsciously builds about women."[44]
All homosexuals have "regressed to the earliest level of psychic development, the 'oral stage.' There are," quite simply "no happy homosexuals; and there would not be even if the outer world left them in
peace,"[45] partly because "all homosexuals harbor a profound *inner* guilt
because of their perversion."[46] Bergler was, as we have seen, an extreme
figure, but more moderate analysts also held his views. Bychowski
denied the possibility that homosexuality could be found in a well-adjusted, healthy character and insisted that "the personality of most
homosexuals is deeply disturbed."[47] And the pseudonymous "Hewitt"
was even more categorical:

Psychoanalysis reveals that all homosexual behavior proceeds as
an escape from heterosexual relations based on the fear of such
relations. This unequivocally means that all homosexual behavior
is abnormal and springs from fear. . . . All homosexuals have
severe personality disorders.[48]

One wonders how Kubie could maintain that psychiatrists are "far
from believing that homosexuality is in and of itself an index of psychopathology," while "Hewitt" was insisting that "all homosexuals have
severe personality disorders." But when we look more closely we see a
systematic softening of the general shrill tone. Rather than enter into
disagreement with these polemicists, many analysts chose instead to
recast extreme views into more moderate, acceptable forms. For example, Bergler had impugned the reliability of Kinsey's subjects and questioned their motives: "Some of the volunteers, undoubtedly, were
pathological exhibitionists, hunting for thrills," while many others
"gladly used the opportunity of proving, by volunteering, that 'every-

body' has homosexual tendencies—thus seeking to *diminish their own inner guilt.*" For him, Kinsey was "duped."[49] But this is how an analyst paraphrased Bergler's article in the *Psychoanalytic Quarterly*:

> Kinsey's information was supplied by volunteers, and secondarily interested other volunteers who, consciously in good faith and inspired by noble intentions, unconsciously may have used this opportunity to prove that "everybody" has homosexual tendencies, thus justifying their own trends.[50]

This failure of the psychoanalytic community to provide a check on the excesses of some of its members by monitoring and correcting mistaken or dishonest views has to be deemed a lapse of professional responsibility. Professional courtesy is one thing, but the reluctance to call a lie a lie is quite another. Many irresponsible and reckless statements were made concerning the Kinsey Report, some of which border on dishonesty. These involve not only claims about "unanimous" psychoanalytic opinion, but also false characterizations of what Kinsey said. Thus, while some criticisms of Kinsey were cogent and important—in particular, Kubie's and Knight's[51]—others were inaccurate and even mendacious. It is embarrassing to read statements of respected analysts and find opinions masquerading as facts that should have been corrected by professional colleagues competent to do so.

Some of the criticism was due to either ignorance or dishonesty, especially regarding Kinsey's statistics. Soon after the Report came out, two sociologists, Hobbs and Lambert, undertook an extensive criticism of the statistics.[52] The extreme bias of the senior author became apparent when he and another sociologist, Kephart, later criticized the second Report on female sexuality. They cited disproportions in the sample and insufficiencies in Kinsey's reliability checks, and pointed out that Kinsey's reliance on the statistical mean in reporting his data, instead of the median or mode, tended to inflate his figures. And they accused him of conflating the data for preadolescent homosexual "play" with adult homosexual experience.[53]

Ramsey, a clinical psychologist sympathetic to Kinsey, discussed these objections and found many of them to be without substance.[54] He pointed out that Kinsey was quite aware of the disproportional representation of certain groups in his sample and corrected for it. While admitting that Kinsey's reliability studies were not conclusive, he observed that they compared favorably with other sociological and psychological research that had not been similarly criticized. As for Kinsey's use of the norm, Ramsey found no practices that were irregular. Kinsey had, in fact, reported the mode or median when it was appropriate and had used the mean because it is a more sophisticated and manipulable statistic and also because the median or mode was sometimes not usable, as when it equaled zero. Finally, it simply was not true that Kinsey failed to distinguish between prepubertal and adult sexual activity. His figures arc for "overt homosexual experience to the point of orgasm between adolescence and old age." The figures for preadolescent sexual activity are quite separate.

Despite this, the same criticisms were made and remade in the year following the publication of the Report and much later. Kubie repeated Hobbs and Lambert's charge that Kinsey had conflated preadolescent and adult sexual activity,[55] and Hoch[56] agreed with Bychowski, who repeated Kubie's charge.[57] Despite Ramsey's clarification, Bergler repeated his earlier charges unchanged six years later.[58] Kubie pointed out that Kinsey's reliance on the statistical mean did give the appearance of inflating his figures, just as his cumulative incidences might "cause readers to confuse *current* with *past* experiences," but his caution was directed at how naive readers might misunderstand perfectly appropriate statistical presentation.[59] Knight voiced similar concern about the same problem for the "uncritical reader,"[60] as did Murphy.[61]

This litany of criticism became so formulaic that its precise meaning began to be misunderstood. Bergler finally accused Kinsey of being dishonest in using the mean: "It is difficult to avoid the impression that statistics on homosexuality were used for sensational purposes by Kinsey." He advocated using the statistical mode, which he ignorantly claimed "represents the typical figure for the large majority." Bergler's criticisms are full of inaccuracies, and while some of them can be explained by his haste to be the first to respond to the Report or by his failure to have read it carefully, his repeating these falsehoods fully six years later, despite Ramsey's explanations, cannot. Kinsey was simply not guilty of "not distinguishing between occasional prepubertal and consistent adult homosexual activity," nor did he include preadolescent homosexuals acts in his figure of thirty-seven percent, which Bergler called "gerrymandering." Finally, Kinsey did not claim that thirty-seven percent of males were homosexual, a figure Bergler pointed to with disbelieving horror.[62] Here he conflated the two distinct findings of

Kinsey's regarding the number of males who had had at least one homosexual experience since adolescence and the number who considered themselves to be at least as homosexual as they were heterosexual. Yet no one in psychoanalytic circles ventured to correct Bergler's misstatements.

Of course, psychoanalytic writers framed many important and valid criticisms of Kinsey's survey. The interview technique, for all Kinsey's talent at it, was not really reliable. Kinsey did neglect questions of motivation as well as the meaning of behavior for the individual. In addition, his use of frequencies and cumulative incidences did lead to a confusion of "normal" with "common." It is true that Kinsey was not very sophisticated in his understanding of such psychoanalytic concepts as pregenital sexuality or sublimation, and that his pugnacious stance toward psychoanalysis only exacerbated this deficiency. These criticisms were made repeatedly by Bergler, Bychowski, Kardiner, Knight, Kubie, Menninger, and Wortis,[63] and it is to be regretted that Kinsey did not respond to them adequately.[64]

But much of the psychoanalytic criticism of Kinsey, even when it was accurate and intended to be helpful, was unreasonable. Eisenbud, while approving of Kinsey's method of gathering and presenting data, thought he had attempted too much. He thought that while the Report was a valuable addition to our knowledge, it had only an oblique relation to psychoanalytic ideas and judgments. Kinsey, he thought, was not competent to make estimates of psychological adjustment or psychopathology.[65] Margolin, on the other hand, thought Kinsey had not attempted enough. He called for a more elaborate assimilation of psychoanalytic ideas in all future studies and suggested a longitudinal study to complement Kinsey's survey.[66] And Kubie, while hailing the study as "the most important . . . addition . . . to our information," found serious omissions in the data, wanting to know more about such issues as menstruation, penis size, breast size, circumcision, and the like. He concluded by advising that "it would be essential to make intensive individual physiologic, anatomic, psychiatric and social studies of individuals who would constitute a statistically adequate random sample of each form of sexual behavior."[67]

But, as Levy pointed out, "Kinsey's is not the study of total man—it is a study of certain aspects of his behavior," an approach that is quite appropriate for the social sciences.[68] While it was unreasonable to ask Kinsey to conduct a psychoanalytic study, it was not unreasonable to expect psychoanalysis to consider his findings as important information. Several analysts did so: among them were Knight, Kubie, Levy, Murphy, and, in his vague way, Margolin.[69] But others were challenged and offended. Kardiner, for example, found his fellow participants in a symposium organized to discuss and evaluate Kinsey's findings "in collusion to put over a certain point," and characterized Kinsey's figures as "entirely misleading."[70] For these analysts, whenever Kinsey's empirical findings clashed with psychoanalytic ideas, or their version of them, the former were dismissed. Thus Bychowski claimed that "clinical observation shows" what Kinsey's findings impugned.[71] Kardiner curiously dismissed the data as "the product of a particular set of social conditions prevailing in Western culture."[72] Bergler sweepingly claimed that some of Kinsey's findings were "simply at odds with clinically observable facts," and referred repeatedly to "the following facts," such as that nine tenths of all infidelity in women is caused by frigidity, and the like.[73]

This dismal performance indicates that no evidence whatsoever was adequate to challenge what some analysts knew from their clinical practice, their theoretical deductions, or even their commonsense suppositions. Kinsey reported on fifty-three hundred subjects, and he made considerable efforts to ensure that they were representative of the population as a whole. Bergler dismissed these findings, claiming he had analyzed "more than 100" homosexuals,[74] a figure that had risen from the "dozens" he had claimed to have analyzed earlier.[75] In any case, the possibility that the subpopulation of psychoanalytic patients might be atypical of the population as a whole seemed never to have occurred to him.

This imperviousness of opinion to evidence revealed itself in the dreary stereotypes some analysts invoked in disputing Kinsey. Kardiner, in discussing the occurrence of homosexuality in cultures that do not restrict sexual behavior, an exception to his theory that the social control of sexuality leads to sexual deviance, implied that homosexuals had to be "males [who] are genetically females and vice versa."[76] And Rado, who in all other matters argued for scientific objectivity and clear-sightedness, challenged his opponents to explain "the most conspicuous fact of observation": why homosexual males "seek out a male who pretends to be a female." It was, according to him, impossible to account for homosexuality by invoking constitutional bisexuality, since if homosexuality were simply "a male's desire for a male," then why did homosexuals "impersonate a female?"[77] And Bergler firmly declared that "passive homosexuals, therefore, dress, walk, talk and adorn themselves like women," an assertion he repeated almost verbatim in two versions of the same article.[78] The level of such discourse is shockingly low, as we find Kardiner echoing the ideas of Hirschfeld, which Freud had successfully refuted in 1905, and Rado and Bergler trading in ignorant and vicious stereotypes. The primitiveness of such notions was matched by the obstinacy with which they were held in the face of evidence that, if it did not deny their truth, at least required that they be reconsidered.

Many analysts who thought it their responsibility to safeguard the morals and reputation of the nation adopted a queasy moralistic tone. Karl Menninger lamented Kinsey's cold antihuman procedures and assumptions: "the word 'love' rarely appears in his book." As for defending Kinsey because his Report would relieve some people of their guilt at being alone in their sexual deviance, Menninger thought that some guilt should not be removed: "and in this instance," he concluded, "surprising as it may be to some, most psychoanalysts and psychiatrists will be definitely on the side of religion."[79] His article was originally published in G.P., a journal for the general practice of medicine, and reprinted three months later in Pastoral Psychology. Hobbs, a sociologist publishing in the American Journal of Psychiatry, was impassioned and inflammatory. In the provocatively titled "Professor Kinsey: His Facts and His Fantasy," he attempted to rescue American women from the dangers posed by an uncritical acceptance of Kinsey's findings. Women, he urged,

> might attain romance before marriage through chastity, through
> the very differences which endow them, in addition to capabilities
> for greater sexual restraint, with charm, with grace, with other
> sometimes irritating but frequently endearing qualities which
> make the Mona Lisa's smile a mystery still. Old fashioned or not,
> there may be some marital and socially integrative value in view-
> ing females as women—perhaps even as ladies.[80]

Finally, Bergler saw the danger as political. He accused Kinsey of pleading "rather emotionally," but ended his own attack with a warning:

> Last but not least, Kinsey's erroneous conclusions pertaining to
> homosexuality will be politically and propagandistically used

against the United States abroad, stigmatizing the nation as a whole in a whisper campaign, especially since there are no comparable statistics available for other countries.[81]

Today's reader may smile with amusement at this misplaced patriotism or he may more wisely attribute it to the political crisis of the time. But if he does either, he will overlook the centrality of this psychoanalytic tradition of moral safeguarding. No one rebuked Bergler for his excessive views or for the inappropriate tone he used in expressing them, and Bergler seemed so pleased with his rhetoric that he twice quoted it verbatim six years later, and his estate reprinted it in the posthumous *Selected Papers*.[82] Many psychoanalysts thought it part of their professional responsibilities to make judgments about morality, politics, and "civilization as we know it." And these judgments, embedded in the undifferentiated mass of psychoanalytic theory, experience, and opinion, were thought somehow to be exempt from empirical tests and contrary evidence.

Still, some analysts had a sensible and intellectually responsible reaction to Kinsey's findings. Knight understood the importance of Kinsey's large sample: "psychiatrists' impressions about . . . the whole population are likely to be highly subjective, and to be based on a particular, not necessarily typical acquaintance with human behavior."[83] Hoch, in his discussion of a symposium on the Kinsey Report, which included the participation of Bychowski and Rado,[84] concluded that "the idea that all sexual behavior which has to do with procreation is natural and other behavior which does not is abnormal, is untenable and will have to be revised."[85] This position was put more honestly and clearly by Levy in the same symposium:

> Kinsey's findings are naturally disturbing to an analyst when he finds a discrepancy between his assumed norms and the supposedly true norms. True, the finding that a certain item of behavior is more frequent than you supposed does not mean that it is not a neurotic symptom in any particular individual. Nevertheless, the possibility that some of your subjective social values may be illusory calls for a critical reevaluation. It may mean recasting a number of other ideas you have worked with on the basis that they are generally accepted social values. You begin to wonder about the particular segment of the population represented by yourself and your patients, out of which your world of social val-

ues, your clinical norms of values and behavior have been derived. It is a jolt, but it is also an important corrective of those
"norms" that may represent arbitrary and dogmatic standards.[86]

The rhetoric of this passage is remarkable. Not so much making a
general statement on the Kinsey Report, Levy seems to be addressing
and rebuking his colleagues. The shift from the general "analyst" to
"you" suggests a narrowing of focus to his intended audience, and the
use of quotation marks around "norms" indicates that Levy understood
and embraced the larger implications of the Report for psychoanalytic
theory. But the indirection and discretion of the passage are also noteworthy. His remarks are forceful, but they function as a peremptory
statement, without inviting a response. None came.

In general, the Kinsey Report did not receive an adequate response
from psychoanalysis, despite the promptness of the reaction and the
selective enthusiasm some analysts expressed for it. While the Report
may have changed private opinions and attitudes, analytic publications
after Kinsey show no evidence that they were affected. Few refer to him,
let alone use his findings to reformulate analytic ideas and norms, as
Hoch and Levy had urged. Still, it is likely that Kinsey's results remained in the background of analytic research as a kind of nagging and
unacknowledged reproach. Though analysts had, to their satisfaction,
demonstrated that the method of the Report was so flawed as to render
the results invalid, they could not point to any positive empirical results
of their own that could claim a scope comparable to Kinsey's. The
challenge was taken up by Bieber and his colleagues fourteen years
later,[87] and if the Kinsey Report had any effect on psychoanalysis, it was
in the way analysts were eager to hail Bieber's work, which in certain
ways denied Kinsey's, as the vindication of their own ideas.

In the end, the publication of the Kinsey Report and the psychoanalytic response to it do mark a climax in this history, though in a way
that could not have been predicted. The very fact that the Report had so
little substantive effect on psychoanalytic thinking about homosexuality
shows that it had by this time become impervious to influence from
outside psychoanalysis. Henceforth, the relation analytic thought on
homosexuality would have to other disciplines would be distrust and
enmity. The evolution of this theory had been primarily internally
generated from the beginning, but it was only in 1948 that the widespread indifference to nonanalytic ideas became apparent and articu-

lated. The motivation behind such recalcitrance was only partially a scrupulousness about the coherence and integrity of analytic theory. It was also, and perhaps primarily, a brittle and exaggerated solicitude for conventional social values. The disruption in American family styles and in wage earning during the war, as well as the larger intellectual and moral trauma of the catastrophes of the time, undoubtedly contributed to such a startled and shrill reaction. But we can see that in the forty or so years from the time of the publication of Freud's *Three Essays* to that of the Kinsey Report, the original revolutionary fervor of Freud's discoveries and the hope that new knowledge could make society more humane had changed into a reactionary attempt to preserve old values and old institutions, even at the expense of honestly acknowledging evidence to the contrary, or of the human sympathy and concern that had motivated the psychoanalytic movement from the very beginning.

CHAPTER **VII**

CONSERVATIVE
DEVELOPMENTS: 1948–1962

The period from the first Kinsey Report in 1948 to the important Bieber study in 1962 was principally one of consolidating and applying the theoretical insights of the preceding period. There were a few important new ideas, such as Ovesey's notion of "pseudohomosexuality," but, for the most part, the theory of perversion as outlined by Glover and the interest in the oral precursors of the Oedipus complex continued to provide the most useful sources of psychoanalytic ideas about homosexuality. Nevertheless, the amount of writing on homosexuality increased, and by the mid-fifties as many as half a dozen articles on the subject appeared annually.

Kinsey's effect on this discourse was minimal. It is, perhaps, suspicious that only four articles on male homosexuality appeared in the four years following the publication of the Report, and that the tide of analytic writing began to swell only by 1952. Of seventy or so articles published in this period, not counting those by Bergler or those specifically on Kinsey, only eleven mentioned the Kinsey Report at all; and of them, eight did so only to disparage it. Only three articles acknowledged that their ideas were influenced by the Report.[1] In the published report of the panel on perversion held by the American Psychoanalytic Association in 1954, it was noted that "all participants demonstrated little use for the findings of Kinsey."[2]

In general, this period was characterized by an increasingly moralistic tone and a growing emphasis on conventional social values, especially

128

by so-called holistic approaches to psychoanalysis. Important refinements in theory were published in the *International Journal of Psychoanalysis* or *Psychoanalytic Quarterly*, which maintained high levels of discourse. Such advances became the property, after a suitable delay, of less sophisticated practitioners who called themselves analysts and frequently published in psychiatric journals, but who revealed at times some very questionable opinions. This simplification of sophisticated psychoanalytic ideas is fairly common in this period, sometimes allowing writers to vent their own moral and social views. Feldman's muddled version of the development of heterosexuality, for example, depended on his notion that "heterosexuality is an anatomically inborn and inevitable fate for both sexes." In treatment, the therapist should labor to "convince" the homosexual patient "that man is born for woman and woman is born for man."[3] Similarly, Berg began with a plea for sympathy for the plight of the homosexual, proceeded through a popularized version of analytic ideas, and ended with the old, dreary stereotypes: the homosexual is unstable, prone to alcoholism and suicide; homosexuality is close to schizophrenia; "homosexual murder is common."[4] In the same way, Fried promised a new approach to homosexuality, concentrating on the function of the ego and the patient's "interpersonal" relations, but traded in the same silly and ignorant clichés, expressed in a prissy and moralistic tone.[5] Hewitt, presumably not the pseudonymous "Hewitt" of the previous chapter, adopting a "holistic" approach and invoking the authority of Horney, offered a long list of disagreeable traits that characterized all forms of homosexuality: passivity and timidity, preoccupation with appearance, sadomasochism, alienation from the self, impaired awareness of emotions, low self-esteem, and unconscious effeminacy.[6] Analysts of the Horney school elaborated the topos of the sad, dark world of the homosexual, making preliminary gestures toward anthropological information or literary culture, only to reaffirm, sometimes quite inconsistently, their own cherished opinions and values. Such cliché-mongering also characterized the several panels convened to discuss various aspects of homosexuality in men.[7]

While such writers claimed to be "humanistic" and "holistic" in approach, their soft-mindedness really concealed conservative, bourgeois values that revealed themselves in their moralistic tone. Their "humane" approach finally blamed the patient for having betrayed his self and his higher goals and possibilities. Much of the discussion of the homosexual's need to "want" to be cured can be seen as a subtle way of seeing homosexuality as a self-induced and willful aberration. In certain ways, such "humanistic" analysts reverted to pre-Freudian views of homosexuality as a moral deficiency. Horney herself put the matter succinctly, although here she was not dealing specifically with homosexuality:

> Sexual problems, although they may sometimes prevail in the symptomatic picture, are no longer considered to be in the dynamic center of the neuroses. Sexual difficulties are the effect rather than the cause of the neurotic character structure. Moral problems on the other hand gain in importance.[8]

This pseudohumane moralizing was admirably criticized by Marcuse in the epilogue to *Eros and Civilization*, where he connected it to a revisionism that both denied the biological basis of Freud's psychology and its metapsychological structure, while attempting an *embourgeoisement* of psychoanalytic ideas. He characterized this tone as "elevated and yet clear, permeated with good will and tolerance and yet moved by an *esprit de sérieux* which makes transcendental values into facts of everyday life." Singling out Horney, Sullivan, Fromm, and Thompson as representatives, Marcuse saw their shying away from the biological and sexual basis of Freud's ideas as part of a larger movement within liberal culture to deny the irreducible conflict between the individual and society that informed, most of all, Freud's late works.[9]

In general, there was a reluctance in this period to acknowledge the importance of constitutional issues and an eagerness to consider environmental factors instead. This development may be partly a geographical issue, as the center of psychoanalysis shifted first from Vienna to London, and then to New York City, and the world view of psychoanalysis became more American. In addition, the consolidation of social values in the United States after World War II found its correlative in an emphasis by certain groups within psychoanalysis on such liberal ideals as the progress of civilization and the amelioration of human ills. The belief in the latter also found a vehicle in American behaviorism, and it is curious to see two such ideological foes as psychoanalysis and behaviorism joining ranks in this one area.

The single most striking characteristic of the theory of homosexuality in this period was the attempt to deny the constitutional basis for psychological deviance and to minimize the importance of sexuality in human motivation. In fact, the entire psychoanalytic movement can be seen as splitting on this. There had always been a centrifugal tendency in psychoanalysis away from Freud's theory of instinct and its emphasis on sexuality, as early as the schisms with Jung and Adler. But by the fifties, with the rise of ego psychology and the social orientation implicit in the "interpersonal" school, the split was quite marked. Such classical analysts as Balint[10] and Edoardo Weiss[11] continued to affirm the importance of constitutional bisexuality in the development of homosexual object choice, but others with a more "modern" outlook bemoaned the reactionary refusal of classical analysts to consider "holistic" approaches dealing with the "total personality." Of them, Kardiner was closest to classic analysis, but he nevertheless cited Rado approvingly and rejected Freud's notion of constitutional bisexuality as "tautological."[12] And Feldman thought that bisexuality was a symptom and not a cause of homosexuality.[13] The pages of revisionist psychoanalytic journals are filled with similar reproaches aimed at the narrowness of classic psychoanalysis. Gershman reiterated these views, and he was supported by his colleague Frederick Weiss in rejecting bisexuality as a constitutional factor.[14] Another analyst of the "adaptational" school presented the successful cure of a homosexual in only sixty-five sessions over an eight-month period. Rejecting the notion of constitutional bisexuality and citing with approval Rado's article, he claimed that only by freeing oneself from the shackles of an outmoded idea could one counter Freud's own pessimism about the possibility of curing homosexuals.[15]

Of great theoretical importance was the specific denial that certain other components of sexuality were constitutional in nature. The negative Oedipus complex, for example, was no longer seen by certain analysts as an irreducible stage of psychosexual development, but rather as a secondary, defensive mechanism against the prior, irreducible positive variety.[16] And narcissism was discussed not as a constitutional endowment but as a defense against aggression toward the libidinal object,[17] an idea that had been developed by the Budapest school of analysis, most notably by Balint, who flatly claimed that "narcissism is always secondary."[18] Finally, the very notion of homosexuality was really "pseudohomosexuality" and involved issues of power and dependence and not those of sex at all.[19]

Just as interest in the oral precursors of the Oedipus complex was the distinguishing mark of analytic theory in the thirties, the movement from intrapsychic, instinctual conflict "outward" to the arena of "interpersonal" and social interaction and development was the defining characteristic of psychoanalytic thought in the fifties. But while developments in the earlier period resulted in a deepening of analytic understanding, there was no corresponding "broadening" in the later period.

Meanwhile, the usual work of psychoanalysis went on, and most analysts adhered to classic formulations and ideas. Anna Freud continued to treat her homosexual patients in the classic manner. Unfortunately, she did not publish the texts of the addresses she delivered on her therapeutic technique, so the reader must rely on abstracts and summaries. She stressed the importance of unconscious fantasies in homosexual behavior and the oscillation of active and passive homosexual yearnings. She urged the analyst to interpret to the patient that an active homosexual indulged passive, feminine wishes in his passive partner, while a passive homosexual appropriated his alienated masculinity by projecting it onto an active partner. She emphasized the importance of grandiose narcissistic fantasies of an omnipotent phallus. She also insisted on the attainment of full object-love of the opposite sex as the requirement for a "cure."[20] Lagache similarly emphasized the vicissitudes of various forms of homosexual yearning within a single individual, who used homosexual jealousy to defend against another kind of homosexuality that was intolerable to his consciousness.[21]

As the coauthor of the important article "The Breast Complex," Eidelberg stressed the strong oral fixation, the identification with the phallic mother, and the defense against aggression by displacing libido onto men. He used the case of one "Mr. Wurmer," whose treatment was "so typical" that it could serve as a kind of prototype. Men, for the patient, represented women without breasts, and the penis substituted for the lost breast.[22] Silber also presented a prototypical case to illustrate Freud's idea of the development of homosexual object choice through the reaction formation of feelings of murderous rivalry with a sibling. Here the hated brother became a love object, and his sudden death led his homosexual sibling to seek in an erect penis the unconscious assurance of his brother being alive.[23] M. Miller found a characteristic split between submission and aggression in male homosexuality, caused by "a stimulus that provokes aggression," which in turn caused a fear of retaliation. The inability to handle such aggressive reactions, Miller thought, was due to a difficulty in identifying with the father. In such cases, submission served to mask an unintegrated aggressiveness, although the dynamics behind such an outcome were classically oedipal.[24]

The most striking theory, however, was that of Thorner, who, under the influence of Klein's ideas, derived homosexuality from a disturbance at the earliest infantile paranoid-schizoid position. For Thorner, homosexuality was "a symptom of a general neurosis rather than an illness in its own right, or a perversion." He insisted that it "receives its significance not from the choice of a love object . . . but from the content of the unconscious phantasy material which breaks through in the homosexual activity." The significance of homosexual thoughts and actions depended on the dynamics of the patient at particular points in the therapy, as passive homosexuality shifted to an active form, or as fear of attack oscillated between oral and anal concerns. In all cases, homosexual activity was a defense against anxiety and prevented the development of a stable psychic organization or a rich and integrated affective life.[25] In a similar vein, Ehrenwald found both paranoia and homosexuality stemming from the refusal of the mother to relinquish her symbiotic ties to her son. Paranoid delusions, he found, were "in essence the regressively distorted counterpart of the early symbiotic model of communication."[26]

Other analysts approached the subject from special points of view or tried to adapt psychoanalytic ideas to novel techniques. Fine wondered why none of his seven homosexual patients ever entertained homosexual feelings toward him. Instead, their objects always represented the narcissistic self or the idealized father, but interpreting this to his patients "had no effect whatsoever." By noting, however, that the analyst had been split off "from the world of accessible homosexual objects," Fine was able to circumvent the analysis of the homosexual acting out and to interpret the patient's fear of homosexuality directly.[27] Hadfield claimed to have cured homosexuality by having his patients relive childhood experiences in as few as five sessions. But even he could do nothing for homosexuals who did not want to be cured, and could not explain why certain treatments failed "for no apparent reason."[28] Hadden urged group therapy for homosexuality in order to confront patients' rationalization of their sexual aims and to lead to an anxiety that was therapeutically useful. In addition, such suitably motivated patients could derive additional ego strength from each other.[29] Finally, Regardie, although claiming that his most difficult cases involved homosexuality and alcoholism, offered a complete cure of the former in only forty sessions through the use of hypnotic suggestion. While hypnotized, the patient was told to dream, to produce transference dreams, to dream about various other topics, and finally to attempt sexual intercourse with his wife. The article is quite superficial, employing simplified oedipal dynamics. Regardie never attempted to interpret or explain the patient's difficulty with free association, nor did he seem to think it significant that the patient proved so amenable to hypnotic suggestion after his former lover had undergone hypnosis by Regardie.[30]

The tendency in this period to minimize the importance of purely intrapsychic processes in determining homosexual object choice revealed itself in a handful of articles that attempted to attribute it to particular events in the child's psychological environment. Lewinsky presented two papers on the analysis of a homosexual who showed no evidence of a passive attitude toward the father. Fixated at the stage of the Oedipus complex because of an inability to handle murderous feelings of rivalry toward father and brothers, the patient felt his heterosexuality threatened by castration both by the father and by the mother's menacing vagina. But his actual homosexual choice of objects was determined by a severe prohibition against masturbation, which the patient understood as permitting him to touch the penis of another man.[31]

Lewinsky's case presented, as it were, a novel twist to traditional theories, but her presentation of her patient's dynamics was quite conventional and would not have surprised Freud and his circle. Similarly, Hamilton derived homosexual object choice from fear of incest. He claimed that the homosexual male had during infancy experienced a heterosexual attachment "of abnormal intensity" with the mother who loved her child "too erotically." Homosexuals were, therefore, "victims of incestuous mothers," forced to regress from phallic erotism to earlier stages. Such an etiology represented nothing new in psychoanalytic theory, and, in fact, can be taken as affirming Ferenczi's notion of 1909 that homosexuality was determined by "excessively powerful heterosexuality (intolerable to the ego)."[32] But what marked Hamilton's article as typical of its period was the extremely negative view he took of the homosexual character: the homosexual is "preponderantly narcissistic, incapable of object-love, still hobbled in his emotional life . . . and more or less fixed at the anal level of libidinal development . . . due to a regression from the phallic stage."[33]

A clear sign of the times was two related articles arguing that deviant sexual behavior in children is caused by parents who "unwittingly seduce them and encourage their aberrant behavior."[34] This notion was elaborated in another article that dealt with homosexual acting out in psychoanalytic treatment. Here too the parents were accused of having unconsciously encouraged their children to act out their own perverse tendencies. Such an idea had important implications for treatment, since the therapist should be alert to the dangers of recapitulating in treatment the original parents' own teasing permissiveness: "overt homosexual activity may occur in an individual with strong latent homosexuality when the therapist inadvertently behaves permissively." Hence the therapist should be quite firm with "a well-timed prohibition of self-destructive homosexual activity" and threaten to end treatment if such activity continues.[35] These ideas were illustrated and magnified by Gillespie, who considered them important in accounting for the participation of defective superego functions in the formation of this particular perverse activity.[36]

In addition, the perennial psychoanalytic interest in the relation between homosexuality and paranoia continued. Bychowski continued to elaborate it, as well as the relation between homosexuality and addiction to alcohol and drugs. It is difficult to determine whether he thought that all cases of homosexuality involved the ego weaknesses, exaggerated narcissistic object relations, and fluid ego boundaries characteristic of schizophrenia. Most of his data on homosexuality are from cases of latent or overt psychosis, and he claimed that "latent homosexual constellation is a constant and most significant element of latent schizophrenia."[37] And elsewhere he adumbrated the "structural kinship" between homosexuality and psychosis, emphasizing the "primitive discharge of impulse in homosexual 'acting out.' "[38] The "humanistic" Gershman, who thought that homosexuality differed from psychosis only in the degree of disturbance, repeated this conclusion.[39] But Grauer, who could find homosexual content in the delusions of only four cases in his sample of 24 paranoid schizophrenics, denied such conclusions.[40] Yet another analytic researcher provided general confirmation of the traditional analytic connection in a sample of 150 cases and controls, although the evidence was more equivocal in the instance of female schizophrenics.[41]

Rosenfeld, using Klein's ideas, contributed a sophisticated account of three cases of homosexuality that involved marked paranoid features. All were quite disturbed, and one became overtly psychotic. Rosenfeld stressed the defensive function of homosexuality against paranoia, and noted that when paranoid anxiety becomes too intense, homosexual defenses break down and psychotic decompensation ensues. Similarly, homosexual behavior serves as a defense against paranoid projection and projective identification, as the paranoid seeks to appease his imagined persecutor by submitting to him sexually.[42] Socarides developed these ideas in a similar vein, treating homosexuality as a fusion of libidinal and aggressive impulses and as a defense against the anxiety resulting from primitive introjection and projection. Here too psychosis was avoided by the development of a perversion, but only at the price of a split in the object and the ego of the homosexual. The former could alternately represent the infantile narcissistic self or the castrated mother, and the latter could sustain two distinct ego states.[43]

Such work expanded and refined certain theoretical notions about the dynamics of homosexual object choice, but the use of grossly disturbed case material reinforced the informal and unexamined connection between homosexuality and severe emotional disturbance. While certain forms of homosexuality provided an insight into serious emotional disturbance, it was never shown that all homosexuality was necessarily so grossly disturbed, although such writers as Bergler maintained that it was. Several large-scale studies that employed disturbed subjects did foster such a view. P. Miller proposed three "causes" for homosexual object choice: a "predisposing" cause, involving rejection by one or both parents; a "precipitating" cause, involving homosexual seduction in late childhood; and a "perpetuating" cause, involving the satisfaction of security needs and an ongoing feminine identification. His data, however, were derived from the study of fifty prisoners.[44] Glueck used "the homosexual sex offender" as his subject and found that three quarters employed "some type of schizophrenic adaptation," and that they suffered a grave impairment in their superegos and in the capacity for abstract thought and fantasy. He concluded that psychoanalytic treatment was ineffective in such cases, and urged "some of the therapeutic efforts utilizing organic therapies, particularly electroshock."[45]

This association of homosexuality with psychosis or serious criminal activity reinforced the old stereotype of the homosexual as a sick or vicious psychic cripple. The present writer could compile a varied *florilegium* of such assertions, but a small sample will have to suffice. It includes such innocuously offensive notions as that of Allen, who thought he was a champion of understanding and tolerance, and expressed the enlightened view that the homosexual "is ill in much the same way as a dwarf is ill—because he has never developed."[46] Hamilton emphasized the intrinsic connection of homosexuality to alcoholism, and claimed that the homosexual is "preponderantly narcissistic, incapable of love [and] . . . hobbled in his emotional life."[47] Gershman elaborated at length the conventional pious clichés about the loneliness and misery of the homosexual's life.[48] Homosexuals are "severely alienated people . . . [with] a core of petrified patterns of living . . . automatonlike. Zest for living, and the capacity to face the unknown, seem atrophied."[49] Fried, another "holistic" analyst, contributed her own rhetorical embellishments: "most . . . homosexuals do not feel like adults. Rather they see themselves as children or adolescents; their ego-superego structure is badly damaged"; and they have only "a limited capacity for relations with other human beings." In addition, she thought it odd that "homosexual collectives" exist only for "mutual support," while heterosexual groups "are more likely to pursue a goal—to find social entertainment, to accomplish something in the community, to enjoy a sport." Finally, it seemed sinister that homosexual hobbies involve objects that are either large or small, thus revealing the castration anxiety lurking behind such joyless existences.[50] Berg, another pleader for tolerance, emphasized the connection of homosexuality to instability, alcoholism, suicide, and schizophrenia, and hinted darkly at the dangers the analyst might face alone in the treatment room with a homosexual.[51] Kardiner did not resist such stereotypes: "In many there is in addition a compensatory vindictiveness and a hatred of all people. The common judgment that homosexuality is a form of antisocial activity is not altogether unwarranted." He went on to remark on the similarity of the Nazi's hatred of Jews with the homosexual's "notorious" hatred of women, and called attention to the "predilection of the Nazi hierarchy for homosexuality" and that other attribute shared by both groups, "cruelty against other human beings."[52] Bergler, of course, provided a whole bestiary of homosexual monstrosities,[53] but he surpassed Kardiner in vicious silliness by relating the lurid story of one of his patients, a Hungarian Nazi in love with a Negro.[54]

Although first-rate writers had more enlightened views, the estimate of the character of "the typical homosexual" at this time was perhaps at its lowest in our history. Many writers acknowledged that some creative artists had been homosexual—a correspondence that Freud remarked upon many times and that occupied him in his two monographs on Leonardo da Vinci and the *Moses* of Michelangelo. But such writers insisted that these artists were creative and productive despite their homosexuality, not because of it. Bychowski, in two separate articles, respectively, claimed both that Walt Whitman had failed to control his sexual predilections and so suffered artistically, and that he had succeeded at sublimation, thus achieving his artistic vision. But in either case, homosexuality was seen as inimical to true creativity and not as one of its components.[55]

A similar point of view informed psychoanalytic discussions of that historical anomaly, Greece in the Golden Age, when homosexuality was the norm, at least among the upper classes.[56] Flournoy, for example, discussing an analytic session, claimed that Socrates thought that the love of boys "should always remain on a spiritual plane," and that Plato, though he admired his teacher, could not follow his precepts. He concluded that it was "apparent that the moral and intellectual grandeur of the two philosophers was not a derivative of their instincts as such, but a function of their repression and sublimation." He made several such assertions, quite without authority and often quite mistakenly,[57] and maintained that homosexuality was not native to Athens, but had been imported from the Doric states,[58] a bit of classical gossip he had probably unknowingly picked up at several removes from *The Laws* of Plato, who was in no position to know. Flournoy's judgment recalls Boehm's assurance more than thirty years earlier that the ancient Germanic tribes never practiced homosexuality until they were corrupted by the decadent Romans.[59] Gershman offered his own contradictory opinions by first praising homosexuality in ancient Greece as healthy and productive but later condemning any "homosexual behavior [that] continues to be persistent and preferential . . . [as] an expression of severe emotional disorder."[60]

But the most vigorous campaign against connecting homosexuality with creativity was led by Bergler, who returned to the subject of homosexual artists throughout his career, attempting each time to denigrate their achievement, from dress designers[61] to literary critics and the greatest of writers. Melville, Hawthorne, Stendhal, and Proust all fell before his onslaught: "If a homosexual is a great artist, this is so *despite*, and not because of his homosexuality. In the great artist who is a homosexual, a small autarchic corner has been rescued from the holocaust of illness."[62] By "great artist" he presumably meant Shakespeare, although he does not mention the sonnets, since he dismissed Oscar Wilde as a "gossip columnist" who plagiarized his *Picture of Dorian Gray* from "the work of half-a-dozen predecessors,"[63] and considered Proust a "schizoid" injustice collector,[64] dismissing his work by quoting Somerset Maugham on the superficiality of homosexuals.[65] He likewise condemned Melville for his moral masochism: "Did he expect to make a living as a writer by using incest as a theme [in *Pierre*]?"[66]

The attentive reader will perceive by now that the level of such discussion was not very high. Both the "humanistic" analysts of the day, such as Gershman and Fried, and the popularizers and propagandists were responsible for this coarsening and vulgarization of psychoanalytic ideas, as well as for their moral brutalization. This occurred during a period of marked social conformity and political repression, which vulgarized psychoanalysis played a role in formulating and imposing. Nowhere is this process exemplified more unambiguously than in the case of Bergler, who began his career by making important contributions to psychoanalytic theory and by serving as assistant director of the Psychoanalytic Freud Clinic in Vienna during its tragic last four years, but ended as a shrill and monotonous promoter of his own work and opinions. By contrast, Glover continued to make important theoretical contributions to psychoanalysis, but also worked diligently and carefully to bring such ideas into the realm of educational and penal reform.

Bergler continued to expound his notion of the "breast complex" in a curiously exclusive and combative way. According to him, the shock at weaning can cause a chronic attempt to repeat that trauma in order to blame the depriving mother, thus resulting in "moral masochism" and "injustice collecting," as well as corresponding character traits of spite, aggression, dishonesty, ingratitude, and the like. So important did Bergler think this formulation that he later came to reject any other explanation as superficial and inconsequential:

> I would like to register *my conviction that there is only one basic neurosis and that neurosis is oral in genesis. All other nosologic groups, based on anal and phallic regression, are but rescue stations from the oral "danger."* [67]

He consequently neglected most contemporary developments in ego psychology or in the refinement and deepening of the theory of oral fixation, just as he had previously urged an abandonment of "super-ficial" interpretations of psychic disorder based on the Oedipus complex.[68]

He repeated these ideas for thirty years, and his bibliography contains approximately three hundred articles and two dozen books. From the end of World War II to the mid-1950s, he published an average of more than fourteen articles annually. In one, "Logorrhea," he presented several examples of patients who could not control their verbal produc-tion, including one "suffering from an obsession of publishing . . . from severe writing diarrhoea." It turns out that his behavior was prompted by the denial, "I am not a peeping Tom; I am an exhibitionist."[69] The reader, however, should not be misled. Bergler invariably repeated himself, often literally quoting previous publications for pages on end. References at the end of his articles direct the reader, almost without exception, to Bergler's own works, and he rarely acknowledged any other writer, except when someone quoted him. He frequently pub-lished in *Pageant, Cosmopolitan, Coronet,* or *Charm* such articles as "The He-Man Exposed," "The Psychology of the Kill-joy," and "Reduce Your Tensions to Nuisances." He also appeared on the radio, adopting a tone that suggested both the wise guy and the *au courant* wise professor. He wrote widely on literature, but seems to have had no real appreciation of literary values. His sensibility was decidedly middlebrow and anti-intellectual, and he often would dismiss a difficult idea or problem with a Groucho Marx–like quip. Or he might refute something Proust thought with a quotation from Somerset Maugham, "certainly based on first-hand observation."[70]

His abiding interest, however, was homosexuality, and he returned to the subject in almost all his writings. His three monographs on the subject are *Counterfeit-Sex, Homosexuality: Disease or Way of Life,* and *One Thousand Homosexuals.*[71] One of his last articles, submitted one month before his death, "The Aristocracy among Homosexuals: Lovers of 'Trade,' " continued his project of exposing and "deglamorizing" homosexuality.[72] Bergler's ideas on the etiology and treatment of ho-mosexuality did not change much, but his tone became more strident. His "transcripts" of analytic sessions are trully appalling, as "the analyst . . . serenely and with assurance mows down his 'opposition' and again proves that he 'knows best.' "[73] He would tell patients what other patients, even their former lovers, had said about them in treatment.[74] His impatience with and distaste for his homosexual patients are apparent throughout his work, and he seemed to have felt no qualms about his feelings:

> I have no bias against homosexuality . . . [but] homosexuals are
> essentially disagreeable people, regardless of their pleasant or un-
> pleasant manner . . . [which contains] a mixture of supercilious-
> ness, false aggression, and whimpering. . . . [They are]
> subservient when confronted with a stronger person, merciless
> when in power, unscrupulous about trampling on a weaker
> person.[75]

His only substantive addition to his ideas about homosexuality occurs in his later compendium of clinical experience, *One Thousand Homosexuals*, in which he emphasized the importance of interpreting the masochism behind homosexual behavior and urged that the therapist not forbid homosexual acting out during treatment. In a chapter entitled "The Tragedy of Parents of Young Homosexuals," he categorically denied that parents have any responsibility for their children's homosexuality. For Bergler, the development of homosexual object choice was entirely an intrapsychic occurrence: "educational mistakes cannot produce homosexuality."[76]

Bergler oscillated between seeing homosexuality as a disease and seeing it as moral corruption. As an analyst he claimed to have labored to cure the former, and as a private individual concerned with his civic duty he strove to alert a dangerously tolerant American public to the dangers posed by predatory and unscrupulous homosexuals:

> If information is unavailable, if false statistics are left uncontradic-
> ted, if new recruits are not warned by dissemination of the fact
> that homosexuality is but a disease, the confirmed homosexual is
> presented with a clear field for his operations—and your teen-age
> children may be the victims.[77]

By the end of his life, Bergler became an embarrassment to many serious analysts. His views at conferences and symposia were reported without remark,[78] or they were softened and their offensive edge blunted.[79] Few analytic articles refer to his work, apart from the paper he wrote with Eidelberg on the breast complex. In the period we are discussing, only three use his ideas: one in quite a general way,[80] one to disagree with the notion of the unimportance of the Oedipus complex,[81] and one as part of a survey of analytic ideas on homosexuality.[82] A review of his posthumous *Selected Papers* was decidedly cool, criticizing his constant repetition of the theme of oral masochism, his reductionism, his ignorance of other developments in psychoanalytic theory, and his "insistent polemic." The reviewer did not even mention homosexuality, although it probably accounts for more of Bergler's writing than any other topic.[83]

Bergler's actual contributions to the psychoanalytic theory of homosexuality could have been summarized in a paragraph or two and his career characterized as a disappointment and perhaps as an embarrassment. Although he did not articulate widely held analytic ideas, and most analysts kept their distance from him, he continued to be published despite his vile tone and the low level of much of his discourse, in some of the most prestigious psychoanalytic journals. Whatever his former association with Freud was, many of his articles are a disgrace to the journals in which they appear, and their editors must bear the accusation of bad judgment or pusillanimity. The most flagrant offenders are *Psychiatric Quarterly, American Imago, Psychoanalytic Review*, and, for publishing the most loathsome article of all, the *Bulletin of the Philadelphia Association for Psychoanalysis.*[84] These journals helped provide sanction for his bigoted and ignorant opinions. Notions of a "conspiracy" of homosexuals seeking to "recruit" innocent children are poisonous and untrue. They have been used perennially to exclude and persecute minorities. Educated and thoughtful people know this, and psychoanalysts should have repudiated such notions. Bergler's extreme opinions encouraged the expression of similar ideas, although they may have been phrased more moderately. We have already noted the intemperate, hateful, and foolish ideas of Robbins and Silverberg, but we may also note similar ideas, masked by false solicitude, expressed by Gershman and Fried.

In addition, Bergler exemplifies the insularity and imperviousness to criticism sometimes characteristic of psychoanalytic ideas. Even when he acknowledged honest disagreement, he labeled it resistance and refused to consider the argument on its own merits. Similarly, Bergler continued to insist on the representativeness of his own clinical experience and called discrepant information such as Kinsey's "fantastic."[85] Finally, his strident tone precluded any thoughtful consideration of genuinely difficult and complicated issues. The question of why homosexuals who were content with their orientation should be "cured" could not be posed as long as it was maintained that treatable patients must experience guilt and that its absence was evidence of extreme sociopathic trends or the kind of sadistic perversion that necessarily excluded guilt. All this, however, was articulated by others under the guise of tolerance and ameliorative goals. Even the movement to decriminalize homosexual activity between consenting adults, which Bergler did not oppose but which left him indifferent, was used to replace criminal sanctions with medical ones. Thus, the reluctance to be "cured" amounted to a willful refusal to rejoin the larger community of normal people, and homosexuality could again be considered a moral failure. Such conclusions did not, of course, represent all psychoanalytic opinion, though psychoanalysis did little to prevent its enormous prestige from being used to endorse them.

It is a pleasure to note that some analysts labored long and painstakingly for truly humane ends. The most prominent of them was Glover. In addition to his theoretical work, he is noteworthy for his attempts to have psychoanalysis contribute to enlightened social policy regarding criminal and sexual deviancy. As editor of the *British Journal of Delinquency*, on whose editorial board Anna Freud also sat, he represented the most informed and engaged psychoanalytic opinion, particularly in regard to homosexuality. His papers and public statements on the subject from 1940 to 1959 were collected in "The Problem of Male Homosexuality," which was published the following year in *The Roots of Crime*.[86] He also contributed a sympathetic introduction to a volume expressing prohomosexual views,[87] and frequently addressed concerned but nonanalytic readers. His most public achievement was probably his influence on the Wolfenden Commission Report, which recommended the decriminalization of homosexual acts between consenting adults in England, following the spirit of Freud, who had petitioned for similar redress.[88]

Like Bergler, Glover returned to the subject of homosexuality throughout his long career, but, unlike Bergler, he continued to reconsider, modify, and refine his ideas. He had argued that certain forms of homosexuality correspond, in the quality of their object relations and their capacity for true object love, to essentially normal heterosexual conditions:

> In many cases apart from the denial of heterosexual genital and reproductive function, the manifestation of homosexual

love-feeling and the attitude to the love object cannot be distinguished from those associated with normal heterosexual love.[89]

Thus, he expressly denied the psychoanalytic consensus that the homosexual choice of object is necessarily disturbed and represents a dimi-
nution of the capacity to love:

> Some analysts have, however, [maintained] that *every* homosexual
> presents signs of neurosis. This is certainly not true of the homo-
> sexual group as a whole. . . . It is no doubt common to find neu-
> rotic formations in those cases who come voluntarily to private
> treatment but it is doubtful whether of those private homosexuals
> who do not come for treatment and are capable of social discre-
> tion in their homosexual activities clinical disorders exist in more
> than a tithe of the cases.[90]

Such misapprehension on the part of analysts, Glover thought, "in all
probability is due to the particular range of cases observed." He frequently called attention to the lack of reliable statistics and to the "fact
[that] very few analyses of undisturbed homosexuals have been carried
out," and that analytic knowledge of homosexuality had been derived
from either disturbed cases or unconscious and conflict-ridden
homosexuals.[91]

   None of the instinctive repulsion to homosexuality that largely characterizes the analytic writing of the period seems to have infected
Glover's views:

> Manifest homosexuality is but one end-result of the activity of
> forces that constitute a substantial part of the instinctual heritage
> of the race and give rise to at least as many if not more creative
> and social processes as they do to destructive and anti-social
> manifestations.[92]

We hear in such pronouncements the echoes of Freud's cosmopolitanism and that of his followers. Glover was clear, as Bergler was not, about
the "countertransference" difficulties necessarily involved in discussing
homosexuality.[93] He finally concluded:

> It is indeed more than likely that the answer to this problem, if it
> be a problem, is in the development of greater tolerance amongst

the sections of the community which at present tend to make a scapegoat of homosexuality. In this sense the treatment of homosexuality as a whole should be directed as much at the "diseased" prejudices of society as at the "diseased" propensities of the individual homosexual. [94]

It is important to record that Glover advanced the most sophisticated and subtle argument for considering homosexuality a mental disturbance, yet he also spoke out most forthrightly and clearly for a range of adaptation within homosexuality that extended from the psychoses to the essentially "normal."

The psychoanalytic community did not publicly share these views, however, and when we look at publication during this period, we find that there is neither a widely agreed upon and coherent theory of homosexuality nor much original and incisive speculation on the subject. In fact, the only major shift was a tendency to "deinstinctualize" dynamic formulations and to see psychic mechanisms and results as the products of defensive operations rather than as the unfolding of constitutional factors. But the subject of homosexuality began to assume importance despite the lack of general agreement on the theory, and, among the most prominent analysts, important refinements in the theory began to be made and possibilities that had lain dormant for decades began again to be discussed. Two symposia were held by the American Psychoanalytic Association, one on perversion[95] and the other, six years later, on overt male homosexuality.[96] Another was held by the International Psychoanalytic Congress.[97] In addition, an important volume of articles on perversion appeared, growing out of the 1954 conference, which presented the most current psychoanalytic thought on the subject.[98] Finally, a survey article on overt male homosexuality appeared that reviewed psychoanalytic thought on the subject from Freud onward.[99]

Still, none of these presented a unified or coherent view of male homosexuality. Apart from their contempt for Kinsey's findings, participants in the three symposia could find little else to agree upon. In the first meeting, Devereux and Muensterberger presented relevant anthropological data, but it was not clear how such information should be used. Rado, as might be expected, urged a return to biology as the basis for psychoanalytic theory, but others disagreed. Participants were also divided·on whether to emphasize oral or oedipal material and on the importance of such familial events as conscious or unconscious parental seduction. Arlow, the compiler of the published report, thought, however, that three important themes emerged that all could assent to: the importance of aggression in the determination of homosexual object choice, the recourse to narcissistic object choice as a defense against aggression directed toward the libidinal object, and the resultant distorted object relations and damaged superego.[100]

A similar conceptual disarray characterized the second meeting, where the clash between proponents of oedipal dynamics and those of oral determinants was even sharper. Still, Socarides was able to list three factors that most participants could acknowledge: characteristic primitive defense mechanisms, the simultaneous fear of separation from the mother and the wish to rejoin her, and narcissistic object choice.[101] Wiedemann concluded his survey, which he originally presented at the second symposium, with an understated confession of theoretical failure:

> If we examine the literature with the aim of finding a typical picture of pregenital libidinal fixation in homosexuality, we will find that any disturbance or combination of disturbances of the libidinal development, be it oral, anal, or phallic, may become manifest in overt homosexuality. . . . The analytic literature does not disclose any single genetic or structural pattern that would apply to all or even a major part of cases of inversion.[102]

Lorand and Balint's collection is similarly mununified conceptually and even incoherent. The most discussed perversion in the volume is homosexuality, but there is no real connection between the theory of perversion, as discussed by Alexander, Balint, and Gillespie in introductory essays, and the specific theory of homosexuality and its therapy, as it appears in the articles that follow them.[103]

Some analysts maintained primary interest in oedipal dynamics. We have already noted Hamilton's derivation of homosexuality from the fear of incest[104] and Lewinsky's emphasis on oedipal rivalry and the prohibition of infantile sexual activity.[105] Flournoy likewise pointed to the conventional factors in the etiology of homosexuality: the attachment to the phallic mother, the identification with her, the complementary narcissistic choice of objects, the overvaluation of the penis and the fear of the castrating father.[106] Saul and Beck provided a neat overview of the various oedipal mechanisms and dynamics involved in homosexual object choice, although they noted an occasional oral trend in their case material. Their article, while offering few new ideas, was quite useful in proposing helpful distinctions, such as seeing male homosexuality as due to excessive sexual interest in men, as opposed to the lack of interest in women. In addition, it clearly distinguished between homosexuality as a defense and as a channel for certain kinds of gratification. In all cases, however, they assumed the pathological nature of the condition. Significantly, they affirmed the importance of constitutional bisexuality in the development of homosexual object choice, although they emphasized that this concept was psychological in nature and not necessarily biological. [107]

These, however, were old ideas. Edoardo Weiss and Loewenstein proposed important additions to the theory based on quite conventional classical approaches. Weiss suggested that certain homosexuals, out of a feeling of phallic deficiency, externalize their own narcissistic concerns onto an object with a penis. Hence, their own phallic erotism is transformed into homosexual object choice, and ego libido into narcissistic object libido. Such a "resonance identification" makes treatment especially difficult, since the renunciation of such object choice is experienced as castration. [108] Loewenstein, utilizing purely oedipal dynamics, emphasized the conflict between libidinal and aggressive striving during the Oedipus complex. Castration fear puts an end to genital striving, but only by increasing the urgency of masochistic trends and by causing a regression from phallic erotism to early stages, where masculinity and femininity are identified with inflicting suffering and suffering, respectively. In boys whose negative Oedipus complex is particularly strong, the homosexual attachment to the father is augmented by the attempt at "appeasing castration and surrendering incestuous wishes," while the identification with the mother is designed to seduce the sexually aggressive and threatening father. [109] Also working within a conventional psychoanalytic framework, D. Brown proposed a simple yet essential distinction between inversion and homosexuality, the former indicating an identification with the object of the opposite sex, the latter the choice of an object of the same sex. Such a distinction goes back to the earliest analytic theory of homosexuality, particularly Ferenczi's distinction between "subject" and "object" homoerotics, but for most of our history, the two categories were so conflated that Brown's article was thought to be an important original contribution. [110]

Another group espoused a more nearly oral approach to the problem of homosexual object choice. Bychowski continued to stress its preoedipal determinants and to draw connections between homosexuality and psychosis.[111] The homosexual object represents the externalization of the subject's own ego as well as parental imagoes that have not been adequately introjected. The resulting unstable ego structure is unable to bind instinctual energies and resorts instead to primitive forms of discharge.[112] In addition, the oral aggression directed at both the objects and the ego itself results in intense ambivalence toward parental introjects. Homosexual acts are attempts by the ego to master libidinal and aggressive impulses, but these maneuvers use such large amounts of instinctual energy that the ego is depleted and unable to engage in other high-level functions such as sublimation.[113]

Socarides adopted a similar approach, concentrating on the ego's attempts to master libidinal and aggressive impulses by primitive mechanisms of introjection and projection. The projection of oral aggression onto the depriving breasts results in a paranoid fear of persecution, which can be neutralized only by being fused with libido, just as the fantasy of a good breast can be maintained only by projective identification with a homosexual object. These mechanisms, however, result in splitting of both object and ego, the former into the idealized boy with the good breast, and the latter into two or more distinct ego states.[114] Eidelberg presented a case with similar dynamics, employing a strong oral fixation, an identification with the phallic mother, and an overwhelming rage against the breasts, which was neutralized by displacing it into men with penises and by then libidinizing the resulting anxiety.[115]

The orientation around the oral stage was even clearer in two articles that explicitly used Klein's formulations and derived homosexual object choice from fixation at the paranoid-schizoid position of infantile development. Thorner presented a case of a male homosexual who reassured himself against his terror of his mother's sinister insides by projecting onto damaged persecuting homosexual objects, whom he appeased by submitting to them passively. In addition, Thorner sought to derive his patient's relations to his objects and the very choice of object from these dynamics.[116] Rosenfeld, in a subtle and sophisticated article, explained homosexuality as a defense against paranoid anxiety, thus reversing Freud's formulation in the Schreber case. Rosenfeld's patient projected his depression and persecution onto the outer world, but they returned in the form of persecuting voices, which were appeased by the patient's idealizing and anally submitting to his objects. In all maneuvers, the importance of projective identification was emphasized. [117]

Several analysts attempted a reconciliation of sorts between oral and oedipal schools of thought. Lorand rather weakly suggested that the Oedipus complex was more important in the development of homosexual object choice, but that the oral phase was also significant. Lorand, however, allied with the theoreticians of the Oedipus complex, as can be seen in his claiming prior significance for the penis, which could be represented by the breast. [118] Such an interpretation set him at odds with theoreticians of the oral stage who conversely saw the penis as a substitute for the breast. Gillespie asserted the importance of the Oedipus complex, but acknowledged the significance of oral precursors, warning, however, against "the danger that the fascination of more recent discoveries may lead to the neglect of earlier, well-established findings":

> We are not dealing . . . either with defense against castration anxiety or defense against some earlier, pregenital danger situation—but rather with a specific modification of castration anxiety, determined in its form by earlier, pregenital, and especially oral developments. [119]

Bak made a sophisticated attempt at integrating the two views, proposing that perversions could be considered as the dominance of pregenitality resulting from a regression from phallic to prephallic stages and a consequent increase in aggression. This regression could be due to either constitutional or environmental factors, but the reaction to either depended upon the achieved stage of structural development and the level of object relations attained. In particular, psychosexual development was partly a question of differentiating between aggressive and libidinal drives. Since the Oedipus complex requires clear differentiation, the issue of whether perversions are primarily oedipal or preoedipal in origin can be determined by deciding whether sufficient differentiation has occurred to allow the Oedipus complex to operate. [120] Implicit in such a view, by the way, is the possibility of arranging the perversions in a series according to the extent to which libido and aggression have been differentiated, much as Glover had proposed earlier, with respect to the completeness of the object being defended against.

The most interesting attempts either to provide a coherent view or to establish a particular notion of the perversions in a theoretical context were made in three important articles originally presented at the 1955 panel on perversion held in Geneva by the International Psychoanalytic Association. In the first, Glauber dealt with the "teleological significance" of the rebirth motif in homosexuality. Deriving it from the failure to have emerged entirely from the mother-child symbiosis, Glauber attributed to homosexual object choice a severe distortion in identification that involved part-object identification with the phallus or breast of the phallic mother. The final, full identification is yearned for as a rebirth that is also felt as "cataclysmic," since the complementary part identifications are experienced as mutually annihilating. In these terms, homosexual "acting out" does not result in psychic change or real satisfaction, but only in a reduction of tension, achieved through the projection and magical reappropriation of ego fragments. [121]

In the second paper, Nacht and his colleagues attempted to find common structures and defenses of the ego in the perversions, which they defined as the need to maintain distance from the desired but feared object, so that the subject can both escape anxiety and experience orgasmic gratification. They emphasized the idea that, contrary to early psychoanalytic theory, the perversions are not simple survivals of component instincts of infantile sexuality, but highly elaborated and refracted instinctual impulses. The motivating anxiety is essentially oedipal, involving fear of castration by the father, or an identification with the phallic mother, or flight from her. Similarly, the conscious fantasy represents an elaboration of a sadomasochistic primal scene of parental sexual intercourse. They were unable to point to any structure or ego mechanism common to all the perversions, except for the eroticization of the defense mechanisms themselves, although they insisted, in the case of homosexuality, on the incapacity for love or for enduring love relationships. [122]

The most impressive and thoughtful article of the three was Gillespie's, which, while providing a historical sketch of the psychoanalytic theory of the perversions, offered a way of reconciling the oral and the oedipal viewpoints. In Freud's early works, the perversions represented the survival of infantile component instincts at the expense of adult genital striving. As Gillespie correctly pointed out, such a view does not allow for further explanation and consequently supports a "gloomy" prognostic outlook. In his later works, however, Freud began to see the perversions as defensive maneuvers, but it remained for Sachs to articulate a coherent oedipal etiology for them. Sachs emphasized the refraction of the component instincts through the Oedipus complex, whereby they underwent elaboration and refinement, so that they would become capable of oedipal cathexes. They survived by retaining only one element to which sexual pleasure now attached itself. This element escaped repression and aided the ego in repressing other elements of infantile sexuality. But even for Sachs, the selection of the element that would survive depended on the particular constitutional sexuality.[123] Gillespie found this explanation coherent as far as it went, but it ignored the contributions of the superego, which Gillespie claimed was responsible for selecting the element that would survive. Thus "the perversion . . . preserves a modicum of sexual outlet and pleasure whilst at the same time it avoids the unpleasure of anxiety and guilt feelings that would otherwise arise." In addition, Sachs's theory ignored the importance of the oral period, which had later been convincingly demonstrated by Klein, Nunberg, Glover, and, most of all, Jones in his paper on the phallic phase. According to Jones, with the onset of the phallic phase during the Oedipus complex, the mother becomes for the first time the object of active phallic sadism, due to both a fear of losing the offending organ and an identification with the castrated mother.[124] Thus, Gillespie concluded, perversions could finally be considered as caused by fear of castration at the oedipal level, which in turn was due to sadistic components of oral origin.[125]

Still, although the general theory of perversion had evolved into a more satisfactory state, the specific theory of homosexuality remained relatively incoherent and the subject of much disagreement. There did not even develop a generally accepted definition of sexual perversion or a clear rationale for considering homosexuality a form of that disorder. The lack of an integral and coherent theory revealed itself in the essays that form an introduction to Lorand and Balint's volume on the perversions.[126] There, Gillespie observed that perversion could be defined only against a standard of normal sexuality, and thus defined it as "any way of sexual life which interferes with the procreative function." He admitted that such a biological standard ignored "the psychological relation to the sexual object," but was unable to incorporate a normative psychological relation into his definition. Instead he resorted to Sachs's "Zur Genese der Perversionen," which described the survival of certain component instincts by their being incorporated into the ego and their aiding the repression of other component instincts. This idea, however, did not provide a rationale for considering homosexuality a perversion, since it is not apparent which partial instinct has gone unrepressed in the case of overt homosexuality, nor what limitations corresponding object relations must necessarily suffer. [127]

Bak, in his essay, saw the problem clearly. The perversions involved the dominance in sexual life of a pregenital drive, but in some kinds of homosexuality, "highly developed object relations" were involved. He finally adduced narcissism, a heightened castration complex, an intense attachment to the mother leading to an identification with her, and a reaction-formed or libidinized aggressive rivalry as the determining characteristics of homosexual perversion. [128] Alexander focused on the inability of the pervert to sublimate pregenital forms of nonreproductive sexuality. Any impulse carried out for its own sake "assumes an erotic or sexual connotation," and, conversely, when it is assimilated into a more integrated "goal structure," it loses its erotic quality. The presence, then, of unsublimated forms of instinctual drives distinguished the perversions. It remained to be demonstrated, however, that they could invariably be found in all forms of overt homosexuality. [129]

Balint established three classes of perversion, all of which he found "inexact and misleading." The first was sexual activity not pursued in order to propagate the species, but this standard was clearly insufficient and tautological. The second, which stipulated the survival of infantile forms of sexual gratification, "unfortunately" did not include forms of homosexuality that clearly were "not survivals of infantile forms of sexuality but later developments." The third, requiring the "lack of proper love for a human object," was similarly unsatisfactory since in homosexuality "we may find practically the whole scale of love and hatred that is exemplified in heterosexuality." He finally established six categories of sexual perversion: homosexuality, sadomasochism, surviving component instincts, the replacement of a human object by an inanimate one, bestiality, and the near-psychotic forms of necrophilia and pedophilia. In other words, the only way Balint could establish homosexuality as a form of sexual perversion was to define it tautologically as one of his six categories. He admitted, however, that homosexual object choice can be "as rich and diversified as . . . heterosexual[ity]," but still insisted that the homosexual's claim of contentment with his condition was a sign of his "overpretense and denial." [130]

Nacht, Diatkine, and Favreau arrived at a similar tautology in their article on perversion at the nineteenth International Psychoanalytic Conference, held in Geneva in 1955. They too established three categories of perversions—sadomasochism, "overt homosexuality," and others involving a flight from object relations felt to be dangerous—but they too could offer no theoretical reason for including the second category, except that it took the place of a normative heterosexuality. While admitting the lack of adequate clinical material on satisfied homosexuals, they nevertheless offered the same tired stereotypes and common opinions:

> There prevails in homosexual circles a special atmosphere of unfaithfulness, jealousy, multiple sexual frivolity and procuring, which show how the best adapted homosexuals rarely find a satisfying object, which again stresses the precariousness of homosexual ties.

They concluded that the ego of homosexuals was similar to that of other perverts in one major respect: "Incapacity to love is of course a common characteristic of all the patients we have observed, which confirms, if it be necessary, the immaturity of their personality."[131]

These theoretical essays, intended to provide a conceptual framework for a discussion of the etiology and treatment of the perversions, failed to justify including homosexuality in that category of disorder. Le Coultre maintained that the distinguishing characteristic of the perversions was the absence of guilt, thus reverting back to Rank's idea that sadism was the prototype of all the perversions since it excluded guilt,[132] but in doing so he was faced with the same perplexing heterogeneity in homosexuality.[133] This attention to the absence of guilt seems to have been fairly widespread. Eissler, for example, remarked on the difficulty of using traditional analytic technique with perverts instead of neurotic patients. The pervert's deviation was "ego-syntonic," and in order for treatment even to begin, he urged the analyst to labor to "create a conflict between [the pervert] and his urge for sexual gratification through his perversion."[134] In any case, the discussion of homosexuality that followed these preliminary essays did not adhere to their stipulations. Freeman showed at length that even his sample of three homosexual patients failed to fulfill the psychoanalytic requirement of disturbed object relations or structural damage to the psyche, since one of them, Mr. Y., "approximates to what may be termed a 'normal' ego."[135]

It seems odd that analysts were not willing to omit some varieties of homosexuality from the category of the perversions in order to maintain the integrity of the theory. Most striking was Balint, whose five categories of perversions fitted nicely into the current theory, but who nevertheless felt compelled to add the sixth tautological category of the various forms of homosexuality with no theoretical justification whatever and in a way that contradicted clinical experience.

This period can be characterized as searching for a coherent theory of the perversions, a need made more pressing by the important insights achieved in the previous period and by contemporary theoretical refinement. In fact, the only important development in the theory of perversions was the trend to deinstinctualize the determinants of deviant sexual behavior. In general, it took the form of denying a constitutional basis for many etiological factors—the negative Oedipus complex, narcissism, bisexuality, and identification with the mother—and of seeing them instead as defensive maneuvers. In particular, and most significant for our history, it sought to deny the sexual nature of some forms of homosexuality itself.

In the first thirty years of the psychoanalytic movement, psychosexual development was conceived of as the unfolding and mutual interaction of certain innate potentialities. Environmental events were, of course, important, but an etiological explanation was felt to have been achieved only when a certain behavior could be related to "constitutional" factors. In the case of homosexuality, although familial and environmental factors were adduced, Freud felt that constitutional factors were by far more determinative of later object choice:

> The decision about the final sexual behavior falls after puberty
> and is the result of an as yet unknown series of factors which are
> partly constitutional and partly accidental in nature. . . . The
> narcissistic object choice and the fixation of the erotic significance
> of the anal zone appear as their most essential (constitutional)
> characteristics.[136]

And in the same essay, Freud pointed to "the congenital differences in the sexual constitution, to which probably falls the main importance." Although various "accidental factors" could account for later homosexual object choice, none of them was specific to or determinative of homosexuality. The reason why one child's sexual nature was affected by a particular set of events in the family and another's was not finally reduced to an issue of constitution and innate predisposition.

Three factors seemed to be most crucial: the lingering significance of the anal erotic zone, a tendency toward narcissistic object choice, and a reservoir of constitutional bisexuality. These factors could result in three psychic mechanisms: the predominance of the negative or "inverted" Oedipus complex, the identification with the mother, and a tendency toward homosexual choice of objects. Such notions continued to be employed throughout our history to describe the etiology and dynamics of homosexuality, but by the fifties, these notions began to be conceived of not as constitutional but as developmental, defensive maneuvers. The tendency to identify narcissistically with a libidinal object was no longer seen as a preexperiential predisposition, but as a defensive strategy used to preserve the object from aggression. Bak emphasized the inability of certain children to neutralize aggression toward the oedipal object, which could then be preserved only by identifying with it.[137] And in a later paper, he derived the negative Oedipus complex from the undermining of the phallic phase by prephallic destructive impulses directed toward the object. Since the positive Oedipus complex could thus never fully effloresce, its subsidiary, negative form predominated.[138] In a similar manner, Loewenstein saw the passive sexual attitude toward the father not as constitutionally determined, but as functioning to appease the castrator by seducing him.[139] These ideas were repeated by individual writers and were agreed upon as summary conclusions of the symposia to which we have already referred. On the other hand, Devereux proposed a further refinement of the notion of the negative Oedipus complex, the so-called Laius complex, named after the father of the mythical hero, which involves the striving for a homosexual triumph over a feminized father.[140] Devereux seems to have been a somewhat peripheral member of psychoanalytic circles, however, contributing a kind of cosmopolitan anthropological cachet to symposia and the like. The notion of the Laius complex never took hold, and no one, as far as I know, refers to it.

The issue of constitutional homosexuality divided psychoanalytic opinion even more clearly. We have seen how central a notion constitutional bisexuality was for Freud and how by the forties a reaction had set in against seeing bisexuality as an innate proclivity. In certain ways, the concept provides a convenient touchstone to distinguish analysts of a classical orientation from those of a more contemporary bent. Thus, Edoardo Weiss continued to affirm its centrality to psychoanalytic thinking.[141] And the notion of a universal inclination to homosexual object choice continued to be a commonplace in, for example, the psychology of adolescence[142] or in psychoanalytic anthropology.[143]

Others, however, denied its relevance or even its very existence. Kardiner was the most vocal, praising Rado's "significant contribution" in showing bisexuality to possess "no value" in psychoanalytic discourse. For him, the "enormous" increase in the prevalence of homosexuality in contemporary society was not primarily a biological or psychological phenomenon, but "a symptom that the society is not functioning properly." Specifically, homosexuality represented a retreat from the onerous demands of competitive masculinity and heroic heterosexual activity. Adducing the importance of dominant mothers and weak fathers in the etiology of homosexual object choice, and the consequent "belittlement" of maleness, Kardiner saw homosexuality not primarily as a sexual phenomenon, but as one involving modern social roles and conditions, the dislocation of familial values, and the consequent need "to relax from the high demands of masculinity."[144]

Kardiner found a theoretical foundation for his views in the work of Ovesey, who, employing "adaptational analysis," promulgated the notion of "pseudohomosexuality." Ovesey began his influential article on homosexual conflict by reviewing Freud's conception of homosexuality, which emphasized constitutional issues and saw homosexuality as a phase of normal psychosexual development. But approving Rado's article, Ovesey bemoaned Freud's neglect of "the crucial role of societal forces" and sought to derive homosexual object choice from the interaction of "the needs of the individual and the societal demands." Ovesey proposed that homosexuality, rather than being an irreducible instinct in its own right, really occurs when heterosexual function is inhibited through "fear" and displaced onto a "safer" object. The central issue in such a mechanism is not sex, but competence. The series of transformations from incompetence to apparent homosexuality is as follows: "*I am a failure = I am castrated = I am not a man = I am a woman = I am a homosexual.*" Furthermore, the sense of masculine failure can relate to three kinds of goals: sexuality, dependence, and power. But a failure in the last two is not sexual at all. These, Ovesey urged, should be considered "pseudohomosexual" issues. It was important to maintain this distinction, since interpreting an issue of power or dependency to a patient in terms of constitutional bisexuality could be "catastrophic."[145]

These views were illustrated the following year in a case in which the patient used homosexual acts to symbolize failures in other realms. Ovesey told the patient "flatly" that he was not homosexual, and the patient was cured without Ovesey's ever having observed "a true homosexual motivation."[146] Several years later, in cooperation with Karush, Ovesey further elaborated these views and showed how homosexual fear in men can stem from dependency needs. In the transference, the wish to incorporate the therapist's penis orally is really a wish to appropriate his omnipotence and not so much a desire to indulge in homosexual gratification.[147] Finally, Kardiner, Karush, and Ovesey spelled out the implications of this point of view. They rejected Freud's biological basis for bisexuality as "tautological" and insisted that notions of masculinity and femininity are really "adaptational responses to the environment." Homosexuality occurs because infantile sexuality was "intimidated" through discipline or threats of castration or annihilation. The child withdraws from heterosexuality and chooses a "safer" homosexual object. They concluded that sexual orientation is a function of "the integration of assertion [and] mirrors the extent of childhood intimidation, not ancestral inheritance of a bisexual disposition."[148]

The emergence of these ideas in the 1950s marks an important shift. Related to the "holistic" psychology of the Horneyans and to the "interpersonal" school of psychoanalysis, these writers attempted to make psychoanalysis more relevent and responsive to modern social conditions. But to do so, they denied the biological basis of psychoanalysis, and one result of such a strategy, as Marcuse demonstrated,[149] was, paradoxically, to have psychoanalysis engulfed by the very society it was to have criticized and from which it was to have maintained a distance. For Kardiner, Karush, and Ovesey, homosexuality was not simply a disorder, but the sexual manifestation of a nonsexual conflict. Having thus denied the sexual basis of that orientation, they could now accuse homosexuals themselves of "sexualizing" their social problems. Arieti, discussing Gershman's paper, of which he entirely approved, made exactly this point:

> Many homosexuals see everything in an aura of sexuality. Every action is either masculine or feminine. For the male homosexual

to take the initiative, to be assertive, to complete a task, to be competitive, to fight—all are masculine characteristics. To do the opposite—to be feminine.[150]

Let us recall that it was Freud himself who argued for such equations, though he also warned that they were "clearly insufficient, empirical and conventional"[151]:

What we speak of in ordinary life as "masculine" or "feminine" reduced itself from the view of psychology to the qualities of "activity" and "passivity"—that is, to qualities determined not by the instincts themselves but by their aims.[152]

Behind the decision of "adaptational" analysts to desexualize and deinstinctualize homosexuality was neither a long intellectual tradition nor even a compelling body of clinical experience, but a lingering reluctance to consider the possibility that normative notions of psychosexual development did not correspond to the lives of real human beings. And behind that lurked personal fears and defenses that are not revealed in published articles. It is, of course, socially inconvenient that such heterogeneity should exist, and in much of the psychoanalytic "alarm" at the reports of the high prevalence of homosexuality and in their outrage at Kinsey's claims, we may observe a longing for orderly and conventional social values and even, perhaps, for an avoidance of the irreducible conflict between heterosexuality and homosexuality, which, according to Freud, was the last impediment in men to a completed analysis.[153] It is not at all clear why telling a patient that he is in conflict over his love for another man should be "catastrophic," while telling him that he wishes to be dependent upon him or to subjugate and humiliate him should not. One suspects that such a judgment depends more on the analyst's own values, fear, and countertransference than it does on the patient's supposed horror at discovering that he has sexual feelings for a member of his own sex. Recall the "several dozen" analysts participating in Kinsey's study who claimed to have had no experience whatever of homosexual arousal in their lives.[154] Serota, in the 1960 symposium on homosexuality, urged all analysts to be clear even before they meet their patients that homosexuality is the result of conflict and that a heterosexual solution is both possible and desirable, no matter what the patient claims.[155] By this point, we are no longer dealing with a system of free scientific inquiry, but with a closed, propagandistic set of social norms. If psychoanalysis were composed solely of such ideologues, there would be little new to learn. Luckily, many continued to learn from their patients and to readjust their ideas. Faergemann's study of menstruation fantasies in men[156] and Muensterberger's anthropological compilation[157] are such attempts, as is Fain and Marty's difficult, subtle, and provocative paper on the homosexual transference as a "synthetic function."[158]

Although this period witnessed a marked constriction in the range of its discourse and can boast of few important achievements with respect to the problem of homosexuality, we may nevertheless detect the beginnings of a more open approach. For the first time since the twenties, analysts began to publish accounts of homosexuals who were essentially "normal" and "healthy" despite their deviant choice of objects. Glover had long insisted on this point: "Amongst the more discreet homosexuals the total function of the ego will be found to stand comparison with that of so-called 'normal' persons."[159] And Fine had similarly stressed the wide range of functioning among homosexuals: "Several were on the verge of psychosis, while others had made excellent social adjustments."[160] But only Freeman published a somewhat detailed account of a homosexual in analysis, Mr. Y., who "approximates to what may be termed a 'normal' ego." He concluded his article by observing that "it is equally possible, as has been seen, for homosexuality to occur in the presence of a relatively intact ego."[161]

The reader will notice how qualified such claims are. Why such circumspection seemed to be necessary or why analysts did not accept such clinical findings as suggesting important additions to the theory is not revealed in the published writing of the period. But it is instructive to look at more informal exchanges of ideas. In the 1960 symposium on overt male homosexuality, Edoardo Weiss raised the question of the "healthy homosexual" who does not "reveal unrealistic immature traits or neurotic symptoms." Bychowski, who read his paper, "The Ego and Object of the Homosexual," at that meeting, was clear in his view, which was paraphrased by the reporter, Socarides:

There seem to be certain well-integrated productive individuals who although intensely homosexual seem to be capable of pro-

longed "love" relationships rather than pursuing momentary gratification. A study of such individuals might lead to a revision of
our concepts of male homosexuality.[162]

The reader can appreciate how important such a study would in fact
have been. But Bychowski himself seems to have backed off from the
implications of his speculation. In the published version of his paper, he
admitted only that such stable homosexual relations differed little "on
the surface" from "the so-called normal heterosexual situation," and
immediately plunged into a consideration of "clinical observations,"
which he consistently applied to "the homosexual."[163] The existence of
a group of "well-integrated" homosexuals thus hovered as a possibility at
the fringes of analytic discourse, but few thought them worth studying
or presenting.

CHAPTER VIII

THEORETICAL OVERVIEW II

From around 1930 to 1962, two ideas about homosexuality developed that radically diverged from their formulations in the earlier period. They are simple to state, but the reasons for their genesis are more knotted and convoluted. In contradistinction to the previous notion that psychosexual development following the operations of the Oedipus complex could result in several alternative outcomes, the later period assumed that psychosexual development, if it was not blocked, stunted, or displaced, would inevitably result in heterosexual object choice. Any other result had to be thought of as a perversion. Hence the second idea: homosexuality was a perversion and not a separate nosologic entity or part of the whole series of psychic organizations, as Freud had thought, and as many analysts such as Glover continued to think. Behind the emergence of these two ideas was the interest in preoedipal development, a shift in understanding of the idea of narcissism, and a new conceptualization of the perversions. But far more important was the conceptual confusion regarding the theory of male homosexuality I pointed to in my last chapter, which was due to the grafting of new ideas and viewpoints onto the classic core of psychoanalytic ideas, without much attention having been paid to how coherent that grafting was. Several ideas that arose out of it were, in fact, internally inconsistent.

The broadest shift in psychoanalytic thinking in our history so far was the general displacement of interest from the phallic stage around the Oedipus complex to the earlier anal and especially oral stages. As we have several times observed, for Freud psychoanalysis was primarily the analysis of the Oedipus complex, the mechanism of momentous psychosexual developments. But, paradoxically, just because of its focal

161

importance in such developments, it only partially determined postoe-dipal results. The other great determinant was preoedipal psychic orga-nization, which in certain important ways was thought not susceptible to change through psychoanalytic treatment in the way that oedipal developments were. Thus, it was conceived of in early psychoanalytic theory as relatively immutable, the sum total of what Freud referred to as the individual's "constitutional disposition," sharing certain charac-teristics with the individual's biological endowment, both temperamen-tally and anatomically.

But if homosexual object choice can be shown to have developed as a result of a preoedipal "constitutional" psychic organization, it would be unanalyzable. Hence Freud's pessimistic prognosis. Constitutional factors favoring the development of homosexual object choice include a predisposition to narcissistic (as opposed to anaclitic) object choices, a related tendency to identify with libidinal objects, an overvaluation of the penis, an unusually strong or long-enduring anal erotism, and a large passive component of constitutional bisexuality. Particular config-urations of these factors determine the outcome of the Oedipus com-plex. The complex transforms them, but the form of the final outcome results, at least partially, from the preexisting condition on which the complex operates.

In these terms, it is at least theoretically possible that heterosexual and homosexual results of the complex are alternative and equivalent, be-cause the complex utterly transforms preoedipal psychic organization and reverses the direction of certain psychic tendencies. All results of the complex, no matter how statistically normative, are the neurotic and conflicted result of trauma, and the phallic substage that occurs as the complex is passed through, the so-called deuterophallic stage, is a "neurotic compromise formation."[1] Consequently, homosexual object choice cannot be distinguished from its heterosexual equivalent on the basis of its being a thwarting or distortion of "normal" psychosexual development. At times Freud thought that homosexuality was an alter-native outcome of the Oedipus complex equivalent to the heterosexual variety, at times not; sometimes that homosexuality was treatable through psychoanalysis, sometimes not. This richness or equivocation can be observed in the several theories for the etiology of homosexual object choice that Freud proposed at various times in his career, as I indicated in my first chapter. Related to all this is the crucial issue of whether homosexual object choice represents a single nosologic entity or a feature of several entities. Freud seems to have espoused the latter view, but he never discussed the issue systematically or at length.

As psychoanalysis became more sophisticated in theory, and as it collected more detailed clinical experience, it began to resolve prematurely the ambiguity characterizing some of Freud's ideas. In particular, it grounded itself in the conviction that there was a "natural" result of the Oedipus complex and that psychosexual development moved toward an implicit telos in adult genital heterosexuality. But while it took this important step, without, by the way, offering any justification for doing so, it also clung to certain of Freud's formulations that were posited implicitly on the opposite view of psychosexual development. No one seems to have recognized this at the time, but we can now see its results in certain incoherences and contradictions in the theory of sexual deviance.

There are in Freud three distinct classes of explanations for the development of homosexual object choice. The least complex specifies love of father- or brother-substitutes as the result of reaction-formed feelings of murderous rivalry for the attention of the mother. This is clearly an oedipal matter. Strictly speaking, this form of homosexuality cannot be considered a perversion, since it does not involve the survival of preoedipal homosexual trends, an identification with the mother, or a fear and loathing of female genitalia.[2] This form is both the least pathological and the most susceptible to treatment by psychoanalysis. It is, however, not clear whether it should be treated, since apart from the denial of heterosexual genital functioning, it does not, according to Freud, involve any other necessary limitation of psychic functioning, such as the avoidance of women or the denial of sexual differences, and its defensive style involves such high-level mechanisms as reaction formation and sublimation. And even these mechanisms act not on erotic impulses, but on aggressive ones.

The other two classes, however, are more equivocal. The first is associated with Freud's early thought on sexual aberration and finds its most complete expression in the *Three Essays*.[3] There Freud saw all the perversions as the survival of a portion of infantile sexuality at the expense of the full development of mature genital striving. This line of thought was developed and elaborated by Sachs in his enormously important paper, "Zur Genese der Perversionen,"[4] in which he argued that one component of infantile sexuality survives the repression that sets in at the Oedipus complex and draws to it all the sexual pleasure that originally accrued to the infant's entire sexual nature. It enters the service of the newly formed ego, which it then aids in repressing other aspects of that infantile sexuality. But the proper fate of all such components is repression and sublimation, and their survival implies a structurally defective superego and an impaired capacity for ego-building defense mechanisms.

Yet even this view, for all its clarity and coherence, contains several ambiguities and inconsistencies. It is not at all clear, for example, whether homosexuality should be considered a perversion in these terms. Freud seemed to acknowledge this difficulty when he almost consistently distinguished between perversion and inversion, or homosexuality. In particular, he recognized that at least some forms of homosexuality represented genuine oedipal-level genital organizations and not the survival of some component of infantile sexuality. The quality of sexual and affective experience associated with many forms of homosexual love was simply too refined and differentiated to correspond to infantile pleasure-seeking. In addition, some types of adult homosexuality were obviously types of alloerotism with their own external objects and unified component instincts. They were, therefore, essentially oedipal in nature. If homosexuality, then, represented a form of oedipal genital sexuality, it should not and indeed could not serve as the material for sublimation. Fenichel, in an important addition to the theory of perversions, pointed out that only pregenital part-instincts could be so sublimated:

> It is highly improbable that a sublimation of adult genital sexuality exists: the genitals represent an apparatus for the achievement of full—that is, unsublimated—orgastic discharge. Pregenital strivings are the object of sublimation.[5]

As soon as one recognizes that some forms of homosexuality operate at the oedipal level, one can no longer require that they be sublimated. According to Fenichel, they are not capable of such a process. Thus, the traditional theory of these forms of homosexuality does not provide a coherent reason for considering them perversions or emotional disturbances, nor does it, *a fortiori*, specify why they should be treated and cured.

The issue, however, is more difficult with respect to the third class of etiological theories, which treat homosexuality as the result of a defensive regression from oedipal dynamics to more primitive psychosexual organizations. Expressed most clearly in the monograph on Leonardo da Vinci[6] and the essay on the beating fantasy,[7] this view emphasizes the relinquishing of a prime heterosexual stance under the onslaught of castration anxiety through regression to an earlier fixation point, most commonly at the anal stage, where the anal zone reassumes dominance, and the child, in order to preserve the erotic tie to the mother, identifies with her and narcissistically chooses objects resembling himself. Freud did not clearly elucidate how such an etiology differed from the others, but implicit in this view is the notion that the Oedipus complex, instead of being determined by preoedipal psychosexual organizations, is itself the cause of these "constitutional" factors. In other words, such factors as narcissism, a pronounced anal erotism, and the tendency toward identification and narcissistic (as opposed to anaclitic) object choices are defensive secondary maneuvers.

The last two classes of etiologies are mutually compatible, as I argued in Chapter IV, but exactly how they fit together was never articulated in the early period. Instead, as psychoanalytic theory progressed, the etiologies that regarded any but the normative heterosexual variety of object choice as a defensive regression came to represent the psychoanalytic consensus. In these terms, homosexuality represented a libidinal outcome "less dangerous" than normative heterosexuality. Thus, there were four possible fates for infantile incest: a "refraction," which led to normative heterosexuality; a "repression," which led to neurosis; a "displacement" of object onto an inanimate object, which led to most perversions; and a similar "displacement" onto a same-sex object, which led to homosexuality.

This last view assumed prominence through positing an outcome of heterosexual object choice for the Oedipus complex. Freud himself did not believe that psychosexual development and outcome were self-apparent, and he was as puzzled by the normative result as he was by its aberrant varieties: "In the psychoanalytic sense the exclusive interest of the man for the woman is also a problem requiring an explanation, and is not something that is self-evident."[8] This open-mindedness provides, perhaps, the greatest contrast to the self-assuredness of later analysts who were sure about what Nature intended as the outcome of psychosexual development. Feldman, for example, roundly declared that "heterosexuality is an anatomically inborn and inevitable fate for both sexes." Claiming erroneously that all children start out as heterosexuals, he sententiously concluded

> that man is born for woman and woman is born for man. Anything else in the picture means only that, once upon a time, a trouble arose which diverted the individual from his normal path in life.[9]

Kardiner was similarly confident when he ended an article by quoting the last lines of the second part of *Faust*, "The eternal feminine draws us on."[10]

But resorting to lame and Philistine rhetoric is an abrogation of scientific responsibility. In addition, these ideas fly in the face of the simple observable fact that at least half the race—little girls—start out in life as functional homosexuals, a fact that provoked Freud into elaborating his early notions of the Oedipus complex and the psychological consequences of anatomical differences.[11] Moreover, whatever real relationship little girls have to their mothers during infancy, the theory on which such analysts as Feldman and Kardiner based their conclusions posits the infantile assumption that all people, men and women, possess a "phallus." Thus all children, before the discovery of genital differences, are psychically male homosexuals.[12] It is precisely because of this infantile homosexuality that the Oedipus complex assumes such importance, since one of its functions can be to transform it into heterosexuality for both boys and girls.

Another important shift in attitude involves the very nature of infantile sexuality. Several attempts have been made since the early days of psychoanalysis to deny the importance or even the existence of infantile homosexuality, but the resulting debate has been inconclusive, and it remains for analysts to choose what they wish to believe. Nonetheless, to deny the existence of constitutional bisexuality has several important implications. First, the notion of how the Oedipus complex operates changes radically. Instead of being a mechanism of trauma, transforming instinctual trends and sometimes reversing their direction, it becomes an instrument of focus and consolidation, ensuring a smooth and continuous transition from preoedipal to oedipal phases and the endurance of preoedipal trends. But while this view retains the skeleton of Freudian metapsychology, the emphasis on instinct and "dynamic" thrust has been enervated. Thus, we see in quite theoretical terms an instance of the general softening of radical psychoanalysis observed by Marcuse to have taken place in the 1950s.

Second, this mollified revisionist position leads to another contradiction. If constitutional homosexuality does not exist, even in the infantile period, then homosexuality cannot be considered a perversion in the classic sense. For all the subtle elaborations of Freud's basic notions by Sachs and Gillespie, perversions essentially still represented for psychoanalysis the survival of a component of infantile sexuality. If, however, there is nothing in infantile sexuality corresponding to an irreducible homosexual component, it is not possible to claim that adult homosexuality represents a survival of such a component. It might represent a disturbance in psychosexual development, but it cannot, strictly speaking, be a perversion. Instead, it would have to be a product of oedipal mechanisms.

Third, if homosexual object choice is an oedipal development, existing at the phallic stage at the least, it cannot be sublimated, as several analysts required. The persistence of homosexual object choice, therefore, cannot be taken as evidence that the patient is incapable of sublimation, because the requirement that homosexual impulses be sublimated and desexualized can be maintained only if they are pregenital. This contradiction, resulting from grafting an oral psychoanalysis upon an oedipal basis, informs, for example, some of the confusions in Alexander's article on the perversions.[13]

Fourth, it is implicit in this view that the Oedipus complex is traumatic only when it has aberrant outcomes. But since, according to these analysts, there is nothing in preoedipal organization to determine such a result, the forces causing disturbance have to be found in the child's psychological environment. Here again, we see a turning away from intrapsychic dynamics to social and interpersonal factors, as in the family orientation of the work of Kolb and Johnson[14] and Lewinsky,[15] as well as in the larger shift in emphasis seen in the work of Sullivan.[16]

Another extremely important shift in theoretical orientation involved seeing constitutional "causes"—narcissism or a strong homosexual component—as "results" of other processes, which could be either preoedipal or oedipal, but which resulted from a regression to preoedipal organization. This reversal of the direction of causality can be observed in several crucial psychoanalytic concepts. For example, we saw in Chapter IV how early analysts saw the final outcome of the

Oedipus complex as partly determined by the relative predominance of constitutional narcissism. Constitutional narcissism and constitutional bisexuality acted through the Oedipus complex to result in a final homosexual stance. With the interest in preoedipal psychic and libidinal organization, however, this causality could be read backward, although many analysts adhered to the traditional point of view. It was the Oedipus complex, acting under the pressure of interpersonal conflict, as well as under the intrapsychic pressure of aggression, that caused such psychic configurations as narcissism or homosexual object choice. The tendency toward a narcissistic choice of objects was no longer seen as the fulfillment of a constitutional predisposition, but as a defensive maneuver that ensured the integrity of the libidinal object against the subject's oral aggression, as did identification with the lost libidinal object. Such configurations as the negative Oedipus complex were also seen not as alternative mechanisms but as defensive and derivative.

This view also allowed for an even more decisive departure from classic Freudian ideas—the attempt to desexualize psychic dynamics. We may see this in the general emphasis on aggression at the expense of libido from 1930 to the 1960s, and in the notion of "pseudohomosexuality." In fact, the entire reaction against Freud's postulate of a universal bisexuality from Rado onward was possible only through a conceptual narrowing of Freud's notion. Rado denied the existence of biological bisexuality, and Ovesey insisted on drives other than aggressive and sexual ones, because they conceived of bisexuality as the concurrence of homosexual and heterosexual object choices. But for Freud, this was only one of the manifestations of bisexuality. Essentially the concept meant for him the simultaneous occurrence of active and passive sexual aims, which might be applied to any of the goals Ovesey thought were nonsexual in nature. [17]

A similar conceptual narrowing can be observed in the new understanding of narcissism. I discussed in Chapter IV how ambiguous this concept was in Freud. It referred to a stage of psychosexual development midway between autoerotism and object-relatedness, in which the object of the drives is the ego or the body of the subject. It also referred to a mode of object selection wherein objects are chosen on the basis of their resemblance to the self. Starting around 1930, however, these two senses of the term *narcissism* were conflated in the psychoanalytic discourse concerning male homosexuality. It began to be claimed that homosexuality, because of its narcissistic object choices, necessarily had a more primitive erotic organization than heterosexuality, and that it involved a defective superego.[18] But this is based on a confused understanding of what *narcissism* and *narcissistic object choice* mean. For Freud, narcissistic object choice was ubiquitous and especially characteristic of female sexuality. But many later analysts, as we have seen, came to consider it as a pathological defensive and regressive mode of object relations inferior to the anaclitic mode. Hence, for them, homosexuality, because of its close affinities with narcissism, was necessarily a more primitive sexual orientation than heterosexuality.

Yet another change was the widespread analytic notion that homosexuals necessarily have defective superegos, an idea expressly denied by Freud on many occasions. By the 1960s, however, this had become a cliché in certain psychoanalytic circles. The earliest expression of the idea seems to have been that of Benedek, who, elaborating ideas formulated by Jones, claimed that homosexuals introject the figure of the mother instead of the father into their superegos, and that the development of this structure is therefore "premature."[19] Such a notion represents a conclusion drawn from three earlier assertions: first, that the development of a superego requires a departure from narcissism,[20] an idea that is erroneous, since the superego requires great amounts of narcissism for its functioning; second, that "the road to homosexuality passes through narcissism"[21]; and, third, that the introjection of the mother into the superego predisposes to homosexuality. Jones formulated this third idea first, but he made no claims about the appropriateness of introjecting either parent. For him, the nucleus of the emerging superego was the image of the forbidding parent,[22] an idea echoed by Fenichel, who observed that the superego is formed out of the image of the parent who provided the "most impressive frustration."[23]

All these early theorists agreed on the irreducible nature of the negative Oedipus complex, in which the father is the primary object and the mother the more "impressive" prohibitor of libidinal striving. For a child whose negative Oedipus complex is more dominant than its positive form, the superego necessarily coalesces around the introjected image of the mother. But it is not this introjection that causes homosexuality, but a preexisting negative Oedipus complex, which itself determines both the kind of introjection and later object choice. This is the view of such sophisticated theorists as Glover, who also noted the correspondence of a maternal superego and homosexual object choice, but who offered no judgment on its supposedly defective character.[24] So the notion that a superego crystallized around the introjected image of the mother is necessarily defective follows from seeing the Oedipus complex only in its simplified positive form, wherein the mother serves only as libidinal object. In the case of the full fourfold Oedipus complex, on the other hand, the image of the mother as prohibitor of incestuous striving for the father can also serve as a satisfactory nucleus for a well-structured superego.

We may see that it is the very maternal nature of the superego that allows the possibility of a homosexual object choice that is ego-syntonic, orgasmic, and, most important, not perverse. Narcissistic object choices predispose to identifications with objects, which, because they are truly external, become the introjects out of which the superego will form. In these terms, some homosexual object choices are quite tolerable to the ego, which must mediate the demands of a maternal superego, which differ from those emanating from a statistically more common paternal superego. Several analysts have adduced the absence of guilt as a sign of the perverse nature of homosexuality, but this misses the critical theoretical point. Homosexual striving that operates under a maternal superego is guiltless not because a portion of guilt-provoking infantile sexuality has evaded repression, but because postoedipal homosexual striving is perfectly compatible with the subject's psychic structure as a whole, including its sexual identification and its superego.

In conclusion, the classic theory of sexual perversion as articulated by Freud and Sachs cannot be used to justify including all forms of homosexuality among the perversions. It does allow us to place certain forms of homosexual object choice there, but only those varieties in which a portion of infantile sexuality survives—only preoedipal homosexual organizations. And it is precisely such organizations—schizophrenic, criminal, or drug-addicted—that have constituted the published clinical material on which the psychoanalytic theory of all male homosexuality has been largely based, especially those later, more sophisticated theories based on Klein's ideas.

The issue psychoanalysis has never faced squarely, at least up to this point in our history, is the possibility that the difference between heterosexuality and homosexuality does not correspond to that between neurotic-oedipal and disturbed-oral. In the early period, this possibility was entertained, simply because one set of theories for the etiology of homosexual object choice was oedipal. But, as we have seen, the interest in oral determinants in later theory forced analysts to offer preoedipal etiologies for all forms of homosexuality. The possibility of an oedipal-level homosexual organization floundered because of a lack of a theory for nonperverse homosexuality and an absence of a large body of corresponding clinical material.

Any clinician with even limited experience can recognize the difference in quality of erotic experience between psychotic and borderline patients and more nearly neurotic and normal ones. Yet psychoanalytic theory has failed to acknowledge and account for the latter. As analysts from Freud to Glover have pointed out, such patients are rarely seen in analytic practice. Their absence in the analytic literature caused them to be assimilated into the category of clearly more disturbed patients. By 1960, however, analytic theory was robust and sophisticated enough to allow these distinctions to be made, and such analysts as Glover and Freeman began to make them. But in 1962, the history of the analytic theory of male homosexuality was partly advanced and partly retarded by the publication of Bieber's immensely influential but deeply flawed study of the origins of male homosexuality.[25]

CHAPTER **IX**

THE TURNAROUND: 1962–1973

The debates and uncertainties of the postwar period seemed to have been silenced, at least temporarily, by the publication in 1962 of Bieber's influential monograph, *Homosexuality: A Psychoanalytic Study of Male Homosexuals.*[1] Almost every article after that date, except for certain erudite discussions appearing in the mandarin *International Journal of Psychoanalysis* and *Psychoanalytic Quarterly,* refers to it with approval and satisfaction. For many, it seemed the much-awaited confirmation of psychoanalytic ideas, and, for a while, it signaled an apparent formalization of the psychoanalytic theory about homosexuality. Nevertheless, ten years later, after perhaps the most compressed and confusing period in the history we are tracing, both the Board of Trustees of the American Psychiatric Association and its general membership, as well as the American Psychological Association, explicitly repudiated several of Bieber's central claims. And in 1973 the American Psychiatric Association (APA) deleted homosexuality from its official list of psychiatric disorders. The reasons why the psychoanalytic theory of homosexuality should have been undermined so soon after the publication of Bieber's study are the principal themes of this chapter.

Two articles appeared at the extremes of the period we are discussing, offering an overview and synopsis. Both were by George Wiedemann, and both appeared in the *Journal of the American Psychoanalytic Association,* so that the differences between them are suggestive of the larger changes we are considering. The first was a standard review article, beginning with the first recorded use of the term *homosexuality* in 1869, going through Freud and the early Freudians, pausing for novel developments in the 1930s, and noting the most recent ideas. Several im-

172

portant topics were covered, including the etiology of and prognosis for homosexuality, as well as its relation to other disorders. The article ends critically: "The analytic literature does not disclose any single genetic or structural pattern that would apply to all or even a major part of cases of inversion." But in general it saw psychoanalytic knowledge as expanding and refining itself. One might well be reading a history of quantum mechanics.[2]

By 1974, however, the situation had changed. Concentrating primarily on ideas since 1962, Wiedemann noted a "flood of writing," but added that "contributions by analysts to the problem of homosexuality have been less than abundant." After again reviewing the contributions of Freud and his circle, Wiedemann presented five important areas of new development. But only two of them, the work of Bieber and Socarides, were, strictly speaking, psychoanalytic. The other three represented alternative approaches to the subject: the studies of Money, Eberhardt, and Stoller on hormonal anomalies resulting in gender disturbance; Karlen's general literary and anthropological overview[3]; and Hatterer's therapeutic endeavors, a fusion of simplified psychoanalytic ideas and behavior modification techniques.[4] The article ended by admitting the failure of psychoanalysis to deal adequately with certain basic issues, including the question of whether aberrant object choice necessarily involves disturbances in other areas of behavior or experience. The generally optimistic and progressive tone of the earlier article was quite absent, and Wiedemann lamented the APA's decision, which he felt came "very close to being a political rather than a scientific issue."[5]

Though several analysts—most notably Stoller, Bak, and Khan—made important contributions in this period, their ideas, for the most part, remained peripheral to the larger debate conducted within psychiatric and sociopolitical circles. The important discourse thus passed from the analytic community and took on a more social or general orientation, and the long-neglected issues of the intrinsic psychopathology of homosexuality and the ethical questions raised by the therapy of deviant groups were discussed by nonanalytic writers. As we shall see, most analysts continued to repeat, even well beyond this period, the old, dreary clichés that were out of fashion even before our history began.

The drift of psychoanalysis to the periphery of discussion resulted from developments within psychoanalysis. As we have seen, a split began to appear between the classical, orthodox school, whose primary organs were the *International Journal of Psychoanalysis* and *Psychoanalytic Quarterly*, and a revisionist school, whose major statements appeared in such publications as the *Journal of the American Academy of Psychoanalysis* and the *American Journal of Psychoanalysis*. The important large areas of dispute were precisely those that concern us: the status of constitutional bisexuality, the mechanism of the Oedipus complex, the importance of primary aggression in psychosexual development, and the relative weight given to intrapsychic and interpersonal dynamics.

The orthodox school continued to refine and deepen its understanding, but these developments were either too recondite (Bak's notion of the phallic mother[6]) or too subtle (Khan's work on perverse object relations[7]) to have had much effect. Occasionally, orthodox contributions verged on the fanciful, such as Bell's speculation on the role of the scrotum in prephallic psychosexual development and the importance of "testicular anxiety."[8] All of this only served to confirm the general suspicion that psychoanalysis was a calcified, outmoded, and irrelevant approach in the face of the larger cultural shifts occurring in the 1960s.

The revisionist school criticized orthodox analysts for continuing to affirm untested and untestable notions and to refuse to acknowledge new "holistic" developments.[9] Bolstered by the findings of Bieber and his colleagues, revisionists declined to acknowledge important methodological and conceptual criticisms leveled at Bieber's work. They dismissed both the larger moral and philosophical issues raised by various homophile spokesmen as "propaganda" and the contrary evidence presented by nonanalytic psychologists and psychiatrists[10] as superficial and irrelevant. In these terms, the APA decision was a rebuke to both analytic schools, as the heterogeneous organization of psychiatrists accepted the arguments of those outside the analytic establishment over those who had for three quarters of a century articulated the most informed and profound ideas on the subject.

Still, the usual work of psychoanalytic thought and publication continued independent of Bieber's study and the APA decision. Several important analytic symposia, conferences, and study groups were conducted on the subject of homosexuality. In 1963, an International Psychoanalytic Congress was held in Stockholm[11] and reported to the public,[12] and the next year the Association for the Advancement of Psychoanalysis held a symposium[13] that included contributions by Frederick Weiss, Ovesey, and Gershman.[14] In 1968 another International

Psychoanalytic Congress was held on the topic of homosexual "acting out."[15] The decision of the APA in 1973 was prepared for by exchanges in the previous year in both the *International Journal of Psychiatry* and the *American Journal of Psychiatry*, and much of the groundwork for the discussion was laid by the National Institute of Mental Health Task Force on homosexuality and the publication of its working papers,[16] which featured psychoanalytic views prominently.[17] After the decision itself, a transcript of discussions by a study group of analysts was published, although the decision itself is not discussed, and the discussion seems not to have been affected by the debate.[18] In addition, several collections of essays on sexual deviation appeared. Rosen's large collection attempted to cover the topic fully for professionals.[19] The next year Marmor attempted the same for a rather more popular audience.[20]

Among the published articles, a fair proportion did not add appreciably to psychoanalytic ideas. Moore and Selzer toiled away at the old problem of the relation of homosexuality to paranoia and schizophrenia and announced a vague confirmation of traditional psychoanalytic ideas.[21] Marberg presented an account of a brief analytic therapy of a patient who was behaviorally heterosexual, but whose dynamics were typically homosexual. Her description was quite superficial, and she seemed to be unaware of any but the most simple psychoanalytic theories.[22] P. Thompson's account of a male homosexual's transference illustrated generally accepted psychoanalytic ideas and can, in fact, be taken as a quick summary of them.[23] De Monchy provided a similar overview with treatment recommendations.[24] Gillespie tied together various strains of analytic thought on homosexuality, from Freud's earliest contributions to Kolb and Johnson's observations on the superego.[25] In the same year, he also raised several important questions on the position of homosexuality in normal development and in animal biology.[26] And Fairbairn contributed a note on the etiology of male homosexuality, venturing the idea that "the substitution of the penis for the breast provides the essential basis of male homosexuality," a notion as old as Freud's formulation.[27] It is unlikely that such an article would have been thought worthy of publication had it been written by anyone less eminent than Fairbairn, and its publication suggests the repetitive quality of a good proportion of psychoanalytic theorizing.

Psychoanalytic writers continued to apply their ideas to cultural and literary subjects in this period. Kubie contributed a long exegesis of Virginia's Woolf's *Orlando* from the point of view of its representation of bisexual strivings.[28] Roy, reviewing the newly published biography of Lytton Strachey by Michael Holroyd, emphasized the masochistic basis of homosexual "love" and claimed that "the homosexual drive is not really sexual at all," but an attempt to be hurt. For Roy, the biography contained elements "so complete and striking that [they] . . . sound exactly like Bergler's clinical observations." His paper resembles certain mediocre undergraduate performances that flatten and simplify a subject by trying to apply the ideas of a previous thinker.[29] Henry Ebel, who appears not to be an analyst, discussed Shakespeare's *Julius Caesar* from the point of view of its pervasive homosexual ethos. Although published in the *Psychoanalytic Review*, the article is an exercise in literary criticism and explicitly refers to Freud only in an appendix.[30] Gonen illustrated his notion of the "negative identity" of homosexuals with two of Gide's novels, *The Immoralist* and *Lafcadio's Adventures*.[31] Jaffe, discussing the pathological identifications with women that lies behind homosexual object choice, cited anthropological evidence for the universality of male envy of the procreative power of women,[32] and Kardiner, in his gloomy sociological overview, presented a selected sample of homosexual practices among such cultures as the Tanda of Madagascar.[33] By virtue of his extensive cross-cultural study of homosexuality,[34] Karlen, also not an analyst, delivered the expert opinion that no society ever fully accepted it.[35]

Such negative views were one aspect of an attempt by certain analysts centered around Kardiner and the *Journal of the American Academy of Psychoanalysis* to see homosexuality as a symptom of a contemporary "social stress syndrome." For Hendin, "homosexuality, crime, and drug and alcohol abuse appear to be barometers of social stress," and he offered the vulgar cliché that homosexual object choice was a threat to community values ("Criminals help produce other criminals, drug abusers other drug abusers, and homosexuals other homosexuals"), thus denying the widely accepted analytic notion that object choice is established well before latency.[36] Gonen too saw homosexuals as having developed a "negative identity" in reaction to social disruption in familial patterns. Venturing no criticism of society, he urged the therapist to help the homosexual patient abandon his negative and "totalistic thinking."[37] The fullest statement of this view was, however, Kardiner's, which, although published in 1978, repeated the views that he had articulated twenty-five years earlier.[38] They represented a lifetime's experience with homosexual patients. For him, the increase in homosexuality was just one aspect of a general rise in crime, murder, and racism. Damning everything from atonal music and *Sesame Street* to the late work of Picasso and women's liberation, he attempted to come to the aid of the middle class, "the group under the greatest pressure today." Homosexuals engaging in "predatory activity" simply "do not make good citizens in any society," and he compared them at length to Hitler's Jew-baiters.[39] The breakdown of society was most apparent in New York City, where "women wear trousers, men wear long hair with or without beards," and in the loss of sexual identity and the weakening of the institution of the family, the "one form of social patterning with consistent success."[40] The fact that Kardiner should think such views worthy of restatement in 1978 represents a fairly typical response of many analysts to the social upheavals of the 1960s and 1970s. Instead of considering new ideas carefully and providing clarification and discussion based on analytic insights, they fell back on vulgar notions and cultural clichés older than psychoanalysis itself. More serious, instead of buttressing their position with sophisticated ideas and evidence, they ended up validating social prejudice and ignorance: "The common judgment that homosexuality is a form of antisocial behavior is therefore not altogether unwarranted."[41]

The fly in the ointment of such unctuous opinion was, of course, homosexuality in Greece during the Golden Age. Although many analysts confessed their perplexity over this conundrum, others felt entitled to pass definitive judgment on an issue about which they were quite misinformed. Gershman thought that homosexuality could not have been accepted then since the society would simply have died out.[42] Hendin was similarly sure and superficial. Not troubling to read the relevant literature, he simply applied what he knew to an alien culture: "Pederasty in such cultures both expresses and conceals ambivalent feelings of admiration, envy, competition and hostility felt by the older generation toward the younger. That similar emotions were a factor in Greek pederasty seems likely."[43] Socarides, in the first of his two magna opera, was also quite confidently speculative: "In certain civilizations and in certain eras, for instance Hellenistic Greece [sic], it was profitable socially, politically and competitively to join those groups who freely announced their homosexual behavior."[44] Such ignorant and overweening confidence and refusal to learn from other disciplines helps account for the growing irrelevance of psychoanalysis to larger intellectual debates.

Responsible analysts, however, used their more refined understanding of homosexual object choice to illuminate other areas of psychological interest. For example, the function and significance of homosexual trends in adolescence and childhood were the subject of a series of analytic articles. Fraiberg offered an overview illustrated with an account of a patient named Eric. Drawing on the previous work of Peter Blos,[45] she claimed that a certain amount of homosexual feeling and behavior was "allowable" during adolescence, and that in most cases it would disappear through sublimation. This was less likely, however, if the adolescent became attached to an older man rather than a peer. In addition, an enduring homosexual identity could be sealed by an experience of homosexual love during adolescence. Her theoretical stance was quite traditional, as she continued to affirm that homosexual object choice represented a passive feminine identification and a failure to achieve masculinity. Significantly, Eric was not cured of his homosexuality, having kept his passive longings secret from his analyst, although he improved his self-esteem and academic performance.[46]

Two years later, Sprince, also working within a traditional analytic framework, discussed the therapy of a sixteen-year-old borderline adolescent whose confusing oedipal dynamics masked a mere "flirtation" with the oedipal phase. Basing his work primarily on the ideas of Bychowski, Sprince emphasized the usual identification with the mother and the defenses against it, the narcissistic choice of objects, and the failure in ego and superego formation. In the case he presented, an unstable positive Oedipus complex regressed to a negative form, which, through overstimulation by the mother, led to a recalcitrant oral fixation. Here again, the patient seemed not to have been cured of his homosexuality, although he did experience significant improvement and relief from other symptoms.[47]

Gadpaille offered a more general statement of his views on homosexuality in adolescence, omitting a detailed account of treatment. Also working within a traditional psychoanalytic framework, he announced that "erotic preference for the same sex does not fall within the biological norm," although transient adolescent homosexual experience does allow exploration and comparison and provides "an outlet" at an age when "responsible" heterosexual activity would be premature. The endurance of a homosexual orientation is hard to predict, he claimed, although age and frequency of such activity seem significant, as well as the occurrence of "the 'in love' phenomenon." He ended his article with the warning that physicians should be extremely careful in making referrals, since certain therapists unfortunately may consider homosexual object choice uncurable and hence urge their patients to learn to adjust to it.[48] Seven years later, he offered a nosology of adolescent homosexuality: adolescents who experiment with homosexual activity, pseudohomosexual adolescents who labor under a conflict about gender role, and genuine erotically motivated homosexuals, the last being the most difficult to treat. Gadpaille considered all forms of true homosexuality as stemming from a feminine identification, and so did not list a category of masculine adolescents who are genuinely aroused by other boys. He cautioned that analytic treatment of adolescents can never be complete and that more thoroughgoing therapy must wait until adulthood.[49] But another analyst urged prompt treatment of any form of adolescent homosexual activity, lest it become rewarded and fixed.[50]

Accounts of other therapies included Pao's six-year-long case[51] and Bonime's case of a homosexual who entered treatment at his parents' insistence when they heard of his homosexuality, although he had been severely depressed before. Bonime's long-term interest was depression, and his discussion concentrated on it and not primarily on sexual variation. Still, he emphasized the controlling and vindictive quality of the patient's homosexuality and depression as he attempted both to hurt his parents and to express his hatred of his analyst. Although these were interpreted to the patient, as well as his attempt to "escape from responsibility," Bonime only witnessed negative therapeutic reactions, which he attributed to the patient's defensiveness. There is no mention of a cure.[52]

A more sophisticated presentation was that of Khan, who treated a homosexual who had a fetish for foreskins. The patient seemed severely disturbed, although he was capable of a high level of social and professional achievement. The patient equated the erect penis with the excited breast, and the foreskin symbolized both the penis and the labia. Khan subtly and complexly explicated the overdetermined nature of the fetish, clearly seeing his patient as suffering from a fetishistic perversion with homosexual features. Khan claimed to have conducted a successful treatment, since the patient finally became capable of something approaching object love, although he remained distinctly homosexual. It is a measure of Khan's sensitivity that he could describe his patient's achieved homosexual object love with such sympathy and understanding.[53]

P. Thompson devoted an article to describing the shifts in transference in the analysis of a homosexual patient. Using Greenson's notion of "screen identity," as well as the work of Bychowski and Bieber, he emphasized traditional oedipal dynamics, as well as the importance of the patient's oral regression. His article represents a summary and illustration of traditional psychoanalytic ideas, but Thompson did not mention whether the patient was cured.[54] Kolb offered advice on the treatment of homosexuals and urged different treatment modalities, but he did not discuss rate of cure.[55] Brown also offered general advice, and his article is remarkable for its sympathetic tone, but he too did not mention how successful his efforts proved.[56] De Monchy reviewed the standard analytic theory and applied it to treatment, but of the eight patients he treated, though seven benefited from his ministrations, all remained homosexual.[57]

In the year following the APA decision, Ostow published excerpts from a psychoanalytic workshop on sexual deviation that had been meeting for six years and discussing the analysis of six patients, three of whom were homosexual. The orientation of the group was distinctly classical and orthodox, as they assumed "norms suggested by biologic— that is, reproductive—function," an assumption borne out by "an aggregate of clinical experience," which found "other signs of mental illness" accompanying sexual deviation. According to the group, all perversions, including homosexuality, involve narcissism, infantilism, and acting out. In all the cases they discussed, they found the traditional dynamics: libidinized anxiety, the attempt to master traumatic situations in a perverse ritual, castration anxiety, phallic narcissism, and a desire to protect women from violent fantasies of revenge. Still, the group's adherence to classical psychoanalytic ideas did not prevent it from advancing several novel theories and observations. One member called attention to "an unusually vivid, almost eidetic quality of visual experience" in homosexuals, which they attributed to a "visual incorporative mode." In addition, homosexuals were "limited in their capacity for abstract thought," and hence involved themselves in the more concrete activities of "feeling and doing." Finally, the curious reader may be interested to learn that "Dr. Blos notes that virtually all of the male homosexuals that he has treated have been convinced that their penises were smaller than 'normal.' " Of the three homosexual cases discussed, none underwent a successful treatment, and one got appreciably worse. For all their theoretical insight, these analysts seemed unable to effect any change in their patients' sexual orientation. The reasons for their lack of success are not apparent, but perhaps the clarity and sureness of their convictions may have interfered with their own therapeutic empathy. According to them, all their homosexual patients were unhappy, despite their analysts' repeated attempts to point out the "embarrassing, threatening and harmful consequences of [their homosexual] behavior."[58]

In all these accounts only two analysts claimed to have effected a cure—that is, a change in sexual orientation and the achievement of real heterosexual object love. Wallace, while stressing the importance of therapeutic neutrality and an "atmosphere of free inquiry . . . free of the preformed opinions of the therapist," nevertheless informed his patient that his homosexuality would be treated and that it would be best if he refrained from homosexual activity during treatment. The patient, feeling accepted "like an adult for the first time in his life," experienced surprisingly quick results. In the fourth hour, after discovering that he was searching for a father, he ceased his homosexual behavior and began a relationship with a woman. And later in treatment, after a few minutes of wanting to cry, he suddenly felt his homosexual interest was at an end, and he began termination. Six months later, he married and eventually had a child. Wallace had since heard no word from him, and wondered if perhaps such positive results might have represented a transference cure. He does not discuss why, if the patient's disturbance was so severe, such dramatic change occurred so quickly.[59]

In the period we are presently discussing, the only substantial and convincing claims for an analytic change in sexual orientation were made by Socarides. After reviewing a history of the psychoanalytic treatment of male homosexuality, in which he could find only five accounts of a successful cure, Socarides presented an account of a four-year analysis of a preoedipal exclusive homosexual who was restored to heterosexual functioning and object love after eight months of treatment. The salient aspects of the treatment were: the interpretation of homosexual activity as the identification with a partner who represented the patient's lost masculinity; the importance of preoedipal anxiety and the fear of engulfment by the mother, stemming from a failure to have passed through the separation-individuation phase; a distorted body image; the penis-breast equation; the yearning for the father's love; and the repression of heterosexuality due to guilt over aggressive and incestuous wishes toward the mother. In addition, Socarides emphasized the therapeutic efficacy of the patient's identification with his analyst. Throughout, the influence of the ideas of Bergler is prominent.[60]

It is important to note that the ten articles I have summarized involved twelve patients in all, but fully seven experienced no change in their sexual orientation. It is striking that no one thought to account for such a dismal therapeutic record. Bieber claimed a cure rate of twenty-seven percent, but he did not present any details of treatment.[61] Either the dynamic theory was defective, the technique inadequate, the analysts' attitudes and assumptions inappropriate, or the relation of homosexual object choice to psychopathology not understood. In any case, none of these possibilities was fully discussed within analytic circles, except that the lack of success was blamed on the patient's resistance. But as we shall see, the obvious discrepancy between theory and outcome was beginning to be acknowledged, though only grudgingly.

Several analysts advocated group therapy. Hartman reported on two groups that he found effective in mediating the development from symbiosis to individuation and in establishing firm ego boundaries, all leading to important intrapsychic and interpersonal changes.[62] Gershman summarized his fourteen-year experience with two groups of homosexuals. Agreeing with Socarides that the failure to resolve the mother-child symbiosis leads to a faulty gender identity, he maintained that the cause of homosexuality was therefore preoedipal. His treatment goals were consequently modest, and he urged the therapist not to attempt "to convert the homosexual to heterosexuality unless he so desires, but to make him more of a whole person to himself and to those about him." To accomplish these aims, the therapist should use as a model Gershman's own "feelings of openness, compassion and honesty."[63] In his "Discussion," Kaye commended such self-congratulation for its "holistic" approach and its "wisdom."[64] Finally, Toby Bieber, a member of the team that produced the 1962 monograph, urged group treatment for homosexuals, provided it was preceded by individual treatment. She claimed that such an approach was efficacious in resolving interpersonal difficulties as well as shifting to a heterosexual object choice.[65]

As for more substantial developments, as theoretical and technical ideas developed, more analysts began to report their findings, many engaging in the bad psychoanalytic habit of generalizing from a small, special sample. In a series of three articles, for example, Bell stressed the importance of the scrotum and testes in psychosexual development. For her, their most salient physical characteristic was their tendency to disappear during defecation. Hence, "testicular anxiety" was a precursor of castration fear, associated with the loss of feces during the anal phase. In addition, since these organs are located between penis and anus, they facilitate the regression to the anal period noted frequently in the analytic literature. As evidence, Bell pointed to the importance of "ball games" for adolescent males, which represented attempts to master moving objects in space, whose prototypes were the testicles. She concluded her article by decrying the massive repression on the part of analysts of their own testicular anxiety. The analysis of male homosexuals could not be complete "until the taboo is lifted and the role of the testicles and scrotal sac fully explored."[66] Four years later, she further developed and expanded these ideas, relating them to psychosexual changes during adolescence, which could revive pregenital fantasies of growing breasts, becoming female, and bearing children, all of which could lead to a defensive turning away from women and the development of homosexual object choice. Once again, she concluded by remarking on the massive repression of such anxiety revealed in the analytic literature.[67] Finally, she presented her ideas as a formal theory in the *International Journal of Psychoanalysis*, where she posited a testicular phase of psychosexual development in boys corresponding to the phallic phase in girls. Here the testicles in the sac correspond to the fetus in the mother, and the boy passively waits for the testes to descend after they have retracted into the body during cold and fear. These feminine identifications and fantasies of testicular pregnancy are a spontaneous and normal part of psychosexual development and serve as the "root" of bisexuality in the male.[68]

Berent offered a new explanation for the origin of homosexual object choice in presenting a patient who feared having injured his mother at birth. To avoid repeating this "original sin," he subsequently avoided all women as sexual objects and became homosexual. Because the patient's fears predated his oedipal phase, Berent denied that he had simply projected his castration anxiety onto the mother. Although basing this idea in one patient, Berent suggested that this fear might be "ubiquitous." He also offered the novel suggestion that the patient's apparently effeminate gestures were not a caricature of women, but of children, as he strove to deny his mature phallic capacities. Berent ended his article urging that such patients witness childbirth in hospitals in order to dispel such unrealistic fantasies. He made no mention of how successful treatment was.[69] Another analyst found that the fear of infanticide provoked the development of homosexual object choice. Expanding on ideas from an earlier paper,[70] Bloch claimed that children will desperately maintain the conviction of their parents' love, even in the face of apparent infanticidal threats, experienced by the child as a jealous reaction on the part of the same-sexed parent. Blaming himself, a child unconsciously assumes the identity of the opposite sex and begins to act seductively toward the same-sexed parent. Bloch thought that these mechanisms underlay "the seemingly bewildering symptomatology of homosexuality." Implicit is the belief that all homosexual men attempt to maintain a feminine identity and to seduce the father passively. She proposed that "the similarity of the dynamics in all instances suggests that they may account for a large proportion of the cases of homosexual identity," omitting to remind the reader that for her "all instances" amounted to precisely four cases.[71]

Even more specific features were adduced to explain the development of homosexual object choice. Bieber claimed that, although the child's relation to his mother could assume many forms, in no case did he find the presence of a "warmly related and consistently constructive" father in the homosexual's childhood.[72] Hence he claimed that although the basis for homosexuality lies in the general family constellation, a "supportive, warmly related father *precludes* the possibility of a homosexual son."[73] Friedman, attempting to replicate a large study of homosexuals that repudiated Bieber's study,[74] found no evidence of behavioral aggression with peers during preadolesence in his sample of seventeen homosexuals. He urged that the development of "sex-typed aggressive skills" during latency would "markedly diminish the likelihood that an exclusive, enduring homosexual orientation will occur."[75] Neither study, we must note, claimed that the failure to achieve a masculine identity and behavior causes homosexual object choice, only that achieving it precludes or is inconsistent with such an outcome. In any case, the emphasis in both studies was on developmental achievements in latency, long after the important developments during pregenital and oedipal phases that had been stressed by analytic writers from the beginning.

Apart from these novel and large claims, much useful and suggestive work went on within classical psychoanalytic theory. Rubinstein continued to emphasize and elaborate the complexities of various identifications and object choices, although his cases were primarily transvestites and pedophiles. Stressing the importance of "dual identifications" primarily with mother and father, but also with other children, he traced their correspondence with narcissistic object choices or "identification love."[76] Proceeding along similar lines, Greenson specified the stages leading to a stable gender identity, which he thought was determined by the genitalia, by parental attitudes, and, borrowing from Stoller's work, by an obscure biological force. Attempting to link gender identity with object choice, a connection never really addressed in the psychoanalytic literature, Greenson outlined a three-stage process. The first stage is the development of the conviction that "I am me," which is followed by the conviction that "I am a boy," which, in turn, is consolidated by the discovery that "I like to do things with girls sexually." In this scheme, homosexuals are "fixated" at the second stage, and although they attempt to achieve stage three, they are traumatized and regress. Because of this phobia of heterosexuality, they develop into "rigid homosexuals."[77] The article, however, falls short of its promise, since it does not discuss the possibility of a firm masculine identity compatible with a homosexual choice of object. In fact, most of Greenson's clinical material derives from his treatment of heterosexual males who experienced homosexual panic and who neurotically believed that gender identity was determined by the gender of their object. One wonders if Greenson would have posited a fourth stage in which gender identity can be maintained independent of the sex of the object.

Also using classical psychoanalytic formulations, Morgenthaler thought that gender identity could go awry because of a discrepancy in the correspondence of developmental lines. Claiming that homosexuals characteristically view sexual differences regressively as a set of dichotomies between superiority and inferiority, strength and weakness, omnipotence and helplessness, and that they maintain a stereotyped notion of these differences based on power, Morgenthaler thought that regression was caused by a premature discovery of sexual differences before certain achievements in object-self differentiation had occurred.[78] Greenson reached compatible conclusions. Observing that gender disturbances are far more common among men than women, he cogently pointed out that just as the oedipal girl must shift her libidinal object from mother to father, the preoedipal boy must accomplish the more basic task of shifting his identification from the mother to the father. This process of "dis-identifying" with the mother and "counter-identifying" with the father leads to the characteristic uncertainty in men about their masculinity. Although Greenson's clinical material involved primarily heterosexual transsexuals, he nonetheless claimed that homosexuals harbor the same unconscious wish to be women.[79]

Edgcumbe and Burgner observed that optimal resolution of identity occurs when stages of object relations and phases of drive development progress in parallel. A crucial period occurs during the phallic-narcissistic phase, which just precedes the oedipal period proper. Drawing on the work of Jones and Loewenstein, as well as Mahler,[80] they spelled out the crucial characteristics of this period, in which the most prominent drives are exhibitionistic and scopophiliac, and in which object relations are typically dyadic, as opposed to the triangular ones of the oedipal phase. Because the primary tasks here are separation-individuation and the resolution of the bisexual identification that precedes sexual differentiation, castration anxiety involves threat from both the mother and the father and activates envy and anger respectively. With a failure at this stage, the Oedipus complex cannot be resolved adequately. Hence fixation at this phase or regression to it leads to a lack of reciprocity in object relations, to an inability to recognize the real qualities of objects, and to a generally hysterical character structure.[81] Finally, A. Goldberg attempted to apply Kohut's formulation of psychoanalytic ideas[82] to perverse behavior, which he presented as "attempts to supply substitutes for the absent narcissistically invested self-object" by sexualizing "pathological narcissistic constellations." Such deficits do not, strictly speaking, cause perversion, but they are expressed in perverse activity.[83]

Of great importance for later writers on sexual perversion was Bak's exegesis of the importance of the fantasy of the phallic mother. Elaborating on Freud's ideas in his essay on fetishism,[84] Bak, while admitting the importance of preoedipal phases, reaffirmed the centrality of the Oedipus complex. All perversions had in common "the dramatized or ritualized denial of castration . . . through the regressive revival of the fantasy of the maternal or female phallus." This fantasy, he thought, was not maintained, as Freud had claimed, through "splitting,"[85] but through defensive uncertainty. Perverse activity allowed for the gratification of sexual instincts, the undoing of separation from the mother, and the libidinization and gratification of aggression. Also, the identification with the phallic mother and the threat of incest led to an exacerbation of the negative Oedipus complex and prevented the formation of an adequate superego. Agreeing with Glover, Bak claimed that perverse fantasies patched over flaws in the reality sense—in this case, the acknowledgment of sexual differences and the resultant castration anxiety.[86]

McDougall reached similar conclusions in her explication of the role of the primal scene in perversion, although her article was about female homosexuality, her abiding interest. For her, perverse activity was an attempt to prolong the relation to the preoedipal mother, who is experienced as both the provoker and prohibitor of sexual activity. In these terms, the Oedipus complex is a "disorganizing experience," and not the focus and consolidation of psychosexual development. Fetishism, the paradigm of all perversions, is an attempt to deny sexual relations between the parents, leading to a consequent failure of symbolic function and to a need for concrete and compulsive sexual acting out. Every perverse act, therefore, represents "a condensed primal scene involving three people."[87]

Finally, analysts again began to provide a useful classification of homosexual object choice informed by psychoanalytic theory. W. Brown suggested a rather perfunctory list of four types he had encountered in his work with imprisoned homosexuals: facultative (i.e., *faute de mieux*), psychoneurotic (i.e., immature or severely symptomatic), psychotic, and psychopathic.[88] Scott used a similar population and offered five categories, which, surprisingly, included homosexuals with "relatively intact personalities" and "latent and well-compensated homosexuals."[89] But the most convincing and enduring distinction, which became quite widespread in our period, was between oedipal and preoedipal homosexuals. Weissman was the first to distinguish between those who had regressed from an oedipal level of object relations and those who labored under preoedipal identification with the mother.[90] Two years later, Gillespie adopted this distinction, but correctly pointed out that the latter group, the "natural" homosexuals, did not conform to the analytic theory of perversion.[91] But the fullest elaboration is found in the work of Socarides, who claimed, however, to have discovered the distinction in 1968 and who concentrated, for the most part, on the preoedipal group.[92]

It is important to note that contributions such as these represented a reaffirmation of classical psychoanalytic ideas and especially the vexed issues of primary bisexuality and the centrality of the full, fourfold Oedipus complex, wherein the mother and father are each libidinal objects and prohibitors of sexuality. This was a response to the emphasis placed on preoedipal development beginning with the work of Klein and her followers in the 1930s and the tendency in later "revisionist" schools to shift away from intrapsychic conflict to familial determinants occurring during latency. The former school was finally assimilated into psychoanalytic theory; the latter was, for the most part, simply ignored. It is difficult to document this counterrevisionist movement within psychoanalysis, since it is a matter of tone and vague references to misplaced emphases and slightings of important aspects of dynamics. This return to the cornerstone of psychoanalytic theory continues beyond the period we are discussing, and a polemical intent can be discerned in the decision by the editors of the *International Journal of Psychoanalysis* to devote an entire issue to the Oedipus complex.[93]

Both Bak and Greenacre began their articles on sexual perversion by emphasizing the centrality of the Oedipus complex, although they acknowledged the importance of preoedipal precursors.[94] Bak, Hornstra, and Pasche also emphasized the negative Oedipus complex as "unavoidable" and not just a defensive maneuver,[95] and Hornstra devoted an article to the complexities that could evolve in such a fourfold mechanism.[96] Interestingly, the problematic quality of this notion was illustrated by Jaffe, who devoted an entire article to the importance and universality of the negative Oedipus complex, feminine identification, and the envy of woman's procreative function,[97] but who, fifteen years later, saw the negative Oedipus complex as "defensive."[98] Similarly, all these writers maintained the notion of a primary and irreducible bisexuality, as did Limentani, who rejected biological bisexuality, but insisted on its psychological aspect as a "reality" based on identification with both parents.[99] Weissman also continued to affirm the reality of "normal" bisexuality in psychosexual development and to stress the importance of passive yearnings for the father.[100]

This reaffirmation of orthodox views is especially important and interesting in this period since two of the three major contributors to the theory of homosexuality—Bieber and Stoller—espoused revisionist views, and one—Socarides—was influenced by them. And a long list of analysts explicitly rejected several important psychoanalytic concepts. In 1964, the Association for the Advancement of Psychoanalysis held a symposium on homosexual trends in therapy, reported in the *American Journal of Psychoanalysis*. Such figures as Bieber, Gershman, and Ovesey explicitly repudiated the notion of constitutional homosexuality, a theme that occurs throughout our period, with approving references to Rado's earlier refutation. For them, homosexual object choice was an "adaptational" consequence of the prohibition of heterosexual activity involving issues of power rather than sexuality per se, a view reiterated by Ovesey time and again.[101] Writers as diverse as Lief and Mayerson,[102] Salzman,[103] and, surprisingly, Marmor,[104] who will figure prominently in the evolution of a positive psychoanalytic view of homosexuality, agreed.

But the rejection of classical psychoanalytic ideas extended beyond issues of constitutional homosexuality. Gershman, in his discussion of the evolution of gender identity, accepted the ideas espoused by Ovesey and rejected both primary aggression and penis envy as universal and irreducible components of psychic organization,[105] a view seconded by Stoller.[106] Finally, Kardiner in exasperation professed having no use at all for many of Freud's later writings such as *Totem and Taboo*, *Civilization and Its Discontents*, *The Future of an Illusion*, and *Moses and Monotheism*, which was "pure fantasy."[107] Yet these writers never formally addressed the problem of what could legitimately remain of psychoanalytic theory if such "cornerstones" were removed.

Though he accepted the revisionist ideas of Bieber and Stoller on gender disturbance, Socarides remained within classical psychoanalytic discourse. Several of his articles began with a historical survey of psychoanalytic theories of homosexuality, emphasizing especially the work of Freud and Sachs. Equally important to his own position, especially after 1968, were the contributions of theorists who attended to preoedipal development. Nevertheless, he did not deal in any detail with Klein and her followers, while the influence of Bergler was felt throughout in his concept, tone, and even specific phrases. Socarides's amalgam of different approaches caused certain inconsistencies and contradictions. For example, though he fully accepted the idea that a homosexual orientation is established before the age of three,[108] he also accepted Bieber's findings on the determining influence of events during latency,[109] and was concerned that homosexual "propaganda" might succeed in legitimating that condition and hence lead the unwary astray.[110]

Socarides's major contribution was his argument that homosexual object choice is the result of preoedipal disturbance, specifically at the separation-individuation phase. He later admitted that some homosexuals do not undergo trauma at that early stage, but can best be thought of as having been disrupted in their psychosexual development at the oedipal stage. For him this condition was not "true" homosexuality.[111]

Significantly, he never dealt at length with these oedipal pseudohomosexuals, but referred curtly to the negative Oedipus complex and fear of the father's power,[112] relinquishing this group to Ovesey and the adaptational school. Thus, his frequent insistence that there are absolutely no homosexuals free of psychopathology, though phrased in an unqualified manner, was somewhat ambiguous. It is not clear if he was characterizing all those with a homosexual object choice or only those "true" homosexuals who have never adequately negotiated the separation-individuation phase. If it was the latter, his position was clearly tautological.

According to Socarides, the failure to pass unscathed through this phase leaves the future homosexual "fixated" on the mother at a stage of undifferentiation of self and object. Hence he maintains "a primary identification with the mother and a faulty gender identity."[113] But this identification is highly ambivalent, as the "demonified mother" is experienced simultaneously as forcing premature separation and a loss of love and as working against complete separation. This leads to an increase in anxiety and frustration, a partial withdrawal of libido from the object, and an increase in aggression toward it. Under the pressure of this highly charged ambivalence, the ego suffers a serious split as it attempts to love narcissistic objects and also to vent the rage and sadism aroused by the mother.[114] In these terms, homosexual acts are unconscious attempts to undo separation by returning to the symbiotic mother-child bond and also to defend against the fear of engulfment and the loss of ego boundaries.[115] Homosexuals never really enter into the oedipal stage, which requires a previously established differentiation of self and object, but instead maintain a psychic organization that is essentially borderline in character. In working out the details of this etiology and in explicating the meaning of homosexual acts, Socarides was able to draw on the insights of previous classical analysts, reaffirming the centrality of the breast-penis equation and the attempt to appropriate a lost masculinity in the homosexual partner.

With a dozen works on homosexuality extending over a twenty-five-year period, Socarides became the leading expert and spokesman for psychoanalysis, a position he relished and encouraged. He claimed to have seen 63 homosexual patients in psychoanalytic treatment and to have done consultations for 350.[116] Like Bergler, he claimed that the range and validity of his clinical experience permitted him to accept or dismiss evidence that had been systematically obtained. According to him, Kinsey's figures were exaggerated, while Bieber's one- to two-percent prevalence was accurate. When his etiological theory was challenged by an analyst discussing a patient who presented developmental characteristics corresponding to Socarides's schema but who was not homosexual,[117] Socarides rejected the argument, claiming that closer scrutiny would confirm his theory.[118] Similarly, he rejected other contrary nonanalytic evidence out of hand as "behavioristic" and consequently irrelevant.[119] As for criticism of the analytic sample, he simply claimed that it was not skewed.[120]

By the time of the APA decision and well afterward, Socarides's tone became quite shrill and his treatment of sources and statistics rather careless. Homophile arguments were "mere propaganda," and his accounts of homosexual viciousness and desperation rivaled Bergler's in intemperateness, though he lacked Bergler's smugness and cruelty: "Homosexuality . . . is filled with aggression, destruction, and self-deceit. It is a masquerade of life . . . [involving] only destruction, mutual defeat, exploitation of the partner and the self."[121] In claiming that homosexuality was a perversion of a borderline level of severity, he claimed agreement with Glover, who, the reader may remember, failed to find such a place for the perversions on a continuum of psychopathology.[122] In buttressing his claim for the necessary psychopathology of homosexual orientation, Socarides referred to Bieber's "findings" that "one-third are schizophrenic, one-third, neurotic and one-third, character disorders."[123] But Bieber's sample consisted of homosexual males in treatment, and his study had been criticized at length precisely because its sample had been preselected on the basis of psychopathology.[124] Finally, Socarides's embattled position can best be illustrated by his response to a paper that assumed a rather agnostic tone with respect to the question of pathology and tried to clarify how homosexuality could be considered deviant.[125] Socarides began his response: "There is such a total lack of scientific veracity in the Green paper that it would hardly merit discussion by any busy and seriously committed physician. However, to prevent the damage that can be done by such a travesty of medical reporting," he deigned to repeat his previous assertions.[126] Such a tone and such tactics, though they had a long history, caused to a great extent both the enmity between psychoanalysis and homosexuals and the partial failure of thoughtful discussion surrounding the APA decision. But even beyond such public events, the accuracy of his findings is questionable because of his personal investment in the debate, which has no place in psychoanalytic research and treatment. If Socarides was so militant in his public utterances, one wonders what his demeanor was like in the treatment room and how he may have distorted the process of treatment and the evidence he derived from it. His experience that "other homosexuals, greatly fearing to face the overwhelming anxiety, will prematurely terminate psychoanalytic treatment in a period of resistance and with many rationalizations for premature interruption"[127] and that one of his patients "came to the realization that homosexuality is valueless, cheapening, aggressive, asocial, demoralizing and self-destructive"[128] probably has as much to do with his own attitudes and behavior, which can be grouped under the idea of countertransference, as it does with the recalcitrance and fearful defensiveness of patients.

In quite another spirit, Stoller pursued his important work on gender disturbance, displaying an openness to new ideas, preserving an agnostic stance when evidence or theory was inconclusive, and manifesting a willingness to reevaluate his convictions. He began his work interested not in homosexuality but in gender disturbance, particularly in transsexuals, and became drawn into the controversy over homosexuality because others—Gershman and Tyson, for example[129]—used his ideas, and because his work led him to consider the problem of sexual perversion. His first book, on gender disturbance,[130] and his second, on perversion, explicitly exclude homosexuality from the category of perversions.[131] He addressed the subject of homosexuality only during the APA debate[132] and in a later article on the treatment of boyhood effeminacy and its relation to adult homosexuality.[133] He thought the question of whether homosexuality was necessarily perverse "a large issue beyond my present understanding,"[134] but admitted that homosexuality as practiced in ancient Greece did not involve hostility and revenge, just as it did not necessarily have to in present times.[135]

His work, apart from its intrinsic merits, is particularly interesting because it attempts to reconcile the analytic studies of Greenson, with whom he collaborated, with the endocrinological investigation of Money. This project necessarily led him to espouse certain views that we have labeled "revisionist." Throughout, he stressed the importance of family constellations to the neglect of intrapsychic mechanisms to account for sexual aberration, and dealt with the Oedipus complex only in its "simplified" form. In addition, he accepted the notion of constitutional bisexuality, but not as conceptualized by Freud, whom he accused of "biologizing." He also denied the centrality of the penis and of penis envy in psychosexual development.[136] Most important, he maintained that castration anxiety was not crucial for the development of gender identity,[137] since the latter is established by the age of two or three, well before entry into the Oedipus complex.[138] In any case, he redefined castration threat as directed not against the genitals per se, but against the establishment of gender.[139] Still, his work is quite analytic, with its emphasis on the struggle against symbiosis.

A firm libertarian stance allowed him to raise some of the larger issues that had, for the most part, remained undiscussed by analysts since the time of Schilder. He undertook a discussion of pornography[140] and attempted to admit moral judgment into an analytic discussion of perversion.[141] He similarly called attention to the lack of clear conceptualization of normalcy, and frequently pointed out, along with Freud, that heterosexuality itself was in need of explanation, thus rebuking such writers as Gershman and Socarides who thought that it was not: "Until we understand heterosexuality instead of taking it for granted as a given, we will not understand perversion . . . ; we must begin by recalling that heterosexuality is an acquisition; we cannot brush the issue aside by saying that heterosexuality is preordained, necessary for the survival of the species and therefore biologically guaranteed." For Stoller, the very establishment of masculinity required a reaction formation against the pull toward femininity and so "require[s] Anlagen of femininity." Finally, he saw the general, unreasoned hatred and fear of homosexuals as pathological, but, in discussing it, was able to suggest how homosexuals themselves are complicit in their own discrimination by virtue of their self-hatred, their hatred of society, and their challenge to heterosexual institutions.[142]

For Stoller, gender identity is established preoedipally by anatomy and the physiology of external genitalia, the attitude of others, and an obscure biological force that can operate independently of the two.[143] Citing the evidence of anatomical anomalies, he claimed that an unstable gender identity can lead to cross-sex impulses and behavior, such as are associated with transsexualism and transvestism.[144] In his later work, which dealt with the perversions in general, he considered how interpersonal and intrafamilial threats to gender identity could lead to perversions. Beginning in 1970 with a series of articles later collected in *Perversion: The Erotic Form of Hatred,* he showed how the thwarted struggle to emerge from symbiosis with the mother represented such a threat. Perversion, in these terms, was the attempt to avenge the self for the childhood trauma inflicted on developing sexuality. The defining characteristic of perversion, therefore, was not object choice or any particular act, but the meaning the perverse fantasy had for the individual, which, Stoller claimed, was invariably hostility, hatred, and the desire to hurt. Thus, he affirmed Rank's contention fifty years earlier that sadism was the prototype of all true perversions. The degradation and reification of love objects was therefore a necessary component of all perverse activity, but they could not be inferred from any particular act. Stoller reversed the logic that had characterized most analysts' thought on such deviant sexual behavior as homosexuality. For them, since homosexuality was perverse, it necessarily involved hatred and aggression. For Stoller, only if the underlying fantasy involved such desires could it be considered truly perverse. Thus he classified two forms of sexual aberration: the "perversions," which are erotized hatred; and the "variants," which deviate from statistical norms but do not involve hostility or the desire to injure the object. [145]

From such a view, the question of object choice could have only a secondary importance. Stoller claimed not to know if homosexual object choice was necessarily perverse in the sense in which he defined the term, [146] although he specifically exempted its ancient Greek manifestation from the charge. [147] Consequently, he urged the deletion of homosexuality from the APA list of sexual disturbances, since it did not represent a category of psychic organization, [148] but only a feature of true diagnostic categories: "there is no such *thing* as homosexuality." At the most, one could speak legitimately only of "homosexualities." [149] Stoller was influential in the APA decision, but his importance as a theoretician should not be qualified by his political and social influence. His findings were consistent with the more nearly pure analytic conceptualizations of Greenson and lent particular plausibility to the speculations of later theorists on such topics as the phallic narcissistic phase of psychosexual development. His work also provided the basis for later elaboration, which included that of politically neutral clinicians and engaged analysts who drew conclusions opposite to his.

But the most influential and lasting work of this period was Bieber's 1962 monograph, *Homosexuality: A Psychoanalytic Study of Male Homosexuals*. Though flawed and deviating in several important ways from traditional psychoanalytic theory, it came to be regarded, shortly after its publication, as vindicating the psychoanalytic theory of male homosexuality. Almost every analytic writer, with the exception of the most orthodox, refers to it approvingly, and it continues to be read and taught in psychopathology courses in universities. Its success earned Bieber the status of psychoanalytic expert on homosexuality. He contributed a chapter to Marmor's first collection,[150] which represented the hard-line analytic view, and he wrote the articles on sexual deviation and homosexuality for Freedman and Kaplan's *Comprehensive Textbook of Psychiatry*,[151] which remained the official view of homosexuality until they were replaced in the second edition by Marmor's article after the APA decision.[152] In his many articles following the publication of his monograph, Bieber referred to himself at length, often in more detail than his discussion of Freud.[153] He figured prominently in the debate preceding the APA decision, where he urged retaining homosexuality on the list of emotional disturbances,[154] a position he continued to espouse well after the battle was lost.[155] With the passage of time, he claimed even greater expertise, by virtue of his claim of having treated 850 cases,[156] a figure that exceeded Socarides's but did not challenge Bergler's record of more than 1,000. Fifteen years after the publication of *Homosexuality*, he presented a retrospective view, in which he reiterated his findings and buttressed them with new data, while ignoring the serious objections raised to the sampling method he used in his first study.[157] Other members of the original team also assumed authoritative roles. Gundlach[158] refuted a criticism of the 1962 study,[159] and Toby Bieber reiterated those findings,[160] and also applied them to the idea of group therapy for homosexuals.[161]

The 1962 study represented a ten-year investigation of the etiology of male homosexuality. It employed the services of eight psychoanalysts and one clinical psychologist who surveyed the analytic treatment of 106 male homosexuals compared with an unmatched sample of 100 heterosexual male patients in analytic treatment. Working with a grant of only five thousand dollars, they gathered "voluminous data" from a 450-item questionnaire, which they developed and submitted to treating therapists. These items concern the family constellations of patients as they were reported in therapy, and answers were provided by the therapists, not by the patients themselves. Specifically, information was gathered regarding the relation of the patients with their mothers, fathers, siblings, and peers, in such areas as feelings toward these important figures, the perceived effects of these figures on aggressive, sexual, and independent activity, and remembered activities and preferences during childhood and latency. The novelty and strength of the study was

its amassing an enormous amount of data, which satisfied the psychoanalytic need for subtle and sophisticated information gathered from a
large clinical experience. In addition, contrary data gathered by nonanalytic workers[162] could be refuted. The findings confirmed a great deal
of psychoanalytic theory about the etiology of male homosexuality,
although several important aspects of that theory were either disconfirmed or refuted. Here, it was thought, was a clear, focused, and
empirical substantiation of claims made theoretically or based on extremely limited clinical material. Specific findings occupied three broad
areas: mother-son relationships, father-son relationships, and developmental patterns.

First, a significantly greater proportion of homosexuals had what
Bieber and his team termed "close-binding-intimate mothers," who
were seductive to their sons and also overcontrolling and inhibiting.
The sons were, by their own account, the most important persons in the
lives of their mothers, who "encouraged reciprocal alienation between
father and son." "On the whole, these mothers encouraged the development of homosexuality in their sons by interfering with their heterosexual development, with the father-son relationship, with the son's
peer relationships and with the son's developing sense of indepen-
dence." Second, and perhaps more important, while not all of the
mothers of future homosexuals necessarily fit this characterization, a
significantly higher proportion of homosexuals reported detached, hostile, or rejecting fathers whom they hated or feared during childhood.
Fathers who did not fit this description were sometimes seductive toward
their sons, but in all cases "profound interpersonal disturbance" characterized relations between fathers and sons. Not one father in 106 cases
could be found who was "warmly related" to his son. Third, boys who
grew up to be homosexual fit the stereotype of the sissy during latency
and adolescence, fearing physical injury and avoiding aggressive activity.

From these findings, the Bieber team drew several large conclusions.
Most important, a family constellation that included a close-binding-
intimate mother and a hostile, detached, and rejecting father strongly
predisposed a child to later homosexual orientation. In addition, the
group rejected constitutional factors as playing an important role. In
particular, they entirely rejected Freud's insistence on the centrality of
constitutional bisexuality and accepted Rado's refutation. The group
went further, however, and denied a homosexual phase in psychosexual

development, having found that fully forty-one percent of the hetero-sexual controls reported no homosexual "problem" whatsoever. In these terms, "latent" homosexuality simply did not exist, and homosexuality could be profitably considered as "latent heterosexuality." Thus, their rejection of Kinsey's figures for the incidence of homosexuality seemed borne out by their theoretical conclusions, and Bieber here and else-where claimed a lower incidence of one to two percent.

Others tried to replicate these findings. One study did not find the pattern of close-binding-intimate mothers in the childhood of homo-sexuals.[163] Another replicated Bieber's findings with disturbed ho-mosexuals, but could find few differences between the childhoods of undisturbed homosexuals and heterosexuals.[164] A series of major non-analytic studies of nonpatient homosexuals rejected Bieber's conclusions, though they did find a rough corroboration of some of his findings. They too found poor parental relationships, although they thought that this might be a retrospective finding. Importantly, they found that one fifth of all homosexuals enjoyed good relations with their fathers. In general, they could not distinguish nonpatient homosexuals from heterosexuals on the basis of psychopathology.[165] This last series of studies too was subjected to attempts at replication, and one of its findings—that mas-culine homosexuals did not go through a period of adolescent sissiness—was not borne out.[166] Another analyst qualified some of Bieber's findings, but he did not present new data,[167] and another researcher aptly pointed out that disturbed family relations were neither a necessary nor a sufficient cause of homosexual object choice.[168]

The Bieber study is flawed and its results vitiated, however, by serious methodological errors, and its applicability to psychoanalytic concep-tualization is qualified by certain explicit and implicit theoretical as-sumptions. The most serious and irremediable error is the sample, which consisted of patients in analytic therapy. These subjects had been preselected for psychopathology, so the question of the emotional dis-turbance of the homosexual population at large could not really be addressed. Bieber himself provided the diagnoses of his sample, apart from their sexual orientation: 28 of 106 were schizophrenic, 31 were neurotic, and 42 character disordered. While similar proportions ob-tained in the control group (although only eighteen percent of the controls were diagnosed as schizophrenic), Bieber's comparison in effect involves two groups of moderately to severely disturbed males. In addi-tion, ninety percent of the homosexual sample were "eager to conceal" their sexual orientation, and sixty-four percent wanted their homosexuality "cured." Thus, the Bieber team simply ignored the difficulties in obtaining a "normal" homosexual sample, which were outlined by workers such as Kinsey, Hooker, and Bell and Weinberg.[169] This omission was criticized at length,[170] but Bieber seems not to have understood or accepted the objection, dismissing it out of hand.[171] He continued to argue for the general applicability of his data, citing studies of homosexual adolescents committed to Bellevue Hospital, of soldiers during World War II arrested for homosexual activities, or of prison populations,[172] and later referring to a study done among low socioeconomic classes at "a municipal hospital."[173] It is dismaying to see a major study repeat the chronic psychoanalytic error of generalizing from disturbed patients to the general population.

Even more seriously limiting are certain overt and hidden assumptions that inform the study. Bieber announced in the first pages of the study that homosexuality was selected as a topic of investigation because it "would not present any diagnostic difficulties," an assumption that may astonish the attentive reader of the present history. In addition, Bieber assumed *a priori* that adult homosexuality was "psychopathologic," here and elsewhere repeating the usual clichés about the desperate viciousness of the unhappy homosexual.[174] Thus, beginning with the assumption that all homosexuals were disturbed and using a preselected disturbed sample, he found that indeed all homosexuals were disturbed.

Moreover, Bieber's adherence to the "revisionist" school led to ambiguities and uncertainties about his data and the conclusions that could legitimately be drawn from them. Bieber participated frequently in discussions centered on the Columbia school and the *American Journal of Psychoanalysis*, which explicitly rejected many of Freud's basic postulates about intrapsychic conflict and emphasized instead the interpersonal dynamics associated with the "adaptational" school. As we have seen, Bieber and his team entirely rejected the importance of constitutional factors in the development of homosexual object choice and dealt with the Oedipus complex only in its "simplified" positive form, neglecting its negative variety. They misunderstood Freud's ideas on narcissism, conflating it with autoerotism. They also claimed that the oral stage did not possess a sexual character.

Adhering to this revisionist form of psychoanalysis, they concentrated on family dynamics, seeing development as proceeding by the effect of interpersonal stress on a biological constitution that naturally pressed to normative heterosexuality. Nothing intrapsychic drew the developing psyche toward nonnormative outcomes, so for them any deviance was *ipso facto* evidence for severe interpersonal trauma. Thus, their attention was shifted away from biology, intrapsychic forces, and preoedipal development and toward events that occurred after the Oedipus complex had been negotiated. Their questionnaire is remarkable as a psychoanalytic document for its almost unqualified probing of events that transpired during latency and adolescence. It is important, therefore, to reexamine their conclusions, since it is not at all clear if such disturbance is the cause or result of homosexual object choice. This objection was raised from the discipline of clinical psychology and general psychiatry,[175] but it was rejected without argument by a member of Bieber's original team.[176]

By eliciting information about homosexuals' history at latency or after and by concentrating on characteristics of the family after the subject had passed through the Oedipus complex, the Bieber study implicitly assumed that later object choice had been determined by particular family constellations operating after the complex, and it interpreted its data in conformity with that assumption. It thereby avoided dealing with two alternative explanations: a more moderate one that sees the family system as maintaining and supporting a previous individual psychic development, and a more extreme one that views the family system not as the cause but as the result of that development. For example, the study found that seventy-two percent of homosexuals remembered their fathers as detached and hostile. It is not clear, however, if the father's withdrawal, assuming that it was accurately recalled, was the cause of the son's failure to have identified with him or the result of the son's sexual advances, an occurrence documented in a case presented by the Ostow study group.[177]

Nevertheless, the Bieber study became the standard investigation of male homosexuality, and for many it came to be regarded as the definitive psychoanalytic pronouncement. Still, it occupied a particularly vulnerable position in the range of psychological discourse, that of revisionist psychoanalysis. Classical, orthodox analysts rarely refer to it, and the advances in subtlety and profundity achieved by the latter group were largely unaffected by Bieber's research, as indeed they had to be, considering Bieber's rejection of many classical analytic assumptions. But Bieber's study also isolated itself from the developing discourse on homosexuality conducted by clinical psychologists, general psychiatrists, and sociologists. In the debate that preceded the APA decision, revisionist analysts found themselves pitted against this more general group of investigators without the powerful conceptual aid of more classical analysts, who, with the exception of Socarides, remained aloof from the fray.

CHAPTER **X**

A NEW BEGINNING: 1973–1982

By the 1970s, psychoanalysis was able to provide a coherent and searching theory of the perversions in general. Psychoanalytic theory on the whole continued to progress, adding greater refinements and qualifications to its knowledge. Such analysts as Gillespie and Khan could speak with great authority on the dynamics and phenomenology of the transformations of love that led to perverse sexual behavior. In addition, they were able to account clearly for certain types of homosexuality, especially those associated with psychotic, borderline, and fetishistic conditions. Still, there were obviously other forms of homosexuality that could not be so easily accommodated within the general theory of perversions. Responsible analysts acknowledged these difficulties, and the weight of accumulated clinical impressions began to force the revision of a monolithic theory that was becoming increasingly unusable.

But the relations of psychoanalysis to the rest of society began to be politicized, and there was a shift within psychoanalysis of the group that claimed the most public voice. The general upheaval of values in the 1960s included an important critique of the institutions of psychiatry and psychoanalysis, most notably by Szasz[1] and more profoundly by Foucault,[2] both of whom questioned the very notion of mental disease and pointed out the political nature of psychiatric discourse. Classical psychoanalysis did not respond to these issues in any substantial manner, although a shift in tone can be discerned in the work of many individual analysts, particularly on the theory of femininity and the notion of normalcy. Analysts of what we have been calling the "revisionist" school, however, did respond by attempting to include in their discourse a consciousness of larger social values and change. They turned away from emphasizing purely intrapsychic mechanisms, "biologizing" psychological concepts, and using such unproven and unprovable notions as primary aggression, constitutional bisexuality, and the like.

Because analysts of this school attempted to answer challenges from outside psychoanalysis, they participated primarily in the debate on the APA list of mental disorders urged by the homophile movement and by sympathetic psychological and sociological investigators. For the most part, classical analysts did not involve themselves. The major analytic spokesmen for both sides were revisionists: Marmor and Stoller in favor of deleting homosexuality from the list; Bieber and Socarides (who was more classical in orientation), joined by Gershman and Kardiner, against. Thus, the final outcome of the debate affected psychoanalysis only within the revisionist school, and, as we shall see, did not dramatically affect the larger—one might say glacial—ongoing movement of orthodox psychoanalysis. In fact, the changes we can discern in classical psychoanalytic discourse about homosexuality after the mid-1970s can be accounted for by possibilities that had evolved before the APA debate took shape.

Nowhere can the grounds for disagreement be seen more clearly than in the wide range of opinions expressed concerning the social and psychological adaptation of less disturbed homosexuals. Some analysts were quite definite that homosexual object choice could coexist with a "normal" and "healthy" psychological adjustment. Rosen, the editor of two volumes on sexual perversions, cited "cases . . . mainly of oedipal type . . . where there is no particular pathology of internal object relations, with a stable self and object representational world."[3] Spitzer, who oversaw the compilation of the third edition of the *Diagnostic and Statistical Manual* of the APA, but who was not an analyst, was equally clear about his reasons for recommending the deletion of homosexuality from the list: "a significant portion of homosexuals" were satisfied with their homosexuality, showed no significant signs of pathology, and could function well.[4] One French analyst, in an article devoted to showing the faulty ego-ideal of homosexuals and their typically fraudulent variety of creativity, nonetheless admitted that some were capable of true creativity and that "the object relations of homosexuality var[y] greatly according to the individual, stretching from an obvious part-object love to a total object-love closer to genitality."[5] Lachman argued forcefully that the development of deviant object choice could occur quite independently of other lines of development and cited the example of Mr. E., who was homosexual, but whose object relations were "complex, emotionally rich and with an appreciation of individual differences."[6] W. Brown agreed that some homosexuals were capable of "genuine affection, friendliness and cooperation,"[7] and Pasche claimed that homosexuality could not be considered a perversion since homosexual love, unlike true perversion, could involve a "full cathexis" of the object, including "tenderness, protectiveness and admiration."[8] Even the orthodox Bak knew of cases of "stable object relations" with "no appreciable defect in the psychic structure (either ego or superego)."[9] The fact that analysts finally could recognize the possibility of full homosexual love in their patients is manifested in Wiedemann's two summary articles. The earlier one ended with the statement that homosexual psychic organization, despite surface appearance, invariably utilizes "primitive psychical mechanisms,"[10] while the later admitted that "the development of the gender identity and of heterosexual orientation" may be disturbed "without an impairment of the capacity to work, to relate to others, to be creative in an artistic field, etc."[11] But the clearest and most unequivocal statement was Marmor's: "Many homosexuals, both male and female, function responsibly and honorably, often in positions of the highest trust, and live emotionally stable, mature and well-adjusted lives, psychodynamically indistinguishable from well-adjusted heterosexuals, except for their alternative sexual preferences."[12]

Still, for the most part, such acknowledgment of the capacity of homosexuals to employ mature object relations and a sound ego structure was qualified and grudging. Some analysts no longer urged a change in object choice as the sign of a successful treatment, but only an improvement in functioning in other areas of life. None of de Monchy's eight homosexual patients became heterosexual, but seven experienced a decrease in loneliness and reckless behavior.[13] Khan wrote movingly of the emotional achievement of his severely disturbed homosexual fetishistic patient, who could, as a result of treatment, endow a homosexual relationship with full object love.[14] Robertiello concluded that his patient's "perversion strikes me as a rather healthy compromise and I have encouraged him to accept it, since I think it is the best his ego can do at this point."[15] Such a qualified view, though it represented an important shift, still espoused the position that homosexual object choice was clearly *faute de mieux*. Wakeling claimed at most that homosexuals could escape "profound neurotic disorder,"[16] and even Socarides remarked on the high level of emotional, interpersonal, and creative achievement of some homosexuals. But for him such accomplishment was apparent only to "superficial examination"; another view emerged when they were "subjected to penetrating investigation of their defensive system."[17] Such a shift was exemplified by Gilbert, who contributed two cases he treated in 1966 and 1977 respectively, in which his view of optimal therapeutic outcome had changed under the influence of feminism and consciousness of population growth.[18] Three years later, he argued again for "therapeutic flexibility and cultural awareness" as "ingredients for a successful outcome" of treatment. But while generally urging a broader, relativistic view of "normal" psychosexual adjustment, he still held hopes for therapeutic cure in the case of adolescents, since they are "probably more amenable to treatment than the adult with similar problems."[19]

Still, most analysts, both orthodox and revisionist, continued to express the traditional themes of the disordered, unhappy, and vicious homosexual, employing reified notions of "*the* homosexual" and "*the* homosexual relationship." Many affirmed that "the homosexual" was capable of only a superficial and guilty relationship, and they painted dreary or lurid pictures of the viciously desperate "gay" life of the cities,[20] where "a small elite with money, power and prestige" prey on their helpless fellows instead of attempting to "change their pathological sexual pattern."[21] Kestenberg, in an angry, contemptuous article, characterized the typical homosexual as one who "falls in love violently like an adolescent . . . [d]ressing up in fancy clothes like a toddler," and classed him with "his relatives, the fetishists, transvestites and transsexuals."[22] Gershman denied any true creativity to the homosexual, except for such pseudocreative activities as "interior decorating and woman's hair dressing,"[23] a position advanced by another analyst from great Olympian heights.[24] For Kardiner, homosexuality, "aided [by] powerful lobbies and an indifferent press," allied itself with crime, murder, and racism to make modern life intolerable,[25] to which list his disciple Hendin added "suicide . . . and drug and alcohol abuse."[26] Toby Bieber warned her readers of "homosexuals who know they have venereal disease [and] will attempt to infect as many partners as possible."[27] Such analysts as Bieber, Kardiner, Gershman, and Hendin, even as they adopted sympathetic and libertarian stances, employed condescending and smarmy tones that would be offensive to anyone with minimal self-respect, and much of their sympathetic protestation concealed a profound distaste for homosexuals and a strategy to "cure" them.[28]

As a historian of the APA decision pointed out, the essentially negative view of homosexuality could not change as long as the norm of "natural" heterosexuality remained in force. Given this assumption, homosexuality had to be thought of as a deviation caused by trauma, and, given the centrality of sexuality in psychoanalytic theory, it necessarily involved defects in other areas of ego functioning and behavior: "it was the perspective on homosexuality that determined the meaning of observed clinical data, and not the other way around."[29] Ostow, in presenting the most informed psychoanalytic opinion, admitted that his study group "seemed to be adopting norms suggested by biologic—that is, reproductive—function. Yet," he added, "this judgment was rooted in an aggregate of clinical experience."[30] Such views could finally be challenged only when the place of sexuality in psychological organization was debated[31] and when the notion of "naturalness" was subject to critical examination.[32]

Yet the widespread opinion that all homosexuals suffer from a defective superego continued to be expressed, in disregard of contrary evidence and testimony, and based on a misunderstanding of psychoanalytic theory. Such analysts as Bieber and Socarides insisted on the primitive and defective superegos of homosexuals. For Socarides, it was this very defect that caused a defensive regression from sadistic heterosexuality to homosexual object choice.[33] Such convictions were reinforced by ideas such as that of Blos, who maintained that narcissistic and homosexual libidos have to be neutralized to permit the formation of the ego ideal.[34] Ostow accepted this formulation and drew the usual conclusions, since homosexuals do not "neutralize" their homosexuality and continue to make narcissistic object choices.[35] Chasseguet-Smirgel provided a more sophisticated explanation. The ego ideal is the heir of primary narcissism, but homosexuals remain fixated at that stage by having cathected the father narcissistically and by having identified with the mother. Hence the ego ideal can never be internalized but remains projected onto a masculine partner, from whom it is magically and primitively incorporated.[36] None of these analysts explained, however, why narcissistic objects could not serve as the nuclei for the superego or why an identification with the mother could not lead to an adequate moral ego ideal, an omission quite striking since such mechanisms serve well for all normal women. Gillespie, adumbrating a conflict theory for the development of homosexual object choice, thought that homosexual activity became possible and necessary because it avoided more dangerous heterosexual activity and because the superego permitted such a regressive choice of objects.[37] Other analysts like Limentani agreed,[38] citing earlier work that implicated the repressed homosexual strivings of the parents in inculcating and permitting homosexual activity in their children.[39]

This permissiveness supposedly revealed the defective nature of the superego,[40] but such a position contains an unexamined confusion. While it may be true that these parental figures, who are introjected to form their children's superegos, condone such deviance, the resulting superegos are not defective in a structural sense, but can be said only to contain values different from social norms. Gillespie's sophisticated argument, then, is not metapsychological at all, but really social in its preference for one set of values above another. An even stranger argument claims that since homosexuals do not conform to social pressures, they must labor under a weak or defective moral sense.[41] The implications of such a position are that a man whose homosexual orientation has been firmly established since childhood should, despite that orientation, marry a woman on false terms, raise children in such a family, and attempt to present himself as what he is not. One can legitimately wonder who has the defective moral sense. All these arguments were apparently unconvincing to many analysts, and the orthodox Bak, for example, simply asserted that he could find no defect in the superegos of some homosexuals.[42]

By the mid-1970s analysts of all persuasions were deeply divided on the most basic issues that had united them earlier, and claims made by some were denied by others, without any acknowledgment of disagreement or any attempt to resolve the debate either empirically or theoretically. For the first time, surveys of homosexuality, such as Wiedemann's, called for further research, while suggesting an uncertainty and rather deep discomfort with the range of inconclusive and contradictory ideas and evidence. In the paper he contributed to the NIMH Task Force publication on homosexuality, Marmor called for further research on such analytic notions as feminine identification and narcissistic object choice—a surprising admission of ignorance, considering the fact that these ideas had served as cornerstones of analytic theory for over half a century.[43] Another analyst urged empirical research on early object choice and child-rearing practices, so that the issues of the pathological nature of homosexuality could finally be settled.[44]

The startling fact was the inability of analysts to assert convincingly whether homosexual object choice necessarily represented an emotional disorder. For Stoller, homosexuality was "a large issue beyond my present understanding."[45] Socarides was sure of his convictions, based on fifteen years of clinical experience, but to maintain them he had to reject all the contrary evidence based on psychological testing, which he found naive and superficial.[46] He accepted Bieber's conclusions without criticism, but urged that a more rigorous methodology be employed by psychological investigators.[47] Friedman rejected Bieber's study for just these reasons—sampling errors and obvious bias—and concluded that nothing had been settled by the Bieber team.[48] Marmor called Socarides's evidence "essentially meaningless."[49] Everyone called for further research, but no one attempted to solve the formidable problems of sampling and bias.

But this conceptual disarray was due not only to inconclusive and contradictory evidence; three quarters of a century of discussion still had not resulted in a rigorous methodology. Despite the clear and frequent criticism of Bieber's sampling techniques, the same errors continued to be made. Rubinstein generalized his notion of "dual identification" from his experience with pedophiliacs who had been arrested,[50] and Scott actually attempted a classification of the forms of homosexuality using "material seen in hospital clinics, prisons and remand houses."[51] Bloch offered an entirely new etiology for "the seemingly bewildering symptomatology of homosexuality," and, while admitting that "other patterns also exist," she did not seem troubled that her entire sample consisted of four cases.[52] And Bieber remained entirely unaffected by the methodological criticism his study had encountered.[53]

In addition, many analysts continued to espouse the vulgar and ignorant notion that male homosexuals were not real men. Gershman referred to the homosexual's "fear of not being a man," and repeated this characterization several times later.[54] Bloch's new theory assumed that homosexuality was not a question of object choice but of a traumatic sexual reversal.[55] A similar error was made by analysts who assumed that homosexual object choice was a symptom of gender disturbance. Wiedemann made such an assumption in his enthusiastic review of Stoller's work, [56] and even Marmor tacitly subscribed to this view by including in his first volume on homosexuality Stoller's work on core gender disturbance resulting in cross-sex identity. [57] This conceptual conflation resulted in serious distortions of theory, particularly in articles in which homosexual object choice was grouped with transvestism and transsexualism. Kestenberg's distasteful article formalized the confusion, as he wrote of the homosexual "and his relatives, the fetishists, transvestites and transsexuals." [58]

The challenge that shook the APA had such a powerful and unexpected effect because it attacked psychoanalytic theory at a point where it was most incoherent and vulnerable. It was mounted by homophile groups whose spokesman, George Weinberg, was distinctly antianalytic in his views. Still, the larger questions they raised—most importantly, the notion of normalcy and the ethical issues implicit in treatment— seemed significant enough that they were taken up by certain analysts. The group that resisted the challenge, however, consistently refused to consider such issues and responded, for the most part, by reiterating traditional ideas. Thus, though the debate involved serious intellectual issues, the actual outcome was largely political in nature. The history of the debate was well told by Bayer. [59] He referred to it as "that bitter dispute," whose legacy of "lingering hostility" informed reminiscences years later. [60] It involved angry and circuslike disruptions of psychiatric conferences, wherein Bieber was called "a motherfucker" and one psychiatrist of a behavior modification bent was accused of having done his residency at Auschwitz.

Though almost submerged by more colorful political maneuverings, the intellectual debate is preserved in two sets of articles appearing in the March 1973 issue of the *International Journal of Psychiatry* and in the November 1973 issue of the *American Journal of Psychiatry*. But the grounds for the debate had been laid earlier. The very incoherence and inconclusiveness of the psychoanalytic theory of homosexuality was perhaps the most important precondition for the challenge. Kinsey's surveys of the sexual behavior of Americans, although they were not assimilated into psychoanalytic discourse, impugned the psychoanalytic notion of normalcy for many outside the discipline. Ford and Beach's studies of animal sexual behavior [61] challenged the biological argument psychoanalysis had used since Freud. And Hooker's investigations of the adaptation of homosexuals further undermined the analytic position. [62] Marmor, himself an analyst, had moved from a mild libertarian stance regarding homosexuality to an agnostic one to finally a vigorous combative position against prevailing psychiatric views,[63] and he continued to argue for a relative and culturally determined notion of normalcy.[64]

Green, who claimed not to be committed to a strict analytic position, began the debate by raising the question of how homosexuality could legitimately be considered a "deviant" form of sexual development. He claimed that neither the view that homosexuality was deviant nor the one that it was normal had been proven.[65] His position was affirmed by Bell, who thought that the question of object choice was not the most interesting one to pose[66]; by Davison, who urged that attention be paid to the quality of the relationship and not to the choice of object[67]; and by Hoffman, who decried the moralistic tone of much writing on the subject, and who pointed out that the etiology of homosexuality was not known.[68] Green went on to argue for a classification of sexual disorders of both homosexual and heterosexual varieties, in which homosexuality itself could not be taken as a sign of psychopathology.[69] Stoller was in basic agreement, arguing that homosexuality was not a diagnosis, properly speaking, since it represented only a sexual preference and not a constellation of symptoms, and since different sets of psychodynamics could give rise to that sexual preference. He, like Green, urged a classification based on personality types, with homosexual and heterosexual varieties, but seemed finally to want to junk the entire classification system.[70] Marmor completed the argument for deletion by denying that all homosexuals were emotionally disturbed, and he rejected Socarides's and Bieber's findings based on a patient sample as "essentially meaningless" for the current debate.[71] For him, the psychiatric labeling of deviance was essentially a moral activity and basically incompatible with the task of psychiatrists, who should be "healers of the distressed, not watchdogs of our social mores."[72] The acrimony of the debate appalled him, and he scolded his colleagues: "The cruelty, the thoughtlessness, the lack of common humanity in the attitudes of many conservative psychiatrists is I think a disgrace to our profession."[73]

These arguments were brushed aside by the spokesman for retention. Bieber insisted that homosexuality was not a normal variant, but the result of heterosexuality thwarted by "fear." He urged the classification of homosexuality as a kind of "sexual inadequacy" and was unimpressed by claims that any diagnosis added to the problems of homosexuals.[74] Socarides adopted a more combative tone, reaffirming that all homosexuals were in agony over their condition. He attacked Green's sensible and moderate questions as revealing "a total lack of scientific veracity."[75] Bieber, according to Socarides, was simply correct in his conclusions, and he rejected the evidence derived from nonanalytic research. Against contrary evidence, Socarides insisted that the sample on which analytic theory was based was not skewed and that only analysts were qualified to judge whether or not any condition was pathological. He was convinced that all homosexuals were severely handicapped since homosexual activity "does not occur between a male and a female, does not involve the penetration of the male organ into the female . . . and is, of course, ineffective for reproduction," an aim "determined by two-and-a-half billion years [sic] of human evolution."[76] His concession to the opposition was to urge the repeal of antihomosexual laws "at once."[77]

As the reader will have noticed, this exchange of views did not constitute a real debate. Instead, one view was merely set against its contrary. Nothing was decided, except that deep disagreement divided the psychiatric community, within which analysts—with the exception of those such as Marmor and Stoller—were the most conservative and resistant to modifying their views.[78] In such a situation, Spitzer, chairman of the APA Task Force on Nomenclature and Statistics, who was in charge of the revision of the *Diagnostic and Statistical Manual*, was left to decide. Impressed by the methodological criticism of Bieber's study, on which the conservative group had based much of its argument, he turned instead to a large nonanalytic psychiatric study of nonpatient homosexuals that found that "homosexuality constitutes the only 'asymptomatic' difference that reliably distinguishes between the homosexual male and his heterosexual counterpart."[79] He concluded, therefore, that "a significant portion of homosexuals" were satisfied with their homosexuality, showed no significant signs of pathology, and could function well interpersonally, socially, and vocationally. While he could not claim that homosexuality was "normal," the manual he edited should classify only disorders and not "sub-optimal organizations," and it should not imply certainty about issues where there was none. Mental disorders would be identified by the distress an individual felt or by an impairment of functioning. He therefore ruled that homosexuality would be deleted from the list of mental disorders and that a listing of "ego-dystonic homosexuality," that is, homosexuality that causes distress to the individual, would be included. Finally, this revision in the nomenclature, he thought, could provide the possibility of finding a homosexual to be "free of psychiatric disorder."[80]

In 1973, the Board of Trustees of the American Psychiatric Association affirmed Spitzer's decision, and, several months later, after a challenge led by Socarides, the general membership assented to the change. This represented an enormous political victory for one side and a stinging rejection of mainstream analytic views by the majority of practicing clinicians, since the American Psychological Association followed suit shortly. Still, few specific and concrete changes followed these decisions. The standard *Comprehensive Textbook of Psychiatry*[81] replaced Bieber's articles on homosexuality[82] with Marmor's.[83] While the former asserted that "dysfunction in heterosexual intercourse and orgasm indicates a neurotic disorder," the latter claimed that "many homosexuals, both male and female, function responsibly and honorably, often in positions of the highest trust, and live emotionally stable, mature, and well-adjusted lives, psychodynamically indistinguishable from well-adjusted heterosexuals, except for their alternative sexual preferences."

Despite these formal changes, however, the APA decision did not seem to cause any major change in attitude. An editorial appearing in the *American Journal of Psychotherapy* took strong issue with the decision, which it characterized as a capitulation to "coercive tactics" and an "unscientific" denial of "those genetically determined biologic mechanisms that guarantee heterosexuality which in turn guarantees the propagation of all higher animal species." The editor concluded by expressing concern that "well-meaning pseudointellectual parents" might bestow legitimacy on their offspring's "homosexual propensities."[84] Kardiner saw evidence of the rise of sexual anarchy and the collapse of civilization itself.[85] Socarides, reviewing the debate several years later, thought it a denial of scientific responsibility and the result of a "behavioristic" view of psychological events.[86] And Bieber, in a similar article, again rejected Hooker's findings and offered his own, concluding with a dark admonition against "homophile propaganda and misinformation."[87] Finally, four years after the APA decision, a survey polled psychiatrists' views of homosexuality. Although a majority of the voting members of the APA had favored deleting homosexuality from the *DSM III*, sixty-nine percent of the respondents to the survey thought homosexuality was "usually a pathological adaptation," and sixty percent thought homosexuals less capable of mature loving relations than heterosexuals. Significantly, it was not asked if they thought homosexuality was necessarily a pathological condition, which was the only point the APA decision actually addressed. In addition, the use of the word *adaptation* in the first question suggests a "revisionist" bias and intention in the survey itself.[88] In any case, although the APA had formally concluded its debate, the more general issues were still far from resolved.

Like the Kinsey Report before it, the APA decision had little specific effect on subsequent psychoanalytic thinking and writing. On the other hand, warnings that deleting homosexuality from the list of emotional disturbances would lead to a neglect of investigation into that condition proved to be unfounded. In the years following the APA decision, two important volumes appeared containing articles on homosexuality written from a variety of perspectives. Marmor revised his 1965 collection and retitled it *Homosexual Behavior: A Modern Reappraisal*. While providing an interdisciplinary approach within the social sciences for the general reader, its tone was decidedly more positive than the earlier volume.[89] And Rosen published a sequel to his earlier volume on sexual deviation, which contained important analytic articles on perversion in general and on specific aspects of homosexuality.[90] In addition, previously uninvestigated aspects of homosexuality and homosexual lifestyles began to provide material for psychoanalytic discussion. Altschuler presented information on males over the age of forty-five,[91] and Gershman attempted to illustrate the wide range of adaptation among stable homosexual couples.[92] Gilberg, after delivering a veiled plea for tolerance in the treatment of adolescent homosexuals,[93] presented two contrasting cases, illustrating the evolution of his notion of treatment goals from 1966 to 1977, ending with the conviction that homosexuals should be helped to adapt to their condition.[94]

But all articles after 1973 did not suddenly become homophiliac. Much psychoanalytic writing was directed toward reaffirming traditional notions of the necessary pathology of homosexual object choice. Bieber went on to represent his old findings,[95] and also attempted to combine psychoanalytic ideas with notions he borrowed from a behavior modification approach.[96] Socarides also continued to reaffirm his position, adducing his experience with greater numbers of homosexual patients.[97] Additional evidence for this position came from an unexpected source when Friedman, who had earlier criticized Bieber's study, reported his failure to replicate some of Saghir and Robins's findings, which had figured so prominently in the APA rejection of Bieber's evidence.[98] In addition, several analysts continued to espouse the view of homosexuals as undermining traditional social and cultural values,[99] and some used the freer debate inaugurated by the APA decision again to find some common sense in popular prejudice against homosexuals. One analyst was concerned lest "decriminalization" of homosexual acts be confused with "social institutionalization" and concluded that "the negative ego-alien affect of rejection of homosexual acts is to be expected in the heterosexual,"[100] a view seconded by another, who thought that the "common judgment that homosexuality is a form of antisocial behavior is therefore not altogether unwarranted."[101] None of these analysts seemed to think that the unreasonable hatred and fear of homosexuals was a phenomenon worth describing or condemning.

The APA decision did affect analytic writing, however, in the way some analysts began to acknowledge certain questions raised by the debate. In one general psychiatric overview of sexual deviation, Wakeling accepted deviation from heterosexual genital sexuality as a working definition of perversion, and claimed that it usually involved hatred and guilt, although "some individuals can suffer from sexual symptoms in the absence of profound neurotic disorder." He criticized Bieber's study, but pointedly declined to address the question of the possibility of a healthy homosexuality.[102] Riess, however, began an overview of psychological testing by questioning whether homosexuality was a "syndrome." He concluded that no tests could distinguish reliably between homosexuals and heterosexuals or between masculine and feminine homosexuals, although he noted studies that found a greater incidence of psychopathology among the latter.[103]

Riess's initial question was elaborated theoretically by Lachman, who argued that homosexuality was not a diagnostic category since sexual functioning, ego development, and object relations do not necessarily evolve in parallel lines. He traced the erroneous idea that they did back to Karl Abraham and Robert Fliess, who developed an "ontogenetic table" of parallel lines of development on which an individual could be located at a single level of fixation.[104] Lachman concluded that homosexual behavior had limited predictive value for other areas of psychological functioning, and presented the case of Mr. E., who was homosexual, but whose object relations were "complex [and] emotionally rich."[105] A similar argument was advanced by Tyson, who implicitly reached different conclusions. She attempted to account for the development of gender identity by seeing it as the composite of "core gender identity," "gender role identity," and "sexual partner orientation," all three of which could be considered "separate strands."[106] Still, the crucial question of whether an abnormality in one strand could exist independent of the other more normatively developed strands was untouched, and her article proved not to be useful in determining the possibility of "healthy" homosexual object choice.

The growing conviction that homosexuality was not a single clinical entity allowed analysts to attempt more sophisticated classification schemes. Even Socarides proposed that three levels of homosexuality be distinguished based on "level of libidinal fixation or regression . . . stage of maturation . . . and an inventory of ego functions." These were oedipal, preoedipal, and "schizo-homosexual." Most of his writings, however, concerned the second level, and he had little to say about the first. [107] The complexities of such a project of classification were outlined by Limentani in three articles. In the first, he dealt with the problem of "actual bisexuality," which represented an oscillation between narcissistic and anaclitic object choices, itself corresponding to a split in the preoedipal object. The "pseudogenitality" of such a condition represented a "severe preoedipal disturbance," which was handled by homosexuality and heterosexuality defending against each other. Under successful treatment, such bisexuality resolved into homosexuality. [108] In a later article he proposed that homosexual behavior be divided into three types: homosexuality against a background of hysterical, obsessional, or other personality types; "true" homosexuality as a symptom of borderline conditions and narcissistic and schizoaffective disorders; and actual bisexuality, which had its own specific psychopathology. [109] He developed this classification in the third article. The first type represented a kind of "latent heterosexuality" and a flight from the opposite sex under severe oedipal conflict and castration anxiety. Guilt was always present in this condition, and treatment, which was often successful, proceeded as with other neurotic disorders. The second represented "true" perversion, which warded off depression, overwhelming separation anxiety, and psychotic fantasies of mutilation. Such a condition did not involve guilt and was, in Limentani's experience, always incurable. The third, actual bisexuality, had been described in his first article. In all three types, however, Limentani saw the commonality of a homosexual "syndrome," and he accepted the norm of heterosexual genitality. [110] Marmor did not attempt a formal classification, but listed the varieties of homosexual behavior he had encountered, and the richness of his list seemed to preclude any clear and orderly classification. He concluded that it was possible to change overt behavior by treatment, but that the question of sexual arousal eluded theoretical understanding.[111]

Because of the APA decision, there was now authority to recognize varieties of homosexual organization and behavior that had previously gone unnoticed because they had not fit into generally accepted analytic theory. Even when writers declined to alter their theories, a new tone of tolerant curiosity and an appreciation for variety entered into analytic discourse. Khan continued his sensitive and subtle work on foreskin fetishism,[112] and "revisionist" analysts, even while they were attacking Freud's notion of passivity or the primacy of the penis, argued for the positive value of certain aspects of homosexual organization that had previously been thought of as pathological and maladaptative. I. Ross saw the development of "paternal identity" as based on what orthodox analysis had termed passive wishes to bear a child, which, according to Ross, were really active.[113] Even orthodox analysts, while advancing quite traditional points of view, assimilated the lessons of the acrimonious debate preceding the APA decision. Rosen claimed that all perversions were a clinical entity and shared certain defensive maneuvers and ego defects, but his careful and complex unraveling of the phenomenology of perverse identification with the mother revealed a new and humane attitude toward perverse behavior. Perhaps recalling some of the well-founded accusations leveled against psychiatry by homophile spokesmen, he began his article with the reminder that "psychoanalysts . . . treat patients, teach, and research into sexual problems with tolerance and respect."[114]

This openness also informed two important articles that directed attention to psychoanalysis itself. In *Psychiatry*, Mitchell attempted to rectify the mistaken notion that psychoanalysis was biased against seeing homosexuality as a natural variant of sexual organization and development, thus responding to some of the objections raised by homophile groups, as well as affirming the approach and methodology of analytic investigation. According to Mitchell, while psychoanalysis began by trying to account for psychopathological conditions, its complete task had always been to address all mental functioning, pathological and healthy. The identification of dynamic causes in itself does not imply the labeling of pathology, and Mitchell cited the example of interracial marriage, which, while it often had its roots in a fear of incest, could nevertheless rise above such preconditions into the realm of unconflicted functioning. He assented to the criticism that analytic investigation had been based on unrepresentative samples and employed biased language and metaphors, and urged that the analytic evaluation of mental functioning be based on the "relative weights of defensive and adaptive aspects in the behavior, the quality of interpersonal relationships, and the degree of development and integration of the self."[115]

The most interesting article of the period, and a fitting conclusion to our survey, is Kwawer's on the countertransferential aspects of psychoanalytic writing on homosexuality. It is extraordinary that it took fully three quarters of a century for psychoanalysis finally to recognize this issue. Generally speaking, it had been well recognized that the theory of psychoanalysis as well as the very data upon which it is constructed depends on the ability to conduct analytic sessions without the unconscious anxiety of the analyst distorting clinical material. Although Freud had pointed out that the acknowledgment of passive homosexual wishes in a man was the last impediment to a thorough analysis,[116] no one thought to attribute the intemperate and angry judgments of such ideologues as Bergler, Robbins, Silverberg, and Kardiner to countertransferential distortions. Kwawer began by observing just such lapses in self-scrutiny and sensitivity in some analytic writings on homosexuality, ranging from Bergler's vile tone to the generally accepted notion that homosexuality should be "cured." Although other views began to be voiced in more recent psychoanalytic writing, only Clara Thompson[117] had previously ventured such a divergent opinion from an authoritative stance. Kwawer insisted on the crucial difference between understanding and describing a condition and judging it, which, he observed, was a countertransferential act.[118]

Kwawer offered rather limited examples. Our own survey contains a larger sample. We have seen several analysts blithely report patients angrily or fearfully bolting treatment and attribute it to "resistance," without recognizing the demeaning language and attitudes they themselves employed in treatment. An example is Socarides's sanctimonious advice to physicians: "I ask you when you take a sexual history to respond with interest and compassion to efforts on the patient's part to communicate his shame and despair in the guilty revelation of behavior so demeaning and injurious to pride."[119] Gershman's reference to the "masculine bankruptcy" of his homosexual patients reveals a similar unwillingness to listen attentively to what exactly they might have wanted to tell him,[120] despite his profession of "feelings of openness, compassion and honesty."[121] In this light, Ovesey's insistence that the "latent" homosexuality of normal heterosexuals is not sexual at all but a form of "pseudohomosexuality" and Bieber's denial of constitutional bisexuality, whatever the objective merit of these claims, constitute evidence for an alienation and denial of those wishes in analysts themselves. Irving Bieber thought that Kinsey had overestimated the prevalence of homosexuality among American males, but he added his own flourish: homosexuals were underrepresented among Jews.[122] We recall Boehm's analogous claim that the pristine Germanic tribes never practiced such deviant behavior until they were corrupted by the decadent Romans.[123] In the entire history of analytic ideas about male homosexuality until Kwawer, there had not been one article that described and discussed countertransferential feelings that arose from the analyst's own uncertainties and anxieties.

The reader would now be finishing quite a different history if Kwawer's article, or one following a similar approach, had figured prominently at its beginning. The material for it existed in Freud's writings, in its attention to an ineluctable homosexual component in all psychic organizations and to the necessary anxiety it causes, as well as in its acknowledgment of uncertainty and the incompleteness of his knowledge. The history we have traced, alongside impressive insights and painstaking attention to detail and nuance, is at least partly the history of analytic countertransference and anxiety. The APA decision, though it was not conducted according to analytic rules of discourse, and although it contained much that was polemical and angry, did finally open up new possibilities for more profound and subtle understanding. In certain ways, then, it can be viewed as the beginning of a new history, with a promise of acknowledging the involvement of analytic procedures in the very data of psychoanalysis, and thereby of transforming what had been largely a discourse based on distance and judgment into a genuine dialogue in which troubled people can speak unguardedly to listeners who are open to hearing.

CHAPTER **XI**

CONCLUSIONS

Readers may now congratulate themselves for having emerged from a long wandering in the tangled underbrush of our history. Despite the dismaying profusion of names, theories, and influences, readers may, nevertheless, have been able to discern some larger trends and developments. But even if they assume clarity and serve to provide some organization for the proliferation of detail in our history, readers will still not think of it as a progressive and unitary narrative. Instead, the primary effect has been to reveal conflicting tendencies and issues that are either more or less clearly articulated and discussed. While specific areas of knowledge about homosexual object choice have indeed grown in clarity and incisiveness, the general topic has neither assumed a conceptual clarity nor commanded universal agreement among analysts, who, after all, in most respects share common assumptions and methods. Yet, despite these deep divisions, individual schools of psychoanalysis have claimed ever-increasing clarity and formalization of their theory.

On the whole, the progressive rigidification of psychoanalytic attitudes toward homosexuality represents not so much the advancement of knowledge and information as it does something else. The most general point to make about the psychoanalytic theory of male homosexuality is that it was not based, as scientific theories supposedly are, on an unbiased inspection and ordering of its data, but on the confluence of that approach with historical accident, unexamined moral and social judgment, and the vagaries of the history of psychoanalysis and psychoanalytic discourse at various points in its evolution. To be sure, it is now generally recognized that even in the "hard" sciences, theories are not

218

formulated by the mere objective and unbiased inspection of neutral data, but that the data themselves are collected and ordered according to *a priori* assumptions. In this respect, psychoanalytic theory is neither remarkable nor objectionable. What does distinguish it from other, more nearly scientific and validly formulated theories, however, is the flaws and defects in its development and the refusal of psychoanalysis to look critically at its own methods and discourse.

From the beginning, most analysts have acknowledged that their clinical data have been biased. Freud himself observed that "perverts who can obtain satisfaction rarely have occasion to come in search of analysis,"[1] and he was aware that his patients represented a subgroup of sexual deviants who were unhappy with their condition or who could not reconcile their sexual proclivities with other social and personal requirements. Yet no attempt was ever made within psychoanalysis to rectify this error in sampling, and even recently some went so far as to deny that the psychoanalytic sample was in any way skewed.

The rigidification of analytic ideas based on limited evidence can be seen more clearly if we consider how the ideal of the bourgeois nuclear family has fared in psychoanalytic discourse. From the beginning, it was seen as the breeding ground of emotional disturbance. But more significant, as family therapy began to be established as a discipline, more compelling data were derived indicating its pathological nature. If analytic judgment of the family as a social institution had been based on clinical experience, we might expect most analysts to have condemned it for its pathogenic workings, since families seen in therapy are necessarily disturbed. Yet this was not the case. Instead, we find analysts, even when the institution of the nuclear family was under the greatest attack in the 1960s, claiming that it was an optimal arrangement. Kardiner, for example, in decrying the social forces subverting civilized life, praised the family as "one form of social patterning with consistent success."[2] The reasons why many analysts found merit in an institution that was clinically so pathological must lie in a prior allegiance to it and to the larger cultural patterns in which it was embedded. It seemed to be self-apparent that the families seen in therapy represented a deviation from the healthy norm. Yet such an allowance was, after the early years of psychoanalysis, never made for sexual deviation.

It is a striking fact of our history that both the conviction that homosexual object choice was necessarily psychopathological and the extremity of negative characterizations of homosexual general functioning became prominent in the years following World War II. At the risk of committing a *post hoc propter hoc* error, I suggest that the historical trauma of the war was one cause of this shift in opinion. Along with the geographical move of psychoanalysis from Berlin and Vienna first to London and then to New York City, the attack on liberal institutions by Fascism resulted in a reaffirmation of bourgeois values, especially those of an American variety. It is remarkable how many times in the postwar period homosexuals were compared to Nazis,[3] when quite the opposite comparison could as easily have been made. In addition, the rejection of Kinsey's impugning of the myth of American sexuality frequently employed calls to patriotism and warnings against cooperating with foreign propaganda.[4] The anxiety returned, however, in the repeated use during this period of the chilling phrase *a solution to the problem of homosexuality*. It is as if psychoanalysis, having found refuge in a new homeland, sought to demonstrate its relief, gratitude, and worthiness by subscribing to and by lending its weight to the consolidation of American values and institutions. This led to a narrowing of the more nearly cosmopolitan European stance of the early Freudians. We may see evidence of this in the general tendency of British analysts to entertain alternative social arrangements and sexual orientations, in comparison with more nearly American tendencies to see their own institutions as natural and universal.

This Americanization of psychoanalytic discourse can be discerned in other trends within psychoanalysis as well. The very ability to see homosexuality as a clinical entity depended on defining it not by its dynamics or phenomenology, but by its characteristic behavior. In this clear operationalization of an analytic concept, American psychoanalysis drifted toward a kind of American positivism and, startlingly, closed ranks with its sworn enemy, behaviorism. By turning away from intrapsychic dynamics, by rejecting the determining value of constitutional factors, and by emphasizing instead familial events, psychoanalysis became firmly ameliorational in its outlook and ideals. It was simply un-American to continue to think that fate or biology determined individual destinies. To be sure, these revisionist schools developed powerful criticisms of the family, but they did so not so much to reject it as pathogenic as to allow it to attain an optimal form. In these terms, psychoanalysis denied its function as radical critic of cultural forms in order to become an ameliorative agent of a particular society.

In other words, as psychoanalysis developed, it became less and less critical, politically and socially. To be sure, Freud was quite conservative in his personal life and artistic tastes and, for the most part, eschewed any involvement in the political issues of his day. But his intellectual stance located him clearly outside the particular cultural values and institutions of his lifetime, and he continued to maintain that individual strivings and satisfactions existed in an irreducibly inimical relation to society in any of its forms.[5] In particular, he saw that participation in civilized life required instinctual renunciation and necessarily resulted in emotional disturbance.[6] The triangulation of psychoanalysis with the individual's biological nature and his civilized values allowed such later thinkers as Marcuse to frame a radical critique of bourgeois society.[7] By the time of the 1950s, however, the most vocal spokesmen for psychoanalysis had traversed the distance separating their discipline from social institutions and had assumed the stance of defenders of those institutions. Kardiner's praise of the nuclear family and his alarm at the forces undermining social life as he defined it are examples of this *embourgeoisement* of psychoanalytic values.[8] It is in this period after World War II that we read repeatedly of "the heroic task of heterosexuality," a phrase that simultaneously sets up bourgeois social forms as an almost spiritual ideal and suggests that such forms are under attack and in need of strenuous and wearisome support.

Once particular social forms had been assimilated into the values of psychoanalysis, all those phenomena that lay outside these forms or threatened them had to be alienated and reified. Hence, we begin reading accounts of "the homosexual." In addition, though some analysts claimed that they were laboring for the good of both society and the sexual deviant (such as Silverberg with his proposal for "enlightened policy"),[9] their allegiance was clearly with the former. Starting especially with Bergler, who argued that the presence of guilt, conscious or unconscious, in the homosexual determined whether treatment would succeed,[10] the dismayingly low rates of "cure" for homosexual object choice began to be attributed not to deficiencies in analytic knowledge or technique, nor to the possibility that such a condition could not or should not be treated, but to the moral recalcitrance of the homosexual himself. For treatment to succeed, a homosexual patient had to feel guilty and ashamed of his sexuality. Thus, fifty years after Freud had removed sexual deviance from the category of moral failure, some analysts replaced it there, and the persistence of homosexual activity in the face of offered treatment was again seen as the manifestation of immoral and vicious proclivities. Psychoanalysis had thus become a moral discipline, adhering to a particular set of social values that, although they had no necessary place in analytic theory, became assimilated into the personal values of many analysts and finally infiltrated analytic theory itself.

We have seen the distorting effect of this in the various pronouncements analysts felt entitled to make regarding subjects about which they had no particular competence to speak. Bergler constantly passed negative literary and moral judgments on the achievements of Proust and Melville,[11] Roy on Lytton Strachey,[12] and a whole list could be compiled of analytic opinions on homosexuality in the ancient world.[13] For the most part, analysts' opinions were extremely vulgar and ignorant. Whereas the early group of analysts looked to classical and Oriental civilizations as a test of their own cultural experience, later analysts, especially after the war, simply denied these discrepant values and institutions, judging them to be psychopathological.

When Bychowski claimed that clinical observation showed the personality of the homosexual to be disturbed,[14] he directly contradicted Freud, who explicitly denied the truth of such a generalization. He was, to be sure, more sophisticated than Freud in technique and theory, but his pronouncement derived primarily from his personal values and experience, not from his sophistication as an analyst. It is a blank fact that, with very few exceptions,[15] the familiarity with the world and with a larger cosmopolitan culture revealed by most analytic writers is quite limited and provincial compared with that of groups of humanists for whom the homosexuality of figures from Plato and Sophocles, through Michelangelo and Leonardo, to such contemporary writers as Barthes and Wittgenstein is a casually accepted aspect of their artistic and intellectual achievement.[16] For many analysts, the progressive refinement of their technique and theory served as justification for narrowing the range of values they could entertain.

We have seen that for Freud and his contemporaries, all varieties of psychic organization were neurotic compromise formations. Some, to be sure, were more disturbed than others, but all necessarily required instinctual renunciation severe enough to cause inhibition in social, interpersonal, or vocational functioning. This was so because the Oedipus complex, as the principal determinant of subsequent psychosexual development, was a mechanism of trauma and the producer of distinctly human, nonnatural organization. All outcomes, including the normative heterosexual form, were, strictly speaking, unnatural and neurotic. But later analysts, especially those associated with the *Journal of the American Academy of Psychoanalysis*, explicitly denied this view, and their positing only one outcome of the Oedipus complex as normative corresponds to their espousing the values and institutions of bourgeois American society as ahistorically optimal, natural, and even universal.

Despite the vocal pronouncements of these analysts, there remained within the orthodox tradition of psychoanalysis another viewpoint that freely admitted an inability to delineate the contours of such concepts as health or normalcy. Freud was explicit on the matter: "it is not scientifically feasible to draw a line of demarcation between what is psychically normal or abnormal; so that the distinction, in spite of its practical importance, possesses only a conventional value."[17] And recently, one of the most orthodox of analysts made the same point:

> . . . both the normal and the pathological arise from psychic conflicts that originate in the same childhood instinctual wishes— both are vicissitudes of the same drive derivatives. If the resulting compromise formation permits a substantial degree of pleasure, a minimum of inhibition of function, little or no unpleasure, and does not involve the individual in any serious difficulties with his or her environment, both human and nonhuman, it qualifies as normal. . . . It is not the fact that something in mental life is related to psychic conflict that marks it as neurotic. All that we enjoy and prize in mental life— all that we rightly call normal—is as closely related to the same or similar conflicts originating in childhood instinctual wishes as is what we call pathological.[18]

Starting in the 1930s, however, and gathering strength after the war, a shift in analytic views can be discerned. Specifically, most analysts claimed without reservation that heterosexual genitality was the only natural and healthy result of psychosexual development, that homosexuality was a perversion in the technical sense, and that all homosexuals necessarily suffered from primitive object relations, impaired ego functions, and a defective superego. Significantly, these claims were never set out in an orderly fashion nor were their empirical or theoretical bases clearly delineated. Instead, they were merely asserted and propagated. Thus, in the present history, we cannot point to a specific contribution that determined this change in doctrine; we can only refer generally to a shift in opinion.

Why such a self-conscious discipline as psychoanalysis should have thus committed itself must ultimately be ascribed to the nature of homosexuality and to the place it occupies in the psychic organization of analysts themselves. Freud claimed that the acknowledgment by a man of his passive homosexual yearnings was the final impediment to a completed analysis,[19] so it is not entirely surprising that psychoanalysis has failed to deal with the subject of homosexuality with its customary equanimity. In fact, for the most part, psychoanalysis' relation to that condition has been one of alienated enmity. Such a relation did not obtain in the early years of psychoanalysis. Freud contributed to the Festschrift for Magnus Hirschfeld, the homosexual activist and investigator of sexual deviance, and the Hirschfeld Institute regularly published psychoanalytic articles on homosexuality with approving prefatory notes by the editors. Freud and Rank expressly opposed the exclusion of homosexuals from analytic candidacy on the basis of their sexual orientation alone.[20] Brill and Ferenczi were extremely sympathetic to the condition of homosexuals, and they entertained a range of alternative viewpoints that would not appear again in our history until the 1970s. When early analysts revealed irritation or shock at homosexual behavior, it was primarily at the sociopathic activities of latent or repressed homosexuals, such as Boehm observed in the drinking bouts of the *Burschenschaften* or in the infamous whorehouses of the time. But the homosexuality they were describing was a universal component of human nature, and they were alert to detect it in the highest achievements of the race as well as in their own experience. These early analysts felt comfortable in keeping open the relation between object choice and more general psychic structure and functioning.

But there was from the beginning a tendency, which became more pronounced later, to see homosexuals as deeply flawed and incomplete human beings.[21] The mechanisms described that led to homosexual object choice—identification with the mother and the narcissistic choice of objects—though they did not apply to all forms of homosexuality, established an affinity between homosexuals and that other group of people who would forever remain incomplete—women. It is, in fact, remarkable how many characteristics ascribed to homosexuals were also applied to neurotic women: the conviction of having been castrated, the search for the lost penis in the father, the attempt to be loved instead of striving actively to love. It had never been shown how a constellation of mechanisms that were normative for half the race could be psycho-

pathological for another group (although Waelder distinguished neurotic compromises on the basis of whether they were determined by
"impossibility" or "anxiety").[22] But the endurance of the habit of seeing
homosexuals as ambiguous in their sexual identity reinforced the fashionable and erroneous view advanced by Hirschfeld himself that homosexuals were an intermediate sex, a group of women trapped in the
bodies of men.

In certain important respects, the analytic failure in dealing with
homosexuality can be viewed as at least partly the result of an initial
gynecophobic stance. Homosexuals were seen as deeply flawed and
defective because they shared certain psychic characteristics with
women. A history comparable to the present one could be written on
psychoanalytic ideas about femininity since, from the beginning, analysts were biased toward regarding women as essentially inferior to men.
The centrality of the penis, the notion that both sexes begin their
psychosexual development as little boys, the psychic consequences of
imagined castration, the trait of masochism, the supposedly underde-
veloped superego, and the transformation of love into passive forms all
served to establish women as defective men. Though Freud himself was
at pains to deny any intention to disparage feminine psychic organization, the ethos of early psychoanalysis was clearly masculine in its
orientation and values.

What distinguishes the psychoanalytic theory of femininity from that
of homosexuality, however, is the fact that almost from the beginning
the former theory was elaborated, challenged, and qualified by such
women analysts as Bonaparte, Deutsch, and Thompson, who kept it
from falling into the hands of men whose cultural values and countertransference would have rendered it a system of alienated observation
about reified objects. Without women, the theory could easily have
become a distanced system of observation, judgment, and, as Foucault
shows,[23] control, operated by men with women as their objects of study.
But from an early stage, those who were primarily affected by such a
developing discourse took part in its formulation. Horney, writing about
the universal fear of female genitalia, could observe with authority that
the countertransference of male analysts had previously caused the
acknowledgment of such fears to be repressed,[24] just as in the present
period, Bell ventured a similar critical observation with regard to "testicular anxiety."[25] This participation by the objects of discourse in the
discourse itself raised it to the level of a real dialogue of intersubjectivity,

in which the distinction of subject and object constantly shifts. Hence, femininity is now no longer considered to be a position of inferiority, but a particular point of view, with its own advantages and perquisites.

The present history allows me now to make the claim that the essentially gynecophobic stance of early psychoanalysis, having been purged from the theory of femininity, found refuge in the theory of homosexuality, which, unlike the former discourse, did not permit its objects to participate in its formulation. There has not been in the history I have sketched a single analytic writer who could identify himself as a homosexual. Indeed, according to Marmor in 1980, no major analytic institute will admit a homosexual to candidacy.[26] The psychoanalytic discourse on homosexuality has been and still is formulated by nonhomosexuals about homosexuals, and the direction of observation, judgment, and control extends in one direction only. Just as some early analysts were at pains to claim implicitly that they were not women—they had penises, identified with their fathers, chose objects on an anaclitic basis, and possessed superegos that were capable of real fair-mindedness and the upholding of civilized values—many later ones claimed that they were not homosexuals. In terms of formal discourse, this required the distancing and reification of their object, "the homosexual." Intrapsychically, it required the alienation and repudiation of any trace of homosexual trends in their own psychic nature. When Ovesey and his colleagues advanced the notion of "pseudohomosexuality," they were attempting to come to the aid of men troubled by feelings of inferiority and powerlessness, to whom the charge of latent homosexuality would be "catastrophic,"[27] just as Bergler earlier had striven to relieve "the Milquetoast" of "unjust" impugnings of his masculinity.[28] But the judgment that the yearning to love another man is horrendous, while the desire to subjugate or humiliate him is not, represents a kind of countertransferential distortion. Similarly, Rado's repudiation of the notion of constitutional bisexuality[29] and its general acceptance by revisionist analysts point to a similar belief that homosexuality is not an irreducible component in human emotional life but an extirpatible product of maladaptation. These analysts, in claiming that such a constellation of impulses and wishes did not necessarily exist in their patients, were also protesting that they themselves suffered no taint of a condition that impugned their masculinity. It is in these terms that we should understand Irving Bieber's quite groundless claim that Jews were underrepresented among the population of homosexuals.[30]

Given this need to alienate and repudiate homosexual strivings, the psychoanalytic representation of homosexuality assumed fictional forms, bearing only a passing resemblance to its natural manifestations. The conviction that homosexuality was a single clinical entity arose without the aid of supporting evidence and contradicted clinical experience, the testimony of authoritative analysts, and the difficulties others encountered when they attempted to use such a unitary concept. In addition, the frequent ignorant portrayal of the sad and desperate lives of practicing homosexuals had its roots more in imaginative literature than in clinical experience or knowledge of the world at large. These vicious stereotypes found their models in anti-Semitic and racist propaganda, and they served a similar function in relieving anxiety by projecting and castigating tendencies that were alien and fearful. Hence the unreasoning rejection of evidence that contradicts such judgments. Many analysts were convinced of what they knew or thought they knew, and no evidence could shake their convictions, based as they were on unacknowledged intrapsychic conflict, anxiety, and defense.

This projection of analysts' own alienated impulses was coupled with an attack on homosexuals conducted with an intemperance, ferocity, and lack of empathy that is simply appalling in a discipline devoted to understanding and healing. The range of hostility includes Bergler's sadistic onslaughts, Gershman's false and queasy solicitude, and Hornstra's magisterial scorn. The denial of any true creativity in homosexuals or the insistence on their inability to sustain mature object relations forms part of this campaign of enmity. Throughout our history, so-called factual claims have been phrased in provocative and offensive language. It is one thing to claim that every homosexual has a fetishistic relation to his partner's penis, and quite another to observe rhetorically that "the urinal is the temple and marketplace of penises."[31] What is equally remarkable is the failure of other analysts who had no stake in this dreary campaign to rebuke the offensive stance and tone of their more voluble colleagues. It cannot be claimed in defense of the analytic establishment that analysts were unaware of the situation, since review articles of such work as Bergler's or Socarides's deliberately muted or ignored extravagant claims and vicious language.[32]

From the time of Freud's first contact with the emotionally disturbed in Charcot's clinic, the analytic stance has consisted of the neutral and sympathetic act of listening. Since only the analysand himself can provide information about the particular experience of his life, the analyst must purge himself of all values and expectations—including, according to Schafer,[33] even the hope that the analysand improve—so that he might enter fully into the world of his patient. The evolving discourse is essentially the analysand's, clarified and bolstered by his attentive listener. The analysand is therefore both subject and object of that discourse, and the analyst himself, having engaged his empathic capacities, plays a similar dual role. It is in these terms that we can speak of the analytic dialogue as being intersubjective. This is what distinguishes psychoanalysis from other more nearly scientific disciplines that require the clear demarcation of subject and object and the positing of a stance of observation apart from the object, as well as the purging of any subjectivity. But revisionist analysts have hopelessly muddled this project by setting themselves apart as distant and authoritative observers and evaluators of their objects, listening only for confirmation of their theories and rejecting other information as denial or resistance. But they have also failed to purge themselves of their own subjectivity and have thereby allowed the countertransference described by Kwawer to determine the shape and values of analytic discourse. Intersubjectivity has thus collapsed into solipsism.

Similar failures can be observed in the history of other humane disciplines such as literary criticism and anthropology, but part of their scholarly tradition has included the critical examination of previous approaches and formulations, as well as the sincere invitation to other disciplines to judge and influence discourse. Psychoanalysis by its very nature cannot afford such checks on its excesses and errors. Its methods are necessarily hermetic, and its data are not replicable. For an outside observer to be competent to judge and criticize psychoanalytic discourse, he must be part of the institution in need of such judgment and criticism. But psychoanalysis has formally forbidden this participation of homosexuals. Their only permissible stance is that of troubled and guilty supplicants. Anything else is resistance and sociopathy.

The only safeguards psychoanalysis can avail itself of are internal: the cogency of its theory and the integrity of its method. It must be attentive to the plausibility of its claims and open to qualifications from biology, on the one hand, and the social sciences, on the other. The exact limits of analytic formulations must be delineated with great precision, especially in regard to judgments of "normalcy" and "naturalness." In addition, the coherence of the theory must be clearly and precisely examined, ambiguities clarified, and extratheoretical judgments purged.

Innovations in theory must be rigorously examined to determine how compatible they are with the stock on which they are to be grafted. And it is the responsibility of the community of analysts to be alert to violations of analytic norms of neutrality and empathy and constantly to strive to maintain the intersubjective nature of their discipline.

Whether literary criticism distorts the meaning of a poet dead several centuries or anthropology misunderstands the values of a remote culture is a small matter compared to the human suffering and desperation caused by analytic failures. Analytic goals are understanding and healing, not judgment and conversion. Insofar as analysis settles for the latter, inferior set of goals, it denies both the scientific and humane bases of its privileged position. The impressive achievements we have traced in this history all stem from an adherence to more demanding requirements, and the work of such analysts as Freud, Glover, Gillespie, and Khan are human achievements of the highest order. The return of psychoanalysis to the methods and values of these analysts and its repudiation of egregious deviations from that ideal would mark the beginning of a new stage of understanding and healing.

NOTES

CHAPTER I. INTRODUCTION

1. Bergler, 1956a.
2. Ibid.
3. S. Goldberg, 1982.
4. Lewy, 1967.
5. Hitschmann, 1933.
6. C. Thompson, 1947.

CHAPTER II. FREUD

1. S. Freud. 1905a.
2. S. Freud, 1911.
3. Gay, 1968; Schorske, 1981.
4. Schorske, 1981.
5. Binion, 1968.
6. Salis, 1964.
7. Blaukopf, 1973.
8. S. Freud, 1930b.
9. S. Freud, 1933.
10. S. Freud, 1910a.
11. S. Freud, 1905a.
12. S. Freud, 1910a.
13. Ibid.
14. S. Freud, 1908c.
15. S. Freud, 1910b.
16. S. Freud, 1905a.
17. S. Freud, 1914a.
18. S. Freud, 1920a.
19. S. Freud, 1922.
20. S. Freud, 1910a.
21. S. Freud, 1920a.
22. S. Freud, 1905a, 1908d.
23. S. Freud, 1916b.
24. Nágera, 1970.
25. S. Freud, 1919a.
26. S. Freud, 1905a.
27. S. Freud, 1919a.
28. S. Freud, 1940a.
29. S. Freud, 1905a.
30. E.g., S. Freud, 1930a.
31. S. Freud, 1908d.
32. S. Freud, 1940a.

33. S. Freud, 1910a, 1914b.
34. S. Freud, 1908d.
35. S. Freud, 1911.
36. S. Freud, 1922.
37. S. Freud, 1930b.
38. S. Freud, 1905a.
39. S. Freud, 1903.
40. S. Freud, 1935.
41. S. Freud, 1921b.
42. S. Freud, 1935.
43. S. Freud, 1920a.
44. S. Freud, 1919a.
45. E.g., Bergler, 1944a.
46. S. Freud, 1918.
47. S. Freud, 1918, 1919a, 1930a.
48. S. Freud, 1920a.
49. S. Freud, 1905a.
50. S. Freud, 1909a.
51. S. Freud, 1910a.
52. S. Freud, 1908c, 1910a, 1923b.
53. S. Freud, 1926.
54. S. Freud, 1905a.
55. S. Freud, 1927, 1940b.
56. S. Freud, 1905a, 1915a, 1916b.
57. S. Freud, 1914a.
58. S. Freud, 1909a.
59. S. Freud, 1905a, 1908a.
60. S. Freud, 1905a.
61. S. Freud, 1910a.
62. S. Freud, 1921a.
63. S. Freud, 1922.
64. S. Freud, 1917.
65. S. Freud, 1921a.
66. S. Freud, 1925, 1931, 1933.
67. S. Freud, 1918.
68. S. Freud, 1908b.
69. S. Freud, 1918.
70. S. Freud, 1937.
71. S. Freud, 1913a.
72. S. Freud, 1923a.
73. S. Freud, 1922.
74. Ibid.
75. S. Freud, 1917.
76. S. Freud, 1937.
77. S. Freud, 1940a.
78. S. Freud, 1905a, 1908d, 1910c, 1940a.
79. S. Freud, 1905a, 1919a.
80. S. Freud, 1905a.
81. Plato, 1961a.
82. S. Freud, 1920a.

CHAPTER III. THE EARLY FREUDIANS: 1900–1930

1. Jones, 1926.
2. Boehm, 1922.
3. Nachmansohn, 1922.
4. S. Freud, 1905a, 1910a.
5. S. Freud, 1922.
6. Rank, 1922; Sachs, 1923.
7. Ferenczi, 1914b.
8. Sadger, 1908a, 1908b, 1910a, 1910b, 1913, 1914, 1919, 1921.
9. Boehm, 1920, 1922, 1926, 1933.
10. Boehm, 1921a, 1923, 1930.

11. Boehm, 1921b, 1924.
12. Boehm, 1933.
13. Ferenczi, 1914b.
14. Boehm, 1920.
15. Boehm, 1921a.
16. Hitschmann, 1923.
17. Sadger, 1910a.
18. Sadger, 1913.
19. E.g., Bergler, 1944a; Socarides, 1968a.
20. Sadger, 1908b.
21. Sadger, 1908a.
22. Rank, 1922.
23. Boehm, 1933.
24. Ferenczi, 1914b.
25. Brill, 1913.
26. Rank, 1922.
27. Sadger, 1908b.
28. Brill, 1913.
29. S. Freud, 1921b.
30. Ferenczi, 1914b.
31. Sachs, 1923.
32. Sadger, 1913.
33. Boehm, 1920.
34. Hitschmann, 1923.
35. Hárnik, 1924.
36. S. Freud, 1905a.
37. Hoenig, 1976.
38. Foucault, 1978.
39. Hirschfeld, 1914.
40. S. Freud, 1905a.
41. S. Freud, 1905a, 1908d, 1910a, 1911.
42. Sadger, 1908b, 1913.
43. Ferenczi, 1909.
44. Brill, 1913.
45. Nachmansohn, 1922.
46. Sherman and Sherman, 1926.
47. Henry, 1937.
48. S. Freud, 1910a.
49. S. Freud, 1922.
50. S. Freud, 1911.
51. Boehm, 1921b.
52. Sadger, 1910a.
53. Boehm, 1926.
54. Burrow, 1917.
55. E.g., Socarides, 1968b.
56. Boehm, 1926.
57. Fenichel, 1930.
58. Sadger, 1921.
59. Brill, 1913.
60. S. Freud, 1914a.
61. Fenichel, 1930.
62. Boehm, 1933.
63. Jekels, 1913.
64. Boehm, 1926.
65. Ferenczi, 1914b.
66. Boehm, 1922.
67. Sadger, 1919.
68. Staerke, 1920; Ophhuijsen, 1920; Boehm, 1933.
69. Nachmansohn, 1922.
70. Sadger, 1913.
71. Sadger, 1910b.
72. Hitschmann, 1923.
73. E.g., Boehm, 1926.
74. S. Freud, 1911.
75. Gardner, 1931.
76. E.g., Morichau-Beauchant, 1912; Ferenczi, 1912, 1914a; Hitschmann, 1913; Shackley, 1914; Staerke, 1920; Ophhuijsen, 1920; Gardner, 1931; Brill, 1934.
77. Chalus, 1977.
78. Rank, 1922.
79. Jekels, 1913.
80. Hárnik, 1924.

81. Hitschmann, 1923.
82. Boehm, 1920, 1921a.
83. Riggal, 1923.
84. Gardner, 1931.
85. Henry, 1937.
86. Boehm, 1922.
87. Sadger, 1908a.
88. Klein, 1932; Boehm, 1926.
89. Sadger, 1921.
90. Boehm, 1924.
91. Boehm, 1920.
92. Sadger, 1908a.
93. Ferenczi, 1914b.
94. Sadger, 1908b.
95. Boehm, 1926.
96. Fenichel, 1945.
97. Rado, 1940.
98. Benedek, 1934.
99. S. Freud, 1905a.
100. S. Freud, 1940a.

101. Brill, 1913.
102. Rank, 1922; Ferenczi, 1914a.
103. Benedek, 1934.
104. Brill, 1913.
105. Sadger, 1919.
106. Vinchon and Nacht, 1929.
107. Ferenczi, 1914b.
108. Boehm, 1933.
109. Fenichel, 1945.
110. S. Freud, 1920b.
111. Sprague, 1935.
112. Vinchon and Nacht, 1929.
113. Ferenczi, 1914b.
114. Brill, 1913.
115. Ferenczi, 1914b.
116. Rank, 1922.
117. Boehm, 1933.
118. Boehm, 1926.
119. Sadger, 1908b.

CHAPTER IV. THEORETICAL OVERVIEW I

1. Dover, 1978.
2. Boswell, 1980.
3. Brill, 1913.
4. Boehm, 1933.
5. Shackley, 1914.
6. E.g., Bergler, 1944.
7. S. Freud, 1914a.
8. S. Freud, 1916a.
9. S. Freud, 1916b.
10. Sadger, 1910a.
11. Brill, 1913.
12. S. Freud, 1916b; Ferenczi, 1914b; Brill, 1934.

13. Ferenczi, 1914b.
14. Fenichel, 1930.
15. Boehm, 1933.
16. S. Freud, 1914a.
17. Ibid.
18. S. Freud, 1940a.
19. Kernberg, 1975.
20. S. Freud, 1923a, 1928, 1940a.
21. S. Freud, 1923a.
22. Jones, 1926.
23. E.g., Shackley, 1914.
24. S. Freud, 1935.
25. S. Freud, 1905a.

26. S. Freud, 1940a.
27. S. Freud, 1924a.
28. E.g., Laufer, 1982; Lebovici, 1982.
29. S. Freud, 1924a.
30. S. Freud, 1923a, 1924a.
31. S. Freud, 1933.
32. Jones, 1933.
33. Boehm, 1930.
34. Loewenstein, 1935.
35. Benedek, 1934.
36. S. Freud, 1930a.
37. E.g., Rado, 1940; I. Bieber et al., 1962.
38. S. Freud, 1924a, 1925; Jones, 1933; Loewenstein, 1935.
39. S. Freud, 1918.
40. S. Freud, 1921a, 1923a.
41. Benedek, 1934.
42. S. Freud, 1923a.
43. Ibid.
44. E.g. Hárnik, 1924.
45. Fenichel, 1945.
46. Bollmeier, 1938.
47. S. Freud, 1918.
48. Boehm, 1930.
49. Jones, 1933.
50. Benedek, 1934.
51. Loewenstein, 1935.
52. Jones, 1933.
53. S. Freud, 1924a.
54. S. Freud, 1937.
55. S. Freud, 1905a.
56. Ostow, 1974.
57. Erikson, 1950.
58. S. Freud, 1920a.
59. S. Freud, 1913a.
60. S. Freud, 1905a.
61. E.g., Stoller, 1974a.

CHAPTER V. THE THEORISTS OF THE ORAL PERIOD: 1930–1948

1. A. Freud, 1946.
2. Hartmann, 1958.
3. Erikson, 1950; C. Thompson, 1951; Horney, 1937; Sullivan, 1953.
4. S. Freud, 1924a.
5. S. Freud, 1905b.
6. Fenichel, 1945.
7. E.g., E. Glover, 1933.
8. Segal, 1979.
9. Klein, 1932.
10. Alexander, 1948.
11. E. Glover, 1939.
12. Karpman, 1938.
13. Bychowski, 1945.
14. Nunberg, 1947.
15. Wittels, 1944.
16. Boehm, 1920.
17. Horney, 1932.
18. Wulff, 1941.
19. Bergler, 1944a; Flournoy, 1953.
20. Lorand, 1930.
21. Lagache, 1950.
22. A. Freud, 1949.

23. Klein, 1932.
24. Kaufmann, 1934.
25. Nunberg, 1938.
26. Rosenfeld, 1949.
27. Sprague, 1935.
28. Bryan, 1930.
29. Rado, 1940.
30. E.g., Federn, 1934, 1943.
31. Klein, 1932.
32. Waelder, 1936.
33. Eidelberg, 1933.
34. Eidelberg and Bergler, 1933.
35. S. Freud, 1919a.
36. Bergler, 1938.
37. Bergler, 1948a.
38. Wulff, 1941.
39. Nunberg, 1938.
40. Bergler, 1947.
41. Bibring, 1940.
42. E. Glover, 1933.
43. E. Glover, 1939.

44. E. Glover, 1932.
45. E. Glover, 1933.
46. Bergler, 1944a.
47. A. Freud, 1951a.
48. S. Freud, 1920a.
49. Bergler, 1947, 1948b.
50. Bergler, 1947.
51. Bergler, 1944a.
52. Boehm, 1933.
53. Bergler, 1947.
54. Bergler, 1944a.
55. Bergler, 1947.
56. Silverberg, 1938.
57. Bergler, 1944a.
58. Robbins, 1943.
59. Eidelberg, 1933.
60. Bychowski, 1945.
61. Nunberg, 1938.
62. A. Freud, 1949, 1951a.
63. Bergler, 1944a.
64. Schilder, 1942.

CHAPTER VI. ANALYTIC RESPONSES TO THE KINSEY REPORT

1. Kinsey et al., 1948.
2. Knight, 1948.
3. Kubie, 1948.
4. Kinsey et al., 1954.
5. S. Freud, 1919a.
6. *Pace* F. Hewitt, 1948.
7. Bergler, 1948b.
8. Bergler and Kroger, 1954.
9. A. Deutsch, 1948; Hoch and Zubin, 1949.
10. Bergler and Kroger, 1954.

11. Kubie, 1948; Knight, 1948.
12. Kardiner, 1949; Menninger, 1953.
13. F. Hewitt, 1948.
14. Bergler, 1948b.
15. E.g., Hoch, 1949; Levy, 1949.
16. E.g., Bychowski, 1949.
17. Kardiner, 1949.
18. F. Hewitt, 1948; Wortis, 1948.
19. Menninger, 1953.
20. Trilling, 1948.

21. Berliner, 1949.
22. Margolin, 1948.
23. Goolker, 1948.
24. F. Weiss, 1949.
25. Fava and Chall, 1955.
26. Gebhard and Johnson, 1979.
27. Kinsey, 1949.
28. Menninger, 1953.
29. Fromm, 1955.
30. Kinsey, 1949.
31. Hamilton, 1929; Ramsey, 1943; Finger, 1947.
32. Gebhard and Johnson, 1979.
33. Gebhard, 1972.
34. R. Ross, 1950.
35. Ford, 1949.
36. Liddicoat, 1956; Curran and Parr, 1957.
37. Bergler, 1948b; Bergler and Kroger, 1954.
38. S. Freud, 1937.
39. Fenichel, 1945.
40. Henry, 1937.
41. Robbins, 1943.
42. Trilling, 1948.
43. Kubie, 1948.
44. Bergler, 1948.
45. Bergler, 1954d.
46. Bergler and Kroger, 1954.
47. Bychowski, 1949.
48. F. Hewitt, 1948.
49. Bergler, 1948b.
50. Berliner, 1949.
51. Kubie, 1948; Knight, 1948.
52. Hobbs and Lambert, 1948.
53. Hobbs and Kephart, 1954.
54. Ramsey, 1950.
55. Kubie, 1948.
56. Hoch, 1949.
57. Bychowski, 1949.
58. Bergler, 1954a.
59. Kubie, 1948.
60. Knight, 1948.
61. Murphy, 1948.
62. Bergler and Kroger, 1954.
63. Bergler, 1948, 1954a–c; Bychowski, 1949; Kardiner, 1949, 1954b; Knight, 1948; Kubie, 1948; Menninger, 1953; Wortis, 1948.
64. Kinsey, 1949; Kinsey et al., 1954.
65. Eisenbud, 1955.
66. Margolin, 1948.
67. Kubie, 1948.
68. Levy, 1949.
69. Knight, 1948; Kubie, 1948; Levy, 1949; Murphy, 1948; Margolin, 1948.
70. Kardiner, 1949.
71. Bychowski, 1949.
72. Kardiner, 1949.
73. Bergler and Kroger, 1954.
74. Ibid.
75. Bergler, 1947.
76. Kardiner, 1949.
77. Rado, 1949.
78. Bergler, 1948b, 1954c, 1954d.
79. Menninger, 1953.
80. Hobbs and Kephart, 1954.
81. Bergler, 1954c.
82. Bergler, 1948b, 1954c, 1954d, 1969.
83. Knight, 1948.
84. Hoch and Zubin, 1949.
85. Hoch, 1949.
86. Levy, 1949.
87. I. Bieber et al., 1962.

CHAPTER VII. CONSERVATIVE DEVELOPMENTS: 1948–1962

1. Berg, 1958; Gershman, 1957; E. Glover, 1945.
2. Arlow, 1954.
3. Feldman, 1956.
4. Berg, 1958.
5. Fried, 1960.
6. C. Hewitt, 1961.
7. Gershman, 1952; Hulbeck, 1948.
8. Horney, 1939.
9. Marcuse, 1956.
10. Balint, 1956.
11. Socarides, 1960; E. Weiss, 1958.
12. Kardiner et al., 1959.
13. Feldman, 1956.
14. Gershman, 1953, 1957.
15. Poe, 1952.
16. Lagache, 1950.
17. Eidelberg, 1956.
18. Balint, 1953.
19. Ovesey, 1954, 1955a; Karush and Ovesey, 1961; Kardiner et al., 1959.
20. A. Freud, 1949, 1951a, 1951b.
21. Lagache, 1950.
22. Eidelberg, 1956.
23. Silber, 1961.
24. M. Miller, 1956.
25. Thorner, 1949.
26. Ehrenwald, 1960.
27. Fine, 1961.
28. Hadfield, 1958.
29. Hadden, 1958.
30. Regardie, 1949.
31. Lewinsky, 1949, 1952.
32. Ferenczi, 1909.
33. Hamilton, 1954.
34. Litin et al., 1956.
35. Kolb and Johnson, 1955.
36. Gillespie, 1956a.
37. Bychowski, 1956b.
38. Bychowski, 1954.
39. Gershman, 1957.
40. Grauer, 1955.
41. Klaf and Davis, 1960; Klaf, 1961.
42. Rosenfeld, 1949.
43. Socarides, 1959.
44. P. Miller, 1958.
45. Glueck, 1956.
46. Allen, 1958.
47. Hamilton, 1954.
48. Gershman, 1957.
49. Gershman, 1953.
50. Fried, 1960.
51. Berg, 1958.
52. Kardiner, 1954b.
53. Especially Bergler, 1956a, 1958b, 1959.
54. Bergler, 1962.
55. Bychowski, 1945, 1949.
56. Hadas, 1954.
57. Cf. Dover, 1978.
58. Flournoy, 1953.
59. Boehm, 1920.
60. Gershman, 1957.
61. Bergler, 1953b.

62. Bergler, 1956a.
63. Bergler, 1956b.
64. Bergler, 1953a.
65. Bergler, 1954a.
66. Bergler, 1954d, 1956a.
67. Bergler, 1949.
68. Bergler, 1944a.
69. Bergler, 1944b.
70. Bergler, 1956b.
71. Bergler, 1958a, 1956a, 1959.
72. Bergler, 1962.
73. Bergler, 1959.
74. Bergler, 1958a.
75. Bergler, 1956a.
76. Bergler, 1958b.
77. Bergler, 1959.
78. A. Freud, 1951a.
79. Berliner, 1949.
80. Berg, 1958.
81. Feldman, 1956.
82. Wiedemann, 1962.
83. Grayson, 1971.
84. Bergler, 1954d, 1953a, 1956b, 1947, 1948b, 1962.
85. Bergler, 1956a.
86. E. Glover, 1960.
87. E. Glover, 1952.
88. S. Freud, 1930b.
89. E. Glover, 1939.
90. E. Glover, 1960.
91. Ibid.
92. Ibid.
93. E. Glover, 1945.
94. E. Glover, 1960.
95. Arlow, 1954.
96. Socarides, 1960.
97. Nacht et al., 1956; Glauber, 1956; Gillespie, 1956b.
98. Lorand and Balint, 1956.
99. Wiedemann, 1962.
100. Arlow, 1954.
101. Socarides, 1960.
102. Wiedemann, 1962.
103. Lorand and Balint, 1956.
104. Hamilton, 1954.
105. Lewinsky, 1949, 1952.
106. Flournoy, 1953.
107. Saul and Beck, 1961.
108. E. Weiss, 1958.
109. Loewenstein, 1957.
110. D. Brown, 1958.
111. Bychowski, 1956b.
112. Bychowski, 1954.
113. Bychowski, 1956a, 1961.
114. Socarides, 1959.
115. Eidelberg, 1956.
116. Thorner, 1949.
117. Rosenfeld, 1949.
118. Lorand, 1956.
119. Gillespie, 1952.
120. Bak, 1956.
121. Glauber, 1956.
122. Nacht et al., 1956.
123. Sachs, 1923.
124. Jones, 1933.
125. Gillespie, 1956b.
126. Lorand and Balint, 1956.
127. Gillespie, 1956a.
128. Bak, 1956.
129. Alexander, 1956.
130. Balint, 1956.
131. Nacht et al., 1956.
132. Rank, 1922.
133. le Coultre, 1956.
134. Eissler, 1958.
135. Freeman, 1955.

136. S. Freud, 1905a.
137. Arlow, 1954.
138. Bak, 1956.
139. Loewenstein, 1957.
140. Devereux, 1960.
141. E. Weiss, 1958; Socarides, 1960.
142. Spiegel, 1958.
143. Arlow, 1954; Muensterberger, 1956; Devereux, 1960.
144. Kardiner, 1954b.
145. Ovesey, 1954.
146. Ovesey, 1955a.
147. Karush and Ovesey, 1961.
148. Kardiner et al., 1959.

149. Marcuse, 1955.
150. Gershman, 1957.
151. S. Freud, 1940a.
152. S. Freud, 1913a.
153. S. Freud, 1937.
154. Kinsey et al., 1948.
155. Socarides, 1960.
156. Faergemann, 1955.
157. Muensterberger, 1956.
158. Fain and Marty, 1960.
159. E. Glover, 1960.
160. Fine, 1961.
161. Freeman, 1955.
162. Socarides, 1960.
163. Bychowski, 1961.

CHAPTER VIII. THEORETICAL OVERVIEW II

1. Jones, 1933.
2. S. Freud, 1922.
3. S. Freud, 1905a.
4. Sachs, 1923.
5. Fenichel, 1945.
6. S. Freud, 1910a.
7. S. Freud, 1919a.
8. S. Freud, 1905a.
9. Feldman, 1956.
10. Kardiner, 1954b.
11. S. Freud, 1925.
12. S. Freud, 1914a, 1925.
13. Alexander, 1956.

14. Kolb and Johnson, 1955.
15. Lewinsky, 1949, 1952.
16. Sullivan, 1953.
17. S. Freud, 1913a.
18. Chasseguet-Smirgel, 1974; Ostow, 1974; Socarides, 1968a.
19. Benedek, 1934.
20. Hárnik, 1924.
21. Brill, 1913.
22. Jones, 1926.
23. Fenichel, 1945.
24. E. Glover, 1960.
25. I. Bieber et al., 1962.

CHAPTER IX. THE TURNAROUND: 1962–1973

1. I. Bieber et al., 1962.
2. Wiedemann, 1962.
3. Karlen, 1971.
4. Hatterer, 1970.
5. Wiedemann, 1974.
6. Bak, 1968.
7. Khan, 1965.
8. Bell, 1961, 1965, 1968.
9. Association for the Advancement of Psychoanalysis, 1964.
10. E.g., Chang and Bloch, 1960; Saghir and Robins, 1973; Evans, 1969; Hooker, 1957; N. Thompson et al., 1971.
11. International Psychoanalytic Congress, 1963.
12. Wiedemann, 1964.
13. Association for the Advancement of Psychoanalysis, 1964.
14. Gershman, 1964b.
15. de Maria, 1968.
16. Livingood, 1972.
17. Marmor, 1972a.
18. Ostow, 1974.
19. Rosen, 1964.
20. Marmor, 1965a.
21. Moore and Selzer, 1963.
22. Marberg, 1972.
23. P. Thompson, 1968.
24. de Monchy, 1965.
25. Gillespie, 1964b.
26. Gillespie, 1964a.
27. Fairbairn, 1964.
28. Kubie, 1974.
29. Roy, 1972.
30. Ebel, 1975.
31. Gonen, 1971.
32. Jaffe, 1968.
33. Kardiner, 1978b.
34. Karlen, 1971.
35. Karlen, 1972.
36. Hendin, 1978.
37. Gonen, 1971.
38. Kardiner, 1954b.
39. Kardiner, 1978a.
40. Kardiner, 1978b.
41. Gershman, 1966.
42. Ibid.
43. Hendin, 1978.
44. Socarides, 1968a.
45. Blos, 1953.
46. Fraiberg, 1962.
47. Sprince, 1964.
48. Gadpaille, 1968.
49. Gadpaille, 1975.
50. Salzman, 1974.
51. Pao, 1969.
52. Bonime, 1966.
53. Khan, 1965.
54. P. Thompson, 1968.
55. Kolb, 1963.
56. Brown, 1964.
57. de Monchy, 1965.
58. Ostow, 1974.
59. Wallace, 1969.
60. Socarides, 1969.
61. I. Bieber et al., 1962; I. Bieber, 1967b.
62. Hartman, 1973.
63. Gershman, 1975.
64. Kaye, 1975.
65. T. Bieber, 1974.

66. Bell, 1961.
67. Bell, 1965.
68. Bell, 1968.
69. Berent, 1973.
70. Bloch, 1974.
71. Bloch, 1975.
72. I. Bieber, 1969.
73. I. Bieber et al., 1962.
74. Saghir and Robins, 1973.
75. Friedman, 1980.
76. Rubinstein, 1964.
77. Greenson, 1964.
78. Morgenthaler, 1969.
79. Greenson, 1968.
80. Jones, 1933; Loewenstein, 1935; Mahler, 1968.
81. Edgcumbe and Burgner, 1975.
82. Kohut, 1971.
83. A. Goldberg, 1975.
84. S. Freud, 1927.
85. S. Freud, 1940b.
86. Bak, 1968.
87. McDougall, 1972.
88. W. Brown, 1964.
89. Scott, 1964.
90. Weissman, 1962.
91. Gillespie, 1964a.
92. Socarides, 1968b.
93. Laufer, 1982; Lebovici, 1982.
94. Bak, 1968; Greenacre, 1968.
95. Bak, 1968; Hornstra, 1967; Pasche, 1964.
96. Hornstra, 1966.
97. Jaffe, 1968.
98. Jaffe, 1983.
99. Limentani, 1977, 1979.
100. Weissman, 1962.
101. Ovesey et al., 1963; Ovesey and Gaylin, 1965; Ovesey, 1965, 1969, 1973.
102. Lief and Mayerson, 1965.
103. Salzman, 1965.
104. Marmor, 1965b.
105. Gershman, 1968.
106. Stoller, 1975a.
107. Kardiner, 1978b.
108. Socarides, 1968b, 1970.
109. Socarides, 1973b.
110. Socarides, 1970, 1972, 1978a.
111. Socarides, 1968a, 1968b, 1979b.
112. Socarides, 1968a.
113. Socarides, 1974.
114. Socarides, 1968b.
115. Socarides, 1973a.
116. Socarides, 1979b.
117. Friedman, 1976a.
118. Socarides, 1976.
119. Socarides, 1978b.
120. Socarides, 1972.
121. Socarides, 1968a.
122. E. Glover, 1932.
123. Socarides, 1968a.
124. Friedman, 1976b.
125. Green, 1972.
126. Socarides, 1972.
127. Socarides, 1968b.
128. Socarides, 1968a.
129. Gershman, 1968; Tyson, 1982.
130. Stoller, 1968.
131. Stoller, 1975a.
132. Stoller, 1973a.
133. Stoller, 1978.
134. Stoller, 1974a.
135. Stoller, 1975a.
136. Ibid.
137. Stoller, 1964.

138. Stoller, 1965.
139. Stoller, 1975a.
140. Stoller, 1970.
141. Stoller, 1974a, 1975a.
142. Stoller, 1975a.
143. Stoller, 1964, 1968.
144. Stoller, 1965, 1968.
145. Stoller, 1974a.
146. Stoller, 1974a.
147. Stoller, 1975a.
148. Stoller, 1973a.
149. Stoller, 1975a.
150. I. Bieber, 1965.
151. I. Bieber, 1967a, 1967b.
152. Marmor, 1975.
153. I. Bieber, 1967b, 1969.
154. I. Bieber, 1973.
155. I. Bieber, 1976a.
156. Ibid.
157. I. Bieber, 1977.
158. Gundlach, 1969.
159. Evans, 1969.
160. T. Beiber, 1965, 1967.

161. T. Bieber, 1974.
162. E.g., Kinsey et al., 1948;
Hooker, 1957, 1965b; Chang
and Bloch, 1960.
163. Bene, 1965.
164. Siegelman, 1974.
165. Saghir and Robins, 1970, 1971,
1973.
166. Friedman, 1980.
167. Rubinstein, 1964.
168. Hooker, 1969.
169. Kinsey et al., 1948; Hooker,
1963, 1965b, 1968; Bell and
Weinberg, 1978.
170. Friedman, 1976b.
171. I. Bieber, 1976b.
172. I. Bieber, 1976a.
173. I. Bieber, 1977.
174. I. Bieber, 1965, 1967b, 1968,
1969.
175. Evans, 1969; Wakeling, 1979.
176. Gundlach, 1969.
177. Ostow, 1974.

CHAPTER X. A NEW BEGINNING: 1973–1982

1. Szasz, 1974
2. Foucault, 1965.
3. Rosen, 1979c.
4. Spitzer, 1973.
5. Chasseguet-Smirgel, 1974.
6. Lachman, 1975.
7. W. Brown, 1964.
8. Pasche, 1964.
9. Bak, 1968.
10. Wiedemann, 1962.

11. Wiedemann, 1974.
12. Marmor, 1975.
13. de Monchy, 1965.
14. Khan, 1965.
15. Robertiello, 1971.
16. Wakeling, 1979.
17. Socarides, 1978a.
18. Gilberg, 1978.
19. Gilberg, 1981.

20. I. Bieber, 1968; McDougall, 1972.
21. I. Bieber, 1967b.
22. Kestenberg, 1971.
23. Gershman, 1964a.
24. Chasseguet-Smirgel, 1974.
25. Kardiner, 1978a.
26. Hendin, 1978.
27. T. Bieber, 1965.
28. Gonen, 1971; Robertiello, 1971.
29. Bayer, 1981.
30. Ostow, 1974.
31. Lichtenstein, 1970; Lachman, 1975.
32. Marmor, 1971a.
33. Socarides, 1968b.
34. Blos, 1965.
35. Ostow, 1974.
36. Chasseguet-Smirgel, 1974.
37. Gillespie, 1964a.
38. Limentani, 1976.
39. Johnson and Szurek, 1952; Kolb and Johnson, 1955; Sperling, 1956; Kolb, 1963.
40. Gillespie, 1964b.
41. Marmor, 1965b.
42. Bak, 1968.
43. Marmor, 1972a.
44. Altschuler, 1976.
45. Stoller, 1974a.
46. Chang and Bloch, 1960; Clark, 1975; Hooker, 1957, 1965b, 1969; Riess, 1980; Saghir and Robins, 1970, 1971, 1973; Siegelman, 1974; N. Thompson et al., 1971.
47. Socarides, 1973b.
48. Friedman, 1976b.
49. Marmor, 1973.
50. Rubinstein, 1964.
51. Scott, 1964.
52. Bloch, 1974, 1975.
53. I. Bieber, 1977.
54. Gershman, 1964a, 1964b, 1966.
55. Bloch, 1974, 1975.
56. Wiedemann, 1974.
57. Stoller, 1965.
58. Kestenberg, 1971.
59. Bayer, 1981.
60. Socarides, 1979.
61. Ford, 1948.
62. Hooker, 1957, 1965b.
63. Marmor, 1965b, 1971a, 1972b, 1973.
64. Marmor, 1971a, 1971b.
65. Green, 1972.
66. Bell, 1972.
67. Davison, 1976.
68. Hoffman, 1972.
69. Green, 1973.
70. Stoller, 1973a.
71. Marmor, 1973.
72. Marmor, 1972.
73. Bayer, 1981.
74. I. Bieber, 1973.
75. Socarides, 1972.
76. Ibid.
77. Socarides, 1973b.
78. Bayer, 1981.
79. Saghir and Robins, 1973.
80. Spitzer, 1973.
81. Freedman and Kaplan, 1967, 1975.
82. I. Bieber, 1967a, 1967b.
83. Marmor, 1975.
84. Lesse, 1974.

85. Kardiner, 1978b.
86. Socarides, 1978a.
87. I. Bieber, 1976a.
88. Lief, 1977.
89. Marmor, 1980a.
90. Rosen, 1979a.
91. Altschuler, 1976.
92. Gershman, 1981.
93. Gilberg, 1978.
94. Gilberg, 1981.
95. I. Bieber, 1976a.
96. I. Bieber, 1977.
97. Socarides, 1979b.
98. Friedman, 1980.
99. Kardiner, 1978a, 1978b; Hendin, 1978.
100. Pattison, 1974.
101. Gershman, 1966.
102. Wakeling, 1979.
103. Riess, 1980.

104. Fliess, 1962.
105. Lachman, 1975.
106. Tyson, 1982.
107. Socarides, 1979b.
108. Limentani, 1976.
109. Limentani, 1977.
110. Limentani, 1979.
111. Marmor, 1980b.
112. Khan, 1979.
113. I. Ross, 1975.
114. Rosen, 1979b.
115. Mitchell, 1978.
116. S. Freud, 1937.
117. C. Thompson, 1947.
118. Kwawer, 1980.
119. Socarides, 1970.
120. Gershman, 1968.
121. Gershman, 1975.
122. I. Bieber, 1967b.
123. Boehm, 1920.

CHAPTER XI. CONCLUSIONS

1. S. Freud, 1919a.
2. Kardiner, 1978b.
3. E.g., Bergler, 1959; Kardiner, 1954b.
4. Bergler, 1948b.
5. S. Freud, 1930a.
6. S. Freud, 1908d.
7. Marcuse, 1955.
8. Kardiner, 1978a, 1978b.
9. Silverberg, 1938.
10. Bergler, 1947.
11. Bergler, 1956b.
12. Roy, 1972.

13. E.g., Gershman, 1966; Hendin, 1978; Socarides, 1968a.
14. Bychowski, 1949.
15. E.g., Kubie, 1974.
16. Steiner, 1983.
17. S. Freud, 1940a.
18. Brenner, 1979.
19. S. Freud, 1937.
20. S. Freud, 1921b.
21. Chauncey, 1982.
22. Waelder, 1960.
23. Foucault, 1978.
24. Horney, 1932.

25. Bell, 1961.
26. Marmor, 1980c.
27. Karush and Ovesey, 1961.
28. Bergler, 1959.
29. Rado, 1940.

30. I. Bieber, 1967b.
31. Hornstra, 1967.
32. Grayson, 1971; Wiedemann, 1974; Berliner, 1949.
33. Schafer, 1983.

BIBLIOGRAPHY

The following abbreviations for titles have been used:

247

Int R Med	*International Record of Medicine*
Int R Psa	*International Review of Psychoanalysis*
Int Z aerzt Psa	*Internationale Zeitschrift fuer aerztliche Psychoanalyse*
Int Z Psa	*Internationale Zeitschrift fuer Psychoanalyse*
J Abn Soc Psych	*Journal of Abnormal and Social Psychology*
JAMA	*Journal of the American Medical Association*
J Am Aca Psa	*Journal of the American Academy of Psycho-analysis*
J Am Psa Asn	*Journal of the American Psychoanalytic Association*
Jb Psa	*Jahrbuch der Psychoanalyse*
Jb Psa Psp F	*Jahrbuch fuer Psychoanalytische und Psychopathologische Forschungen*
Jb Sex Zw	*Jahrbuch fuer sexuellen Zwischenstufen*
J Ch Psy Psychiat	*Journal of Child Psychology and Psychiatry*
J Cl Psych	*Journal of Clinical Psychology*
J Cons Cl Psych	*Journal of Consulting and Clinical Psychology*
JH	*Journal of Homosexuality*
J H Med J	*Johns Hopkins Medical Journal*
J Mtl Sc	*Journal of Mental Science*
J Ner Mtl Dis	*Journal of Nervous and Mental Disease*
J Proj Tech	*Journal of Projective Techniques*
Med Asp H Sex	*Medical Aspects of Human Sexuality*
Med-Leg R	*Medical-Legal Review*
MM	*Masses and Mainstream*
N aerzt Z	*Neue aerztliche Zentralzeitung*
Psychiat A	*Psychiatric Annals*
Psychiat Q	*Psychiatric Quarterly*
Psa Q	*Psychoanalytic Quarterly*
Psa R	*Psychoanalytic Review*
Psa St Child	*Psychoanalytic Study of the Child*
Psychiat	*Psychiatry*
PsySom Med	*Psychosomatic Medicine*
R fr Psa	*Revue française de psychoanalyse*
Sal	*Salmagundi*
Sat R Lit	*Saturday Review of Literature*
SE	*Standard Edition of the Complete Psychological Works of Sigmund Freud* (James Strachey, ed. London: Hogarth Press).
ZBl Psa	*Zeitblaetter fuer Psychoanalyse*
Z Sexwis	*Zeitschrift fuer Sexualwissenschaft*

Alexander, F. (1930). The Neurotic Character. *Int J Psa* 11:292–311.
—— (1948). *Fundamentals of Psychoanalysis*. New York: Norton.
—— (1956). A Note on the Theory of Perversions. In Lorand, S., and Balint, M. (eds.), *Perversions: Psychodynamics and Therapy*. New York: Random House.
Allen, C. (1958). Homosexuality: Its Nature, Causation and Treatment. In Berg, C., and Allen, C., *The Problem of Homosexuality*. New York: Citadel Press.
Altshuler, K. (1976). Some Notes and an Exercise with Regard to Male Homosexuality. *J Am Aca Psa* 4 (2):237–48.
American Journal of Psychiatry (1973). A Symposium: Should Homosexuality Be in the APA Nomenclature? *Am J Psychiat* 130 (11):1207–16.
American Psychiatric Association (1980). *Diagnostic and Statistical Manual of Mental Disorders*, Third Edition.
Arlow, J. (1954). Report: Panel on Perversion: Theoretical and Therapeutic Aspects. *J Am Psa Asn* 2:336–45.
Association for the Advancement of Psychoanalysis (1964). The Meaning of Homosexual Trends in Therapy: A Round Table Discussion. *Am J Psa* 24:60–76.
Bak, R. (1956). Aggression and Perversion. In Lorand, S., and Balint, M. (eds.), *Perversions: Psychodynamics and Therapy*. New York: Random House.
—— (1968). The Phallic Woman: The Ubiquitous Fantasy in Perversions. *Psa St Child* 23:15–36.
Balint, M. (1953). *Primary Love and Psycho-Analytic Technique*. New York: Liveright.
—— (1956). Perversions and Genitality. In Lorand, S., and Balint, M. (eds.), *Perversions: Psychodynamics and Therapy*. New York: Random House.
Bayer, R. (1981). *Homosexuality and American Psychiatry*. New York: Basic Books.
Beach, F. (1948). *Sexual Behavior in Animals and Men*. Harvey Lecture Series 43:254–80. New Haven: Yale University Press.
Bell, A. (1961). Significance of Scrotal Sac and Testicles. *J Am Psa Asn* 9:261–86.
—— (1965). The Significance of Scrotal Sac and Testicles for the Prepuberty Male. *Psa Q* 34:182–206.
—— (1968). Additional Aspects of Passivity and Feminine Identification in the Male. *Int J Psa* 49:640–47.
—— (1972). Human Sexuality—A Response. *Int J Psychiat* 10 (3):99–102.

—— (1975). Research in Homosexuality: Back to the Drawing Board. *Arch Sex Beh* 4:421–31.

Bell, A., and Weinberg, M. (1978). *Homosexualities: A Study of Diversity among Men and Women*. New York: Simon and Schuster.

Bene, E. (1965). On the Genesis of Male Homosexuality: An Attempt at Classifying the Role of the Parents. *Brit J Psychiat* 3:803ff.

Benedek, T. (1934). Some Factors Determining Fixation at the "Deutero-phallic Phase." *Int J Psa* 15:440–58.

Berent, I. (1973). "I Didn't Mean to Hurt You, Mother": A Basic Fantasy Epitomized by a Male Homosexual. *J Am Psa Asn* 21 (2):262–84.

Berg, C. (1958). The Foundations of Homosexuality. In Berg, C., and Allen, C., *The Problem of Homosexuality*. New York: Citadel Press.

Berg, C., and Allen, C. (1958). *The Problem of Homosexuality*. New York: Citadel Press.

Bergler, E. (1938). Preliminary Phases of the Masculine Beating Fantasy. *Psa Q* 7:514–36.

—— (1944a). Eight Prerequisites for Psychoanalytic Treatment of Homosexuality. *Psa R* 31:253–86.

—— (1944b). Logorrhea. *Psychiat Q* 18:700–712.

—— (1947). Differential Diagnosis between Spurious Homosexuality and Perversion Homosexuality. *Psychiat Q* 31:399–409.

—— (1948a). Further Studies on Beating Fantasies. *Psychiat Q* 22:209–14.

—— (1948b). The Myth of a New National Disease: Homosexuality and the Kinsey Report. *Psychiat Q* 22:66–88.

—— (1949). *The Basic Neurosis*. New York: Harper and Brothers.

—— (1953a). Proust and the Torture Theory of Love. *Am Imago* 10:3ff.

—— (1953b). *Fashion and the Unconscious*. New York: Robert Brunner.

—— (1954a). Contributions to the Psychology of Homosexuals. *Samiksa* (Calcutta) 8:205–9.

—— (1954b). "Sexual Behavior." *JAMA* 154 (2):167–68.

—— (1954c). Homosexuality and the Kinsey Report. In Krich, A. (ed.), *The Homosexuals: As Seen by Themselves and 30 Authorities*. New York: Citadel Press.

—— (1954d). Spurious Homosexuality. *Psychiat Q* (Supplement) 28 (1):68–77.

—— (1956a). *Homosexuality: Disease or Way of Life*. New York: Hill and Wang.

—— (1956b). "Salome," the Turning Point in the Life of Oscar Wilde. *Psa R* 43:433–41.

—— (1958a). *Counterfeit-Sex: Homosexuality, Impotence and Frigidity, Second Edition*. New York: Grune and Stratton.

—— (1958b). What Every Physician Should Know about Homosexuality. *Int R Med* 171:685–90.

—— (1959). *One Thousand Homosexuals: Conspiracy of Silence, or Curing and Deglamorizing Homosexuals?* Paterson, New Jersey: Pageant Books.

—— (1962). The Aristocracy among Homosexuals: Lovers of "Trade." *B Phil Asn Psa* 12:1–9.

—— (1969). *Selected Papers: 1933–1961*. New York: Grune and Stratton.

Bergler, E., and Kroger W. (1954). *Kinsey's Myth of Female Sexuality: The Medical Facts*. New York: Grune and Stratton.

Berliner, B. (1949). Abstract. *Psa Q* 18:400–401.

Bibring, G. (1940). Ueber eine orale Komponente bei maennlicher Inversion. *Int Z Psa* 25:124–30.

Bieber, I. (1964a). Discussion of Homosexuality and Some Aspects of Creativity. *Am J Psa* 24:29–38.

—— (1964b). The Meaning of Homosexual Trends in Therapy. *Am J Psa* 24:60–76.

—— (1965). Clinical Aspects of Male Homosexuality. In Marmor, J. (ed.), *Sexual Inversion: The Multiple Roots of Homosexuality*. New York: Basic Books.

—— (1967a). Sexual Deviations I. Introduction. In Freedman, A., and Kaplan, H. (eds.), *Comprehensive Textbook of Psychiatry*. Baltimore: Williams and Wilkins.

—— (1967b). Sexual Deviations II. Homosexuality. In Freedman, A., and Kaplan, H. (eds.), *Comprehensive Textbook of Psychiatry*. Baltimore: Williams and Wilkins.

—— (1968). Advising the Homosexual. *Med Asp H Sex* 2:34–39.

—— (1969). Homosexuality. *Am J Nurs* 69 (12):2637–41.

—— (1973). Homosexuality—An Adaptative Consequent of Disorder in Psychosexual Development. *Am J Psychiat* 130:1209–11.

—— (1976a). A Discussion of "Homosexuality: The Ethical Challenge." *J Cons Cl Psych* 44 (2):163–66.

—— (1976b). Psychodynamics and Sexual Object Choice: A Reply to Dr. Richard C. Friedman's Paper. *C Psa* 12 (3):366–69.

—— (1977). Sexuality: 1956–1976. *J Am Aca Psa* 5 (2):195–205.

Bieber, I., Dain, H., Dince, P., Drellich, M, Grand, H, Gundlach, R., Kremer, M., Rifkin, A., Wilbur, C., and Bieber, T. (1962).

Homosexuality: A *Psychoanalytic Study of Male Homosexuals.*
New York: Basic Books.

Bieber, T. (1965). Acting Out in Homosexuality. In Abt, L., and Weissman, S. (eds.), *Acting Out—Theoretical and Clinical Aspects.* New York: Grune and Stratton.

———— (1967). On Treating Male Homosexuals. *Arch Gen Psychiat* 16:60–63.

———— (1974). Group and Individual Psychotherapy with Male Homosexuals. *J Am Aca Psa* 2 (3):255–60.

Binion, R. (1968). *Frau Lou: Nietzsche's Wayward Disciple.* Princeton, New Jersey: Princeton University Press.

Blaukopf, K. (1973). *Mahler.* New York: Praeger.

Bloch, D. (1947). Fantasy and the Fear of Infanticide. *Psa R* 61:1ff.

———— (1975). The Threat of Infanticide and Homosexual Identity. *Psa R* 62 (4):579–99.

Blos, P. (1953). The Treatment of Adolescents. In Heiman, M. (ed.), *Psychoanalysis and Social Work.* New York: International Universities Press.

———— (1965). The Initial Stage of Male Adolescence. *Psa St Child* 20:145–64.

Boehm, F. (1920). Beitraege zur Psychologie der Homosexualitaet I: Homosexualitaet und Polygamie. *Int Z Psa* 6:297–319.

———— (1921a). Homosexualitaet und Bordell. *Int Z Psa* 7:79–82.

———— (1921b). Sexual Perversions. *Int J Psa* 2:435–50.

———— (1922). Beitraege zur Psychologie der Homosexualitaet II: Ein Traum eines Homosexuellen. *Int Z Psa* 8:313–20.

———— (1923). Bemerkungen zum Transvestitismus. *Int Z Psa* 9:497–509.

———— (1924). Review (of Sadger's *Die Lehre* . . .). *Int J Psa* 5:487–92.

———— (1926). Beitraege zur Psychologie der Homosexualitaet III: Homosexualitaet und Oedipuskomplex. *Int Z Psa* 12:66–79.

———— (1930). The Femininity Complex in Men. *Int J Psa* 11:444–69.

———— (1933). Beitraege zur Psychologie der Homosexualitaet IV: Ueber zwei Typen von maennlichen Homosexuellen. *Int Z Psa* 19:499–506.

Bollmeier, L. (1938). A Paranoid Mechanism in Male (Overt) Homosexuality. *Psa Q* 7:357–67.

Bonaparte, M. (1953). *Female Sexuality.* New York: International Universities Press.

Bonime, W. (1966). A Case of Depression in a Homosexual Young Man. *C Psa* 3 (1):1–14.

Boswell, J. (1980). *Christianity, Social Tolerance and Homosexuality.* Chicago: University of Chicago Press.

———— (1982). Revolutions, Universals, Categories. *Sal* 58:89–113.

Brenner, C. (1979). The Components of Psychic Conflict and Its Consequences in Mental Life. *Psa Q* 48:547–67.

Brill, A. (1913). The Conception of Homosexuality. *JAMA* 61 (5):335–40.

———— (1934). Homoerotism and Paranoia. *Am J Psychiat* 13:957–74.

Brown, D. (1958). Inversion and Homosexuality. *Am J OrthoPsychiat* 28:424–29.

Brown, W. (1964). The Homosexual Male: Treatment in an Out-Patient Clinic. In Rosen, I. (ed.), *The Pathology and Treatment of Sexual Deviation: A Methodological Approach.* London: Oxford University Press.

Bryan, D. (1930). Bisexuality. *Int J Psa* 11:150–66.

Burrow, T. (1917). The Genesis and Meaning of 'Homosexuality' and Its Relation to the Problem of Mental States. *Psa R* 4:272–84.

Bychowski, G. (1945). The Ego of Homosexuals. *Int J Psa* 26:114–27.

———— (1949). Some Aspects of Psychosexuality in Psychoanalytic Experience. In Hoch, P., and Zubin, J. (eds.), *Psychosexual Development in Health and Disease.* New York: Grune and Stratton.

———— (1954). The Structure of Homosexual Acting Out. *Psa Q* 23:48–61.

———— (1956a). The Ego and the Introjects. *Psa Q* 25:11–36.

———— (1956b). Homosexuality and Psychosis. In Lorand, S., and Balint, M. (eds.), *Perversions: Psychodynamics and Therapy.* New York: Random House.

———— (1961). The Ego and the Object of the Homosexual. *Int J Psa* 42:255–59.

Chalus, G. (1977). An Evaluation of the Validity of the Freudian Theory of Paranoia. *JH* 3:171–88.

Chang, J., and Bloch, J. (1960). A Study of Identification in Male Homosexuals. *J Cons Cl Psych* 24:307–10.

Chasseguet-Smirgel, J. (1974). Perversions, Idealization and Sublimation. *Int J Psa* 55:349–57.

Chauncey, G. (1982). From Sexual Inversion to Homosexuality. *Sal* 58:114–46.

Clark, T. (1975). Homosexuality and Psychopathology in Nonpatient Males. *Am J Psa* 35:163–68.

Curran, D., and Parr, D. (1957). Homosexuality: An Analysis of 100 Male Cases. *Brit Med J* 1:797–801.

Davison, G. (1976). Homosexuality: The Ethical Challenge. *J Cons Cl Psych* 44:157–62.

de Maria, L. (1968). Homosexual Acting Out. *Int J Psa* 49:219–20.

de Monchy, R. (1965). A Clinical Type of Male Homosexuality. *Int J Psa* 46:218–25.

Deutsch, A. (1948). *Sex Habits of American Men: A Symposium on the Kinsey Report*. New York: Grosset and Dunlap.

Deutsch, H. (1933). Homosexuality in Women. *Int J Psa* 14:34–70.

——— (1944). *The Psychology of Women*. New York: Grune and Stratton.

Devereux, G. (1960). Retaliatory Homosexual Triumph Over the Father. A Further Contribution the Counteroedipal Sources of the Oedipus Complex. *Int J Psa* 41:157–61.

Dover, K. (1978). *Greek Homosexuality*. New York: Random House.

Ebel, H. (1975). Caesar's Wounds. *Psa R* 62:107–30.

Edgcumbe, R., and Burgner, M. (1975). The Phallic-Narcissistic Phase: A Differentiation between Pre-Oedipal and Oedipal Aspects of Phallic Development. *Psa St Child* 30:161–80.

Ehrenwald, J. (1960). The Symbiotic Matrix of Paranoid Delusions and the Homosexual Alternative. *Am J Psa* 20:49–65.

Eidelberg, L. (1933). Zur Theorie und Klinik der Perversion. *Int Z Psa* 19:620ff. Also translated and published as *On the Theory and Clinical Treatment of Perversions. Studies in Psychoanalysis*. New York: International Universities Press, 1952.

——— (1956). Analysis of a Case of a Male Homosexual. In Lorand, S., and Balint, M. (eds.), *Perversions: Psychodynamics and Therapy*. New York: Random House.

Eidelberg, L., and Bergler, E. (1933). Der Mammakomplex des Mannes. *Int Z Psa* 19:547–83.

Eisenbud, J. (1955). A Psychiatrist Looks at the Report. In Himmelhoch, J., and Fava, S. (eds.), *Sexual Behavior in American Society: An Appraisal of the First Two Kinsey Reports*. New York: Norton.

Eissler, K. (1958). Notes on Problems of Technique in the Psychoanalytic Treatment of Adolescence: With Some Remarks on Perversions. *Psa St Child* 13:223–54.

Erikson, E. (1950). *Childhood and Society*. New York: Norton.

Evans, R. (1969). Childhood Parental Relationships of Homosexual Men. *J Cons Cl Psych* 33:129–35.

Faergemann, P. (1955). Fantasies of Menstruation in Men. *Psa Q* 24:1–19.

Fain, M., and Marty, P. (1960). The Synthetic Function of Homosexual Cathexis in the Treatment of Adults. *Int J Psa* 41:401–6.

Fairbairn, W. (1964). A Note on the Origin of Male Homosexuality. *Brit J Med Psych* 37:31–32.

Fava, S., and Chall, L. (1955). Some Published Material Referring to the First Two Kinsey Reports: September, 1947 to August, 1954. In Himmelhoch, J., and Fava, S. (eds.), *Sexual Behavior in American Society: An Appraisal of the First Two Kinsey Reports*. New York: Norton.

Federn, P. (1934). The Analysis of Psychotics. *Int J Psa* 15:209–14.

——— (1943). Psychoanalysis of Psychoses, I–III. *Psa Q* 17.

Feldman, S. (1956). On Homosexuality. In Lorand, S., and Balint, M. (eds.), *Perversions: Psychodynamics and Therapy*. New York: Random House.

Fenichel, O. (1930). Zur Psychologie der Transvestitismus. *Int Z Psa* 16:21–34.

——— (1931). *Perversionen, Psychosen, Charakterstoerungen*. Darmstadt: Wissenschaftliche Buchgesellschaft.

——— (1945). *The Psychoanalytic Theory of Neurosis*. New York: Norton.

Ferenczi, S. (1909). More About Homosexuality. In *Final Contributions to the Problems and Methods of Psychoanalysis*. New York: Basic Books, 1955.

——— (1912). On the Part Played by Homosexuality in the Pathogenesis of Paranoia. In *Sex in Psycho-Analysis*. Boston: Gorham Press, 1916.

——— (1914a). Some Clinical Observations on Paranoia and Paraphrenia. In *Sex in Psycho-Analysis*. Boston: Gorham Press, 1916.

——— (1914b). The Nosology of Male Homosexuality (Homoerotism). In *Sex in Psycho-Analysis*. Boston: Gorham Press, 1916.

Fine, R. (1961). A Transference Manifestion of Male Homosexuals. *Psa R* 48:116–20.

Finger, F. (1947). Sex Beliefs and Practices among Male College Students. *J Abn Soc Psych* 42:57–67.

Fliess, R. (1962). An Ontogenetic Table. In *The Psycho-Analytic Reader*. New York: International Universities Press.

Flournoy, H. (1953). An Analytic Session in a Case of Male Homosexuality. In Loewenstein, R. (ed.), *Drives, Affects, Behavior: Essays in Honor of Marie Bonaparte*. New York: International Universities Press.

Ford, C. (1949). A Brief Description of Human Sexual Behavior in Cross-Cultural Perspective. In Hoch, P., and Zubin, J. (eds.), *Psychosexual Development in Health and Disease*. New York: Grune and Stratton.

Foucault, M. (1965). *Madness and Civilization*. New York: Random House.

———— (1978). *The History of Sexuality*. Volume I: *An Introduction*. New York: Pantheon.

Fraiberg, S. (1962). Homosexual Conflicts in Adolescence. In Lorand, S., and Schnell, H. (eds.), *Adolescents: Psychoanalytic Approach to Problems and Therapy*. New York: Harper and Row.

Freedman, A., and Kaplan, H. (eds.) (1967). *Comprehensive Textbook of Psychiatry*. Baltimore: Williams and Wilkins.

———— (1975). *Comprehensive Textbook of Psychiatry*, Second Edition. Baltimore: Williams and Wilkins.

Freeman, T. (1955). Clinical and Theoretical Observations on Male Homosexuality. *Int J Psa* 36:335–47.

Freud, A. (1946). *The Ego and the Mechanisms of Defense*. New York: International Universities Press.

———— (1949). Some Clinical Remarks Concerning the Treatment of Cases of Male Homosexuality. *Int J Psa* 30:196.

———— (1951a). Clinical Observations on the Treatment of Male Homosexuality. *Psa Q* 20:337–8.

———— (1951b). Homosexuality. *Am Psa Asn B* 7:117–18.

Freud, S. (1899). Letter (No. 125). *SE* 1:280.

———— (1900). *The Interpretation of Dreams. SE* 4–5.

———— (1903). Brief. *Die Zeit* (Vienna), October 27, 1903.

———— (1905a). *Three Essays on the Theory of Sexuality. SE* 7:123–246.

———— (1905b). Fragment of an Analysis of a Case of Hysteria. *SE* 7:3–124.

———— (1908a). Character and Anal Erotism. *SE* 9:167–76.

———— (1908b). Hysterical Phantasies and Their Relation to Bisexuality. *SE* 9:155–66.

———— (1908c). On the Sexual Theories of Children. *SE* 9:205–26.

———— (1908d). "Civilized" Sexual Morality and Modern Nervous Illness. *SE* 9:177–204.

———— (1909a). Analysis of a Phobia in a Five-Year-Old Boy. *SE* 10:1–147.

———— (1909b). Notes upon a Case of Obsessional Neurosis. *SE* 10:153–250.

———— (1910a). *Leonardo da Vinci and a Memory of His Childhood. SE* 11:59–138.

———— (1910b). Contributions to the Psychology of Love: 1. A Special Type of Object Choice Made by Men. SE 11:163–76.

———— (1910c). Five Lectures on Psycho-Analysis: IV. Infantile Sexuality and Neurosis. *SE* 11:40–48.

———— (1911). Psycho-Analytic Notes upon an Autobiographical Account of a Case of Paranoia (*Dementia Paranoides*). SE 12:1–84.

———— (1912). *Totem and Taboo*. SE 13:1–161.

———— (1913a). The Claims of Psycho-Analysis to Scientific Interest. SE 13:165–90.

———— (1913b). The Disposition to Obsessional Neurosis. SE 12:318ff.

———— (1914a). Narcissism: An Introduction. SE 14:73–102.

———— (1914b). The *Moses* of Michelangelo. SE 13:209–38.

———— (1915a). Instincts and Their Vicissitudes. SE 14:109–40.

———— (1915b). The Unconscious. SE 14:159–204.

———— (1916a). On Transformations of Instinct as Exemplified in Anal Erotism. SE 17:125–34.

———— (1916b). The Libido Theory and Narcissism. SE 16:412–30.

———— (1917). Mourning and Melancholia. SE 14:237–58.

———— (1918). From the History of an Infantile Neurosis. SE 17:3–22.

———— (1919a). "A Child Is Being Beaten": A Contribution to the Study of the Origin of Sexual Perversions. SE 17:175–204.

———— (1919b). Lines of Advance in Psycho-Analytic Therapy. SE 17:157–68.

———— (1920a). The Psychogenesis of a Case of Homosexuality in a Woman. SE 18:155–72.

———— (1920b). *Beyond the Pleasure Principle*. SE 18:1–64.

———— (1921a). *Group Psychology and the Analysis of the Ego*. SE 18:67–145.

———— (1921b). Letter (to Jones). *Body Politic* (Toronto, Canada), May 1977, page 9.

———— (1922). Certain Neurotic Mechanisms in Jealousy, Paranoia and Homosexuality. SE 18:221–34.

———— (1923a). *The Ego and the Id*. SE 19:3–66.

———— (1923b). The Infantile Genital Organization of the Libido. SE 19:41 ff.

———— (1924a). The Dissolution of the Oedipus Complex. SE 19:73–79.

———— (1924b). The Economic Problem of Masochism. SE 19:157–72.

———— (1925). Some Psychological Consequences of the Anatomic Distinction between the Sexes. SE 19:241–60.

———— (1926). *Inhibitions, Symptoms and Anxiety*. SE 20:75–176.

———— (1927). Fetishism. SE 21:149–59.

———— (1928). Dostoevsky and Parricide. SE 21:177–94.

———— (1930a). *Civilization and Its Discontents*. SE 21:57–146.

———— (1930b). Open Letter. *Wiener Arbeitzeitung*, May 16, 1930. Translated and reprinted in *Body Politic* (Toronto, Canada), May 1977, page 8.

———— (1931). Female Sexuality. *SE* 21:221–46.

———— (1933). Femininity. *SE* 22:112–35.

———— (1935). Letter. Published in *Am J Psychiat* 107 (1951):786.

———— (1937). Analysis Terminable and Interminable. *SE* 23:216–53.

———— (1939). *Moses and Monotheism*. *SE* 23:7–140.

———— (1940a). *An Outline of Psycho-Analysis*. *SE* 23:144–207.

———— (1940b). Splitting of the Ego in the Process of Defence. *SE* 23:275–78.

———— (1940c). Medusa's Head. *SE* 18:273–74.

Fried, E. (1960). *The Ego in Love and Sexuality*. New York: Grune and Stratton.

Friedman, R. (1976a). Psychodynamics and Sexual Object Choice. *C Psa* 12 (3).

———— (1976b). Psychodynamics and Sexual Object Choice III. A Reply to Drs. I. Bieber and C. W. Socarides. *C Psa* 12 (3):379–85.

———— (1980). Juvenile Aggressivity and Sissiness in Homosexual and Heterosexual Males. *J Am Aca Psa* 8 (3):427–40.

Fromm, E. (1947). *Man for Himself*. New York: Rinehart.

———— (1955). Sex and Character: The Kinsey Report Viewed from the Standpoint of Psychoanalysis. In Himmelhoch, J., and Fava, S. (eds.), *Sexual Behavior in American Society: An Appraisal of the First Two Kinsey Reports*. New York: Norton.

Gadpaille, W. (1968). Homosexual Experience in Adolescence. *Med Asp H Sex* 2 (10):29–38.

———— (1975). Homosexuality in Adolescent Males. *J Am Aca Psa* 3 (4):361–71.

Gardner, G. (1931). Evidence of Homosexuality in One Hundred and Twenty Unanalyzed Cases with Paranoid Content. *Psa R* 18:57–62.

Gay, P. (1968). *Weimar Culture: The Outsider as Insider*. New York: Harper and Row.

Gebhard, P. (1972). Incidence of Overt Homosexuality in the United States and Western Europe. In Livingood, J., *National Institute of Mental Health Task Force on Homosexuality: Final Report and Background Papers*. Rockville, Maryland: National Institute of Mental Health.

Gebhard, P., and Johnson, A. (1979). *The Kinsey Data: Marginal Tabulations of the 1938–1963 Interviews Conducted by the Institute for Sex Research*. Philadelphia: Saunders.

Gershman, H. (1952). Some Aspects of Compulsive Homosexuality. *Am J Psa* 12:100–101.

———(1953). Considerations of Some Aspects of Homosexuality. *Am J Psa* 13:82–83.

———(1957). Psychopathology of Compulsive Homosexuality. *Am J Psa* 17:58–77.

———(1964a). Homosexuality and Some Aspects of Creativity. *Am J Psa* 24:29–38.

———(1964b). The Meaning of Homosexual Trends in Therapy. *Am J Psa* 24:60–76.

———(1966). Reflections on the Nature of Homosexuality. *Am J Psa* 26:46–62.

———(1968). The Evolution of Gender Identity. *AM J Psa* 28:80–90.

———(1975). The Effect of Group Therapy on Compulsive Homosexuality in Men and Women. *Am J Psa* 35:303–12.

———(1981). Homosexual Marriages. *Am J Psa* 41:149–59.

Gilberg, A. (1978). Psychosocial Considerations in Treating Homosexual Adolescents. *Am J Psa* 38:355–58.

———(1981). Treatment of Young Adults with Sexual Maladaptation. *Am J Psa* 41:45–50.

Gillespie, W. (1952). Notes on the Analysis of Sexual Perversions. *Int J Psa* 33:397–402.

———(1956a). The Structure and Aetiology of Sexual Perversion. In Lorand, S., and Balint, M. (eds.), *Perversions: Psychodynamics and Therapy*. New York: Random House.

———(1956b). The General Theory of Sexual Perversions. *Int J Psa* 37:396–403.

———(1964a). Symposium on Homosexuality (1). *Int J Psa* 45:203–9.

———(1964b). The Psycho-Analytic Theory of Sexual Deviation with Special Reference to Fetishism. In Rosen, I. (ed.), *The Pathology and Treatment of Sexual Deviation: A Methodological Approach*. London: Oxford University Press.

Glasser, M. (1977). Homosexuality in Adolescence. *Brit J Med Psych* 50:217–25.

Glauber, I. (1956). The Rebirth Motif in Homosexuality and Its Teleological Significance. *Int J Psa* 47:416–21.

Glover, B. (1951). Observations on Homosexuality among University Students. *J Ner Mtl Dis* 377–87.

Glover, E. (1932). The Principle of Psychiatric Classification. *J Mtl Sc.* Reprinted as A Psycho-Analytic Approach to the Classification of Mental Disorders. In *On the Early Development of Mind*. London: Oxford University Press, 1956, pp. 161–86.

———— (1933). The Relation of Perversion-Formation to the Development of Reality Sense. *Int J Psa* 14:486–504.

———— (1939). *Psycho-Analysis: A Handbook for Medical Practitioners and Students of Comparative Psychology.* London and New York: Staples Press.

———— (1945). The Social and Legal Aspects of Sexual Abnormality. *Med-Leg R* 13:3ff. Reprinted in *The Roots of Crime*. New York: International Universities Press, 1960.

———— (1952). Introduction. In Westwood, G., *Society and the Homosexual*. London: Gollancz.

———— (1960). The Problem of Male Homosexuality: 1940–59. In *The Roots of Crime*. New York: International Universities Press, 1960.

Glueck, B. (1956). Psychodynamic Patterns in the Homosexual Sex Offender. *Am J Psychiat* 112:584–90.

Goldberg, A. (1975). A Fresh Look at Perverse Behavior. *Int J Psa* 56:335–42.

Goldberg, S. (1982). Is Homosexuality Normal? *Policy Review* (Summer).

Gonen, J. (1971). Negative Identity in Homosexuals. *Psa R* 58:345–52.

Goolker, P. (1948). Review: *Sexual Behavior in the Human Male*. *Int J Psa* 29:182–83.

Grauer, D. (1955). Homosexuality and the Paranoid Psychoses as Related to the Concept of Narcissism. *Psa Q* 24:516–26.

Grayson, R. (1971). Review of *Selected Papers* of Edmund Bergler. *Psa Q* 40:153–55.

Green, R. (1972). Homosexuality as a Mental Illness. *Int J Psychiat* 10:77–98.

———— (1973). Should Heterosexuality Be in the APA Nomenclature? *Am J Psychiat* 130 (11):1213–14.

Greenacre, P. (1968). Perversions: General Considerations Regarding Their Genetic and Dynamic Background. *Psa St Child* 23:47–62.

Greenson, R. (1964). On Homosexuality and Gender Identity. *Int J Psa* 45:217–19.

———— (1968). Dis-identifying from Mother: Its Special Importance for the Boy. *Int J Psa* 49:370–74.

Gundlach, R. (1969). Childhood Parental Relationships and the Establishment of Gender Roles of Homosexuals. *J Cons Cl Psych* 33:136–139.

Hadas, M. (1954). *Ancilla to Classical Reading*. New York: Columbia University Press.

Hadden, S. (1958). Treatment of Homosexuality by Individual and Group Psychotherapy. *Am J Psychiat* 114:810–15.

Hadfield, J. (1958). The Cure of Homosexuality. *Brit Med J* (June 7): 1323–26.

Hamilton, G. (1929). *A Research in Marriage*. New York: A. and C. Boni.

———— (1954). Incest and Homosexuality. In Krich, A. (ed.), *The Homosexuals: As Seen by Themselves and 30 Authorities*. New York: Citadel Press.

Hárnik, J. (1924). The Various Developments Undergone by Narcissism in Men and Women. *Int J Psa* 5:66–83.

Hartman, J. (1973). Bisexual Fantasy and Group Process. *C Psa* 9:303–26.

Hartmann, H. (1958). *Ego Psychology and the Problem of Adaptation*. New York: International Universities Press.

Hatterer, L. (1970). *Changing Homosexuality in the Male*. New York: McGraw-Hill.

Hendin, H. (1978). Homosexuality: The Psychosocial Dimension. *J Am Aca Psa* 6:479–96.

Henry, G. (1937). Psychogenic Factors in Overt Homosexuality. *Am J Psychiat* 93:889–908.

Hewitt, C. (1961). On the Meaning of Effeminacy in Homosexual Men. *Am J PsyTher* 10:591–602.

Hewitt, F. (pseudonym) (1948). That Kinsey Report: A Psychiatrist's View. *MM* 1:40–46.

Himmelhoch, J., and Fava, S. (eds.) (1955). *Sexual Behavior in American Society: An Appraisal of the First Two Kinsey Reports*. New York: Norton.

Hirschfeld, M. (1914). *Die Homosexualitaet des Mannes und des Weibes. Handbuch der gesamtem Sexualwissenschaft in Einzeldarstellungen*, 3. Berlin: Lorius Marcus.

Hitschmann, E. (1913). Paranoia, Homosexualitaet und Analerotik. *Int Z aerzt Psa* 1:251–54.

———— (1933 [1956]). Johannes Brahms and Women. In Margolin, S. (ed.), *Great Men: Psychoanalytic Studies*. New York: International Universities Press.

———— (1923). Urethral Erotism and Obsessional Neurosis. *Int J Psa* 4:118–9.

Hobbs, A., and Kephart, W. (1954). Professor Kinsey: His Facts and His Fantasy. *Am J Psychiat* 110:614–20.

Hobbs, A., and Lambert, R. (1948). An Evaluation of *Sexual Behavior in the Human Male. Am J Psychiat* 104:758–64.

Hoch, P. (1949). Discussion (of Clinical and Psychoanalytic Approach). In Hoch, P., and Zubin, J. (eds.), *Psychosexual Development in Health and Disease*. New York: Grune and Stratton.

Hoch, P., and Zubin, J. (eds.) (1949). *Psychosexual Development in Health and Disease*. New York: Grune and Stratton.

Hoenig, J. (1976). Sigmund Freud's Views on the Sexual Disorders in Historical Perspective. *Brit J Psychiat* 129:193–200.

Hoffman, M. (1972). Philosophic, Empirical and Ecologic Remarks. *Int J Psychiat* 10:105–7.

Hooker, E. (1957). The Adjustment of the Male Overt Homosexual. *J Proj Tech* 21:18–31.

—— (1963). Male Homosexuality. In Farberow, N. (ed.), *Taboo Topics*. New York: Atherton.

—— (1965a). An Empirical Study of Some Relations between Sexual Patterns and Gender Identity in Male Homosexuals. In Money, J. (ed.), *Sex Research: New Developments*. New York: Holt, Rinehart and Winston.

—— (1965b). Male Homosexuals and Their "Worlds." In Marmor, J. (ed.), *Sexual Inversion: The Multiple Roots of Homosexuality*. New York: Basic Books.

—— (1968). Homosexuality. In Siles, D. (ed.), *International Encyclopedia of the Social Sciences*, Vol. 14. New York: Crowell, Collier and Macmillan.

—— (1969). Parental Relations and Male Homosexuality in Patient and Nonpatient Samples. *J Cons Cl Psych* 33:140–42.

Horney, K. (1932). The Dread of Women. *Int J Psa* 13:348–60.

—— (1937). *The Neurotic Personality of Our Time*. New York: Norton.

—— (1939). *New Ways in Psychoanalysis*. New York: Norton.

Hornstra, L. (1966). The Antecedents of the Negative Oedipus Complex. *Int J Psa* 47.

—— (1967). Homosexuality. *Int J Psa* 48:394–402.

Hulbeck, C. (1948). Emotional Conflicts in Homosexuality. *Am J Psa* 8:72–73.

International Psychoanalytic Congress (1963). Symposium on Homosexuality. *Int J Psa* 45:214–16.

Jaffe, D. (1968). The Masculine Envy of Women's Procreative Function. *J Am Psa Asn* 16:521–48.

—— (1983). Some Relations between the Negative Oedipus Complex and Aggression in the Male. *J Am Psa Asn* 31:957–84.

Jekels, L. (1913). Einige Bemarkungen zur Trieblehre. *Int Z Psa* 1:439–43.

Johnson, A., and Szurek, T. (1952). The Genesis of Antisocial Acting Out in Children and Adults. *Psa Q* 21:323ff.

Jones, E. (1923). Hass und Analerotik in der Zwangneurose. *Int Z Psa* 1:425–30.

―――― (1926). The Origin and Structure of the Superego. *Int J Psa* 7.

―――― (1933). The Phallic Phase. *Int J Psa* 14:1–33.

Kardiner, A. (1949). Orientation: Discussion. In Hoch, P., and Zubin, J. (eds.), *Psychosexual Development in Health and Disease.* New York: Grune and Stratton.

―――― (1954a). How the Problem Has Been Studied: Freud and Kinsey. In *Sex and Morality.* New York: Bobbs-Merrill.

―――― (1954b). The Flight from Masculinity. In *Sex and Morality.* New York: Bobbs-Merrill.

―――― (1978a). The Social Distress Syndrome of Our Time, I. *J Am Aca Psa* 6 (1):89–101.

―――― (1978b). The Social Distress Syndrome of Our Time, II. *J Am Aca Psa* 6 (2):215–30.

Kardiner, A., Karush, A., and Ovesey, L. (1959). A Methodological Study of Freudian Theory III: Narcissism, Bisexuality and the Dual Instinct Theory. *J Ner Mtl Dis* 129:207–21.

Karlen, A. (1971). *Sexuality and Homosexuality: A New View.* New York: Norton.

―――― (1972). A Discussion of "Homosexuality as a Mental Illness." *Int J Psychiat* 10:108–13.

Karpman, B. (1938). "The Kreutzer Sonata": A Problem in Latent Homosexuality and Castration. *Psa R* 25:20–48.

Karush, A., and Ovesey, L. (1961). Unconscious Mechanisms of Magical Repair. *Arch Gen Psychiat* 5:77–91.

Kaufmann, M. (1934). Projection, Heterosexual and Homosexual. *Psa Q* 3:134–36.

Kaye, H. (1975). Discussion of "The Effect of Group Therapy on Compulsive Homosexuality in Men and Women." *Am J Psa* 35:313–16.

Kernberg, O. (1975). *Borderline Conditions and Pathological Narcissism.* New York: Aronson.

Kestenberg, J. (1971). A Developmental Approach to Disturbances in Sex-Specific Identity. *Int J Psa* 52:99–102.

Khan, M. (1965). Foreskin Fetishism and Its Relation to Ego Pathology in a Male Homosexual. *Int J Psa* 46:64–80.

―――― (1979). Fetish as Negation of the Self: Clinical Notes on Foreskin Fetishism in a Male Homosexual. In *Alienation in Perversions.* London: Hogarth.

Kinsey, A. (1949). Concepts of Normality and Abnormality in Sexual Behavior. In Hoch, P., and Zubin, J. (eds.), *Psychosexual Development in Health and Disease*. New York: Grune and Stratton.

Kinsey, A., Pomeroy, W., and Martin, C. (1948). *Sexual Behavior in the Human Male*. Philadelphia: Saunders.

Kinsey, A., Pomeroy, W., Martin C., and Gebhard, P. (1954). *Sexual Behavior in the Human Female*. Philadelphia: Saunders.

Klaf, F. (1961). Female Homosexuality and Paranoid Schizophrenia. *Arch Gen Psychiat* 4:84–90.

Klaf, F., and Davis, C. (1960). Homosexuality and Paranoid Schizophrenia: A Study of 150 Cases and Controls. *Am J Psychiat* 116:1070–75.

Klein, M. (1932). *The Psycho-Analysis of Children*. New York: Delacorte.

Knight, R. (1948). Psychiatric Issues in the Kinsey Report. In Deutsch, A. (ed.), *Sex Habits of American Men: A Symposium on the Kinsey Report*. New York: Grosset and Dunlap.

Kohut, H. (1971). *The Analysis of the Self*. New York: International Universities Press.

Kolb, L. (1963). Therapy of Homosexuality. In Masserman, J. (ed.), *Current Psychiatric Therapies*. New York: Grune and Stratton.

Kolb, L., and Johnson, A. (1955). Etiology and Therapy of Overt Homosexuality. *Psa Q* 24:506–15.

Krich, A. (ed.) (1954). *The Homosexuals: As Seen by Themselves and 30 Authorities*. New York: Citadel Press.

Kubie, L. (1948). Psychiatric Implications of the Kinsey Report. *PsySom Med* 10:95–106.

——— (1974). The Drive to Become Both Sexes. *Psa Q* 43:349–426.

Kwawer, J. (1980). Transference and Countertransference in Homosexuality: Changing Psychoanalytic Views: *Am J PsyTher* 34:72–80.

Lachman, F. (1975). Homosexuality: Some Diagnostic Perspectives and Dynamic Considerations. *Am J PsyTher* 29:254–60.

Lagache, D. (1950). Homosexuality and Jealousy. *Int J Psa* 31:24–31.

Laufer, M. (1982). The Formation and Shaping of the Oedipus Complex: Clinical Observations and Assumptions. *Int J Psa* 63:217–27.

Lebovici, S. (1982). The Origins and Development of the Oedipus Complex. *Int J Psa* 63:201–15.

le Coultre, R. (1956). Elimination of Guilt as a Function of Perversions. In Lorand, S., and Balint, M. (eds.), *Perversions: Psychodynamics and Therapy*. New York: Random House.

Lesse, S. (1974). To Be or Not To Be an Illness? That Is the Question—
or—the Status of Homosexuality. *Am J PsyTher* 28:1–3.

Levy, D. (1949). Discussion (of Clinical and Psychoanalytic
Approach). In Hoch, P., and Zubin, J. (eds.), *Psychosexual Development in Health and Disease*. New York: Grune and Stratton.

Lewinsky, H. (1949). Notes on Two Special Features in a Homosexual
Patient. *Int J Psa* 30:56.

——— (1952). Features From a Case of Homosexuality. *Psa Q*
21:344–54.

Lewy, E. (1967). The Transformation of Frederick the Great: A Psychoanalytic Study. In Roheim, G. (ed.), *The Psychoanalytic
Study of Society* IV. New York: International Universities Press.

Lichtenstein, H. (1970). Changing Implications of the Concept of
Psychosexual Development: An Inquiry Concerning the Validity
of Classical Psychoanalytic Assumptions Concerning Sexuality. *J
Am Psa Asn* 18:300–318.

Liddicoat, R. (1956). Homosexuality: Results of a Survey. *Brit Med J*
1:1110–11.

Lief, H. (1977). Sexual Survey No. 4: Current Thinking of Homosexuality. *Med Asp H Sex* 11:110.

Lief, H., and Mayerson, P. (1965). Psychotherapy of Homosexuality:
A Follow-up of Nineteen Cases. In Marmor, J. (ed.), *Sexual
Inversion: The Multiple Roots of Homosexuality*. New York: Basic
Books.

Limentani, A. (1976). Object Choice and Actual Bisexuality. *Int J Psa
Psy* 5:205–17.

——— (1977). The Differential Diagnosis of Homosexuality. *Brit J
Med Psych* 80:209–16.

——— (1979). Clinical Types of Homosexuality. In Rosen, I. (ed.),
Sexual Deviance. Oxford: Oxford University Press.

Lippmann, W. (1984). *Rilke: A Life*. New York: Fromm.

Litin, E., Giffin, M., and Johnson, A. (1956). Parental Influence in
Unusual Sexual Behavior in Children. *Psa Q* 25:37–55.

Livingood, J. (ed.) (1972). *National Institute of Mental Health Task
Force on Homosexuality: Final Report and Background Papers*.
Rockville, Maryland: National Institute of Mental Health.
DHEW Publication No. (HSM) 72-9116.

Loewenstein, R. (1935). Phallic Passivity in Men. *Int J Psa* 16:334–40.

——— (1957). A Contribution to the Psychoanalytic Theory of Masochism. *J Am Psa Asn* 5:197–231.

Lorand, S. (1930). Fetishism *in Statu Nascendi*. *Int J Psa* 11:419–27.

———— (1956). The Therapy of Perversions. In Lorand, S., and Balint, M. (eds.), *Perversions: Psychodynamics and Therapy*. New York: Random House.

Lorand, S., and Balint, M. (eds.) (1956). *Perversions: Psychodynamics and Therapy*. New York: Random House.

Mahler, M. (1968). *On Human Symbiosis and the Vicissitudes of Individuation I: Infantile Psychosis*. New York: International Universities Press.

Mahler, M., Pine, F., and Bergman, A. (1975). *The Psychological Birth of the Human Infant*. New York: Basic Books.

Marberg, H. (1972). Fragmentary Psychoanalytic Treatment of Acute Homosexual Panic. *Psa R* 59:295–304.

Marcuse, H. (1955). *Eros and Civilization: A Philosophical Inquiry into Freud*. New York: Random House.

Margolin, S. (1948). Review of *Sexual Behavior in the Human Male*. *Psa Q* 17:265–72.

Marmor, J. (ed.) (1965a). *Sexual Inversion: The Multiple Roots of Homosexuality*. New York: Basic Books.

———— (1965b). Introduction. In Marmor, J. (ed.), *Sexual Inversion: The Multiple Roots of Homosexuality*. New York: Basic Books.

———— (1971a). "Normal" and "Deviant" Sexual Behavior. *JAMA* 217:165–70.

———— (1971b). Homosexuality in Males. *Psychiat A* 1:44–59.

———— (1972a). Notes on Some Psychodynamic Aspects of Homosexuality. In Livingood, J. (ed.), *National Institute of Mental Health Task Force on Homosexuality: Final Report and Background Papers*. Rockville, Maryland: National Institute of Mental Health.

———— (1972b). Homosexuality: Mental Illness or Moral Dilemma? *Int J Psychiat* 10:114–17.

———— (1973). Homosexuality and Cultural Value Systems. *Am J Psychiat* 130:1208–09.

———— (1975). Sexual Disorders: Homosexuality and Sexual Orientation Disturbances. In Freedman, A., and Kaplan, H. (eds.), *Comprehensive Textbook of Psychiatry*, Second Edition. Baltimore: Williams and Wilkins.

———— (ed.) (1980a). *Homosexual Behavior: A Modern Reappraisal*. New York: Basic Books.

———— (1980b). Clinical Aspects of Male Homosexuality. In *Homosexual Behavior: A Modern Reappraisal*. New York: Basic Books.

———— (1980c). Epilogue: Homosexuality and the Issue of Mental Illness. In *Homosexual Behavior: A Modern Reappraisal*. New York: Basic Books.

McDougall, J. (1972). Primal Scene and Sexual Perversion. *Int J Psa* 53:371–84,.

Menninger, K. (1953). One View of the Kinsey Report. *GP* 8:67–72.

Miller, M. (1956). The Relation between Submission and Aggression in Male Homosexuality. In Lorand, S., and Balint, M. (eds.), *Perversions: Psychodynamics and Therapy*. New York: Random House.

Miller, P. (1958). The Effeminate Passive Obligatory Homosexual. *AMA Arch* 80:612–18.

Mitchell, S. (1978). Psychodynamics, Homosexuality and the Question of Pathology. *Psychiat* 41:254–63.

Money, J. (ed.) (1965). *Sex Research: New Developments*. New York: Holt, Rinehart and Winston.

Moore, R., and Selzer, M. (1963). Male Homosexuality, Paranoia and the Schizophrenias. *Am J Psychiat* 119:747–53.

Morgenthaler, F. (1969). Introduction to Panel on Disturbances of Male and Female Identity as Met With in Psychoanalytic Practice. *Int J Psa* 50:109–12.

Morichau-Beauchant, R. (1912). Homosexualitaet und Paranoia. *ZBl Psa* 2:172.

Muensterberger, W. (1967). Perversion, Cultural Norm and Normality. In Ruitenbeck, H. (ed.), *The Psychotherapy of Perversions*. New York: Citadel Press.

Murphy, W. (1948). Review of Sex Habits of American Men. *Psa Q* 17:537–40.

Nachmansohn, M. (1922). Die Psychoanalyse eines Falles von Homosexualitaet. *Int Z Psa* 8:45–64.

Nacht, S., Diatkine, R., and Favreau, J. (1956). The Ego in Perverse Relationships. *Int J Psa* 37:404–13.

Nágera, H. (1970). *Basic Psychoanalytic Concepts*. New York: Basic Books.

Nunberg, H. (1938). Homosexuality, Magic and Aggression. *Int J Psa* 19:1–16.

——— (1947). Circumcision and Problems of Bisexuality. *Int J Psa* 28:145–79.

Ophuijsen, T. (1920). On the Origin of the Feeling of Persecution. *Int J Psa* 1:235–39.

Ostow, M. (1974). *Sexual Deviation: Psychoanalytic Insights*. New York: Quadrangle.

Ovesey, L. (1954). The Homosexual Conflict: An Adaptational Analysis. *Psychiat* 17:243–50.

——— (1955a). Pseudohomosexual Anxiety. *Psychiat* 18:17–25.

—— (1955b). Pseudohomosexuality and the Paranoid Mechanism, and Paranoia: An Adaptational Revision of a Classical Freudian Theory. *Psychiat* 18:163–73.

—— (1956). Masculine Aspirations in Women: An Adaptational Analysis. *Psychiat* 19:341–51.

—— (1964). The Meaning of Homosexual Trends in Therapy. *Am J Psa* 24:60–76.

—— (1965). Pseudohomosexuality and Homosexuality in Men: Psychodynamics as a Guide to Treatment. In Marmor, J. (ed.), *Sexual Inversion: The Multiple Roots of Homosexuality.* New York: Basic Books.

—— (1969). *Homosexuality and Pseudohomosexuality.* New York: Science House.

—— (1973). Gender Identity and Sexual Psychopathology in Men: A Psychodynamic Analysis of Homosexuality, Transsexualism, and Transvestism. *J Am Aca Psa* 1:53–72.

Ovesey, L., and Gaylin, W. (1965). Psychotherapy of Male Homosexuality: Prognosis, Selection of Patients, Technique. *Am J Psy-Ther* 19:385–96.

Ovesey, L., Gaylin, W., and Hendin, H. (1963). Psychotherapy of Male Homosexuality. *Arch Gen Psychiat* 9:19–31.

Pao, P. (1969). Pathological Jealousy. *Psa Q* 38:616–38.

Pasche, F. (1964). Symposium on Homosexuality (II). *Int J Psa* 45:210–13.

Pattison, E. (1974). Confusing Concepts about the Concept of Homosexuality. *Psychiat* 37:340–49.

Plato (1961a). *The Laws.* Translated by C. E. Taylor. Princeton: Princeton University Press.

—— (1961b). *Symposium.* Translated by C. E. Taylor. Princeton: Princeton University Press.

Poe, J. (1952). The Successful Treatment of a 40-year-old Passive Homosexual Based on an Adaptational View of Sexual Behavior. *Psa R* 39:23–33.

Rado, S. (1940). A Critical Examination of the Concept of Bisexuality. *PsySom Med* 2:459–67.

—— (1949). An Adaptational View of Sexual Behavior. In Hoch, P., and Zubin, J. (eds.), *Psychosexual Development in Health and Disease.* New York: Grune and Stratton.

Ramsey, G. (1943). The Sexual Development of Boys. *Am J Psychiat* 56:217–34.

—— (1950). A Survey Evaluation of the Kinsey Report. *J Cl Psych* 6:133–43.

Rank, O. (1922). Perversion und Neurose. *Int Z Psa* 8:397ff.

Regardie, F. (1949). Analysis of a Homosexual. *Psychiat Q* 23:548–66.

Riess, B. (1980). Psychological Tests in Homosexuality. In Marmor, J. (ed.), *Homosexual Behavior: A Modern Reappraisal*. New York: Basic Books.

Riggal, R. (1923). Homosexuality and Alcoholism. *Psa R* 10:157–69.

Robbins, B. (1943). Psychological Implications of the Male Homosexual Marriage. *Psa R* 30:428–37.

Robertiello R. (1971). A More Positive View of Perversions. *Psa R* 58:467–71.

Rosen, I. (ed.) (1964). *The Pathology and Treatment of Sexual Deviation: A Methodological Approach*. London: Oxford University Press.

——— (1979a). *Sexual Deviance*. London: Oxford University Press.

——— (1979b). The General Psychoanalytic Theory of Perversion: A Critical and Clinical Review. In *Sexual Deviance*. London: Oxford University Press.

——— (1979c). Perversion as a Regulator of Self-Esteem. In *Sexual Deviance*. London: Oxford University Press.

Rosenfeld, H. (1949). Remarks on the Relation of Male Homosexuality to Paranoia, Paranoid Anxiety and Narcissism. *Int J Psa* 30:36–47.

Ross, I. (1975). The Development of Paternal Identity: A Critical Review of the Literature on Nurturance and Generativity in Boys and Men. *J Am Psa Asn* 23:783–818.

Ross, R. (1950). Measurement of the Sex Behavior of College Males Compared with Kinsey's Results. *J Abn Soc Psych* 45:753–55.

Roy, D. (1972). Lytton Strachey and the Masochistic Basis of Homosexuality. *Psa R* 59:579–84.

Rubinstein, L. (1964). The Role of Identifications in Homosexuality and Transvestism in Men and Women. In Rosen, I. (ed.), *The Pathology and Treatment of Sexual Deviation: A Methodological Approach*. London: Oxford University Press.

Ruitenbeck, H. (ed.) (1967). *The Psychotherapy of Perversions*. New York: Citadel Press.

Sachs, H. (1923). Zur Genese der Perversionen. *Int Z Psa* 9:172–82.

Sadger, J. (1908a). Fragment der Psychoanalyse eines Homosexuellen. *Jb Sex Zw* 9:339–424.

——— (1908b). Ist der Kontraere sexual Empfindung heilbar? *Z Sexwis* 712–20.

——— (1910a). Ein Fall von Multipler Perversionem mit hysterischen Absenzen. *Jb Psa Psp F* 2:59–133.

———— (1910b). Ueber Urethralerotik. *Jb Psa* 2:409–50.

———— (1913). Ueber Gesaesserotik. *Int Z Psa* 1:351–58.

———— (1914). Sexual Perversionen. *Jb Psa* 6:296–313.

———— (1915). *Neue Forschungen zur Homosexualitaet.* Berlin: Berliner Klinik.

————(1919). Allerlei Gedanken zur Psychopathia sexualis. *N aerzt Z.*

———— (1921). *Die Lehre von den Geschlechtsverwirrungen* (Psychopathia sexualis) *auf psychoanalytischer Grundlage.* Leipzig and Vienna: Deuticke.

Saghir, M., and Robins, E. (1970). Homosexuality III: Psychiatric Disorders and Disability in the Male Homosexual. *Am J Psychiat* 126:1079–86.

———— (1971). Male and Female Homosexuality: Natural History. *C Psychiat* 12:503–10.

———— (1973). *Male and Female Homosexuality: A Comprehensive Investigation.* Baltimore: Williams and Wilkins.

Salis, J. von (1964). *Rainer Maria Rilke: The Years in Switzerland.* Berkeley: University of California Press.

Salzman, L. (1965). "Latent" Homosexuality. In Marmor, J. (ed.), *Sexual Inversion: The Multiple Roots of Homosexuality.* New York: Basic Books.

———— (1974). Sexual Problems in Adolescence. *C Psa* 10:189–207.

Saul, L., and Beck, A. (1961). Psychodynamics of Male Homosexuality. *Int J Psa* 42:43–48.

Schafer, R. (1983). *The Analytic Attitude.* New York: Basic Books.

Schilder, P. (1942). Problems of Homosexuality. In *Goals and Desires of Men.* New York: Columbia University Press.

Schorske, C. (1981). Fin-de-Siècle *Vienna: Politics and Culture.* New York: Vintage.

Scott, P. (1964). Definition, Classification, Prognosis and Treatment. In Rosen, I. (ed.), *The Pathology and Treatment of Sexual Deviation: A Methodological Approach.* London: Oxford University Press.

Segal, H. (1979). *Melanie Klein.* New York: Viking.

Shackley, F. (1914). The Role of Homosexuality in the Genesis of Paranoid Conditions. *Psa R* 1:431–38.

Sherman, M., and Sherman, I. (1926). The Factor of Parental Attachment in Homosexuality. *Psa R* 13:32–37.

Siegelman, M. (1974). Parental Background of Male Homosexuals and Heterosexuals. *Arch Sex Beh* 3:3ff.

Silber, A. (1961). Object Choice in a Case of Male Homosexuality. *Psa Q* 3:497–503.

Silverberg, W. (1938). The Personal Basis and Social Significance of Passive Male Homosexuality. *Psychiat* 1:41–53.

Socarides, C. (1959). Meaning and Content of a Pedophiliac Perversion. *J Am Psa Asn* 7:84–94.

—— (1960). Theoretical and Clinical Aspects of Overt Male Homosexuality. *J Am Psa Asn* 8:552–66.

—— (1968a). *The Overt Homosexual.* New York: Grune and Stratton.

—— (1968b). A Provisional Theory of Etiology in Male Homosexuality: A Case of Preoedipal Origin. *Int J Psa* 49:27–37.

—— (1969). Psychoanalytic Therapy of a Male Homosexual. *Psa Q* 38:173–90.

—— (1970). Homosexuality and Medicine. *JAMA* 212:1199–1202.

—— (1972). Homosexuality. *Int J Psychiat* 10:118–25.

—— (1973a). Sexual Perversion and the Fear of Engulfment. *Int J Psa Psy* 2:432–48.

—— (1973b). Findings Derived from 15 Years of Clinical Research. *Am J Psychiat* 130:1212–13.

—— (1974). The Demonified Mother. *Int R Psa* 1:187–95.

—— (1976). Psychodynamics and Sexual Object Choice. *C Psa* 12:370–78.

—— (1978a). The Sexual Deviations and the Diagnostic Manual. *Am J PsyTher* 32:414–26.

—— (1978b). *Homosexuality.* New York: Aronson.

—— (1979a). The Psychoanalytic Theory of Homosexuality with Special Reference to Therapy. In Rosen, I. (ed.), *Sexual Deviance.* London: Oxford University Press.

—— (1979b). Some Problems Encountered in the Psychoanalytic Treatment of Overt Male Homosexuality. *Am J PsyTher* 33:506–20.

Sperling, O. (1956). Psychodynamics of Group Perversions. *Psa Q* 25:56ff.

Spiegel, L. (1958). Comments on the Psychoanalytic Psychology of Adolescence. *Psa St Child* 13:296–308.

Spitzer, R. (1973). A Proposal about Homosexuality and the APA Nomenclature: Homosexuality as an Irregular Form of Sexual Behavior and Sexual Orientation Disturbance as a Psychiatric Disorder. *Am J Psychiat* 132:1214–16.

Sprague, G. (1935). Varieties of Homosexual Manifestation. In Krich, A. (ed.), *Homosexuals,* pp. 174–87.

Sprince, M. (1964). A Contribution to the Study of Homosexuality in Adolescence. *J Ch Psy Psychiat* 5:103–17.

Staerke, A. (1920). The Reversal of the Libido-Sign in Delusions of Persecution. *Int J Psa* 1:231–34.

Steiner, G. (1983). In Lieu of a Preface. *Sal* 58:4–9.

Stoller, R. (1964). A Contribution to the Study of Gender Identity. *Int J Psa* 45:220–26.

——— (1965). Passing and the Continuum of Gender Identity. In Marmor, J. (ed.), *Sexual Inversion: The Multiple Roots of Homosexuality.* New York: Basic Books.

——— (1968). *Sex and Gender.* New York: Science House.

——— (1970). Pornography and Perversion. *Arch Gen Psychiat* 22:490–99.

——— (1973a). Criteria for Psychiatric Diagnosis. *Am J Psychiat* 130:1207–08.

——— (1973b). The Impact of New Advances in Sex Research on Psychoanalytic Theory. *Am J Psychiat* 130:241–51, 1207–16.

——— (1974a). Does Sexual Perversion Exist? *J H Med J* 134:43–57.

——— (1974b). Symbiosis, Anxiety and the Development of Masculinity. *Arch Gen Psychiat* 30:164–72.

——— (1975a). *Perversion: The Erotic Form of Hatred.* New York: Pantheon Books.

——— (1975b). *Sex and Gender II: The Transsexual Experiment.* London: Hogarth Press.

——— (1978). Boyhood Gender Aberrations: Treatment Issues. *J Am Psa Asn* 26:541–58.

——— (1979). The Gender Disorders. In Rosen, I. (ed.), *Sexual Deviance.* Oxford: Oxford University Press.

Sullivan, H. (1953). *The Interpersonal Theory of Psychiatry.* New York: Norton.

Szasz, T. (1974). *The Myth of Mental Illness: Foundations of a Theory of Personal Conduct,* revised edition. New York: Harper and Row.

Thompson, C. (1947). Changing Concepts of Homosexuality in Psychoanalysis. *Psychiat* 10:183–89.

——— (1951). *Psychoanalysis: Evolution and Development.* New York: Hermitage House.

Thompson, N., McCandless, B., and Strickland, B. (1971). Personal Adjustment of Male and Female Homosexuals and Heterosexuals. *J Abn Soc Psych* 78:237–40.

Thompson, P. (1968). Vicissitudes of the Transference in a Male Homosexual. *Int J Psa* 49:629–39.

Thorner, H. (1949). Notes on a Case of Male Homosexuality. *Int J Psa* 30:31–36.

Trilling, L. (1948). Sex and Science: The Kinsey Report. *B Men C* 13:109–18.

Tyson, P. (1982). A Developmental Line of Gender Identity, Gender Role and Choice of Love Object. *J Am Psa Asn* 30:61–66.

Vinchon, J., and Nacht, S. (1929). Considérations sur la cure psychoanalytique d'une névrose homosexuelle. *R fr psa* 3.

Waelder, R. (1936). The Principle of Multiple Function: Observations on Over-Determination. *Psa Q* 5:46–62.

—— (1960). *Basic Theory of Psychoanalysis.* New York: International Universities Press.

Wakeling, A. (1979). A General Psychiatric Approach to Sexual Deviation. In Rosen, I. (ed.), *Sexual Deviance.* Oxford: Oxford University Press.

Wallace, L. (1969). Psychotherapy of a Male Homosexual. *Psa R* 56:346–64.

Weinberg, M. and Williams, C. (1974). *Male Homosexuals: Their Problems and Adaptations.* New York: Oxford University Press.

Weiss, E. (1958). Bisexuality and Ego Structure. *Int J Psa* 39:91–97.

Weiss, F. (1949). Review: *Sexual Behavior in the Human Male. Am J Psa* 9:80–81.

—— (1964). The Meaning of Homosexual Trends in Therapy. *Am J Psa* 24:60–76.

Weissman, P. (1962). Structural Considerations in Overt Male Bisexuality. *Int J Psa* 43:159–67.

Westwood, G. (1952). *Society and the Homosexual.* London: Gollancz.

Wiedemann, G. (1962). Survey of Psychoanalytic Literature on Overt Male Homosexuality. *J Am Psa Asn* 10:386–409.

—— (1964). Symposium on Homosexuality. *Int J Psa* 45:214–16.

—— (1974). Homosexuality: A Survey. *J Am Psa Asn* 22:651–96.

Wittels, F. (1944). Collective Defense Mechanisms Against Homosexuality. *Psa R* 31:19–33.

Wortis, B. (1948). The Kinsey Report and Related Fields: Psychiatry. *Sat R Lit* 31:19, 32–34.

Wulff, M. (1942). A Case of Male Homosexuality. *Int J Psa* 23:112–20.

INDEX

Abraham, Karl, 213
active sexuality, 26, 67, 75, 80
  negative Oedipus complex and,
    28–29
  phase differences in, 107
"adaptational" school, 131, 156–158,
  190, 198
adolescence, homosexual behavior in,
  178–179, 212
Aesthetic movement, English, 13
aesthetics, 13–15, 31
aggression, 42, 109, 168, 184, 202
  conservative developments and,
    131–133, 148, 149
  Miller's views on, 132–133
  narcissism as defense against, 131
  Nunberg's views on, 95–96
  in oral stage, 91, 92–93, 95–97, 100
  Socarides's views on, 148
AIDS epidemic, 9
alcoholism, 40, 129, 134, 135, 137
Alexander, F., 84, 146, 152, 167
alienation, 137
Allen, C., 137
alloerotism, 60, 164
  sexual instincts in, 61
Altschuler, K., 212
American Imago, 142
American Journal of Psychiatry, 175,
  208
American Journal of Psychoanalysis,
  112, 124, 174, 188, 198

American Journal of Psychotherapy,
  211
American Psychiatric Association
  (APA),
  homosexuality debate in, 172–175,
    191, 192, 194, 195, 200, 202,
    208–213, 215, 217
American Psychoanalytic Association,
  128, 145–149
American Psychological Association,
  172, 211
anaclitic instincts, 78
anaclitic object choice, 62–65, 72, 162,
  165, 214
  mother as, 65
  narcissistic libido and, 69–70
anal erotism, 44, 162, 165
  varieties of, 28, 37, 46–47
anal stage, 23, 26, 77, 78, 83, 91, 161
  narcissism and, 60
  regression to, 93, 165
Andreas-Salomé, Lou, 14
animals, homosexuality in, 76
anus, as vagina, 32
anxiety, 99, 133, 190
  of analytic writers, 6
  aphanisis, 91
  of fetishists, 25
  in Glover's perversion theory, 98, 99
  of heterosexuals, 1, 2, 9, 220
  lack of, 41, 92
  Nacht's views on, 150

275

ABOUT THE AUTHOR

Kenneth Lewes is a clinical psychologist practicing psychoanalytic therapy outside Detroit, Michigan. He has a Ph.D. in clinical psychology from the University of Michigan and a Ph.D. in Renaissance English Literature from Harvard. He has taught literature at Rutgers University. Dr. Lewes resides in Ann Arbor. He is interested in the relations among psychoanalysis, homosexuality, and creativity.